W9-CKR-552

SOCIAL WELFARE
HELP OR HINDRANCE?

SOCIAL WELFARE
HELP OR HINDRANCE?

Leslie Joseph

INFORMATION PLUS REFERENCE SERIES
Formerly published by Information Plus, Wylie, Texas

GALE GROUP

Detroit
New York
San Francisco
London
Boston
Woodbridge, CT

SOCIAL WELFARE: HELP OR HINDRANCE?

Leslie Joseph, *Author*

The Gale Group Staff:

Editorial: John F. McCoy, *Project Manager and Series Editor*; Michael T. Reade, *Series Associate Editor*; Jason M. Everett, *Series Assistant Editor*; Rita Runchock, *Managing Editor*; Luann Brennan, *Editor*; Thomas Carson, *Editor*; Andrew Claps, *Editor*; Kathleen Droste, *Editor*; Nancy Matuszak, *Editor*; Christy Wood, *Associate Editor*; Ryan McNeill, *Assistant Editor*; Jeffrey Telford, *Assistant Editor*

Image and Multimedia Content: Barbara J. Yarrow, *Manager, Imaging and Multimedia Content*; Robyn Young, *Project Manager, Imaging and Multimedia Content*; Dean Dauphinais, *Senior Editor, Imaging and Multimedia Content*; Kelly A. Quin, *Editor, Imaging and Multimedia Content*; Leitha Etheridge-Sims, Mary K. Grimes, and David G. Oblender, *Image Catalogers*; Pamela A. Reed, *Imaging Coordinator*; Randy Bassett, *Imaging Supervisor*; Robert Duncan, *Senior Imaging Specialist*; Dan Newell, *Imaging Specialist*; Christine O'Bryan, *Graphic Specialist*

Indexing: Jennifer Dye, *Indexing Specialist*; Lynne Maday, *Indexing Specialist*

Permissions: Maria Franklin, *Permissions Manager*; Margaret Chamberlain, *Permissions Specialist*; Julie Juengling, *Permissions Specialist*

Product Design: Michelle DiMercurio, *Senior Art Director*; Mike Logusz, *Graphic Artist*; Kenn Zorn, *Product Design Manager*

Production: Mary Beth Trimper, *Composition Manager*; Gary Leach, *Typesetting Specialist*; NeKita McKee, *Buyer*; Dorothy Maki, *Manufacturing Manager*

TABLE OF CONTENTS

Federal, state, and local governments, as well as private institutions, share in the expenditures on social welfare services. This chapter examines the costs and types of programs available to those in need.

The summer of 1996 saw the passage of a new welfare bill which brought about profound changes in the way America handles its welfare programs. This chapter discusses the 1996 welfare law as well as changes that have been made since its passage. Two examples of state welfare-reform programs are also presented.

Millions of Americans suffer from poverty. This chapter examines poverty statistics across a number of societal characteristics. Income, tax relief, and hunger are also explored.

The wealth and earnings gap between the rich and poor continues to increase. Studies of household incomes and household net worth illustrate this unfortunate fact. For most poor Americans, poverty is not a static condition; some stay poor, others manage to improve their economic conditions.

Poor families are more likely to need government assistance to survive than non-poor families. However, the structure of the family usually indicates how much that family needs to rely on welfare. Other factors such as child support payments, unemployment compensation, and the minimum wage affect the poverty status of America's families.

This chapter explores the types of households that participate in welfare programs. Characteristics such as gender, race and ethnicity, age, education level, employment status, and regional differences all factor in to who participates and who doesn't. Not surprisingly, individuals who receive one form of welfare may likely qualify for and receive others.

The welfare-reform law enacted in 1996 ended the entitlement welfare program and replaced it with a block grant program. This chapter provides background on the two programs and examines their similarities and differences. Also examined are the effects of these programs on welfare recipients.

Benefit programs provide cash and/or non-cash aid to individuals who meet certain low-income qualifications. This chapter explores Supplemental Security Income, the Food Stamp Program, National School Lunch and School Breakfast Program, and other major programs designed to assist low-income Americans.

Since the Great Depression, the federal government has created work programs designed to combat unemployment. The passage of the 1996 welfare law laid the foundation for a work-based welfare system. Welfare recipients are now expected to participate in work activities while receiving benefits.

This chapter discusses the successes and failures of welfare since its 1996 reform. A discussion about who left welfare and who remains, employment and earnings, welfare spending, and support services reveals the cautious optimism concerning welfare reform.

PREFACE

Social Welfare: Help or Hindrance? is the latest volume in the ever-growing *Information Plus Reference Series*. Previously published by the Information Plus company of Wylie, Texas, the *Information Plus Reference Series* (and its companion set, the *Information Plus Compact Series*) became a Gale Group product when Gale and Information Plus merged in early 2000. Those of you familiar with the series as published by Information Plus will notice a few changes from the 1999 edition. Gale has adopted a new layout and style that we hope you will find easy to use. Other improvements include greatly expanded indexes in each book, and more descriptive tables of contents.

While some changes have been made to the design, the purpose of the *Information Plus Reference Series* remains the same. Each volume of the series presents the latest facts on a topic of pressing concern in modern American life. These topics include today's most controversial and most studied social issues: abortion, capital punishment, care for the elderly, crime, health care, the environment, immigration, minorities, social welfare, women, youth, and many more. Although written especially for the high school and undergraduate student, this series is an excellent resource for anyone in need of factual information on current affairs.

By presenting the facts, it is Gale's intention to provide its readers with everything they need to reach an informed opinion on current issues. To that end, there is a particular emphasis in this series on the presentation of scientific studies, surveys, and statistics. This data is generally presented in the form of tables, charts, and other graphics placed within the text of each book. Every graphic is directly referred to and carefully explained in the text. The source of each graphic is presented within the graphic itself. The data used in these graphics is drawn from the most reputable and reliable sources, in particular from the various branches of the U.S. government and from major independent polling organizations. Every effort was made to secure the most recent information available. The reader should bear in mind that many major studies take years to conduct, and that additional years often pass before the data from these studies is made available to the public. Therefore, in many cases the most recent information available in 2000 dated from 1997 or 1998. Older statistics are sometimes presented as well, if they are of particular interest and no more-recent information exists.

Although statistics are a major focus of the *Information Plus Reference Series* they are by no means its only content. Each book also presents the widely held positions and important ideas that shape how the book's subject is discussed in the United States. These positions are explained in detail and, where possible, in the words of those who support them. Some of the other material to be found in these books includes: historical background; descriptions of major events related to the subject; relevant laws and court cases; and examples of how these issues play out in American life. Some books also feature primary documents, or have pro and con debate sections giving the words and opinions of prominent Americans on both sides of a controversial topic. All material is presented in an even-handed and unbiased manner; the reader will never be encouraged to accept one view of an issue over another.

HOW TO USE THIS BOOK

Aid for the poor has long been a controversial topic in the United States. Most Americans agree that society should help those who have fallen on hard times, but there are many different opinions as to what is the best method of accomplishing this. The 1990s were a time of particularly heavy debate over this issue, resulting in major changes to the U.S. welfare system in 1996. In this book, both the old and the new welfare systems are examined, and their differences highlighted. This book also describes those who make use of the welfare system, why they use it, and what they get out of it.

Social Welfare: Help or Hindrance? consists of ten chapters and three appendices. Each chapter is devoted to a particular aspect of state of minorities in the United States. For a summary of the information covered in each chapter, please see the synopses provided in the Table of Contents at the front of the book. Chapters generally begin with an overview of the basic facts and background information on the chapter's topic, then proceed to examine sub-topics of particular interest. For example, Chapter 5: Factors Affecting Poverty and Welfare Use begins with an overview of the root causes of welfare use in the United States, such as poverty, family size, and unemployment, and how government programs try to address these issues. The chapter then moves on to examine some of the groups most likely to be using welfare, such as single-parent families and the unemployed, in greater detail. The chapter concludes with a discussion of the factors that can force even those who are employed to see government assistance. Readers can find their way through any chapter by looking for the section and sub-section headings, which are clearly set off from the text. Or, they can refer to the book's extensive index, if they already know what they are looking for.

Statistical Information

The tables and figures featured throughout *Social Welfare: Help or Hindrance?* will be of particular use to the reader in learning about this issue. These tables and figures represent an extensive collection of the most recent and important statistics on welfare. For example, the amount of money spent each year for various government welfare programs, the demographics of poverty, the role of child support payments in preventing poverty, the number of people who use welfare-to-work programs to escape poverty, and much more. Gale believes that making this information available to the reader is the most important way in which we fulfill the goal of this book: To help readers understand the issues and controversies

surrounding social welfare in the United States, and reach their own conclusions about them.

Each table or figure has a unique identifier appearing above it, for ease of identification and reference. Titles for the tables and figures explain their purpose. At the end of each table or figure, the original source of the data is provided. The reader can also find the source information for all of the tables and figures gathered together in the Acknowledgments section.

In order to help readers understand these often complicated statistics, all tables and figures are explained in the text. References in the text direct the reader to the relevant statistics. Furthermore, the contents of all tables and figures are fully indexed. Please see the opening section of the index at the back of this volume for a description of how to find tables and figures within it.

In addition to the main body text and images, *Social Welfare: Help or Hindrance?* has three appendices. The first appendix is the Important Names and Addresses directory. Here the reader will find contact information for organizations that study poverty and social welfare, or play a prominent role in shaping opinions and policies on these issues. The second appendix is the Resources section, which is provided to assist the reader in conducting his or her own research. In this section, the author and editors of *Social Welfare: Help or Hindrance?* describe some of the sources that were most useful during the compilation of this book. The final appendix is this book's index. It has been greatly expanded from previous editions, and should make it even easier to find specific topics in this book.

COMMENTS AND SUGGESTIONS

The editor of the *Information Plus Reference Series* welcomes your feedback on *Social Welfare: Help or Hindrance?* Please direst all correspondence to:

Editor
Information Plus Reference Series
27500 Drake Rd.
Farmington Hills, MI, 48331-3535

ACKNOWLEDGMENTS

Photographs and illustrations appearing in **Information Plus-Social Welfare**, *were received from the following sources:*

Figure 2.1, February 1998, "Ensuring the Well-Being of Children Under Welfare Reform," in **Meeting the Challenges of Welfare Reform: Programs with Promise.** Copyrighted by the National Conference of State Legislatures. Reproduced by permission.

Table 2.2, May 1998, "New Mexico Forges Ahead on Welfare." Copyrighted by the Na

tional Conference of State Legislatures. Reproduced by permission.

Figure 9.4, 1998, **Meeting the Challenges of Welfare Reform: Programs with Promise.** National Conference of State Legislatures. Reproduced by permission.

Table 10.1, February, 1998, "Overseeing Welfare Reform: Accountability, Financing, and Devolution," in **Meeting the Challenges of Welfare Reform: Programs with Promise.** Copyrighted by the National Conference

of State Legislatures. Reproduced by permission.

Focus, table 2.1, Vol. 18, No. 3, Spring 1997: 2. University of Wisconsin-Madison Institute for Research in Poverty. Reproduced by permission.

Hunger 1997: The Faces and Facts, figures 3.6, 3.7, 3.8, 3.9. Second Harvest National Research Study. Reproduced by permission.

The Gallup Poll Monthly, tables 7.1, 7.2, 7.3, May, 1994. Gallup Organization. Reproduced by permission.

CHAPTER 1
HOW MUCH DOES THE NATION SPEND ON WELFARE?

The U.S. Social Security Administration defines social welfare expenditures as the cost of "cash benefits, services, and administrative costs of public programs that directly benefit individuals and families." This broad definition includes expenditures for social security (Old-Age, Survivor's, Disability, and Health Insurance or OASDHI), health and medical programs, education, housing, veterans' programs, and public aid programs.

In fiscal year 1995, federal, state, and local governments spent about $1.5 trillion on social welfare programs, an increase of $69.4 billion (5 percent) from 1994. Social insurance, education, and public aid accounted for almost nine-tenths of the total increase. (See Figure 1.1.) Table 1.1 breaks down all social welfare spending by specific categories and by state and federal spending. The 1995 total expenditure for social welfare was almost 21 percent of the gross domestic product (GDP, the monetary total of the domestic goods and services produced by a country) of the United States. This reflects a 1.1 percentage point growth in social welfare spending over the previous four years. (See Table 1.2.)

The federal government accounted for about 59 percent of total spending on social welfare, while state and local governments spent the remaining 41 percent. But the expenditures in each category of spending were very different. For example, social insurance outlays made up about two-thirds (65 percent) of federal welfare spending (primarily in social security) and one-fifth (20 percent) of state and local welfare spending. On the other hand, education expenditures accounted for very little (less than 3 percent) of the total federal welfare spending, while over half (55 percent) of state and local welfare costs were spent for education. (See Table 1.1.)

Though social welfare expenditures have made up over half of all federal spending since 1985, they have been increasing as a percentage of state and local government costs. State and local spending for social welfare grew from 69 percent in 1985 to 84 percent in 1995. (See Table 1.3.) This continual increase was a major reason for the severe budget problems faced by local and state governments during the early 1990s. However, the strong economy of the mid-1990s made it easier for the states to absorb these costs.

PUBLIC AID

While all classes of American people typically benefit from social welfare spending, most people generally consider welfare to be public aid or public assistance programs designed to help the poor. There are several reasons for this. Except for domestic workers and migrant laborers, almost all workers contribute into the nation's social insurance programs (social security, for example), which account for about half of all social welfare expenditures. Consequently, most Americans look upon social insurance as a right or entitlement, especially OASDHI, better known as social security and Medicare. Furthermore, with so many Americans receiving social security payments, or expecting to in the future, it would be politically unwise to consider these expenditures to be similar to programs like Aid to Families with Dependent Children (AFDC) or Medicaid. Similarly, veterans' programs, which account for about 3 percent of all federal social welfare expenditures, are usually considered justifiably earned by those receiving them.

Public assistance has usually included such programs as AFDC, General Assistance, and Medicaid. The latest complete overview of social welfare spending, "Public Social Welfare Expenditures, Fiscal Year 1994" (*Social Security Bulletin*, vol. 62, no. 2, 1999), was prepared by Ann Kallman Bixby. Virtually all these programs are included under "Public aid." (See Table 1.1.) In 1995 public aid accounted for 16.8 percent of all social welfare spending. More than half of this went for Medicaid and other medical expenses. While total costs for social services increased only a small percentage (in constant dol-

FIGURE 1.1

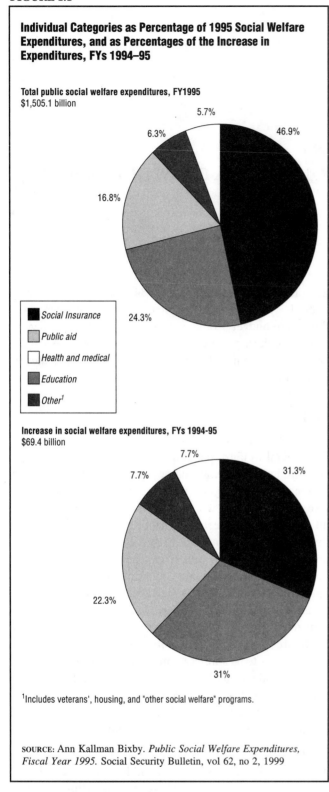

Individual Categories as Percentage of 1995 Social Welfare Expenditures, and as Percentages of the Increase in Expenditures, FYs 1994–95

Total public social welfare expenditures, FY1995
$1,505.1 billion

5.7%
6.3%
16.8%
46.9%
24.3%

- ■ Social Insurance
- ▨ Public aid
- □ Health and medical
- ▨ Education
- ■ Other[1]

Increase in social welfare expenditures, FYs 1994-95
$69.4 billion

7.7%
7.7%
31.3%
22.3%
31%

[1]Includes veterans', housing, and "other social welfare" programs.

SOURCE: Ann Kallman Bixby. *Public Social Welfare Expenditures, Fiscal Year 1995.* Social Security Bulletin, vol 62, no 2, 1999

In 1995 public aid accounted for 3.5 percent of the nation's GDP. From 1975 to 1990, the proportion spent on public aid ranged from about 2.5 to 2.7 percent of GDP. Public health care costs nearly doubled from 3.2 percent of the GDP in 1975 to 6.1 percent of the GDP in 1995. (See Table 1.2.) This increase reflects, among many factors, the growing number of older Americans, who have greater need of medical services, as well as the increasing cost of medical care.

A rapid increase occurred in public spending on health and medical care between the 1970s and 1990s. (See Table 1.4.) In 1975 the government spent $51 billion on health care. A decade later, not accounting for inflation, government spending on health and medical care rose to almost $171 billion, and by 1995, it reached $435 billion. Seventy-two percent of all this spending was on two programs—Medicare and Medicaid. In 1975 the government paid about $15 billion for Medicare; two decades later, in 1995, it spent over $164 billion. Similarly, spending on public assistance medical payments (Medicaid) in 1975 barely exceeded $13.5 billion, but by 1995 Medicaid accounted for over $150 billion. These are huge changes involving enormous sums of money over a relatively short time. This situation helps to explain some of the problems governments face in trying to control their budgets and why health care has become a major national issue.

Welfare Payments

In 1995 the two major categories of public cash benefit payments paid out about $50.6 billion. Public assistance payments (mainly AFDC and general assistance, excluding Medicaid) totaled $22.7 billion, while $27.9 billion was paid out for SSI. Spending has increased dramatically in these areas over just a few years. Between 1985 and 1995 spending on public assistance grew from $15.3 billion to $22.7 billion, a 48 percent rise. Meanwhile, expenditures on SSI have more than doubled, from $11.1 billion to $27.9 billion. Much of this growth reflects the increase in the number of retired Americans, many of whom need Supplemental Security Income in order to live. (See Table 1.5.)

PER CAPITA SPENDING

Another way to look at social welfare spending is to consider per capita spending or how much would theoretically be spent on each person in the United States if the total expenditure were equally divided among the population. In 1995 per capita spending for all government social welfare expenditures reached $5,622. About one-half (47 percent) went for social insurance, mainly social security, and one-fourth (24 percent) went for education. About 6 percent went for health care costs, 4 percent for Veteran programs, 17 percent went for public aid and 2 percent went towards other programs. (See Table 1.6.)

lars, which account for inflation) from 1980 to 1995, the costs of many specific programs had grown tremendously by 1995. Expenditures for Supplementary Security Income (SSI) more than tripled, and spending for food stamps nearly tripled (in current dollars, which do not account for inflation). In addition, medicare spending more than quadrupled. (See Table 1.1.)

TABLE 1.1

Social Welfare Expenditures Under Public Programs, Selected Years 1960–95[1]

[In millions]

Program	1960	1970	1980	1985	1990[2]	1993[2]	1994[2]	1995
				Total expenditures				
Total	$52,519.4	$145,979.2	$492, 212.7	$731,840.1	$1,048,950.8	$1,366,743.1	$1,435,714.3	$1,505,136.4
Social insurance	19,306.5	54,691.2	229,754.4	369,595.2	513,821.8	659,209.9	683,778.7	705,483.3
Old-Age, Survivors, Disability, and Health Insurance (OASDHI)	11,032.2	36,835.4	152,110.4	257,535.1	355,264.5	449,276.8	477,339.7	496,355.8
OASDI	11,032.2	29,686.2	117,118.9	186,150.8	245,555.5	301,183.3	315,947.0	331,642.5
HI (Medicare)[3]	...	7,149.2	34,991.5	71,384.3	109,709.0	148,093.5	161,392.7	164,713.3
Railroad Retirement[4]	934.7	1,609.9	4,768.7	6,275.6	7,229.9	7,920.6	8,025.2	8,106.2
Public employee retirement[5]	2,569.9	8,658.7	39,490.2	63,044.0	90,391.2	112,559.5	119,253.1	128,001.8
Unemployment insurance and employment services[6]	2,829.6	3,819.5	18,326.4	18,343.8	19,973.7	40,720.8	31,251.1	26,302.0
Railroad unemployment insurance	215.2	38.5	155.4	138.4	64.6	60.3	53.5	48.4
Railroad temporary disability insurance	68.5	61.1	68.7	50.6	40.3	25.9	29.3	30.0
State temporary disability insurance[7]	347.9	717.7	1,377.4	1,944.1	3,224.2	3,316.0	3,200.8	3,189.1
Hospital and medical benefits[8]	40.2	62.6	49.6	55.3	62.5	53.7	52.1	43.2
Workers' compensation[9]	1,308.5	2,950.4	13,457.2	22,263.6	37,633.4	45,330.0	44,626.0	43,450.0
Hospital and medical benefits[8]	420.0	985.0	3,725.0	7,080.0	14,305.5	17,712.3	16,200.0	16,700.0
Public aid	4,101.1	16,487.8	72,703.1	98,361.8	146,811.1	220,999.8	238,025.3	253,530.0
Public assistance[10]	4,041.7	14,433.5	45,064.3	66,170.2	105,093.8	160,625.0	171,755.1	187,219.0
Medical payments	492.7	5,212.7	27,570.1	44,182.7	76,115.1	125,138.0	134,204.5	150,869.0
Social services	...	712.6	2,342.8	2,742.8	2,753.2	3,712.9	3,645.2	3,729.0
Supplemental Security Income	...	...	8,226.5	11,840.0	17,230.4	26,506.2	30,085.5	30,138.0
Food stamps	...	577.0	9,083.3	12,512.7	16,254.5	24,496.7	25,273.6	25,319.0
Other[11]	59.4	1,477.3	10,329.0	7,838.9	8,232.4	9,371.9	10,911.1	10,854.0
Health and medical programs[12]	4,690.1	10,030.0	26,762.0	38,643.0	61,684.0	74,706.0	80,130.0	85,507.0
Hospital and medical care	3,079.5	5,407.0	12,286.0	16,373.0	25,971.0	30,617.0	31,562.0	31,904.0
Civilian programs	2,199.4	3,725.0	8,097.0	9,118.0	14,809.0	17,208.0	18,428.0	18,482.0
Defense Department[13]	880.1	1,682.0	4,189.0	7,255.0	11,162.0	13,409.0	13,134.0	13,422.0
Maternal and child health programs[14]	141.4	450.0	870.0	1,222.0	1,865.0	2,185.0	2,272.0	2,348.0
Medical research	448.9	1,684.0	4,924.0	6,903.0	10,848.0	12,779.0	13,988.0	14,982.0
School health	101.0	247.0	575.0	790.0	1,113.0	1,309.0	1,384.0	1,667.0
Other public health activities	401.2	1,312.0	6,484.0	11,223.0	19,354.0	24,772.0	27,685.0	30,808.0
Medical facilities construction	518.1	930.0	1,623.0	2,132.0	2,533.0	3,044.0	3,239.0	3,798.0
Veterans' programs	5,479.3	9,078.1	21,465.5	27,042.3	30,916.2	36,378.3	37,894.8	39,072.0
Pensions and compensation[15]	3,402.7	5,393.8	11,306.0	14,333.0	15,792.6	17,205.2	17,481.0	18,070.4
Health and medical programs	954.1	1,784.1	6,203.9	9,493.2	12,004.1	15,410.5	16,231.4	16,654.4
Hospital and medical care	879.4	1,651.4	5,749.9	8,808.6	11,321.4	14,382.3	15,089.5	15,714.0
Hospital construction	59.6	70.9	323.0	458.0	445.0	749.6	778.8	581.9
Medical and prosthetic research	15.1	61.8	131.0	226.6	237.7	278.6	292.3	289.1
Education	409.6	1,018.5	2,400.7	1,170.8	522.8	937.7	1,098.3	1,118.2
Life insurance[16]	494.1	502.3	664.5	795.5	1,037.8	904.7	971.5	946.3
Welfare and other	218.8	379.4	890.4	1,249.8	1,558.9	1,920.2	2,112.6	2,282.7
Education[17]	17,626.2	50,845.5	121,049.6	172,047.5	258,331.6	331,996.8	344,091.0	365,625.3
Elementary and secondary	15,109.0	38,632.3	87,149.9	120,696.6	199,224.3	252,506.5	261,006.2	277,874.5
Construction	2,661.8	4,659.1	6,524.0	8,358.3	10,636.0	22,288.0	19,692.8	24,809.9
Higher	2,190.8	9,907.0	26,175.9	41,130.4	57,424.3	77,558.1	81,091.2	85,743.8
Construction	357.9	1,566.9	1,528.1	2,346.6	3,953.0	8,990.3	22.8	10,490.3
Vocational and adult[18]	298.0	2,144.4	7,375.2	9,891.2	1,293.3	1,494.9	1,503.8	1,508.0
Housing	176.7	701.2	6,879.0	12,598.5	19,468.5	20,782.3	27,032.0	29,361.1
Public housing	143.5	459.9	4,680.5	9,340.3	14,521.8	15,302.0	24,724.4	24,724.4
Other social welfare	1,139.5	4,145.4	13,599.1	13,551.8	17,917.6	22,670.0	24,762.5	26,557.7
Vocational rehabilitation	96.4	703.8	1,251.1	1,536.7	2,126.6	2,379.1	2,560.1	2,630.3
Medical services	17.8	133.8	279.4	360.0	531.6	594.8	640.0	658.0
Medical research[19]	6.6	29.6	13.5	...	...	...	...	...
Institutional care[20]	420.5	201.8	482.4	379.6	629.4	721.5	783.1	874.0
Child nutrition[21]	398.7	896.0	4,852.3	5,308.5	7,165.4	9,392.4	10,099.1	10,653.4
Child welfare[22]	211.5	585.4	800.0	200.0	252.6	294.6	294.6	292.0
Special OEO and ACTION programs[23]	...	752.8	2,302.7	503.8	169.4	208.3	204.4	222.0
Social welfare, not elsewhere classified[24]	12.4	1,005.6	3,910.6	5,623.2	7,574.2	9,674.1	10,821.2	11,886.0

See footnotes at end of table.

The lower section of Table 1.6 presents per capita spending in constant 1995 dollars that account for increases caused by inflation. From 1980 to 1995 social welfare per capita expenditures under public programs rose 48 percent in constant dollars. The largest increases occurred in total health care costs (113 percent), public aid (69 percent), and social insurance (49 percent). Expenditures for education rose 47 percent,

TABLE 1.1

Social Welfare Expenditures Under Public Programs, Selected Years 1960–95[1] [CONTINUED]

[In millions]

Program	1960	1970	1980	1985	1990[2]	1993[2]	1994[2]	1995
					Federal expenditures			
Total	**$24,956.6**	**$77,130.2**	**$303,152.5**	**$450,604.2**	**$616,640.6**	**$805,335.7**	**$852,875.7**	**$888,357.3**
Social insurance	14,307.1	45,245.6	191,162.0	310,174.7	422,256.6	534,211.9	557,320.7	579,803.7
Old-Age, Survivors, Disability, and								
Health Insurance (OASDHI)	11,032.2	36,835.4	152,110.4	257,535.1	355,264.5	449,276.8	477,339.7	496,355.8
OASDI	11,032.2	29,686.2	117,118.9	186,150.8	245,555.5	301,183.3	315,947.0	331,642.5
HI (Medicare)[3]	...	7,149.2	34,991.5	71,384.3	109,709.0	148,093.5	161,392.7	164,713.3
Railroad Retirement[4]	934.7	1,609.9	4,768.7	6,275.6	7,229.9	7,920.6	8,025.2	8,106.2
Public employee retirement[5]	1,519.9	5,516.7	26,982.9	40,504.0	53,540.4	61,631.6	63,732.9	67,022.3
Unemployment insurance and								
employment services[6]	473.5	1,036.1	4,407.6	2,604.1	3,096.2	12,123.6	4,971.7	5,156.0
Railroad unemployment insurance	215.2	38.5	155.4	138.4	64.6	60.3	53.5	48.4
Railroad temporary disability insurance	68.5	61.1	68.7	50.6	40.3	25.9	29.3	30.0
Workers' compensation[9]	63.1	147.9	2,668.3	3,066.9	3,020.7	3,173.1	3,168.4	3,085.0
Hospital and medical benefits[8]	9.0	20.7	129.5	280.2	456.6	596.6	688.0	668.0
Public aid	2,116.9	9,648.6	49,394.2	63,479.9	92,858.5	151,850.5	162,674.7	170,260.0
Public assistance[10]	2,057.5	7,594.3	23,542.1	33,523.1	54,746.6	95,339.9	100,209.4	107,599.0
Medical payments	199.8	2,607.1	14,550.2	22,677.4	40,690.1	77,367.1	81,192.1	89,113.0
Social services	...	522.0	1,757.1	2,057.1	2,064.9	2,784.7	2,733.9	2,797.0
Supplemental Security Income	...	...	6,439.8	9,605.2	13,625.0	22,642.0	26,280.6	26,488.0
Food stamps	...	577.0	9,083.3	12,512.7	16,254.5	24,496.7	25,273.6	25,319.0
Other[11]	59.4	1,477.3	10,329.0	7,838.9	8,232.4	9,371.9	10,911.1	10,854.0
Health and medical programs[12]	1,737.1	4,568.0	12,827.0	17,842.0	27,206.0	33,189.0	34,770.0	36,767.0
Hospital and medical care	983.5	1,973.0	6,619.0	9,685.0	14,816.0	18,575.0	18,600.0	19,373.0
Civilian programs	103.4	291.0	2,430.0	2,430.0	3,654.0	5,166.0	5,466.0	5,951.0
Defense Department[13]	880.1	1,682.0	4,189.0	7,255.0	11,162.0	13,409.0	13,134.0	13,422.0
Maternal and child health programs[14]	35.3	190.0	351.0	422.0	492.0	595.0	615.0	612.0
Medical research	425.9	1,515.0	4,428.0	5,993.0	9,172.0	10,689.0	11,739.0	12,544.0
Other public health activities	57.3	589.0	1,215.0	1,399.0	2,311.0	3,164.0	3,714.0	3,809.0
Medical facilities construction	235.1	301.0	214.0	343.0	415.0	166.0	102.0	429.0
Veterans' programs	5,367.4	8,951.6	21,253.6	26,704.4	30,427.7	35,806.3	37,261.6	38,384.9
Pensions and compensation[15]	3,402.7	5,393.8	11,306.0	14,333.0	15,792.6	17,205.2	17,481.0	18,070.4
Health and medical programs	954.1	1,784.1	6,203.9	9,493.2	12,004.1	15,410.5	16,231.4	16,654.4
Hospital and medical care	879.4	1,651.4	5,749.9	8,808.6	11,321.4	14,382.3	15,089.5	15,714.0
Hospital construction	59.6	70.9	323.0	458.0	445.0	749.6	778.8	581.9
Medical and prosthetic research	15.1	61.8	131.0	226.6	237.7	278.6	292.3	289.1
Education	409.6	1,018.5	2,400.7	1,170.8	522.8	937.7	1,098.3	1,118.2
Life insurance[16]	494.1	502.3	664.5	795.5	1,037.8	904.7	971.5	946.3
Welfare and other	106.9	252.9	678.5	911.9	1,070.4	1,348.2	1,479.4	1,595.6
Education[17]	867.9	5,875.8	13,452.2	13,796.2	18,374.0	20,454.9	24,084.2	23,472.0
Elementary and secondary	441.9	2,956.8	7,429.6	7,277.6	9,944.3	13,238.0	15,513.8	15,301.0
Construction	70.6	35.9	40.9	23.0	22.9	5.3	8.6	2.0
Higher	293.1	2,154.6	4,467.5	5,102.1	6,746.7	5,284.7	6,576.8	6,164.0
Construction	1.2	466.3	42.1	32.1	...	35.3	22.8	29.0
Vocational and adult[18]	104.5	602.6	1,206.5	1,087.2	1,293.3	1,494.9	1,503.8	1,508.0
Housing	143.5	581.6	6,277.6	11,058.8	16,612.4	18,984.8	24,987.2	27,276.0
Public housing	143.5	459.9	4,680.5	9,340.3	14,521.8	16,414.7	21,396.9	22,522.0
Other social welfare	416.7	2,259.0	8,785.9	7,548.2	8,905.4	10,838.3	11,777.3	12,393.7
Vocational rehabilitation	64.3	567.5	1,006.1	1,186.7	1,660.8	1,830.1	1,962.8	2,031.3
Medical services	11.2	107.0	223.5	275.0	415.2	457.5	491.0	508.0
Medical research[19]	6.6	29.6	13.5	...	...	...	...	...
Institutional care[20]	20.5	22.5	74.2	120.8	143.4	142.6	149.7	152.0
Child nutrition[21]	306.1	710.9	4,209.3	4,348.7	5,469.8	7,139.4	7,626.1	7,992.4
Child welfare[22]	13.4	44.7	57.0	200.0	252.6	294.6	294.6	292.0
Special OEO and ACTION programs[23]	...	752.8	2,302.7	503.8	169.4	208.3	204.4	222.0
Social welfare, not elsewhere								
classified[24]	12.4	160.6	1,136.6	1,188.2	1,209.4	1,223.3	1,539.7	1,704.0

See footnotes at end of table.

while veterans' programs dropped, as did other welfare programs.

STATE EXPENDITURES FOR SOCIAL WELFARE

In fiscal year 1998 state governments spent a total of approximately $826.7 billion. The largest expenditures were on elementary and secondary education (22 percent) and Medicaid (20 percent), followed by higher education (11 percent) and transportation (9 percent). (See Figure 1.2.) About 2.9 percent went for public assistance to the needy, which totaled $23.9 billion, mainly for AFDC.

TABLE 1.1

Social Welfare Expenditures Under Public Programs, Selected Years 1960–95[1] [CONTINUED]

[In millions]

Program	1960	1970	1980	1985	1990[2]	1993[2]	1994[2]	1995
				State and local expenditures				
Total	**$27,562.8**	**$68,849.0**	**$189,060.2**	**$281,235.9**	**$432,310.2**	**$561,418.4**	**$582,943.6**	**$616,779.1**
Social insurance	4,999.4	9,445.6	38,592.4	59,420.5	91,565.2	124,998.0	126,458.0	125,679.6
Public employee retirement[5]	1,050.0	3,142.0	12,507.3	22,540.0	36,850.8	50,927.9	55,520.2	60,979.5
Unemployment insurance and employment services[6]	2,356.1	2,783.4	13,918.8	15,739.7	16,877.5	28,597.2	26,279.4	21,146.0
State temporary disability insurance[7]	347.9	717.7	1,377.4	1,944.1	3,224.2	3,316.0	3,200.8	3,189.1
Hospital and medical benefits[8]	40.2	62.6	49.6	55.3	62.5	53.7	52.1	43.2
Workers' compensation[9]	1,245.4	2,802.5	10,788.9	19,196.7	34,612.7	42,156.9	41,457.6	40,365.0
Hospital and medical benefits[8]	411.0	964.3	3,595.5	6,799.8	13,848.9	17,115.7	15,512.0	16,032.0
Public aid	1,984.2	6,839.2	23,308.9	34,881.9	53,952.6	69,149.3	75,350.6	83,270.0
Public assistance[10]	1,984.2	6,839.2	21,522.2	32,647.1	50,347.2	65,285.1	71,545.7	79,620.0
Medical payments	292.9	2,605.6	13,019.9	21,505.3	35,485.0	47,770.9	53,012.4	61,756.0
Social services	...	190.6	585.7	685.7	688.3	928.2	911.3	932.0
Supplemental Security Income	...	...	1,786.7	2,234.8	3,605.4	3,864.2	3,804.9	3,650.0
Health and medical programs[12]	2,953.0	5,462.0	13,935.0	20,801.0	34,478.0	41,528.0	45,465.0	48,740.0
Hospital and medical care	2,096.0	3,434.0	5,667.0	6,688.0	11,155.0	12,042.0	12,962.0	12,531.0
Maternal and child health programs[14]	106.1	260.0	519.0	800.0	1,373.0	1,590.0	1,657.0	1,736.0
Medical research	23.0	169.0	496.0	910.0	1,676.0	2,090.0	2,249.0	2,438.0
School health	101.0	247.0	575.0	790.0	1,113.0	1,320.0	1,489.0	1,667.0
Other public health activities	343.9	723.0	5,269.0	9,824.0	17,043.0	21,608.0	23,971.0	26,999.0
Medical facilities construction	283.0	629.0	1,409.0	1,789.0	2,118.0	2,878.0	3,137.0	3,369.0
Veterans' programs	111.9	126.5	211.9	337.9	488.5	572.0	633.2	687.1
Education[17]	16,758.3	44,969.7	107,597.4	158,251.3	239,957.6	311,541.9	320,006.8	342,153.3
Elementary and secondary	14,667.1	35,675.5	79,720.3	113,419.0	189,280.0	239,268.5	245,492.4	262,573.5
Construction	2,591.2	4,623.2	6,483.1	8,335.3	10,613.1	22,282.7	19,684.2	24,807.9
Higher	1,897.7	7,752.4	21,708.4	36,028.3	50,677.6	72,273.4	74,514.4	79,579.8
Construction	356.7	1,100.6	1,486.0	2,314.5	3,953.0	8,955.0		10,461.3
Vocational and adult[18]	193.5	1,541.8	6,168.7	8,804.0	...	...	...	...

See footnotes at end of table.

As increased demands were made on state and local funding, much of the impetus for welfare reform came from the states before federal welfare programs were overhauled in 1996. Furthermore, welfare reform became a key goal for President Clinton. In August 1996 he signed into law the Personal Responsibility and Work Opportunity Reconciliation Act of 1996 (PL 104-193). This controversial law repealed the 60-year-old AFDC program and created the Temporary Assistance for Needy Families (TANF) block grant program. Though states must comply with time limits, work requirements, and child protection guidelines, they have been given the flexibility to design their own welfare programs. (See Chapter 2 for more complete information on PL 104-193.) Each state was required to submit a complete plan of implementation no later than July 1, 1997.

Prior to the passage of Public Law 104-193, 43 states were granted federal waivers to set aside federal regulations and guidelines to introduce their own reform proposals. For example, in March 1996 a Texas plan was approved, limiting benefits to a maximum of three years but allowing the recipients to hold more assets, including up to $2,000 in savings, without reducing welfare benefits. For more information on these waivers and how they fit into the new welfare law, see Chapter 2.

FIGURE 1.2

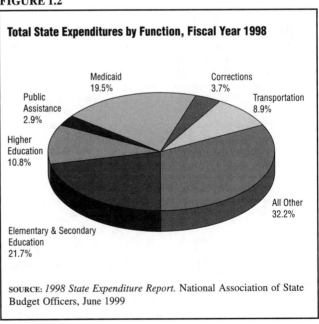

Total State Expenditures by Function, Fiscal Year 1998

Medicaid 19.5%

Corrections 3.7%

Transportation 8.9%

Public Assistance 2.9%

Higher Education 10.8%

All Other 32.2%

Elementary & Secondary Education 21.7%

SOURCE: *1998 State Expenditure Report.* National Association of State Budget Officers, June 1999

The state and federal governments jointly fund cash assistance. In 1998 the federal government provided almost half (42 percent) while the states funded the rest, mostly from general funds. (See Figure 1.3.) State spending for total cash welfare took 2.9 percent of the budget, with state

TABLE 1.1

Social Welfare Expenditures Under Public Programs, Selected Years 1960–95[1] [CONTINUED]

[In millions]

Program	1960	1970	1980	1985	1990[2]	1993[2]	1994[2]	1995
Housing	33.2	119.6	601.4	1,539.7	2,856.1	1,797.5	2,044.8	2,085.1
Other social welfare	722.8	1,886.4	4,813.2	6,003.6	9,012.2	11,831.7	12,985.2	14,164.0
Vocational rehabilitation	32.1	136.3	245.0	350.0	465.8	549.0	597.3	599.0
Medical services	6.6	26.8	55.9	85.0	116.4	137.3	149.0	150.0
Institutional care[20]	400.0	179.3	408.2	258.8	486.0	578.9	633.4	722.0
Child nutrition[21]	92.6	185.1	643.0	959.8	1,695.6	2,253.0	2,473.0	2,661.0
Child welfare[22]	198.1	540.7	743.0	...	...	...	...	...
Social welfare, not elsewhere classified[24]	...	845.0	2,774.0	4,435.0	6,364.8	8,450.8	9,281.5	10,182.0

[1]Expenditures from federal, state, and local revenues and trust funds under public law; includes capital outlays and administrative expenditures unless otherwise noted. Includes some payments abroad. Through 1976, fiscal year ended June 30 for the federal government, most states, and some localities. Beginning in 1977, federal fiscal years end on September 30.

[2]Revised data.

[3]Includes Hospital Insurance and Supplementary Medical Insurance.

[4]Excludes the financial interchange between OASDI and the Railroad Retirement system.

[5]Includes the military retirement system; excludes refunds of employee contributions.
Administrative expenses not available for some programs.

[6]Includes unemployment compensation under state programs, programs for federal employees, trade adjustment and trading allowances, and payments under the extended, emergency, disaster, and special unemployment insurance programs.

[7]Cash and medical benefits in five areas. Includes private plans where applicable and state administrative costs. Data for Hawaii not available.

[8]Included in total directly above.

[9]Cash and medical benefits paid under public law by private insurance carriers. Administrative costs of private carriers and self-insurers not available. Beginning 1960, includes data for Alaska and Hawaii; beginning 1970, includes the federal "Black Lung" program.

[10]Cash payments and medical assistance under the Aid to Families with Dependent Children, Medicaid, emergency assistance, Women, Infants, and Children (WIC), and general assistance programs.
Also includes social services and work incentive activities.

[11]Work relief, other emergency aid, surplus food for the needy, repatriate and refugee assistance, and work-experience training programs. Beginning in 1981, includes Low-Income Home Energy Assistance.

[12]Excludes state and local expenditures for domiciliary care in institutions other than those for tuberculosis.
Also excludes medical services connected with the OASDHI, state temporary disability insurance, workers' compensation, public assistance, veterans', and vocational rehabilitation programs, which are included in the expenditures for those programs. State and local expenditures include amounts for anti-poverty State school health expenditures included in "Hospital and medical care."

[13]Includes medical care for military dependents.

[14]Includes services for disabled children.

[15]Includes burial awards, special allowances for the survivors of veterans who did not qualify for OASDI, and clothing allowances.

[16]Excludes the serviceperson's group life insurance program.

[17]Federal administrative expenditures (Department of Education) and research costs included in total only.

[18]State and local expenditures for vocational and adult education not available after 1985.

[19]No longer available separately after 1980.

[20]Federal expenditures represent primarily surplus food for institutions.

[21]Surplus food for schools and programs under the National School Lunch and Child Nutrition Acts.

[22]Represents primarily child welfare services under the Social Security Act. State and local data not available after 1980.

[23]Includes domestic programs consolidated in 1972 under ACTION and special Office of Economic Opportunity programs. From 1987 to 1994, represents ACTION funds only. Starting 1994, represents Domestic Volunteer Service programs.

[24]Federal expenditures include the administrative and related expenses of the Secretary of Health and Human Services; Indian welfare and guidance, aging and juvenile delinquency, and certain manpower and human development programs. State and local expenditures include amounts for anti-poverty and manpower programs, day care, child placement and adoption services, foster care, legal assistance, care of transients, and other unspecified welfare services.

SOURCE: Ann Kallman Bixby. *Public Social Welfare Expenditures, Fiscal Year 1995.* Social Security Bulletin, vol 62, no 2, 1999

contributions for AFDC representing 2.1 percent of the total. The federal government paid a larger proportion of AFDC (53.2 percent) than they did for all of state welfare. As with overall spending for cash assistance, the AFDC proportion of state spending has dropped in recent years.

Medicaid

The National Association of State Budget Officers observed in the *1996 State Expenditure Report* (Washington, D.C., 1997), "Though Medicaid spending increases are leveling off, the growth of Medicaid continues to dominate as a budget problem for states." As a percent of total state expenditures, Medicaid spending increased from 10 percent in 1987 to 14 percent in 1991 and 20 percent in 1998. Two factors that help explain this dramatic increase are the rate of inflation for medical goods and services and the increased number of persons eligible for Medicaid. "With states experiencing limited revenue growth over the last few years," the *1996 State Expenditure Report* stated, "Medicaid increases absorbed the bulk of additional revenue generated in many states."

TABLE 1.2

Social Welfare Expenditures Under Public Programs as a Percent of Gross Domestic Product (GDP), Selected Years 1950–95

Fiscal year	Gross domestic product in billions)[1]	All programs[2]			Program category						
		Total	Federal	State and local	Social insurance	Public aid	Health and medical programs	Veterans' programs	Education	Other social welfare	Total health care costs[3]
1950	$266.8	8.8	3.9	4.7	1.8	0.9	0.8	2.6	2.5	0.2	1.1
1955	386.4	8.5	3.8	4.7	2.4	.8	.8	1.2	2.8	.2	1.2
1960	524.1	10.0	4.8	5.3	3.7	.8	.9	1.0	3.4	.2	1.2
1965	701.0	11.0	5.4	5.6	4.0	.9	.9	.9	4.0	.3	1.3
1970	1,023.1	14.3	7.5	6.7	5.3	1.6	1.0	.9	5.0	.4	2.4
1975	1,590.8	18.2	10.5	7.7	7.7	2.6	1.0	1.1	5.1	.4	3.2
1980	2,718.9	18.1	11.1	7.0	8.5	2.7	1.0	.8	4.5	.5	3.6
1985	4,108.0	17.8	11.0	6.8	9.0	2.4	.9	.7	4.2	.3	4.2
1990	5,682.9	18.5	10.9	7.6	9.0	2.6	1.1	.5	4.5	.3	4.8
1991	5,861.5	19.8	11.5	8.2	9.6	3.1	1.1	.6	4.7	.3	5.4
1992[4]	6,149.3	20.6	12.2	8.4	10.1	3.4	1.1	.6	4.8	.4	5.7
1993[4]	6,476.6	21.1	12.4	8.7	10.2	3.4	1.2	.6	5.1	.4	5.9
1994[4]	6,837.1	21.0	12.5	8.5	10.0	3.5	1.2	.6	5.0	.4	6.0
1995	7,186.9	20.9	12.4	8.6	9.8	3.5	1.2	.5	5.1	.4	6.1

[1]Revised in 1996 to reflect changes in GDP figures for 1960-93, as released by the Bureau of Economic Analysis, January/February 1996.
[2]Includes housing, not shown separately.
[3]Combines "health and medical" programs with medical services provided under the social insurance, public aid, veterans', and "other social welfare" programs.
[4]Revised data.

SOURCE: Ann Kallman Bixby. *Public Social Welfare Expenditures, Fiscal Year 1995.* Social Security Bulletin, vol 62, no 2, 1999

FIGURE 1.3

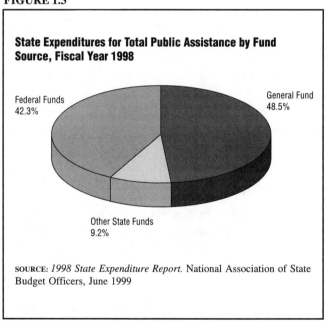

State Expenditures for Total Public Assistance by Fund Source, Fiscal Year 1998

Federal Funds 42.3%
General Fund 48.5%
Other State Funds 9.2%

SOURCE: *1998 State Expenditure Report.* National Association of State Budget Officers, June 1999

FIGURE 1.4

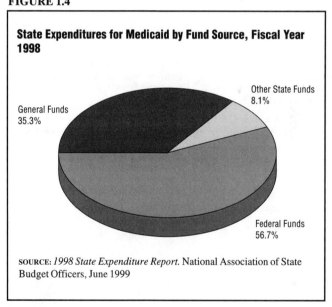

State Expenditures for Medicaid by Fund Source, Fiscal Year 1998

General Funds 35.3%
Other State Funds 8.1%
Federal Funds 56.7%

SOURCE: *1998 State Expenditure Report.* National Association of State Budget Officers, June 1999

In 1998 total spending on Medicaid, not including administrative costs, reached $161 billion, up 3.5 percent from the 1997 level but down from the nearly 10 percent increase between 1994 and 1995. Of the $161 billion total, the federal government paid 57 percent, and the states paid the remaining 43 percent. (See Figure 1.4.) In 1998 the states paid $69 billion, more than double the $32 billion eight years earlier. In addition Medicaid spending has increased since 1970, with expenditures projected to be $86 billion in 2000. (See Figure 1.5.)

PRIVATE WELFARE EXPENDITURES

The private sector is an important source of social welfare funding. These expenditures can be grouped into four program categories: health and medical care, welfare services, education, and income maintenance. In 1994 private spending for welfare services reached $86 billion, more than 3.5 times the almost $23 billion spent in 1980 (in current dollars, which do not account for inflation). As a fraction of total private social welfare outlays, welfare spending increased from 7.9 percent in 1972 to 9.4 per-

TABLE 1.3

Social Welfare Expenditures from Public Funds[1] as a Percent of Government Expenditures for All Purposes, Selected Years 1965–95

Type of fund	1965	1970	1975	1980	1985	1990[2]	1991[2]	1992[2]	1993[2]	1994[2]	1995
					All public social welfare expenditures						
Total as a percent of all government expenditures	42.2	46.5	56.6	57.2	54.4	58.2	60.3	63.7	66.6	64.5	67.5
Federal as a percent of all federal expenditures	32.6	40.0	53.7	54.4	48.7	51.4	52.8	57.4	60.0	57.4	60.2
State and local as a percent of all state and local expenditures[3]	60.4	57.9	61.6	62.9	68.8	74.0	77.4	77.7	80.7	80.4	83.6
					Trust fund social welfare expenditures						
Total as a percent of all government expenditures	14.3	16.4	22.2	24.7	26.0	26.9	27.5	29.1	30.0	29.0	30.0
Federal as a percent of all federal expenditures	17.7	22.0	29.1	31.3	31.4	33.2	33.4	35.5	37.2	35.5	37.2
State and local as a percent of all state and local expenditures[3]	7.8	6.5	10.5	11.1	12.3	12.4	13.9	15.1	14.8	14.4	14.1
					Non-trust fund social welfare expenditures						
Total as a percent of all expenditures from general revenues	27.8	36.6	45.1	44.1	39.3	42.7	45.2	48.8	52.2	50.0	53.6
Federal as a percent of all federal expenditures from general revenues:											
All programs	14.8	23.8	35.8	34.9	26.3	27.2	29.1	33.9	36.3	34.0	36.6
Public aid	3.1	6.6	12.8	13.4	10.4	11.6	13.3	16.5	18.1	17.0	18.4
State and local as a percent of all state and local expenditures from general revenues:[3]											
All programs	52.6	55.0	57.1	58.3	64.5	69.8	73.7	73.7	77.3	77.1	80.9
Education	42.4	44.1	44.3	44.9	50.0	52.4	53.7	53.8	58.3	57.0	59.6
Public aid	4.5	6.7	8.7	9.7	11.0	11.8	14.2	13.7	12.9	13.4	14.5

[1]Excludes that part of workers' compensation and temporary disability insurance payments made through private carriers and self-insurers.

[2]Revised data. In particular, state and local figures reflect revisions in the National Income and Product Accounts reports of total state/local government expenditures. Those figures were revised downward, resulting in higher percentages for social welfare outlays.

[3]From state and local sources, excluding federal grants.

SOURCE: Ann Kallman Bixby. *Public Social Welfare Expenditures, Fiscal Year 1995.* Social Security Bulletin, vol 62, no 2, 1999

FIGURE 1.5

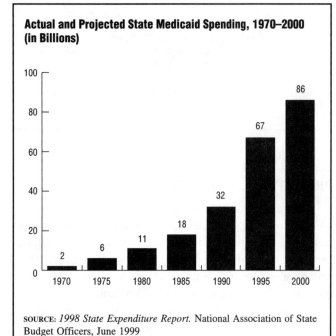

Actual and Projected State Medicaid Spending, 1970–2000 (in Billions)

SOURCE: *1998 State Expenditure Report.* National Association of State Budget Officers, June 1999

cent in 1994. (See Table 1.7.) Welfare services funded by private sources include:

- Individual and family services (counseling and referral services for families and children, family service agencies, adoption services, emergency and disaster services, child day-care services, and senior citizen services).

- Residential care (group foster homes, halfway homes, and housing and shelter for the homeless).

- Recreation and group work (YMCA, YWCA, Boy Scouts, and Girl Scouts).

- Civic, social, and fraternal organizations.

- Job training and vocational rehabilitation, such as sheltered workshops, vocational rehabilitation agencies, and skill-training centers.

TABLE 1.4

All Public Expenditures for Health and Medical Care, Selected Years 1965–95

[In millions]

Program	1965	1970	1975	1980	1985	1990[1]	1991[1]	1992[1]	1993[1]	1994[1]	1995
Total	$9,302	$24,801	$51,022	$99,145	$171,399	$274,472	$314,227	$353,174	$381,710	$408,780	$435,075
Health and medical services	7,531	22,187	46,862	92,598	161,679	260,408	299,692	336,925	364,858	390,482	415,424
Medicare	...	7,149	14,781	34,992	71,384	109,709	116,651	132,246	148,094	161,393	164,713
Temporary disability insurance[2]	51	63	73	50	55	63	66	70	54	52	43
Workers' compensation[2]	580	985	2,470	3,725	7,080	14,306	16,010	17,914	17,712	16,200	16,700
Public assistance medical payments	1,367	5,213	13,551	27,570	44,183	76,175	101,909	117,622	125,138	134,204	150,869
General hospital and medical care	2,510	3,301	6,019	8,105	9,118	14,809	15,511	15,928	17,208	18,428	18,482
Hospital and medical care for Armed Forces and dependents	881	1,682	2,817	4,198	7,455	11,162	12,740	12,769	13,409	13,134	13,422
Maternal and child health programs	239	450	567	870	1,222	1,865	1,981	2,106	2,185	2,272	2,348
School health (education agencies)	140	247	352	575	790	1,113	1,194	1,230	1,309	1,384	1,667
Other public health activities	614	1,312	2,727	6,484	11,223	19,354	20,881	22,976	24,772	27,685	30,808
Veterans' hospital and medical care	1,115	1,651	3,287	5,750	8,809	11,321	12,190	13,452	14,382	15,090	15,714
Medical vocational rehabilitation	34	134	218	279	360	532	559	612	595	640	658
Medical research	1,227	1,684	2,648	4,924	7,130	11,086	11,568	12,869	13,058	14,280	15,271
Medical facilities construction	544	930	1,512	1,623	2,590	2,978	2,967	3,380	3,794	4,018	4,380
Department of Veterans' Affairs	77	71	137	323	458	445	776	845	750	779	582
Total as percent of gross domestic product	1	2.4	3.2	3.6	4.2	4.8	5.4	5.7	5.9	6.0	6.1

[1] Revised data.

[2] Includes medical benefits paid under public law by private carriers and self-insurers.

SOURCE: Ann Kallman Bixby. *Public Social Welfare Expenditures, Fiscal Year 1995*. Social Security Bulletin, vol 62, no 2, 1999

EFFECTS OF NEW WELFARE-REFORM LEGISLATION

The intent of the Personal Responsibility and Work Opportunity Reconciliation Act of August 1996 (PL 104-193) was to reduce future welfare expenditures by changing provisions and requiring work from welfare recipients. The 1997 Balanced Budget Reconciliation Act modified some provisions of PL 104-193 and restored and even added funding for certain programs. Both pieces of legislation brought about sweeping changes in the welfare system. Yet, while most of the new programs have dramatically cut welfare logs, they have not gone without what many consider to be a hitch. The implementation of state plans for welfare reform produced mixed results. While welfare reform advocates claim that the new system has lifted former welfare recipients out of poverty and into gainful employment, critics argue that changes pushed those who left welfare for work deeper into poverty. For information about the provisions and aftereffects of both laws, see Chapter 2.

TABLE 1.5

Public Income-Maintenance Programs, Cash Payment Benefits, 1940–97

Retirement, disability, and survivor benefits. Monthly group: OASDI, Railroad Retirement, Public employee retirement[5] (Federal Civil Service, Other[7]), Veterans' pension and compensation[8]. Lump sum[9]: OASDI, Other[10]. Unemployment benefits: State laws[11], Railroad[12]. Temporary disability benefits: State laws[12], Railroad[13].

Period	Total[1,2]	OASDI[3]	Railroad Retirement[4]	Federal Civil Service[6]	Other[7]	Veterans' pension and compensation[8]	OASDI (lump sum)	Other[10]	State laws[11] (unemployment)	Railroad[12] (unemployment)	State laws[12] (temp. disability)	Railroad[13]	Workers' compensation benefits[14]	Public assistance payments[15]	Supplemental Security income payments[16]
1940	$2,171.4	823.5	$115.6	$62.0	$183.1	$123.5	$11.8	1624.9	$518.7	$16.0	589.3	$28.1	$161.1	$631.3	
1950	8,395.4	928.4	295.1	184.2	600.4	2,223.8	32.7	54.0	1,407.8	59.8	311.3	56.9	415.0	2,073.9	
1960	25,564.0	11,080.5	942.4	804.5	1,793.3	3,436.9	163.3	135.2	2,867.1	157.7	644.6	56.2	860.0	2,953.9	
1970	59,322.9	31,569.8	1,756.2	2.796.6	6,369.4	5,480.1	293.6	288.6	4,183.7	38.7	1,299.8	63.2	1,981.0	4,864.4	
1980	227,853.7	120,271.7	4,866.6	15,042.5	25,558.8	11,358.4	250.2	606.0	18,756.5	176.1	1,807.8	47.3	9,632.0	12,144.4	$7,857.5
1985	328,304.2	186,082.9	6,264.7	22,840.5	40,028.4	14,083.6	142.9	679.5	14,639.2	134.3	3,099.2	57.5	15,170.0	15,276.1	11,107.0
1990	434,752.7	244,756.9	7,258.9	29,395.7	58,348.5	15,717.3	130.8	211.6	18,059.0	61.2	21,226.6	18.502.9	23,029.3	19,271.6	15,175.2
1991	478,224.1	264,216.0	7,571.0	31,777.1	63,316.6	16,245.6	132.3	283.6	25,450.2	25,693.9	22,329.0	22,323.9	27,617.7	21,037.5	
1992	507,012.6	281,393.0	7,747.6	30,691.4	69,208.8	16,315.7	88.0	188.3	24,967.0	27,753.8	3,100.5	48.8	27,426.0	23,270.4	
1993		296,155.6	7,904.3	32,947.8	76,096.1	16,864.8	80.9	(17)	21,547.0	51.3	(17)	55.9	26,750.0	22,712.4	24,730.2
1994		311,496.0	8,001.5	35,715.0	(17)	18,747.4	94.3	(17)	21,645.7	45.4	(17)	54.8			26,077.5
1995		326,670.7	8,085.1	37,689.0	(17)	17,974.5	119.4	(17)	22,009.8	39.7					27,870.7
1996															
September		25,477.5	679.3			1,574.3	9.7		1,405.4	2.3		4-1	53.7	1,676.9	2,428.9
October		28,521.1	678.0			1,536.9	9.6		1,466.5	2.3		4.8	53.3	(17)	2,429.6
November		28,562.7	677.0			1,532.7	9.8		1,371.3	2.4	…	5.1	53.0	(17)	2,481.0
December		29,416.3	668.0			1,608.4	9.8		1,871.7	3.1	…	5.6	52.6	(17)	2,399.1
1997															
January		29,296.8	693.7			1,579.1	3.6		2,242.0	5.0		6 4	53.3	(17)	2,389.7
February		29,356.5	690.2			1,640.6	.8		2,020.2	5.7		5.1	52.9	(17)	2,459.9
March		29,410.3	690.8			1,635.0	0.0		2,058.1	5.4		5.3	52.5	(17)	2,466.8
April		29,450.3	673.8			1,630.0	30.7		1,837.3	4.3	…	5.6	52.1	(17)	2,451.8
May		29,522.6	683.5			1,633.9	19.5		1,495.9	2.7		4.8	51.7	(17)	2,441.4
June		29,558.5	701.7			1,609.5	11.4		1,457.8	2.1		4.6	51.4	(17)	2,485.6
July		29,601.0	680.2			(17)	9.7		1,608.3	1.7	…	4.5	51.0	(17)	2,436.6
August		29,653.4	672.9			(17)	10.6		1,385.0	1.9		4.5	50.7	(17)	2,453.1
September		29,698.0	694.3			(17)	11.1		1,369.6	2.0		5.0	50.4	(17)	2,483.9

1 Emergency relief funds of $1,630.3 million in 1940 total, not included elsewhere. Includes training allowances to unemployed workers under Area Redevelopment Act and Manpower Development and Training Act for 1961-15, *not* shown separately.

2 Beginning December 1980, includes public assistance revisions for 1940-79.

3 Retirement and survivor benefits beginning in 1940; disability benefit beginning in 1957. Beginning October 1966, includes special benefits authorized by 1966 legislation for persons aged 72 or older not insured under the regular or transitional provisions of the Social Security Act.

4 Includes annuities to widows under joint-and-survivor elections before 1947. Beginning February 1967, includes supplemental annuities for career railroad employees.

5 Excludes refunds of contributions to employees who leave service.

6 Beginning January 1988, includes both CSRS and FERS benefits. Beginning 1994, annual data only.

7 Represents Federal contributory systems other than Civil Service, Federal noncontributory systems for civilian employees and career military personnel, and systems for State and local employees. Monthly data not available.

8 Payment to veterans and survivors of deceased veterans, including special allowances for survivors of Veterans who did not qualify under OASDHI (Servicemen's and Veterans' Survivor Benefit Act of 1956) and through June 1973, subsistence payments to disabled veterans undergoing training.

9 Death payment.

TABLE 1.5

Public Income-Maintenance Programs, Cash Payment Benefits, 1940–97 [CONTINUED]

[10] Includes annual and monthly data for Railroad Retirement, Veterans' programs, and Federal Civil Service Retirement. For "other" public employee systems, annual data only. Lump-sum data not available for State and local retirement systems after 1986.

[11] Annual and monthly totals include regular State Unemployment Insurance program and payments made by States as agents of the Federal Government under the Federal Employees' Unemployment Compensation program and under the Ex-Servicemen's Compensation Act of 1958. Annual data only for payment under Servicemen's Readjustment Act of 1944, Veterans' Readjustment Act of 1952, Disaster Relief Act of 1970, and the Temporary and Permanent Extended Unemployment Insurance programs. Beginning in 1961, includes program in Puerto Rico. Beginning in 1981, State Unemployment Insurance and ex-Servicemen's Compensation Act only. Beginning July 1987, state programs only.

[12] Benefits in Rhode Island (from 1943), in California (from 1947). in New Jersey (from 1949), in New York (from 1950), in Puerto Rico (from 1970), in Hawaii (from 1972), including payments under private plans where applicable. Monthly data not available.

[13] Benefit began 1947.

[14] Under Federal worker compensation laws and under State laws paid by private insurance carriers, State funds, and self-insurers. Beginning in 1959, includes data for Alaska and Hawaii. Monthly data refer only to Federal Black Lung Benefits administered by the Social Security Administration (stating in 1970).

[15] Includes Aid to Families with Dependent Children and General Assistance. Through 1973 includes Old-Age Assistance, Aid to the Blind, and Aid to the Permanently and Totally Disabled. Includes payments to intermediate-care facilities (July 1968-December 1971); and payments for emergency assistance, beginning July 1969. Includes money payment under medical assistance for the aged (1960-69). Excludes medical vendor payments. Starting in 1974, includes money payment to the aged, blind, and disabled in Guam, Puerto Rico, and the Virgin Islands under federally aided public assistance programs.

[16] Supercedes the public assistance programs of Old-Age Assistance, Aid to the Blind, and Aid to the Permanently and Totally Disabled in the 50 States and the District of Columbia, beginning in 1974: beginning in 1978, in the Northern Mariana Islands. Annual, but not monthly, totals include payment under State-administered supplementation programs.

[17] Data not available.

SOURCE: Social Security Bulletin, vol 61, no 2, 1998

TABLE 1.6

Total and Per Capita Social Welfare Expenditures Under Public Programs, in Current and Constant (1995) Dollars, Selected Years 1965–95

Fiscal year	Total expenditures		Per capita expenditures for—						
	Amount (in millions)[1]	Per capita[2]	Social insurance	Public aid	Health and medical programs	Veterans' programs	Education	Other social welfare	Total health care costs[3]
					Current dollars				
1965	$76,837.00	$390.69	$142.29	$31.95	$31.30	$30.30	$142.73	$10.50	$47.30
1970	145,183.20	697.91	261.75	79.26	46.18	43.16	244.27	19.93	119.22
1975	288,457.60	1,315.73	558.66	189.05	76.36	76.95	368.56	31.69	232.73
1980	491,597.80	2,126.35	989.95	314.47	117.92	92.02	523.41	58.82	428.84
1985	730,896.70	3,009.79	1,515.98	405.05	162.14	110.53	708.41	55.81	705.81
1990[4]	1,046,498.30	4,124.03	2,017.31	578.55	243.08	119.79	1,017.96	70.61	1,081.64
1991[4]	1,157,039.40	4,520.44	2,184.52	708.48	257.11	126.13	1,082.84	77.28	1,227.66
1992[4]	1,263,322.90	4,868.30	2,376.93	801.36	270.30	133.35	1,125.73	82.97	1,360.98
1993[4]	1,364,067.80	5,237.51	2,523.19	848.56	286.84	137.40	1,274.67	87.04	1,465.62
1994[4]	1,432,756.70	5,446.19	2,590.96	904.78	304.59	141.10	1,307.88	94.13	1,553.85
1995	1,502,234.40	5,622.39	2,631.98	948.88	320.03	143.86	1,368.34	99.40	1,628.35
					Percentage increase to 1995				
1965	1,855.09	1,339.10	1,749.73	2,870.01	922.58	374.72	858.71	846.38	3,342.80
1970	934.72	705.60	905.53	1,097.20	593.04	233.36	460.17	398.81	1,265.82
1975	420.78	327.32	371.13	401.92	319.07	86.96	271.27	213.70	599.69
1980	205.58	164.41	165.87	201.74	171.38	56.33	161.43	68.98	279.71
1985	105.53	86.80	73.62	134.26	97.38	30.16	93.16	78.11	130.71
1990	43.55	36.33	30.47	64.01	31.65	20.10	34.42	40.77	50.54
1991	29.83	24.38	20.48	33.93	24.47	14.06	26.37	28.62	32.64
1992	18.91	15.49	10.73	18.41	18.40	7.89	21.55	19.79	19.65
1993	10.13	7.35	4.31	11.82	11.57	4.70	7.35	14.19	11.10
1994	4.85	3.24	1.58	4.87	5.07	1.96	4.62	5.60	4.79
					Constant (1995) dollars				
1965	330,706.45	1,681.52	612.42	137.51	134.70	130.43	614.30	45.20	203.57
1970	510,513.47	2,454.10	920.40	278.70	162.37	151.75	858.94	70.07	419.22
1975	735,498.53	3,354.81	1,424.44	482.03	194.71	196.21	939.74	80.79	593.39
1980	875,760.32	3,788.01	1,763.56	560.21	210.07	163.94	932.43	104.79	763.96
1985	1,003,118.43	4,130.78	2,080.61	555.91	222.52	151.70	972.25	76.59	968.69
1990	1,203,025.82	4,740.88	2,319.05	665.09	279.44	137.70	1,170.22	81.17	1,243.42
1991	1,286,130.57	5,024.79	2,428.25	787.52	285.80	140.20	1,203.65	85.90	1,364.63
1992	1,359,335.44	5,238.29	2,557.58	862.26	290.84	143.48	1,211.28	89.28	1,464.41
1993	1,429,149.91	5,487.40	2,643.58	889.04	300.53	143.96	1,335.49	91.20	1,535.55
1994	1,465,443.16	5,570.44	2,650.07	925.42	311.54	144.32	1,337.72	96.27	1,589.30
1995	1,502,234.40	5,622.39	2,631.98	948.88	320.03	143.86	1,368.34	99.40	1,628.61
					Percentage increase to 1995				
1965	354	234	330	590	138	10	123	120	700
1970	194	129	186	240	97	-5	59	42	288
1975	104	68	85	97	64	-27	46	23	174
1980	72	48	49	69	52	-12	47	-5	113
1985	50	36	27	71	44	-5	41	30	68
1990	25	19	13	43	15	4	17	22	31
1991	17	12	8	20	12	3	14	16	19
1992	11	7	3	10	10	0	13	11	11
1993	5	2	0	7	6	0	2	9	6
1994	3	1	-1	3	3	0	2	3	2

[1] Excludes expenditures in foreign countries for OASDHI benefits, civil service retirement benefits, veterans' programs, and education.

[2] Includes housing, not shown separately.

[3] Combines "health and medical" programs with medical services provided in connection with social insurance, public aid, veterans', and "other social welfare" programs.

[4] Revised data

SOURCE: Ann Kallman Bixby. *Public Social Welfare Expenditures, Fiscal Year 1995.* Social Security Bulletin, vol 62, no 2, 1999

TABLE 1.7

Welfare Services: Private Expenditures as a Percent of Total Private Outlays: National Income and Product Accounts Data, 1972–94
[Amounts in millions]

Year	Expenditure	Percent of total private outlays
1972	$ 7,545	7.9
1973	8,297	8.0
1974	8,970	7.9
1975	10,067	7.8
1976	11,748	8.1
1977	13,535	8.1
1978	16,590	8.8
1979	19,540	9.0
1980	22,776	9.1
1981	25,728	9.0
1982	28,067	8.6
1983	31,392	8.6
1984	34,749	8.5
1985	38,999	8.4
1986	43,211	8.4
1987	47,601	8.7
1988	52,579	8.8
1989	59,312	8.9
1990	64,583	9.0
1991	68,998	9.0
1992	76,022	9.2
1993	80,899	9.3
1994	86,297	9.4

SOURCE: Wilmer L. Kerns. *Public Social Welfare Expenditures, 1972-1994.* Social Security Bulletin, vol 60, no 1, 1997

CHAPTER 2
RECENT WELFARE-REFORM LEGISLATION

A TIME OF RADICAL CHANGE

The summer of 1996 brought about profound and controversial changes in the way America handles its welfare programs. Much criticism had been directed toward the previous welfare system, based mainly on Aid to Families with Dependent Children (AFDC). This criticism centered on claims that the system produced welfare dependency rather than temporary assistance to help recipients move into a job and off welfare. According to LaDonna Pavetti in *Questions and Answers on Welfare Dynamics* (Urban Institute, Washington, D.C., September 1995), the average length of stay on welfare, counting repeat spells, for families who were enrolled in AFDC at any given moment, was 13 years. In addition to time-limited assistance, welfare-reform issues included child care; child support;

FIGURE 2.1

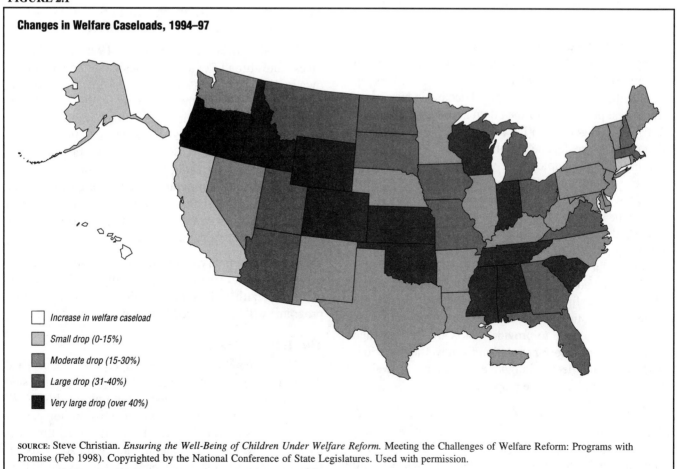

Changes in Welfare Caseloads, 1994–97

Increase in welfare caseload
Small drop (0-15%)
Moderate drop (15-30%)
Large drop (31-40%)
Very large drop (over 40%)

SOURCE: Steve Christian. *Ensuring the Well-Being of Children Under Welfare Reform.* Meeting the Challenges of Welfare Reform: Programs with Promise (Feb 1998). Copyrighted by the National Conference of State Legislatures. Used with permission.

young, unmarried women with children; assistance to immigrants; and welfare costs.

When earlier welfare-reform efforts stalled in the federal government, many states began to explore ways to modify their welfare programs. In President Clinton's first term, 43 states were granted federal waivers, allowing them to experiment with different approaches to welfare and work. State plans generally included stiffer work and time requirements and greater demands of parental responsibility. Many of the programs that developed from those waivers helped to lay the foundation for the new welfare-reform law.

After many proposals, much congressional discussion, and several presidential vetoes, a massive welfare-reform bill, the Personal Responsibility and Work Opportunity Reconciliation Act (PL 104-193), was signed into law in August 1996. Replacing AFDC with Temporary Assistance for Needy Families (TANF), the law requires that a welfare recipient work in exchange for time-limited assistance. It provides $1 billion for performance bonuses to reward states for moving welfare recipients into jobs. PL 104-193 also requires a state "maintenance of effort," a continuation of welfare spending at a level that is at least 80 percent of its 1994 expenditures. The law contains comprehensive child support enforcement and supports for families moving from welfare to work, including increased funding for child care and guaranteed medical coverage.

Overall, the welfare caseload has fallen by 7.2 million recipients from 14.1 million recipients in January 1993, to 6.9 million in March 1999, a drop of 51 percent. This represents the largest welfare caseload decline in history and the lowest percentage of the population on welfare since 1967. (See Figure 2.1.) However, most observers agree that much of the decline was the result of a strong economy in which unemployment was around 4 percent, an unprecedented low, rather than of welfare reform. Most people who found work over the past three years would have done so anyway in a booming economy. Some wonder whether the new welfare system is recession-proof. Others question whether it is fair to everyone. Some critics claim that the new system leads to former welfare recipients, without adequate health care, child care, and affordable housing, slipping through the cracks of the welfare system into destitution and homelessness. States under the new system, unable to provide jobs with a living wage, merely move the poor population from welfare into low-wage work and deeper into poverty. As a result, welfare legislation continues to be proposed.

The Balanced Budget Act of 1997 (PL 105-33) made many modifications and additions to the 1996 welfare-reform law, including changes to the TANF block grant and funding for additional grants (see below). A Senate

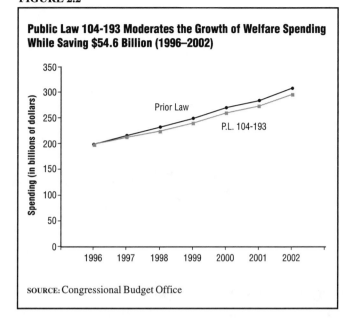

FIGURE 2.2

Public Law 104-193 Moderates the Growth of Welfare Spending While Saving $54.6 Billion (1996–2002)

SOURCE: Congressional Budget Office

agriculture bill, which passed the Senate overwhelmingly in May 1998, included a provision to restore food stamps to 250,000 legal immigrants who were cut from the rolls under the 1996 law. Following passage by the House of Representatives, President Clinton signed the bill into law on June 23, 1998.

THE PERSONAL RESPONSIBILITY AND WORK OPPORTUNITY RECONCILIATION ACT OF 1996

Signed into law on August 22, 1996, PL 104-193 gives states broad flexibility to design and operate their own welfare programs while, at the same time, holding them accountable to the proposed regulations. States were required to implement their block grants programs (see below) by July 1, 1997. According to the Congressional Budget Office (CBO), though welfare spending will continue to grow about 50 percent through the beginning of the twenty-first century, the rate of growth will be reduced. The CBO claims that this drop in the growth of welfare spending will reduce the federal budget deficit by nearly $55 billion. (See Figure 2.2.)

A brief summary of the welfare-reform law, based primarily on information prepared by the U.S. Department of Health and Human Services, follows. Specific programs will be discussed further in later chapters.

Title I: Block Grants

The law combines AFDC, Emergency Assistance, and the JOBS program into a single block grant (a lump sum of money) for each state. Federal funding for this TANF block grant is capped at an estimated $16.4 billion per fiscal years 1996 through 2002. Each state's allotment is based on previous years' federal funding for AFDC benefits and administration, Emergency Assistance, and JOBS.

States have considerable control over how they will implement the programs covered by the block grant, but the act requires that:

- Families on welfare for five cumulative years may no longer receive further cash assistance. States can set shorter time limits and can exempt up to 20 percent of their caseload from the time limits.

- To count toward meeting the work requirement, a state must require individuals to participate in employment (public or private), on-the-job training, community service, work experience, vocational training (up to 12 months), or child care for other workers for at least 20 hours per week. State and local communities are responsible for the development of work, whether by creating community service jobs or by providing income subsidies or hiring incentives for potential employers.

- As part of their state plans, states must require families to work after two years of receiving benefits. In 1998 states were required to have 30 percent of all families, and 75 percent of all two-parent families, engaged in a work activity for a minimum of 20 hours per week for single parents and 35 hours a week for at least one adult in two-parent families. The rates for all families started at 25 percent in 1997 and increase 5 percent each year to 50 percent in 2002. For two-parent families the rates started at 75 percent and increased in 1999 to 90 percent. In 1998 all states met the overall participation rate for all families and 28 of 41 states subject to the two-parent rate met the goal.

- Each state must maintain at least 80 percent of its fiscal year 1994 level of spending on these programs. If a state meets the work requirement percentages, the maintenance of effort level may be reduced to 75 percent of 1994 spending. States must maintain spending at 100 percent of 1994 levels for access to the $2 billion federal contingency fund. This contingency fund was designed to assist states affected by high population growth or severe economic conditions, such as increases in food stamp caseloads or high unemployment rates.

- Unmarried teenage parents (under age 18) are required to live with an adult or with adult supervision and must participate in educational or job training to receive benefits. In addition, the law encourages "second chance homes" to provide teen parents with the skills and support they need and provides $50 million a year in new funding for state abstinence education activities.

None of the block grant funds can be used for adults who have been on welfare for over five years or who do not work after receiving benefits for two years. However, states are offered some flexibility in how to spend their TANF funds (see below).

Title II: Supplemental Social Security (SSI)

The act redefines "disability" for children who receive SSI. A child will be considered disabled if he or she has a medically determinable physical or mental impairment that results in marked and severe functional limitations, which can be expected to cause death or has lasted or can be expected to last at least 12 months. References to "maladaptive behavior" as a medical criterion was removed from the listing of impairments used for evaluating mental disabilities in children.

Title III: Child Support

To be eligible for federal funds, each state must operate a child-support enforcement program that meets federal guidelines. The state must establish centralized registries of child-support orders and centers for collection and disbursement of child-support payments. The state must also establish enforcement methods, such as revoking the driver's and professional licenses of delinquent fathers. To receive full benefits, a mother must cooperate with state efforts to establish paternity. She may be denied assistance if she refuses to disclose the father. Paternity establishments rose to more than 1.4 million in 1998, an increase of over 300 percent since 1992.

Title IV: Restricting Welfare and Public Benefits for Noncitizens

The original law severely limited or banned benefits to most legal immigrants who entered the country on or after the date on which the bill became law. Ineligibility continued for a five-year period or until they attained citizenship. In addition, states had the option of withholding eligibility for Medicaid, AFDC, and other social services from legal immigrants already residing in the United States. Refugees/asylees (those who have come for political or other asylum or sanctuary), veterans, and Cuban/Haitian immigrants were exempted from the five-year ban.

Illegal immigrants had no entitlement to benefit programs, such as AFDC or Medicaid. They could receive emergency medical care, short-term disaster relief, immunizations, and treatment of communicable diseases (in the interest of public health). They could also get community services such as soup kitchens and shelters, some housing programs, and school lunches/breakfasts if their children were eligible for free public education. States established programs to verify the legality of an immigrant before paying benefits and could elect to deny Women, Infants, and Children (WIC) benefits and other child nutrition programs to illegal aliens.

However, the Balanced Budget Act of 1997 (see below) and the Noncitizen Technical Amendment Act of 1998 invested $11.5 billion to restore disability and health benefits to 380,000 legal immigrants who were in the United States before welfare reform became law on

August 22, 1996. The Balanced Budget Act also extended the SSI and Medicaid eligibility period for refugees and people seeking asylum from five years after entry to seven years to give these residents more time to naturalize. In addition the budget bill fixed some of the food stamp provisions in the welfare law by creating work slots and preserving food stamp benefits for those single, able-bodied recipients without dependents who are willing to work but, through no fault of their own, have not found employment.

Title V: Child Protection

The law gives states the authority to use current federal funds to pay for foster care for children in child-care institutions. It extended the enhanced federal match for statewide automated child-welfare information systems through 1997 and appropriates $6 million per year (fiscal years 1996–2002) for a national random sample study of abused and neglected children.

Title VI: Child Care

The law requires that states maintain spending for child care at the level of fiscal years 1994 or 1995, whichever is greater, in order to be eligible for federal matching funds. Mandatory funding is set at $13.9 billion for fiscal years 1997 through 2002, with states receiving an estimated $1.2 billion per year, before matching begins. The remainder of the funds is available for state matching at the Medicaid rate. States are spending more per recipient in 1998 than they did in 1994. In 1998 all states met the minimum spending requirements and 13 states exceeded them.

States must establish standards (as under prior law) for prevention and control of infectious diseases, such as immunization programs, and for building and physical safety in child-care institutions. Child-care workers must also receive minimal training in health and safety.

As a result of more parents working while still on welfare or leaving welfare to work, the critical need for child care became more pronounced. Despite the fact that states are spending virtually all their child care money, of the 14.7 million children potentially eligible for federal support, only 1.5 million children (about 10 percent) received assistance in 1998. According to a report by the Children's Defense Fund in 1998, child care may be a financial burden on the family because state subsidies are often inadequate. The lack of availability of quality child care undermines both family integrity and the desire to enter the workforce.

Title VII: Child Nutrition Programs

The law continues the existing child nutrition programs, such as the school lunch and breakfast programs. Maximum reimbursement is reduced, however, for the Summer Food Service Program and for some institutional food programs. States may decide whether to include or exclude legal immigrants from these programs.

Title VIII: Food Stamps and Commodities

The new law reduces maximum benefits to the level of the "Thrifty Food Plan," an index set by the U.S. Department of Agriculture that reflects the amount of money needed to purchase food to meet minimal nutrition requirements. Benefits are indexed to the rate of inflation so that they increase as inflation rises.

The law also restructures the way certain expenses and earnings are counted in establishing eligibility for food stamps. When recipients' benefits are calculated, their counted monthly income is reduced by several "deductions," including a "standard deduction" and a deduction for excessively high shelter expenses. These deductions raise food stamp allotments. The standard deduction is frozen at the current level, $134 (in the contiguous 48 states and Washington, D.C.). As of fiscal year 2001, the cap on shelter expense deductions gradually increases from $247 per month in 1996 to $300 in 2001 and will be frozen at $300 per month thereafter. State and local energy assistance is counted as income.

All food stamp recipients who are 18 to 50 years old and without children (Able-Bodied Adults Without Dependents; see below) must work for at least three months in a period of 36 months, or they will lose their eligibility for the program. Recipients who were in a workfare program for 30 days, but lost their placement, may qualify for an additional three months of food stamps.

The law increases the penalties for recipients and retailers convicted of fraud or trafficking in food stamps. It also allows states to convert food-stamp benefits to wage subsidies for employers who hire food stamp recipients; the workers then receive salaries rather than food stamps.

STATE FLEXIBILITY REGARDING WAIVERS

Under the welfare-reform law, states that had received approval for waivers prior to July 1, 1997, were given the option to continue those cash assistance programs under some or all of those waivers. States were allowed to retain provisions that were inconsistent with the new law until their waivers expire if they accepted the option of continuing cash assistance programs covered by the waivers. However, the law limited the extent to which inconsistencies apply so as to maintain the law's strong work requirements.

From the first 32 state plans submitted to the Department of Health and Human Services (HHS), at least half indicated an intent to continue one or more waivers. In *Waivers and the New Welfare Law: Initial Approaches in State Plans* (Center of Law and Social Policy, November

1996), Mark Greenberg and Steve Savner summarize the most common areas identified as inconsistencies with the law's provisions. The law's work and participation requirements are the areas most frequently cited. For instance the law states that individuals must be engaged in work within 24 months without expressly providing for any exemptions. Connecticut, Massachusetts, and New Hampshire each indicate that they will use the exemption policies under their waivers. Tennessee allows an extended list of exemptions from its work requirements.

Another inconsistency between the welfare-reform law and state waivers concerns time limits. The law requires the termination of assistance after five years but includes a 20 percent hardship exemption. Connecticut's waiver provides for unlimited extensions for six months at a time, provided the family qualifies. Several state waivers define work activities differently than the federal law. Missouri intends to allow all work activities defined in its waiver to meet the work participation rates as required under the welfare law. Connecticut extends the time for which job search and job readiness activities may be counted as work activities in calculating its participation rate.

Other areas inconsistent with the welfare law's provisions include those related to penalties for noncompliance with work requirements, transitional assistance, teen-parent school attendance, teen-parent living-arrangement requirements, and child-support cooperation penalties. The Department of Health and Human Services must review the state plans and approve the inconsistencies due to waivers.

1997 BALANCED BUDGET RECONCILIATION ACT

The 1997 Balanced Budget Reconciliation Act (PL 105-33) made a number of changes affecting state programs funded under TANF block grants, including partially restoring funding for some of the program cuts made in the 1996 welfare law. SSI benefits were restored to legal elderly or disabled immigrants who were receiving assistance as of August 22, 1996. These benefits were also restored to immigrants who were legally residing in the United States as of that date and subsequently became disabled. Legal immigrants who arrived after the passage of the welfare reform law are not eligible for assistance.

Funding for the food stamp employment and training program was increased so that states could create workfare, or subsidized job slots, for food stamp recipients. Eighty percent of the funds must be spent on food stamp recipients who are 18 to 50 years old and without children (Able-Bodied Adults Without Dependents or ABAWD). With the 1996 law, this group was limited to three months of food stamp assistance during each 36-month period unless the recipient was working at least half-time or engaged in employment and training. The balanced budget act allows states to exempt 15 percent of the ABAWD population from the three-month limit.

This act set a new mandatory penalty for failure to reduce assistance for TANF recipients who refuse to work. This penalty, to be imposed by the Secretary of Health and Human Services, may not be less than 1 percent, or more than 5 percent, of the TANF grant. The act also specified a mandatory 5 percent penalty if a state failed to meet work participation rates. Under the 1996 law, the HHS secretary had the option to penalize states.

Formulas were changed and the cap raised to allow a larger number of individuals participating in vocational education training to count toward the state's TANF work participation rate. Several changes were made in work definitions for the mandatory work requirements.

The 1997 balanced budget act also created two additional grants to aid state welfare programs. A welfare-to-work grant provided $3 billion over two years (1998 and 1999) to be used for job-related activities directed mainly at individuals with significant work barriers, such as lack of education and low skills in reading or mathematics, substance abuse, or a poor work history. In addition, the act created a $20.3 billion child health block grant, the State Children's Health Insurance Program. This money was targeted for assistance to uninsured, low-income children. States could use the new funds to make more children eligible for Medicaid or to purchase other health coverage, or both.

On April 12, 1999, the Department of Health and Human Services (HHS) issued the final TANF regulations. They include many provisions, some of which reflect significant changes from the proposed regulations, which affirm and enhance the flexibility of states to determine how best to use TANF funds to assist low-income families. The regulations, together with the already-existing substantial TANF financial reserves in many states, which resulted from the decreasing number of welfare cases, provide strong support for states to improve their welfare reform approaches. The federal welfare law restricts HHS's authority to regulate state conduct or enforce any TANF provision except to the extent expressly provided in the law. The federal law expressly provides that HHS will impose penalties if a state fails to comply with requirements of the law in a number of areas. For example a state can be subject to penalties if it uses federal TANF funds improperly, if it fails to expend the amount of state funds required under maintenance-of-effort provisions, if it fails to meet work participation rates, or if it fails to comply with time limits applicable to federal TANF funds.

There still is concern, however, that if states do not use their TANF funds they may be taken away by the federal government for other purposes. In 1999 several proposals in the U.S. Congress sought to divert unused

TABLE 2.1

Wisconsin Works: (W-2)

Level of W-2	Basic Income Package	Time Required of Recipients	Program Time Limits	Est. Child Care Copays ($/mo.)	
				Licensed Care	Certified Care
Unsubsidized employment	Market wage + Food Stamps + EITC	40 hrs/wk standard	None	$101-$134	$71-$92
Trial Job (W-2 pays maximum of $300/mo. to the employer)	At least minimum wage + Food Stamps + EITC	40 hrs/wk standard	Per job: 3 mo. with an option for one 3-mo. extension; total 24 mo.	$55	$38
Community Service Job (CSJ)	$673 per mo. + Food Stamps (no EITC)	30 hrs/wk standard; and up to 10 hrs/wk in education and training	Per job: 6 mo. with an option for one 3-mo. extension; total: 24 mo.	$38	$25
W-2 Transition (placement contingent on assessment by the state Vocational Rehab. agency)	$628 per mo. + Food Stamps (no EITC)	28 hrs/wk work activities standard; and up to 12 hrs/wk in education and training	24- mo. limit, but extensions permitted on a case-by-case basis	$38	$25

Notes: The income package and child care copayment are based on Governor Thompson's proposals in the 1997-99 biennial budget. Estimated child care copayments are for a three-person family with two children receiving no child support payments. Department of Workforce Development materials express child care copayments on a weekly basis; the monthly copayments shown in the table assume 4.2 weeks per month. For the purpose of estimating child care copayments, the Trial Jobs position is assumed to pay minimum wage, which, after October 1, 1997, will be $5.15 per hour, or $858 per month, and the unsubsidized-employment package is assumed to range from $6-$7 per hour, or $1,000-$1,170 per month.

SOURCE: Reprinted with Permission from Focus, Newsletter of the University of Wisconsin-Madison Institute for Research in Poverty, vol 18, no 3 (Spring 97): 2

TANF funds to offset other legislative initiatives. While maintaining a surplus is tempting, opponents have urged states to spend more of their allotted money in order to avoid such an occurrence.

TWO STATE PLANS AS EXAMPLES

Wisconsin, considered a national leader among states in welfare reform, implemented its welfare-reform system in early 1996. One program, Self-Sufficiency First, required AFDC applicants to interview with a financial planning resource specialist before completing the AFDC application. During the 30-day application-processing period, each applicant must participate in the state JOBS program (see Chapter 9). Child care was provided if needed. Pay for Performance, an intensive JOBS program, required that AFDC recipients participate 20–40 hours per week, with heavy penalties for those who failed to comply.

Starting on September 1, 1997, Wisconsin Works (W-2) eliminated AFDC and replaced it with cash assistance available only through work. Participation requirements begin when the youngest child is 12 weeks old. Families are still assigned to a financial and employment planner. Following an assessment, the planner will place them on one of four levels of a "self-sufficiency ladder" and help them progress up the ladder to greater independence. Table 2.1 shows the W-2 levels, the requirements for assistance, and child-care copayments. Failure to meet the requirements reduces the income of the participant.

Since implementing its welfare-reform system, Wisconsin's welfare cases fell more than 89 percent, the

TABLE 2.2

The New Mexico Works Act

• Recipients are required to take part in work activities within two years or when the agency deems them work ready.

• Participants and agency personnel will sign a mutual agreement that outlines obligations and requirements. The plan is to be reviewed once a year.

• Cash benefits are subject to a 60-month time limit with up to 20 percent of recipients exempt from the limit.

• Individuals who do not get a federal housing subsidy receive an additional $100 per month.

• Married two-parent families get an additional $100 per month.

• One-third of the state share of child support payments will go into a trust fund for the children's education.

• Families who are not eligible for cash assistance, but earn less than the federal poverty guidelines, qualify for the same services provided cash recipients, including child care, transprotation, job training and education.

• A legislative committee will oversee implementation of the welfare reforms.

SOURCE: Jack Tweedie. New Mexico Forges Ahead on Welfare. State Legislatures, May 1998. Copyrighted by the National Conference of State Legislatures.

steepest in the nation. But while Wisconsin is considered to be leading the nation in welfare reform, it has also become the target of fierce debate. While supporters, like the conservative think tank, the Heritage Foundation, laud Wisconsin's effort as "Wisconsin's Welfare Miracle," Wisconsin's advocates for the poor argue that the reforms have pushed many of the poorest people, particularly children, deeper into poverty.

And the question remains, where have the 89 percent of former welfare recipients gone? Those who hail the program say the former recipients have become gainfully employed in the private sector, while critics contend that many of the families do not have jobs and have ended up in the state's homeless shelters. Regardless, neither group has provided complete evidence to back up their claims.

In a different state, the New Mexico Works Act includes the same strong work requirements of most other states and expands services to help welfare recipients overcome the barriers to finding jobs and supporting their families. The last state to enact major reform, New Mexico borrowed heavily from other states' programs but also created several innovations of its own. One innovation, for example, was making "working poor" families (with incomes no more than the federal poverty level) eligible for the same services provided to welfare recipients. See Table 2.2 for descriptions of the major provisions of this act.

CHAPTER 3

POVERTY

BACKGROUND

The federal government began measuring poverty in 1959. During the 1960s President Lyndon Baines Johnson declared a national War on Poverty. Researchers realized that there were very few statistical definitions available to measure the number of Americans who continued to live in poverty in the most affluent nation in the world. In order to fight this "war," it had to be determined who was poor and why.

During the early 1960s Mollie Orshansky of the Social Security Administration suggested that the poverty income level be defined as the income sufficient to purchase a minimally adequate amount of goods and services. The necessary data for defining and pricing a full "market basket" of goods were not available then, nor are they available now. Ms. Orshansky noted, however, that the U.S. Department of Agriculture (USDA) had published a "Household Food Consumption Survey" in 1955, which showed that the average family of three or more persons spent approximately one-third of its after-tax income on food. She multiplied the USDA's 1961 economy food plan (a no-frills food basket meeting the then-recommended dietary allowances) by three.

Basically this defined a poor family as any family or person whose after-tax income was not sufficient to purchase a minimally adequate diet if one-third of the income was spent on food. Differences were allowed for size of family, gender of the head of the household, and whether it was a farm or nonfarm family. The threshold (the level at which poverty begins) for a farm family was set at 70 percent of a nonfarm household. (This difference was eliminated following the 1982 survey.)

Poverty Thresholds

The poverty guidelines, prepared by the U.S. Department of Health and Human Services (HHS), are based on the poverty thresholds as established by the Bureau of the Census. The poverty thresholds, used for statistical purposes, are updated each year to reflect inflation. People with incomes below the applicable threshold are classified as living below the poverty level.

The poverty guidelines vary by family size and composition. For a family of four in 1999 the poverty guideline was $16,700 in annual income. A person living alone who earned less than $8,240 was considered poor, as was a family of eight members making less than $27,980. Notice, on Table 3.1, that the poverty level is considerably higher in Alaska and Hawaii, where the cost of living is higher than in the contiguous (with borders that touch each other) 48 states and the District of Columbia.

The poverty guidelines set by HHS are very important because various government agencies use them as the basis for eligibility to key assistance programs. HHS uses the poverty guidelines to determine Community Services Block Grants, Low-Income Home Energy Assistance Block Grants, and Head Start allotments. The guidelines are also the basis for funding the USDA's Food Stamp Program, National School Lunch Program, and Special Supplemental Food Program for Women, Infants, and Children (WIC). The Department of Labor uses the guidelines to determine funding for the Job Corps and other employment and training programs under the Job Training Partnership Act. Some state and local governments choose to use the federal poverty guidelines for some of their own programs, such as state health insurance programs and financial guidelines for child support enforcement.

POVERTY—THEN AND NOW

Race and Ethnicity

Table 3.2 shows the nation's poverty rates from 1959 through 1998. Figure 3.1 shows the numbers of poor peo-

TABLE 3.1

Poverty Guidelines for Families of Specified Size, 1965–99[1,2]

Date of issuance[3]	1 person	2 persons	3 persons	4 persons	5 persons	6 persons	7 persons	8 persons	Increment[4]
December 1965	$1,540	$ 1,990	$ 2,440	$ 3,130	$ 3,685	$ 4,135	$ 4,635	$ 5,135	$ 500
August 1967	1,600	2,000	2,500	3,200	3,800	4,200	4,700	5,300	500
September 1968	1,600	2,100	2,600	3,300	3,900	4,400	4,900	5,400	500
September 1969	1,800	2,400	3,000	3,600	4,200	4,800	5,400	6,000	600
December 1970	1,900	2,500	3,100	3,800	4,400	5,000	5,600	6,200	600
November 1971	2,000	2,600	3,300	4,000	4,700	5,300	5,900	6,500	600
October 1972	2,100	2,725	3,450	4,200	4,925	5,550	6,200	6,850	650
March 1973	2,200	2,900	3,600	4,300	5,000	5,700	6,400	7,100	700
May 1974	2,330	3,070	3,810	4,550	5,290	6,030	6,770	7,510	740
March 1975	2,590	3,410	4,230	5,050	5,870	6,690	7,510	8,330	820
April 1976	2,800	3,700	4,600	5,500	6,400	7,300	8,200	9,100	900
April 1977	2,970	3,930	4,890	5,850	6,810	7,770	8,730	9,690	960
April 1978	3,140	4,160	5,180	6,200	7,220	8,240	9,260	10,280	1,020
May 1979	3,400	4,500	5,600	6,700	7,800	8,900	10,000	11,100	1,100
April 1980	3,790	5,010	6,230	7,450	8,670	9,890	11,110	12,330	1,220
March 1981	4,310	5,690	7,070	8,450	9,830	11,210	12,590	13,970	1,380
April 1982	4,680	6,220	7,760	9,300	10,840	12,380	13,920	15,460	1,540
February 1983	4,860	6,540	8,220	9,900	11,580	13,260	14,940	16,620	1,680
February 1984	4,980	6,720	8,460	10,200	11,940	13,680	15,420	17,160	1,740
March 1985	5,250	7,050	8,850	10,650	12,450	14,250	16,050	17,850	1,800
February 1986	5,360	7,240	9,120	11,000	12,880	14,760	16,640	18,520	1,880
February 1987	5,500	7,400	9,300	11,200	13,100	15,000	16,900	18,800	1,900
February 1988	5,770	7,730	9,690	11,650	13,610	15,570	17,530	19,490	1,960
February 1989	5,980	8,020	10,060	12,100	14,140	16,180	18,220	20,260	2,040
February 1990	6,280	8,420	10,560	12,700	14,840	16,980	18,120	21,260	2,140
February 1991	6,620	8,880	11,140	13,400	15,660	17,920	20,180	22,440	2,260
February 1992	6,810	9,190	11,570	13,950	16,330	18,710	21,090	23,470	2,380
February 1993	6,970	9,430	11,890	14,350	16,810	19,270	21,730	24,190	2,460
February 1994	7,360	9,840	12,320	14,800	17,280	19,760	22,240	24,720	2,480
February 1995	7,470	10,030	12,590	15,150	17,710	20,270	22,830	25,390	2,560
March 1996	7,740	10,360	12,980	15,600	18,220	20,840	23,460	26,080	2,620
March 1997	7,890	10,610	13,330	16,050	18,770	21,490	24,210	26,960	2,720
February 1998	8,050	10,850	13,650	16,450	19,250	22,050	24,850	27,650	2,800
March 1999	8,240	11,060	13,880	16,700	19,520	22,340	25,160	27,980	2,820

[1] Except for Alaska and Hawaii. Guidelines for Alaska and Hawaii since 1980 are:

Year	Alaska		Hawaii	
	1 person	Increment	1 person	Increment
1980	$ 4,760	$1,520	$4,370	$1,400
1981	5,410	1,720	4,980	1,580
1982	5,870	1,920	5,390	1,770
1983	6,080	2,100	5,600	1,930
1984	6,240	2,170	5,730	2,000
1985	6,560	2,250	6,040	2,070
1986	6,700	2,350	6,170	2,160
1987	6,860	2,380	6,310	2,190
1988	7,210	2,450	6,650	2,250
1989	7,480	2,550	6,870	2,350
1990	7,840	2,680	7,230	2,460
1991	8,290	2,820	7,610	2,600
1992	8,500	2,980	7,830	2,740
1993	8,700	3,080	8,040	2,820
1994	9,200	3,100	8,470	2,850
1995	9,340	3,200	8,610	2,940
1996	9,660	3,280	8,910	3,010
1997	9,870	3,400	9,070	3,130
1998	10,070	3,500	9,260	3,220
1999	10,320	3,520	9,490	3,240

Separate figures for Alaska and Hawaii reflect Office of Economic Opportunity administrative practice beginning in the 1966–70 period. The U.S. Census Bureau, producer of the primary version of the poverty measure, does not produce separate figures for Alaska and Hawaii.

[2] Before 1983, guidelines are for nonfarm families only.

[3] Guidelines shown are effective from date of issuance.

[4] Add this amount for each additional family member. Before 1973, increments between some of the smaller family sizes differed from the increment shown in the table. Beginning in 1973, the increment has been the same between all family sizes in each year's set of guidelines.

SOURCE: *Annual Statistical Supplement, 1999.* Social Security Administration: Washington, D.C., 1999

TABLE 3.2

Poverty Status of People by Family Relationship, Race, and Hispanic Origin, 1959–1998

[Numbers in thousands. People as of March of the following year]

Year and characteristic	All people			People in families						Unrelated individuals		
				All families			Families with female householder, no husband present					
	Total	Below poverty level		Total	Below poverty level		Total	Below poverty level		Total	Below poverty level	
		Number	Percent		Number	Percent		Number	Percent		Number	Percent
ALL RACES												
1998	271,059	34,476	12.7	227,229	25,370	11.2	39,000	12,907	33.1	42,539	8,478	19.9
1997	268,480	35,574	13.3	225,369	26,217	11.6	38,412	13,494	35.1	41,672	8,687	20.8
1996	266,218	36,529	13.7	223,955	27,376	12.2	38,584	13,796	35.8	40,727	8,452	20.8
1995	263,733	36,425	13.8	222,792	27,501	12.3	38,908	14,205	36.5	39,484	8,247	20.9
1994	261,616	38,059	14.5	221,430	28,985	13.1	37,253	14,380	38.6	38,538	8,287	21.5
1993	259,278	39,265	15.1	219,489	29,927	13.6	37,861	14,636	38.7	38,038	8,388	22.1
1992ʳ	256,549	38,014	14.8	217,936	28,961	13.3	36,446	14,205	39.0	36,842	8,075	21.9
1991ʳ	251,192	35,708	14.2	212,723	27,143	12.8	34,795	13,824	39.7	36,845	7,773	21.1
1990	248,644	33,585	13.5	210,967	25,232	12.0	33,795	12,578	37.2	36,056	7,446	20.7
1989	245,992	31,528	12.8	209,515	24,066	11.5	32,525	11,668	35.9	35,185	6,760	19.2
1988ʳ	243,530	31,745	13.0	208,056	24,048	11.6	32,164	11,972	37.2	34,340	7,070	20.6
1987ʳ	240,982	32,221	13.4	206,877	24,725	12.0	31,893	12,148	38.1	32,992	6,857	20.8
1986	238,554	32,370	13.6	205,459	24,754	12.0	31,152	11,944	38.3	31,679	6,846	21.6
1985	236,594	33,064	14.0	203,963	25,729	12.6	30,878	11,600	37.6	31,351	6,725	21.5
1984	233,816	33,700	14.4	202,288	26,458	13.1	30,844	11,831	38.4	30,268	6,609	21.8
1983	231,700	35,303	15.2	201,338	27,933	13.9	30,049	12,072	40.2	29,158	6,740	23.1
1982	229,412	34,398	15.0	200,385	27,349	13.6	28,834	11,701	40.6	27,908	6,458	23.1
1981	227,157	31,822	14.0	198,541	24,850	12.5	28,587	11,051	38.7	27,714	6,490	23.4
1980	225,027	29,272	13.0	196,963	22,601	11.5	27,565	10,120	36.7	27,133	6,227	22.9
1979	222,903	26,072	11.7	195,860	19,964	10.2	26,927	9,400	34.9	26,170	5,743	21.9
1978	215,656	24,497	11.4	191,071	19,062	10.0	26,032	9,269	35.6	24,585	5,435	22.1
1977	213,867	24,720	11.6	190,757	19,505	10.2	25,404	9,205	36.2	23,110	5,216	22.6
1976	212,303	24,975	11.8	190,844	19,632	10.3	24,204	9,029	37.3	21,459	5,344	24.9
1975	210,864	25,877	12.3	190,630	20,789	10.9	23,580	8,846	37.5	20,234	5,088	25.1
1974	209,362	23,370	11.2	190,436	18,817	9.9	23,165	8,462	36.5	18,926	4,553	24.1
1973.	207,621	22,973	11.1	189,361	18,299	9.7	21,823	8,178	37.5	18,260	4,674	25.6
1972	206,004	24,460	11.9	189,193	19,577	10.3	21,264	8,114	38.2	16,811	4,883	29.0
1971	204,554	25,559	12.5	188,242	20,405	10.8	20,153	7,797	38.7	16,311	5,154	31.6
1970	202,183	25,420	12.6	186,692	20,330	10.9	19,673	7,503	38.1	15,491	5,090	32.9
1969	199,517	24,147	12.1	184,891	19,175	10.4	17,995	6,879	38.2	14,626	4,972	34.0
1968	197,628	25,389	12.8	183,825	20,695	11.3	18,048	6,990	38.7	13,803	4,694	34.0
1967	195,672	27,769	14.2	182,558	22,771	12.5	17,788	6,898	38.8	13,114	4,998	38.1
1966	193,388	28,510	14.7	181,117	23,809	13.1	17,240	6,861	39.8	12,271	4,701	38.3
1965	191,413	33,185	17.3	179,281	28,358	15.8	16,371	7,524	46.0	12,132	4,827	39.8
1964	189,710	36,055	19.0	177,653	30,912	17.4	(NA)	7,297	44.4	12,057	5,143	42.7
1963	187,258	36,436	19.5	176,076	31,498	17.9	(NA)	7,646	47.7	11,182	4,938	44.2
1962	184,276	38,625	21.0	173,263	33,623	19.4	(NA)	7,781	50.3	11,013	5,002	45.4
1961	181,277	39,628	21.9	170,131	34,509	20.3	(NA)	7,252	48.1	11,146	5,119	45.9
1960	179,503	39,851	22.2	168,615	34,925	20.7	(NA)	7,247	48.9	10,888	4,926	45.2
1959	176,557	39,490	22.4	165,858	34,562	20.8	(NA)	7,014	49.4	10,699	4,928	46.1
WHITE												
1998	222,837	23,454	10.5	186,184	16,549	8.9	24,211	6,674	27.6	35,563	6,386	18.0
1997.	221,200	24,396	11.0	185,147	17,258	9.3	23,773	7,296	30.7	34,858	6,593	18.9
1996.	219,656	24,650	11.2	184,119	17,621	9.6	23,744	7,073	29.8	34,247	6,463	18.9
1995	218,028	24,423	11.2	183,450	17,593	9.6	23,732	7,047	29.7	33,399	6,336	19.0
1994	216,460	25,379	11.7	182,546	18,474	10.1	22,713	7,228	31.8	32,569	6,292	19.3
1993.	214,899	26,226	12.2	181,330	18,968	10.5	23,224	7,199	31.0	32,112	6,443	20.1
1992ʳ	213,060	25,259	11.9	180,409	18,294	10.1	22,453	6,907	30.8	31,170	6,147	19.7
1991ʳ	210,133	23,747	11.3	177,619	17,268	9.7	21,608	6,806	31.5	31,207	5,872	18.8
1990	208,611	22,326	10.7	176,504	15,916	9.0	20,845	6,210	29.8	30,833	5,739	18.6
1989	206,853	20,785	10.0	175,857	15,179	8.6	20,362	5,723	28.1	29,993	5,063	16.9
1988ʳ	205,235	20,715	10.1	175,111	15,001	8.6	20,396	5,950	29.2	29,315	5,314	18.1
1987ʳ	203,605	21,195	10.4	174,488	15,593	8.9	20,244	5,989	29.6	28,290	5,174	18.3
1986	202,282	22,183	11.0	174,024	16,393	9.4	20,163	6,171	30.6	27,143	5,198	19.2
1985	200,918	22,860	11.4	172,863	17,125	9.9	20,105	5,990	29.8	27,067	5,299	19.6
1984	198,941	22,955	11.5	171,839	17,299	10.1	19,727	5,866	29.7	26,094	5,181	19.9
1983	197,496	23,984	12.1	171,407	18,377	10.7	19,256	6,017	31.2	25,206	5,189	20.6
1982	195,919	23,517	12.0	170,748	18,015	10.6	18,374	5,686	30.9	24,300	5,041	20.7
1981	194,504	21,553	11.1	169,868	16,127	9.5	18,795	5,600	29.8	23,913	5,061	21.2

TABLE 3.2

Poverty Status of People by Family Relationship, Race, and Hispanic Origin, 1959–1998 [CONTINUED]

[Numbers in thousands. People as of March of the following year]

Year and characteristic	All people			People in families						Unrelated individuals		
				All families			Families with female householder, no husband present					
		Below poverty level			Below poverty level			Below poverty level			Below poverty level	
	Total	Number	Percent	Total	Number	Percent	Total	Number	Percent	Total	Number	Percent
WHITE—Con.												
1980	192,912	19,699	10.2	168,756	14,587	8.6	17,642	4,940	28.0	23,370	4,760	20.4
1979	191,742	17,214	9.0	168,461	12,495	7.4	17,349	4,375	25.2	22,587	4,452	19.7
1982	195,919	23,517	12.0	170,748	18,015	10.6	18,374	5,686	30.9	24,300	5,041	20.7
1981	194,504	21,553	11.1	169,868	16,127	9.5	18,795	5,600	29.8	23,913	5,061	21.2
1980	192,912	19,699	10.2	168,756	14,587	8.6	17,642	4,940	28.0	23,370	4,760	20.4
1979	191,742	17,214	9.0	168,461	12,495	7.4	17,349	4,375	25.2	22,587	4,452	19.7
1978	186,450	16,259	8.7	165,193	12,050	7.3	16,877	4,371	25.9	21,257	4,209	19.8
1977	185,254	16,416	8.9	165,385	12,364	7.5	16,721	4,474	26.8	19,869	4,051	20.4
1976	184,165	16,713	9.1	165,571	12,500	7.5	15,941	4,463	28.0	18,594	4,213	22.7
1975	183,164	17,770	9.7	165,661	13,799	8.3	15,577	4,577	29.4	17,503	3,972	22.7
1974	182,376	15,736	8.6	166,081	12,181	7.3	15,433	4,278	27.7	16,295	3,555	21.8
1973.	181,185	15,142	8.4	165,424	11,412	6.9	14,303	4,003	28.0	15,761	3,730	23.7
1972	180,125	16,203	9.0	165,630	12,268	7.4	13,739	3,770	27.4	14,495	3,935	27.1
1971	179,398	17,780	9.9	165,184	13,566	8.2	13,502	4,099	30.4	14,214	4,214	29.6
1970	177,376	17,484	9.9	163,875	13,323	8.1	13,226	3,761	28.4	13,500	4,161	30.8
1969	175,349	16,659	9.5	162,779	12,623	7.8	12,285	3,577	29.1	12,570	4,036	32.1
1968	173,732	17,395	10.0	161,777	13,546	8.4	12,190	3,551	29.1	11,955	3,849	32.2
1967	172,038	18,983	11.0	160,720	14,851	9.2	12,131	3,453	28.5	11,318	4,132	36.5
1966	170,247	19,290	11.3	159,561	15,430	9.7	12,261	3,646	29.7	10,686	3,860	36.1
1965	168,732	22,496	13.3	158,255	18,508	11.7	11,573	4,092	35.4	10,477	3,988	38.1
1964	167,313	24,957	14.9	156,898	20,716	13.2	(NA)	3,911	33.4	10,415	4,241	40.7
1963	165,309	25,238	15.3	155,584	21,149	13.6	(NA)	4,051	35.6	9,725	4,089	42.0
1962	162,842	26,672	16.4	153,348	22,613	14.7	(NA)	4,089	37.9	9,494	4,059	42.7
1961	160,306	27,890	17.4	150,717	23,747	15.8	(NA)	4,062	37.6	9,589	4,143	43.2
1960	158,863	28,309	17.8	149,458	24,262	16.2	(NA)	4,296	39.0	9,405	4,047	43.0
1959	156,956	28,484	18.1	147,802	24,443	16.5	(NA)	4,232	40.2	9,154	4,041	44.1
WHITE, NOT HISPANIC												
1998	192,754	15,799	8.2	159,301	10,061	6.3	18,547	4,074	22.0	32,573	5,352	16.4
1997	191,859	16,491	8.6	158,796	10,401	6.5	18,474	4,604	24.9	32,049	5,632	17.6
1996	191,459	16,462	8.6	159,044	10,553	6.6	18,597	4,339	23.3	31,410	5,455	17.4
1995	190,951	16,267	8.5	159,402	10,599	6.6	18,340	4,183	22.8	30,586	5,303	17.3
1994	192,543	18,110	9.4	161,254	12,118	7.5	18,186	4,743	26.1	30,157	5,500	18.2
1993	190,843	18,882	9.9	160,062	12,756	8.0	18,508	4,724	25.5	29,681	5,570	18.8
1992ʳ	189,001	18,202	9.6	159,102	12,277	7.7	18,016	4,640	25.8	28,775	5,350	18.6
1991ʳ	189,116	17,741	9.4	158,850	11,998	7.6	17,609	4,710	26.7	29,215	5,261	18.0
1990	188,129	16,622	8.8	158,394	11,086	7.0	17,160	4,284	25	28,688	5,002	17.4
1989	186,979	15,599	8.3	158,127	10,723	6.8	16,827	3,922	23.3	28,055	4,466	15.9
1988ʳ	185,961	15,565	8.4	157,687	10,467	6.6	16,828	3,988	23.7	27,552	4,746	17.2
1987ʳ	184,936	16,029	8.7	157,785	11,051	7.0	16,787	4,075	24.3	26,439	4,613	17.4
1986	184,119	17,244	9.4	157,665	12,078	7.7	16,739	4,350	26.0	25,525	4,668	18.3
1985	183,455	17,839	9.7	157,106	12,706	8.1	16,749	4,136	24.7	25,544	4,789	18.7
1984	182,469	18,300	10.0	156,930	13,234	8.4	16,742	4,193	25.0	24,671	4,659	18.9
1983	181,393	19,538	10.8	156,719	14,437	9.2	16,369	4,448	27.2	23,894	4,746	19.9
1982	181,903	19,362	10.6	157,818	14,271	9.0	15,830	4,161	26.3	23,329	4,701	20.2
1981	180,909	17,987	9.9	157,330	12,903	8.2	16,323	4,222	25.9	22,950	4,769	20.8
1980	179,798	16,365	9.1	156,633	11,568	7.4	15,358	3,699	24.1	22,455	4,474	19.9
1979	178,814	14,419	8.1	156,567	10,009	6.4	15,410	3,371	21.9	21,638	4,179	19.3
1978	174,731	13,755	7.9	154,321	9,798	6.3	15,132	3,390	22.4	20,410	3,957	19.4
1977	173,563	13,802	8.0	154,449	9,977	6.5	14,888	3,429	23.0	19,114	3,825	20.0
1976	173,235	14,025	8.1	155,324	10,066	6.5	14,261	3,516	24.7	17,912	3,959	22.1
1975	172,417	14,883	8.6	155,539	11,137	7.2	13,809	3,570	25.9	16,879	3,746	22.2
1974	171,463	13,217	7.7	155,764	9,854	6.3	13,763	3,379	24.6	15,699	3,364	21.4
1973	170,488	12,864	7.5	155,330	9,262	6.0	12,731	3,185	25.0	15,158	3,602	23.8
BLACK												
1998	34,877	9,091	26.1	29,333	7,259	24.7	13,156	5,629	42.8	5,390	1,752	32.5
1997	34,458	9,116	26.5	28,962	7,386	25.5	13,218	5,654	42.8	5,316	1,645	31.0
1996	34,110	9,694	28.4	28,933	7,993	27.6	13,193	6,123	46.4	4,989	1,606	32.2
1995	33,740	9,872	29.3	28,777	8,189	28.5	13,604	6,553	48.2	4,756	1,551	32.6
1994	33,353	10,196	30.6	28,499	8,447	29.6	12,926	6,489	50.2	4,649	1,617	34.8

TABLE 3.2

Poverty Status of People by Family Relationship, Race, and Hispanic Origin, 1959–1998 [CONTINUED]

[Numbers in thousands. People as of March of the following year]

Year and characteristic	All people			People in families						Unrelated individuals		
				All families			Families with female householder, no husband present					
		Below poverty level			Below poverty level			Below poverty level			Below poverty level	
	Total	Number	Percent	Total	Number	Percent	Total	Number	Percent	Total	Number	Percent
BLACK - Con												
1993	32,910	10,877	33.1	28,106	9,242	32.9	13,132	6,955	53.0	4,608	1,541	33.4
1992ʳ	32,411	10,827	33.4	27,790	9,134	32.9	12,591	6,799	54.0	4,410	1,569	35.6
1991ʳ	31,313	10,242	32.7	26,565	8,504	32.0	11,960	6,557	54.8	4,505	1,590	35.3
1990	30,806	9,837	31.9	26,296	8,160	31.0	11,866	6,005	50.6	4,244	1,491	35.1
1989	30,332	9,302	30.7	25,931	7,704	29.7	11,190	5,530	49.4	4,180	1,471	35.2
1988ʳ	29,849	9,356	31.3	25,484	7,650	30.0	10,794	5,601	51.9	4,095	1,509	36.8
1987ʳ	29,362	9,520	32.4	25,128	7,848	31.2	10,701	5,789	54.1	3,977	1,471	37.0
1986	28,871	8,983	31.1	24,910	7,410	29.7	10,175	5,473	53.8	3,714	1,431	38.5
1985	28,485	8,926	31.3	24,620	7,504	30.5	10,041	5,342	53.2	3,641	1,264	34.7
1984	28,087	9,490	33.8	24,387	8,104	33.2	10,384	5,666	54.6	3,501	1,255	35.8
1983	27,678	9,882	35.7	24,138	8,376	34.7	10,059	5,736	57.0	3,287	1,338	40.7
1982	27,216	9,697	35.6	23,948	8,355	34.9	9,699	5,698	58.8	3,051	1,229	40.3
1981	26,834	9,173	34.2	23,423	7,780	33.2	9,214	5,222	56.7	3,277	1,296	39.6
1980	26,408	8,579	32.5	23,084	7,190	31.1	9,338	4,984	53.4	3,208	1,314	41.0
1979	25,944	8,050	31.0	22,666	6,800	30.0	9,065	4,816	53.1	3,127	1,168	37.3
1978	24,956	7,625	30.6	22,027	6,493	29.5	8,689	4,712	54.2	2,929	1,132	38.6
1977.	24,710	7,726	31.3	21,850	6,667	30.5	8,315	4,595	55.3	2,860	1,059	37.0
1976	24,399	7,595	31.1	21,840	6,576	30.1	7,926	4,415	55.7	2,559	1,019	39.8
1975	24,089	7,545	31.3	21,687	6,533	30.1	7,679	4,168	54.3	2,402	1,011	42.1
1974	23,699	7,182	30.3	21,341	6,255	29.3	7,483	4,116	55.0	2,359	927	39.3
1973	23,512	7,388	31.4	21,328	6,560	30.8	7,188	4,064	56.5	2,183	828	37.9
1972	23,144	7,710	33.3	21,116	6,841	32.4	7,125	4,139	58.1	2,028	870	42.9
1971	22,784	7,396	32.5	20,900	6,530	31.2	6,398	3,587	56.1	1,884	866	46.0
1970	22,515	7,548	33.5	20,724	6,683	32.2	6,225	3,656	58.7	1,791	865	48.3
1969	22,011	7,095	32.2	20,192	6,245	30.9	5,537	3,225	58.2	1,819	850	46.7
1968	21,944	7,616	34.7	(NA)	6,839	33.7	(NA)	3,312	58.9	(NA)	777	46.3
1967	21,590	8,486	39.3	(NA)	7,677	38.4	(NA)	3,362	61.6	(NA)	809	49.3
1966	21,206	8,867	41.8	(NA)	8,090	40.9	(NA)	3,160	65.3	(NA)	777	54.4
1959	18,013	9,927	55.1	(NA)	9,112	54.9	(NA)	2,416	70.6	1,430	815	57.0
HISPANIC ORIGIN¹												
1998	31,515	8,070	25.6	28,055	6,814	24.3	6,074	2,837	46.7	3,218	1,097	34.1
1997	30,637	8,308	27.1	27,467	7,198	26.2	5,718	2,911	50.9	2,976	1,017	34.2
1996	29,614	8,697	29.4	26,340	7,515	28.5	5,641	3,020	53.5	2,985	1,066	35.7
1995	28,344	8,574	30.3	25,165	7,341	29.2	5,785	3,053	52.8	2,947	1,092	37.0
1994	27,442	8,416	30.7	24,390	7,357	30.2	5,328	2,920	54.8	2,798	926	33.1
1993	26,559	8,126	30.6	23,439	6,876	29.3	5,333	2,837	53.2	2,717	972	35.8
1992ʳ	25,646	7,592	29.6	22,695	6,455	28.4	4,806	2,474	51.5	2,577	881	34.2
1991ʳ	22,070	6,339	28.7	19,658	5,541	28.2	4,326	2,282	52.7	2,146	667	31.1
1990	21,405	6,006	28.1	18,912	5,091	26.9	3,993	2,115	53.0	2,254	774	34.3
1989	20,746	5,430	26.2	18,488	4,659	25.2	3,763	1,902	50.6	2,045	634	31.0
1988ʳ	20,064	5,357	26.7	18,102	4,700	26.0	3,734	2,052	55.0	1,864	597	32.0
1987ʳ	19,395	5,422	28.0	17,342	4,761	27.5	3,678	2,045	55.6	1,933	598	31.0
1986	18,758	5,117	27.3	16,880	4,469	26.5	3,631	1,921	52.9	1,685	553	32.8
1985	18,075	5,236	29.0	16,276	4,605	28.3	3,561	1,983	55.7	1,602	532	33.2
1984	16,916	4,806	28.4	15,293	4,192	27.4	3,139	1,764	56.2	1,481	545	36.8
1983	16,544	4,633	28.0	15,075	4,113	27.3	3,032	1,670	55.1	1,364	457	33.5
1982	14,385	4,301	29.9	13,242	3,865	29.2	2,664	1,601	60.1	1,018	358	35.1
1981	14,021	3,713	26.5	12,922	3,349	25.9	2,622	1,465	55.9	1,005	313	31.1
1980	13,600	3,491	25.7	12,547	3,143	25.1	2,421	1,319	54.5	970	312	32.2
1979	13,371	2,921	21.8	12,291	2,599	21.1	2,058	1,053	51.2	991	286	28.8
1978	12,079	2,607	21.6	11,193	2,343	20.9	1,817	1,024	56.4	886	264	29.8
1977	12,046	2,700	22.4	11,249	2,463	21.9	1,901	1,077	56.7	797	237	29.8
1976	11,269	2,783	24.7	10,552	2,516	23.8	1,766	1,000	56.6	716	266	37.2
1975	11,117	2,991	26.9	10,472	2,755	26.3	1,842	1,053	57.2	645	236	36.6
1974	11,201	2,575	23.0	10,584	2,374	22.4	1,723	915	53.1	617	201	32.6
1973	10,795	2,366	21.9	10,269	2,209	21.5	1,534	881	57.4	526	157	29.9
1972	10,588	2,414	22.8	10,099	2,252	22.3	1,370	733	53.5	488	162	33.2

TABLE 3.2

Poverty Status of People by Family Relationship, Race, and Hispanic Origin, 1959–1998 [CONTINUED]

[Numbers in thousands. People as of March of the following year]

	All people			People in families						Unrelated individuals		
				All families			Families with female householder, no husband present					
Year and characteristic		Below poverty level			Below poverty level			Below poverty level			Below poverty level	
	Total	Number	Percent	Total	Number	Percent	Total	Number	Percent	Total	Number	Percent
ASIAN AND PACIFIC ISLANDER												
1998	10,873	1,360	12.5	9,576	1,087	11.4	1,123	373	33.2	1,266	257	20.3
1997	10,482	1,468	14.0	9,312	1,116	12.0	932	313	33.6	1,134	327	28.9
1996	10,054	1,454	14.5	8,900	1,172	13.2	1,018	300	29.5	1,120	255	22.8
1995	9,644	1,411	14.6	8,582	1,112	13.0	919	266	28.9	1,013	260	25.6
1994	6,654	974	14.6	5,915	776	13.1	582	137	23.6	696	179	25.7
1993	7,434	1,134	15.3	6,609	898	13.6	725	126	17.4	791	228	28.8
1992ʳ	7,779	985	12.7	6,922	787	11.4	729	183	25.0	828	193	23.3
1991ʳ	7,192	996	13.8	6,367	773	12.1	721	177	24.6	785	209	26.6
1990	7,014	858	12.2	6,300	712	11.3	638	132	20.7	668	124	18.5
1989	6,673	939	14.1	5,917	779	13.2	614	212	34.6	712	144	20.2
1988ʳ	6,447	1,117	17.3	5,767	942	16.3	650	263	40.5	651	160	24.5
1987ʳ	6,322	1,021	16.1	5,785	875	15.1	584	187	32.0	516	138	26.8

r For 1992, figures are based on 1990 census population controls. For 1991, figures are revised to correct for nine omitted weights from the original March 1992 CPS file. For 1988 and 1987, figures are based on new processing procedures and are also revised to reflect corrections to the files after publication of the 1988 advance report, *Money Income and Poverty Status in the United States: 1988,* P-60, No. 166.

(NA) Not available.

¹People of Hispanic origin may be of any race.

Note: Prior to 1979, people in unrelated subfamilies were included in people in families. Beginning in 1979, people in unrelated subfamilies are included in all people but are excluded from people in families.

SOURCE: Joseph Dalaker. *Poverty in the United States: 1998.* Current Population Reports, Series P60-207. U.S. Bureau of the Census: Washington, D.C., 1999

ple and the poverty rates for the same years. In 1959, 22.4 percent of the nation's population, or nearly 40 million persons, lived below the poverty level. For African Americans, the rate in 1959 was almost triple that of whites— 55.1 percent compared to 18.1 percent. By 1973 the rate of poverty in the United States had been cut in half to 11.1 percent. (See Table 3.2.) The numbers and percentages were reduced for both blacks and whites, but whites saw greater gains. Analysts believe this decline was due both to the growth in the economy and to the success of some of the anti-poverty programs instituted in the late 1960s.

The poverty rate began to increase in the latter half of the 1970s, coinciding with a downturn in household and family incomes for all Americans. The poverty rate rose steadily until it reached an 18-year high of 15.2 percent in 1983, a year during which the country was climbing out of a serious economic recession. The percentage of Americans living in poverty then began dropping, falling to 12.8 percent in 1989. Since then, however, the percentage increased again, reaching 15.1 percent in 1993 (39.3 million people) and then dropped to 12.7 percent in 1998 (34.5 million). (See Table 3.2 and Figure 3.1.)

Poverty has affected whites and minorities differently. In 1959, 18 percent of all whites, or 28.5 million people, lived below the poverty level. By 1970 the rate declined to slightly under 10 percent, about where it remained for the next 10 years. In 1983 the percentage of whites living in poverty reached an 18-year high of 12.1 percent. By 1989 the proportion of whites that were poor had dropped to 10 percent, although it rose significantly to 12.2 percent in 1993 and then dropped back to 11.2 percent in 1995. By 1998 it had dropped further to 10.5 percent. (See Table 3.2.)

In 1998, a year in which the American economy was very strong, over one-fourth (26.1 percent) of all African Americans were poor. This percentage, however, is the lowest poverty rate ever for blacks. African-American children and the elderly have been particularly affected by poverty. In 1996, 40 percent of young blacks less than 18 years of age and 25 percent of black elderly people 65 years or over were poor. (See Table 3.2.)

Among those of Hispanic origin, in 1972 (the first year for which statistics were recorded by the Census Bureau for Hispanic ethnicity), 22.8 percent lived below the poverty level. Between 1972 and 1985, the number of Hispanics living below the poverty level more than doubled, from 2.4 million to 5.2 million. Over this same period, the total Hispanic population rose from 10.6 million to 18.1 million. (Persons of Hispanic origin can be of any race.) The poverty rate among Hispanics reached 29.9 percent in 1982 and

FIGURE 3.1

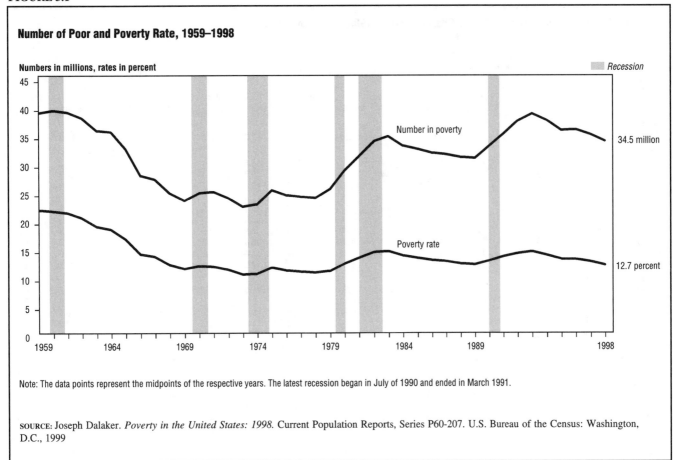

Number of Poor and Poverty Rate, 1959–1998

Numbers in millions, rates in percent

Note: The data points represent the midpoints of the respective years. The latest recession began in July of 1990 and ended in March 1991.

SOURCE: Joseph Dalaker. *Poverty in the United States: 1998.* Current Population Reports, Series P60-207. U.S. Bureau of the Census: Washington, D.C., 1999

then dropped to 26.2 percent in 1989. The poverty rate reached 30.7 percent, its highest point, in 1994, dropping to 29.4 in 1996 and 25.6 in 1998. (See Table 3.2) A large proportion (40.3 percent) of young Hispanics under 18 years of age and about one-fourth (24.4 percent) of those 65 years and older were poor. (See Table 3.3.)

The poverty rate in 1998 for Asian and Pacific Islanders was 12.5 percent, a decline of 1.5 percent from the previous year. (See Table 3.3.)

Although a far higher percentage of blacks and Hispanics than whites were poor, nearly half of the 34.4 million people who were poor in 1998 were non-Hispanic whites. In that year, 45.8 percent of poor Americans were non-Hispanic whites, 26.3 percent were black, 23.4 percent were Hispanic, and 3.9 percent were Asian and Pacific Islander. (See Table 3.3.)

Age

In 1998, 18.9 percent of children under 18 years old were poor; this was a slight drop from the high of 22.7 percent in 1993. (See Table 3.3 and Figure 3.2.) From 1959 to 1998 the number of people 65 years and older living in poverty dropped significantly, from almost 30 percent to 10.5 percent. (See Figure 3.2.)

In 1998 almost 30 percent of the nation's poor were either under 18 years of age (18.9 percent) or 65 years of age and older (10.5 percent). In comparison to the non-poor, children are over-represented among the poor, while the elderly are under-represented. Children make up about 39 percent of the poor even though they represent only a little more than one-fourth of the total population. People over 65 years old made up 12 percent of the total population in 1998 but only 9.8 percent of the poor. (See Figure 3.2.) Most observers credit Social Security for the sharp decline in poverty among the elderly.

CHILD POVERTY. The child poverty rate, at 18.9 percent of the nation's children under the age of 18, was nearly twice the poverty rate for adults. Very young children are at the greatest risk of being poor. According to the National Center for Children in Poverty, the United States has the highest rate of young child poverty of all Western industrialized nations.

In 1998 nearly 20.6 percent of children under the age of six lived in poverty. Close to 55 percent of young children living with a female householder (with no spouse present) were poor, compared to 10.1 percent of children under six years old living with families headed by a married couple. Of the 20.6 percent of young children living

TABLE 3.3

People and Families in Poverty by Selected Characteristics, 1989, 1997, and 1998

[Numbers in thousands.]

Characteristic	Below poverty, 1998				Below poverty, 1997				Below poverty, 1989			
	Number	90-pct. C.I. (±)	Percent	90-pct. C.I. (±)	Number	90-pct. C.I. (±)	Percent	90-pct. C.I. (±)	Number	90-pct. C.I. (±)	Percent	90-pct. C.I. (±)
PEOPLE												
Total	**34,476**	**920**	**12.7**	**0.3**	**35,574**	**931**	**13.3**	**0.3**	**32,415**	**859**	**13.1**	**0.3**
Family Status												
In families	25,370	804	11.2	0.4	26,217	814	11.6	0.4	24,882	765	11.8	0.4
Householder.	7,186	248	10.0	0.4	7,324	252	10.3	0.4	6,895	232	10.4	0.4
Related children under 18	12,845	479	18.3	0.7	13,422	485	19.2	0.7	12,541	454	19.4	0.7
Related children under 6	4,775	309	20.6	1.4	5,049	316	21.6	1.4	5,116	306	22.5	1.4
In unrelated subfamilies	628	66	48.8	6.0	670	67	46.5	5.5	727	67	54.6	6.1
Reference person	247	41	47.4	9.2	259	41	45.0	8.5	284	41	51.8	9.1
Children under 18	361	89	50.5	14.2	403	94	48.9	13.0	430	92	60.5	15.3
Unrelated individual.	8,478	275	19.9	0.7	8,687	280	20.8	0.7	6,807	230	19.3	0.7
Male	3,465	161	17.0	0.8	3,447	161	17.4	0.9	2,577	132	15.8	0.8
Female	5,013	201	22.6	1.0	5,240	206	24.0	1.0	4,230	174	22.3	1.0
Race and Hispanic Origin												
White, total	23,454	776	10.5	0.3	24,396	790	11.0	0.4	21,294	712	10.2	0.3
White, not Hispanic	15,799	646	8.2	0.3	16,491	660	8.6	0.3	15,499	615	8.3	0.3
Black, total	9,091	434	26.1	1.2	9,116	434	26.5	1.3	9,525	423	30.8	1.4
Asian and Pacific Islander, total	1,360	181	12.5	1.7	1,468	186	14.0	1.8	1,032	155	14.2	2.1
Hispanic origin, all races	8,070	411	25.6	1.3	8,308	413	27.1	1.3	6,086	357	26.3	1.5
Age												
Under 18 years	13,467	487	18.9	0.7	14,113	495	19.9	0.7	13,154	462	20.1	0.7
18 to 64 years	17,623	674	10.5	0.4	18,085	681	10.9	0.4	15,950	617	10.4	0.4
18 to 24 years	4,312	201	16.6	0.8	4,416	204	17.5	0.8	4,132	189	15.4	0.7
25 to 34 years	4,582	214	11.9	0.6	4,759	219	12.1	0.6	4,873	212	11.2	0.5
35 to 44 years	4,082	202	9.1	0.5	4,251	207	9.6	0.5	3,115	171	8.3	0.5
45 to 54 years	2,444	158	6.9	0.4	2,439	158	7.2	0.5	1,873	133	7.5	0.5
55 to 59 years	1,165	110	9.2	0.9	1,092	107	9.0	0.9	971	97	9.5	0.9
60 to 64 years	1,039	104	10.1	1.0	1,127	109	11.2	1.1	986	97	9.4	0.9
65 years and over	3,386	179	10.5	0.6	3,376	179	10.5	0.6	3,312	171	11.4	0.6
Nativity												
Native	29,707	860	12.1	0.4	30,336	869	12.5	0.4	NA	NA	NA	NA
Foreign-born	4,769	413	18.0	1.6	5,238	433	19.9	1.6	NA	NA	NA	NA
Naturalized citizen	1,087	199	11.0	2.0	1,111	201	11.4	2.1	NA	NA	NA	NA
Not a citizen	3,682	364	22.2	2.2	4,127	385	25.0	2.3	NA	NA	NA	NA
Region												
Northeast	6,357	385	12.3	0.8	6,474	388	12.6	0.8	5,213	336	10.2	0.7
Midwest	6,501	428	10.3	0.7	6,493	428	10.4	0.7	7,088	429	12.0	0.7
South	12,992	612	13.7	0.7	13,748	628	14.6	0.7	13,277	594	15.6	0.7
West	8,625	505	14.0	0.8	8,858	512	14.6	0.9	6,838	433	12.8	0.8
Residence												
Inside metropolitan areas	26,997	827	12.3	0.4	27,273	829	12.6	0.4	23,726	748	12.3	0.4
Inside central cities	14,921	630	18.5	0.8	15,018	632	18.8	0.8	14,151	589	18.5	0.8
Outside central cities	12,076	569	8.7	0.4	12,255	572	9.0	0.4	9,574	489	8.2	0.4
Outside metropolitan areas	7,479	554	14.4	1.1	8,301	582	15.9	1.1	8,690	571	15.9	1.1
FAMILIES												
Total	**7,186**	**248**	**10.0**	**0.4**	**7,324**	**252**	**10.3**	**0.4**	**6,895**	**232**	**10.4**	**0.4**
White, total	4,829	196	8.0	0.3	4,990	199	8.4	0.3	4,457	179	7.9	0.3
White, not Hispanic	3,264	156	6.1	0.3	3,357	160	6.3	0.3	3,287	151	6.4	0.3
Black, total	1,981	118	23.4	1.5	1,985	118	23.6	1.5	2,108	118	27.9	1.7
Asian and Pacific Islander, total	270	43	11.0	1.8	244	41	10.2	1.8	201	35	12.2	2.2
Hispanic origin, all races	1,648	109	22.7	1.5	1,721	110	24.7	1.6	1,227	89	23.7	1.8
Type of Family												
Married-couple	2,879	146	5.3	0.3	2,821	145	5.2	0.3	2,965	143	5.7	0.3
White	2,400	132	5.0	0.3	2,312	130	4.8	0.3	2,347	125	5.0	0.3
White, not Hispanic	1,639	107	3.8	0.2	1,501	102	3.5	0.2	1,776	107	4.1	0.3
Black	290	44	7.3	1.1	312	46	8.0	1.2	444	53	11.7	1.4
Hispanic origin, all races	775	72	15.7	1.5	836	76	17.4	1.6	592	61	16.4	1.8
Female householder, no husband present	3,831	171	29.9	1.5	3,995	176	31.6	1.5	3,575	158	32.6	1.6
White	2,123	123	24.9	1.6	2,305	130	27.7	1.7	1,886	112	25.8	1.7
White, not Hispanic	1,428	100	20.7	1.6	1,598	107	23.4	1.7	1,341	92	21.7	1.6
Black	1,557	105	40.8	3.1	1,563	105	39.8	3.0	1,553	100	46.7	3.4
Hispanic origin, all races	756	72	43.7	4.7	767	72	47.6	5.1	576	59	48.0	5.7

SOURCE: Joseph Dalaker. *Poverty in the United States: 1998.* Current Population Reports, Series P60-207. U.S. Bureau of the Census: Washington, D.C., 1999

in poverty, nearly half were considered to be extremely poor, living in families with incomes less than 50 percent of the poverty level for 1998.

Childhood poverty is a matter of great concern because strong evidence exists that poverty can limit a child's physical and cognitive development. According to the Children's Defense Fund report, "The High Price of Poverty for Children of the South" (May 1998),

- Poverty is a greater risk to children's overall health status than is living in a single parent family.

- Poor children are twice as likely as non-poor children to be born weighing too little or to suffer stunted growth.

- Poor children suffer more mental and physical disabilities.

- Poverty makes children hungry. Hungry children are more likely to be hyperactive and to have serious behavior problems. They are four times more likely to have difficulty concentrating in school.

- Poor children score lower on reading and math tests and are twice as likely to repeat a year of school as non-poor children.

- Poor children earn 25 percent lower wages when they become young adults.

Regions

In 1998 the Midwest had the lowest poverty rate (10.3 percent) among the nation's four regions, followed by the Northeast with 12.3 percent. The poverty rate was highest in the West (14 percent) and the South (13.7 percent). (See Table 3.3.)

Family Status

Eleven percent of all families in the United States were living in poverty in 1998. Families headed by married couples had the lowest poverty rate (5.3 percent). Almost one-third (29.9 percent) of all families with a female householder (with no husband present) were living in poverty. (See Table 3.3.)

Female-headed households are not only more likely to live in poverty; it is also harder for these families to escape poverty. In *Studies in Household and Family Formation* (U.S. Bureau of the Census, Washington, D.C., 1992), Donald J. Hernandez studied families that had started a year in the mid-1980s in poverty and had ended the same year in poverty. He found that among two-parent families, 59 percent of the whites, 70 percent of the blacks, and 69 percent of the Hispanics that began the year poor had ended the year poor. Among female-headed households, 84 percent of the whites, 88 percent of

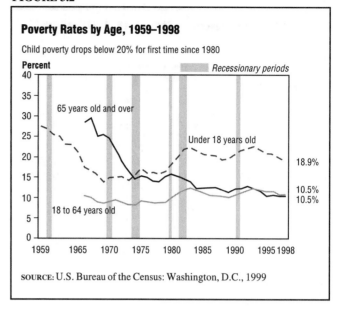

FIGURE 3.2

Poverty Rates by Age, 1959–1998

Child poverty drops below 20% for first time since 1980

SOURCE: U.S. Bureau of the Census: Washington, D.C., 1999

the blacks, and 85 percent of the Hispanics that had started the year in poverty finished it in the same condition.

BY RACE. In 1998 white non-Hispanic families (6.1 percent) had a much lower poverty rate than black (23.4 percent) or Hispanic (22.7 percent) families. White married-couple families (5 percent) were much less likely to live in poverty than black (7.3 percent) or Hispanic (15.7 percent) families headed by married couples. (See Table 3.3.)

While close to one-fourth (24.9 percent) of all white families headed by a female with no husband present were living in poverty in 1998, 40.8 percent of all such female-headed black families were poor and slightly less than one-half of female-headed Hispanic families (43.7 percent) were poor. (See Table 3.3.)

States

State poverty rates vary widely from year to year and should be used very carefully when ranking the states for statistical purposes. However, on average, over the years 1996, 1997, and 1998, New Hampshire, Utah, Maryland, Indiana, and Wisconsin had the lowest poverty rates, while New Mexico, the District of Columbia, Louisiana, and Mississippi had the highest rates. (See Table 3.4.)

Work Experience

The probability of a family living in poverty is influenced by three primary factors: the size of the family, the number of workers, and the characteristics of the wage-earners. As the number of wage-earners in a family increases, the probability of poverty declines. The likelihood of a second wage-earner is greatest in families headed by married couples.

About 6.3 percent of all Americans who worked in 1998 lived in poverty, compared to 21.1 percent of those

TABLE 3.4

Percent of People in Poverty by State, 1996, 1997, and 1998

State	3-year average 1996-98		Average 1997-98		Average 1996-97		Difference in 2-year moving averages	
	Percent	Standard error	Percent	Standard error	Percent	Standard error	Poverty rate	Standard error
United States	**13.2**	**0.15**	**13.0**	**0.18**	**13.5**	**0.18**	*** −0.5**	**0.15**
Alabama	14.7	1.29	15.1	1.52	14.8	1.50	0.3	1.23
Alaska	8.8	1.02	9.1	1.21	8.5	1.16	0.6	0.98
Arizona	18.1	1.29	16.9	1.47	18.8	1.54	−1.9	1.25
Arkansas	17.2	1.34	17.2	1.56	18.4	1.60	−1.2	1.26
California	16.3	0.55	16.0	0.63	16.8	0.64	−0.8	0.53
Colorado	9.3	1.05	8.7	1.18	9.4	1.24	−0.7	1.05
Connecticut	9.9	1.21	9.0	1.37	10.1	1.43	−1.1	1.22
Delaware	9.5	1.18	10.0	1.39	9.1	1.36	0.9	1.13
District of Columbia	22.7	1.73	22.0	2.01	23.0	2.01	−0.9	1.68
Florida	13.9	0.67	13.7	0.77	14.3	0.79	−0.5	0.64
Georgia	14.3	1.12	14.0	1.29	14.7	1.33	−0.6	1.09
Hawaii	12.3	1.33	12.4	1.55	13.0	1.59	−0.6	1.25
Idaho	13.2	1.18	13.8	1.38	13.3	1.38	0.6	1.11
Illinois	11.1	0.67	10.6	0.77	11.6	0.81	−1.0	0.65
Indiana	8.6	1.02	9.1	1.21	8.2	1.16	0.9	0.98
Iowa	9.4	1.09	9.3	1.26	9.6	1.27	−0.3	1.04
Kansas	10.1	1.12	9.6	1.28	10.4	1.33	−0.8	1.10
Kentucky	15.5	1.31	14.7	1.49	16.4	1.56	−1.7	1.26
Louisiana	18.6	1.36	17.7	1.56	18.4	1.59	−0.7	1.35
Main	10.6	1.25	10.2	1.44	10.7	1.48	−0.4	1.22
Maryland	8.6	1.09	7.8	1.21	9.3	1.31	−1.6	1.06
Massachusetts	10.3	0.83	10.4	0.97	11.2	1.00	−0.7	0.76
Michigan	10.8	0.71	10.6	0.82	10.7	0.83	−0.1	0.70
Minnesota	9.9	1.07	10.0	1.25	9.7	1.25	0.3	1.05
Mississippi	18.3	1.38	17.1	1.58	18.6	1.62	−1.5	1.36
Missouri	10.4	1.16	10.8	1.36	10.6	1.36	0.2	1.08
Montana	16.4	1.29	16.1	1.50	16.3	1.51	−0.2	1.26
Nebraska	10.8	1.15	11.1	1.36	10.0	1.31	1.1	1.13
Nevada	9.9	1.12	10.8	1.34	9.6	1.30	1.2	1.05
New Hampshire	8.4	1.17	9.4	1.42	7.7	1.32	1.7	1.11
New Jersey	9.0	0.68	8.9	0.79	9.2	0.81	−0.3	0.66
New Mexico	22.4	1.44	20.8	1.65	23.4	1.71	* −2.6	1.41
New York	16.6	0.61	16.6	0.71	16.6	0.71	−	0.59
North Carolina.	12.5	0.88	12.7	1.03	11.8	1.00	0.9	0.87
North Dakota	13.2	1.26	14.4	1.52	12.3	1.43	* 2.1	1.21
Ohio	11.6	0.72	11.1	0.82	11.8	0.84	−0.7	0.70
Oklahoma	14.8	1.24	13.9	1.42	15.2	1.46	−1.3	1.22
Oregon	12.8	1.26	13.3	1.50	11.7	1.43	1.6	1.25
Pennsylvania	11.3	0.67	11.2	0.78	11.4	0.78	−0.2	0.65
Rhode Island	11.8	1.35	12.2	1.59	11.9	1.58	0.3	1.28
South Carolina	13.3	1.30	13.4	1.52	13.1	1.52	0.3	1.27
South Dakota	13.0	1.23	13.7	1.45	14.1	1.48	−0.5	1.12
Tennessee	14.5	1.29	13.9	1.47	15.1	1.53	−1.2	1.25
Texas	16.1	0.68	15.9	0.78	16.7	0.81	−0.8	0.65
Utah	8.5	0.95	8.9	1.12	8.3	1.09	0.7	0.91
Vermont	10.6	1.26	9.6	1.41	10.9	1.50	−1.4	1.26
Virginia	11.3	1.11	10.8	1.26	12.5	1.36	* −1.7	1.05
Washington	10.0	1.13	9.1	1.26	10.5	1.35	−1.5	1.12
West Virginia	17.6	1.34	17.1	1.54	17.5	1.56	−0.3	1.31
Wisconsin	8.6	1.02	8.5	1.19	8.5	1.18	−	1.00
Wyoming	12.0	1.21	12.1	1.40	12.7	1.43	−0.6	1.13

− Represents zero.

* Statistically significant at the 90-percent confidence level.

SOURCE: Joseph Dalaker. *Poverty in the United States: 1998*. Current Population Reports, Series P60-207. U.S. Bureau of the Census: Washington, D.C., 1999

who did not work that year. In 1998, 41 percent (9.1 million) of poor persons 16 years old and over worked at least some of the year, with only 12.5 percent working year-round and full-time. This compares to 70 percent of all people 16 years old and over who worked, with 68 percent working full-time. (See Table 3.5.)

Most poor children live in families where one or more adults work. However, millions of working parents are not able to earn enough to lift their families out of poverty, even those who work full-time all year. In 1998 approximately 5.6 million families with children in which the parents were not elderly and disabled had incomes

TABLE 3.5

Work Experience During Year by Selected Characteristics and Poverty Status in 1998 of People 16 Years Old and Over

[Numbers in thousands. People as of March of the following year.]

	All workers			Worked full-time, year-round			Not full-time, year-round			Did not work during year		
		Below poverty level			Below poverty level			Below poverty level			Below poverty level	
Characteristic	Total	Number	Percent of total	Total	Number	Percent of total	Total	Number	Percent of total	Total	Number	Percent of total
ALL PEOPLE												
Both Sexes												
Total	**145 566**	**9 133**	**6.3**	**95 772**	**2 804**	**2.9**	**49 794**	**6 330**	**12.7**	**62 211**	**13 122**	**21.1**
16 to 17 years	3 395	254	7.5	78	7	9.3	3 317	246	7.4	4 661	993	21.3
18 to 64 years	137 003	8 709	6.4	94 075	2 755	2.9	42 929	5 953	13.9	30 323	8 914	29.4
18 to 24 years	20 495	2 430	11.9	7 673	432	5.6	12 823	1 997	15.6	5 472	1 883	34.4
25 to 34 years	33 339	2 686	8.1	24 016	798	3.3	9 323	1 888	20.3	5 135	1 895	36.9
35 to 54 years	68 273	3 050	4.5	52 076	1 320	2.5	16 197	1 730	10.7	11 703	3 476	29.7
55 to 64 years	14 896	543	3.6	10 310	205	2.0	4 586	337	7.4	8 013	1 660	20.7
65 years and over	5 168	171	3.3	1 619	41	2.5	3 548	130	3.7	27 227	3 215	11.8
Male												
Total	**76 918**	**4 000**	**5.2**	**56 953**	**1 642**	**2.9**	**19 965**	**2 357**	**11.8**	**23 117**	**4 626**	**20.0**
16 to 17 years	1 688	106	6.3	55	7	(B)	1 633	99	6.1	2 493	530	21.3
18 to 64 years	72 319	3 806	5.3	55 858	1 607	2.9	16 461	2 198	13.4	9 807	3 189	32.5
18 to 24 years	10 590	992	9.4	4 514	241	5.3	6 076	751	12.4	2 347	760	32.4
25 to 34 years	17 686	1 141	6.4	14 353	488	3.4	3 334	653	19.6	1 237	577	46.6
35 to 54 years	35 983	1 402	3.9	30 800	760	2.5	5 183	642	12.4	3 317	1 223	36.9
55 to 64 years	8 060	270	3.4	6 192	118	1.9	1 868	153	8.2	2 907	629	21.6
65 years and over	2 910	88	3.0	1 039	28	2.7	1 871	60	3.2	10 817	907	8.4
Female												
Total	**68 648**	**5 134**	**7.5**	**38 819**	**1 161**	**3.0**	**29 829**	**3 972**	**13.3**	**39 093**	**8 496**	**21.7**
16 to 17 years	1 707	147	8.6	23	–	(B)	1 684	147	8.8	2 168	463	21.3
18 to 64 years	64 684	4 903	7.6	38 217	1 148	3.0	26 468	3 755	14.2	20 516	5 726	27.9
18 to 24 years	9 905	1 437	14.5	3 159	191	6.1	6 746	1 246	18.5	3 126	1 123	35.9
25 to 34 years	15 653	1 546	9.9	9 663	310	3.2	5 989	1 236	20.6	3 898	1 319	33.8
35 to 54 years	32 290	1 648	5.1	21 277	559	2.6	11 013	1 088	9.9	8 386	2 253	26.9
55 to 64 years	6 836	272	4.0	4 118	88	2.1	2 718	185	6.8	5 106	1 031	20.2
65 years and over	2 257	83	3.7	580	13	2.2	1 677	70	4.2	16 410	2 308	14.1
Household Relationship												
People 16 to 64 years old	140 398	8 962	6.4	94 152	2 763	2.9	46 246	6 200	13.4	34 984	9 907	28.3
In families	113 036	6 018	5.3	74 336	2 096	2.8	38 699	3 922	10.1	29 815	6 301	21.1
Householder	51 777	3 853	7.4	39 689	1 426	3.6	12 088	2 427	20.1	8 257	2 594	31.4
In families with related children under												
18 years	64 632	5 148	8.0	41 143	1 826	4.4	23 489	3 322	14.1	17 415	4 625	26.6
Householder	32 036	3 479	10.9	24 196	1 280	5.3	7 841	2 199	28.0	4 496	1 977	44.0
In families with related children under												
6 years	26 844	2 996	11.2	17 691	1 045	5.9	9 153	1 952	21.3	6 990	2 217	31.7
Householder	14 335	2 072	14.5	10 375	714	6.9	3 959	1 358	34.3	2 289	1 052	45.9
In married-couple families	91 175	2 884	3.2	61 157	1 259	2.1	30 017	1 625	5.4	22 126	3 003	13.6
Husband	41 363	1 644	4.0	35 468	977	2.8	5 895	667	11.3	3 433	736	21.4
Wife	34 889	898	2.6	20 572	218	1.1	14 317	680	4.7	12 177	1 610	13.2
Related children	13 546	276	2.0	4 296	43	1.0	9 250	233	2.5	5 900	544	9.2
Other	1 377	66	4.8	822	21	2.5	555	46	8.2	617	113	18.3
In married-couple families with related												
children under 18 years	51 855	2 349	4.5	33 924	1 082	3.2	17 930	1 268	7.1	12 683	2 062	16.3
Husband	24 768	1 394	5.6	21 666	858	4.0	3 102	536	17.3	1 103	376	34.1
Wife	19 323	687	3.6	10 451	170	1.6	8 871	517	5.8	6 688	1 104	16.5
Related children	6 860	218	3.2	1 287	36	2.8	5 572	182	3.3	4 412	490	11.1
Other	904	50	5.5	519	17	3.4	385	32	8.4	479	91	18.9
In married-couple families with related												
children under 6 years	21 880	1 474	6.7	14 999	684	4.6	6 881	789	11.5	5 276	1 045	19.8
Husband	11 717	924	7.9	10 199	559	5.5	1 517	364	24.0	411	159	38.7
Wife	8 366	418	5.0	4 064	102	2.5	4 302	316	7.3	3 798	667	17.6
Related children	1 245	101	8.1	389	14	3.7	855	87	10.2	729	152	20.9
Other	553	31	5.6	347	9	2.7	207	22	10.5	338	67	19.9

below the federal poverty line. Of these families, 3.8 million (73 percent) had a working parent. (See Figure 3.3.)

Education

Not surprisingly, poverty rates drop sharply as years of schooling rise. In 1996 the poverty rate was 24.8 per-

cent for persons who had not completed high school, 10.1 percent for those who had graduated from high school but had not gone to college, and 6.9 percent for those who had completed at least one year of college.

The general relationship between education and welfare applied for all races. But there were some large dif-

TABLE 3.5

Work Experience During Year by Selected Characteristics and Poverty Status in 1998 of People 16 Years Old and Over [CONTINUED]

[Numbers in thousands. People as of March of the following year.]

							Worked during year								Did not work during year		
	All workers			Worked full-time, year-round			Not full-time, year-round										
		Below poverty level			Below poverty level			Below poverty level			Below poverty level						
Characteristic	Total	Number	Percent of total	Total	Number	Percent of total	Total	Number	Percent of total	Total	Number	Percent of total
In families with female householder, no spouse present	16 041	2 760	17.2	9 068	699	7.7	6 973	2 061	29.6	6 037	2 884	47.8
Householder	9 002	2 179	24.2	5 741	595	10.4	3 262	1 583	48.5	2 193	1 436	65.5
Other	7 038	581	8.3	3 327	104	3.1	3 711	478	12.9	3 844	1 448	37.7
In families with female householder, no spouse present, with related children under 18 years	10 112	2 489	24.6	5 415	631	11.7	4 697	1 857	39.5	3 961	2 344	59.2
Householder	6 948	2 080	29.9	4 201	559	13.3	2 747	1 521	55.4	1 666	1 277	76.7
Related children	2 284	302	13.2	666	37	5.5	1 618	265	16.4	1 902	882	46.4
Other	880	107	12.1	548	35	6.5	332	72	21.5	393	185	47.1
In families with female householder, no spouse present, with related children under 6 years	3 980	1 337	33.6	2 030	290	14.3	1 949	1 047	53.7	1 561	1 114	71.4
Householder	2 865	1 165	40.7	1 476	260	17.6	1 389	905	65.1	830	696	83.8
Related children	647	104	16.1	263	13	4.9	384	91	23.7	523	322	61.6
Other	468	68	14.5	291	17	5.7	176	51	28.8	208	96	46.4
In unrelated subfamilies	474	170	35.9	269	34	12.8	205	136	66.3	136	106	78.3
Unrelated individuals	26 889	2 774	10.3	19 547	632	3.2	7 342	2 142	29.2	5 034	3 500	69.5
Male	15 364	1 425	9.3	11 604	404	3.5	3 760	1 020	27.1	2 322	1 573	67.8
Householder	10 453	781	7.5	8 042	204	2.5	2 411	576	23.9	1 553	932	60.0
Female	11 525	1 350	11.7	7 943	228	2.9	3 582	1 122	31.3	2 711	1 927	71.1
Householder	8 421	678	8.1	6 102	136	2.2	2 319	542	23.4	1 914	1 205	62.9

SOURCE: Joseph Dalaker. *Poverty in the United States: 1998*. Current Population Reports, Series P60-207. U.S. Bureau of the Census: Washington, D.C., 1999

ferences between the races. For example, the 1996 poverty rates for black and Hispanic high school graduates, from age 25 and over, who had not gone to college were 21.2 percent and 15.6 percent, respectively, while white graduates had a much lower poverty rate (8.3 percent).

MEDIAN INCOME

In its surveys, the Bureau of the Census differentiates between households and families. A household is an individual living alone or a group of persons living together who may or may not be related, while a family is composed of two or more related individuals. All families are households, but not all households are families. In 1998 there were 103 million households in the United States but only 71.5 million families.

Household Income

In 1998 the median income (half the population earns less than this amount, and half earn more) for all households was $38,885. Black ($25,351) and Hispanic ($28,330) households had much lower median incomes than did white (not Hispanic) households ($42,439). (See Table 3.6.)

Family Income

In 1998 the median income for all families was $47,469. The median family income is more than two-

FIGURE 3.3

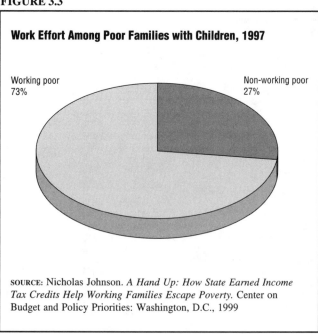

Work Effort Among Poor Families with Children, 1997

Working poor 73%

Non-working poor 27%

SOURCE: Nicholas Johnson. *A Hand Up: How State Earned Income Tax Credits Help Working Families Escape Poverty.* Center on Budget and Policy Priorities: Washington, D.C., 1999

and-a-half times the 1999 average poverty threshold of $16,700 for a family of four. Families headed by married couples of all racial and ethnic backgrounds enjoyed the greatest financial success (a median income of $54,276), with incomes more than twice that of female-headed households ($24,393). (See Table 3.6.)

TABLE 3.6

Comparison of Summary Measures of Income by Selected Characteristics: 1989, 1997, and 1998

[Households and people as of March of the following year.]

Characteristics	1998 Median income Number (1,000)	Value (dollars)	90-percent confidence interval (+/−) (dollars)	Median income in 1997 (in 1998 dollars) Value (dollars)	90-percent confidence interval (+/−) (dollars)	Median income in 1989r (in 1998 dollars) Value (dollars)	90-percent confidence interval (+/−) (dollars)	Percent change in real income 1997 to 1998 Percent change	90-percent confidence interval (+/−)	Percent change in real income 1989r to 1998 Percent change	90-percent confidence interval (+/−)
HOUSEHOLDS											
All households	103,874	38,885	378	37,581	286	37,884	344	*3.5	0.6	*2.6	0.8
Type of Household											
Family households	71,535	47,469	410	46,053	394	45,343	413	*3.1	0.6	*4.7	0.8
Married-couple families	54,770	54,276	530	52,486	388	50,702	458	*3.4	0.6	*7.0	0.9
Female householder, no husband present	12,789	24,393	655	23,399	657	22,662	603	*4.2	2.0	*7.6	2.5
Male householder, no wife present	3,976	39,414	1,633	37,205	1,201	39,717	1,607	*5.9	2.8	−0.8	3.5
Nonfamily households	32,339	23,441	467	22,043	347	22,568	363	*6.3	1.3	*3.9	1.6
Female householder	17,971	18,615	462	17,887	428	18,143	474	*4.1	1.8	2.6	2.2
Male householder	14,368	30,414	559	28,022	770	29,489	660	*8.5	1.8	*3.1	1.8
Race and Hispanic Origin of Householder											
All races[1]	103,874	38,885	378	37,581	286	37,884	344	*3.5	0.6	*2.6	0.8
White	87,212	40,912	336	39,579	413	39,852	320	*3.4	0.7	*2.7	0.7
Non-Hispanic White	78,577	42,439	401	41,209	354	40,792	331	*3.0	0.6	*4.0	0.8
Black	12,579	25,351	653	25,440	720	23,950	789	−0.3	1.9	*5.8	2.7
Asian and Pacific Islander	3,308	46,637	2,135	45,954	2,102	47,337	2,007	1.5	3.2	−1.5	3.7
Hispanic origin[2]	9,060	28,330	898	27,043	792	28,631	882	*4.8	1.8	−1.1	2.7
Age of Householder											
15 to 24 years	5,770	23,564	730	22,935	822	24,401	755	2.7	2.4	−3.4	2.6
25 to 34 years	18,819	40,069	696	38,769	755	39,041	603	*3.4	1.3	*2.6	1.5
35 to 44 years	23,968	48,451	730	47,081	637	49,310	675	*2.9	1.0	−1.7	1.2
45 to 54 years	20,158	54,148	877	52,683	727	54,575	893	*2.8	1.1	−0.8	1.4
55 to 64 years	13,571	43,167	989	42,000	763	40,569	878	*2.8	1.5	*6.4	2.0
65 years and over	21,589	21,729	395	21,084	406	20,719	381	*3.1	1.3	*4.9	1.6
Nativity of the Householder											
Native born	92,853	39,677	390	38,229	381	(NA)	(NA)	*3.8	0.7	(X)	(X)
Foreign born	11,021	32,963	1,230	31,806	802	(NA)	(NA)	3.6	2.3	(X)	(X)
Naturalized citizen	4,877	41,028	1,808	(NA)	(NA)	(NA)	(NA)	(X)	(X)	(X)	(X)
Not a citizen	6,143	28,278	1,199	27,379	971	(NA)	(NA)	3.3	2.8	(X)	(X)
Region											
Northeast	19,877	40,634	772	39,535	877	42,780	709	*2.8	1.5	*−5.0	1.5
Midwest	24,489	40,609	600	38,913	747	37,685	642	*4.4	1.3	*7.8	1.5
South	36,959	35,797	500	34,880	580	33,933	471	*2.6	1.1	*5.5	1.3
West	22,549	40,983	661	39,772	910	40,705	696	*3.0	1.4	0.7	1.4
Residence											
Inside metropolitan areas	83,441	40,983	352	39,994	448	40,776	346	*2.5	0.7	0.5	0.7
Inside central cities	32,144	33,151	638	32,039	456	(NA)	(NA)	*3.5	1.5	(X)	(X)
Outside central cities	51,297	46,402	512	45,364	568	(NA)	(NA)	*2.3	0.8	(X)	(X)
Outside metropolitan areas	20,433	32,022	630	30,525	690	29,393	636	*4.9	1.5	*8.9	1.9
EARNINGS OF FULL-TIME, YEAR-ROUND WORKERS											
Male	56,951	35,345	219	34,199	535	35,727	242	*3.4	0.9	*−1.1	0.6
Female	38,785	25,862	194	25,362	259	24,614	270	*2.0	0.7	*5.1	0.9
PER CAPITA INCOME											
All races[1]	271,743	20,120	199	19,541	202	18,280	132	*3.0	0.7	*10.1	0.8
White	223,294	21,394	237	20,743	239	19,385	147	*3.1	0.8	*10.4	0.8
Non-Hispanic White	193,074	22,952	268	22,246	271	(NA)	(NA)	*3.2	0.9	(X)	(X)
Black	35,070	12,957	322	12,543	346	11,406	253	*3.3	1.9	*13.6	2.1
Asian and Pacific Islander	10,897	18,709	1,094	18,510	1,128	(NA)	(NA)	1.1	4.4	(X)	(X)
Hispanic origin[2]	31,689	11,434	410	10,941	393	10,770	294	*4.5	2.3	*6.2	2.7

*Statistically significant change at the 90-percent confidence level.

rRevised to reflect the population distribution reported in the 1990 census.

[1]Data for American Indians, Eskimos, and Aleuts are not shown separately. Data for this population group are not tabulated from the CPS because of its small size.

[2]Hispanics may be of any race.

SOURCE: *Money Income in the United States: 1998.* Current Population Reports, P60-206. U.S. Bureau of the Census: Washington, D.C., 1999.

Per Capita Income

In *Current Population Survey*, the Census Bureau annually determines the per capita income in the United States. Per capita income is computed by dividing the total money income by the total population. In other words, it represents the amount of income that every man, woman, and child would receive if the nation's total earnings were divided equally among them. In 1998 the median per capita income was $20,120. The 1998 per capita incomes for whites, blacks, and Hispanics were $21,394, $12,957, and $11,434, respectively. (See Table 3.6.) Comparing the median per capita income with the poverty level for a family of four in 1998 ($16,700) reveals that the poverty level for four people is less than the median per capita income of one person.

TAX RELIEF FOR THE POOR

Both conservatives and liberals hailed the Tax Reform Act of 1986 (PL 99-514) as a major step towards relieving the tax burden of low-income families, one group of Americans whose wages and benefits have been eroding since 1979. The law enlarged and "inflation-proofed" the Earned Income Tax Credit (EITC), which provides a refundable tax credit that both offsets taxes and often operates as a wage supplement. Only those who work can qualify. The amount is determined, in part, by how much each qualified individual or family earned. It is also adjusted to the size of the family. To be eligible for the family EITC, workers must live with their children, who must be under 19 years old or a full-time student under 24 years old.

The maximum credit for 2000 was $2,353 for taxpayers with one child, $3,888 for taxpayers with more than one child, and $347 for persons with no children. Families get less if their income is very low because they are also eligible for public assistance. Working families receive the maximum benefit if their earnings are at least $6,800 (for families with one child) or $9,540 (for families with more than one child), up to an adjusted gross income of no more than $12,460. Benefits phase down gradually when income surpasses $12,460 and phase out entirely for families with 2 or more children at $30,580. (See Figure 3.4.)

The largest EITC benefits go to families that are getting off welfare. The gradual phaseout and the availability of the EITC at above-poverty income levels help to stabilize a parent's employment by providing additional money to cover expenses associated with working, such as child care and transportation. Research has found that the EITC has been an effective work incentive and has significantly increased work participation among single mothers.

Those who do not owe income tax, or who owe an amount smaller than the credit, receive a check directly from the Internal Revenue Service (IRS) for the credit due them. Most recipients claim the credit when they file an income tax form. The EITC lifted more than 4.8 million people, including 2.6 million children, out of poverty in 1999.

Although the Tax Reform Act of 1986 has helped ease the burden of federal taxes, most of the poor still pay a substantial share of their income in state and local taxes. To relieve this tax burden, seven states have enacted a state EITC, and eleven others offer state EITCs based on the federal credit. These state programs boost the income of families that move from welfare to work and prevent states from taxing poor families deeper into poverty.

HOW ACCURATE IS THE "POVERTY LEVEL"?

Almost every year since the Bureau of the Census first defined the poverty level, observers have been concerned about the accuracy of the estimated poverty level. The figure had been based on the finding that the average family in the mid-1950s spent about one-third of its income on food. That cost was multiplied by three to allow for expenditure on all other goods and services. This represented the after-tax money income of an average family relative to the amount it spent on food. (See above.) Since 1965 the poverty threshold has been adjusted each year only for inflation.

Since that time, living patterns have changed, and food costs have become a smaller percentage of family spending. For example, the Bureau of Labor Statistics, in its *Consumer Expenditures in 1995* (Washington, D.C., 1997), reported that in 1995 the average family spent about 14 percent of its total expenditures on food, while housing accounted for about one-third (32.4 percent) of family spending. Based on these changes in buying patterns, should the amount spent on food be multiplied by a factor of seven instead of three? Or should it be based on housing or other factors? What about geographical differences in the cost of living?

The proportion of family income spent on food is not the only change in family living since the 1950s. Both parents in a family are far more likely to be working than they were a generation ago. There is also a much greater likelihood that a single parent, most likely a mother, will be heading the family. Child-care costs, which were of little concern during the 1950s, have become a major issue for working mothers and single parents at the beginning of the twenty-first century.

Critics of the current poverty calculations tend to believe that the poverty levels have been too low since they are based on a 50-year old concept of American life that does not reflect today's economic and social realities. Most feel the poverty level should be raised, probably to about 130 to 150 percent of the current levels. A 1989

FIGURE 3.4

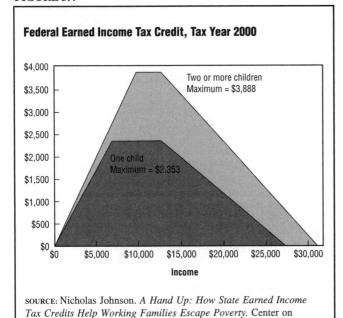

Federal Earned Income Tax Credit, Tax Year 2000

Two or more children
Maximum = $3,888

One child
Maximum = $2,353

Income

SOURCE: Nicholas Johnson. *A Hand Up: How State Earned Income Tax Credits Help Working Families Escape Poverty.* Center on Budget and Policy Priorities: Washington, D.C., 1999

study prepared by the Joint Economic Committee of Congress cited the example of a working mother with two children earning an income right at the poverty level. If the mother spent just $50 per week on child care, spent no more than 30 percent of her earnings on housing. This is the proportion which the U.S. Department of Housing and Urban Development (HUD) has established as the basic affordability standard. In this particular example, 30 percent of her income would equal about $226 a month for rent and utilities. Unless this woman lived in public or subsidized housing (more than two-thirds of the poor do not live in public or subsidized housing) finding an apartment for her family for this amount would be very hard. If she spent a bare minimum on food, she would have about $30 left after taxes. This $30 would have to cover medical care, clothing, personal care items, and an occasional ice cream cone for her two children.

Some are concerned because the poverty threshold is different for elderly and non-elderly Americans. When the poverty threshold was first established, it was thought that older people did not need as much food. Therefore, the value of their basic food needs was lower. Consequently, when this figure was multiplied by three to get the poverty rate, it was naturally lower than the rate for non-elderly people. (The U.S. government, however, uses the poverty rate for the non-elderly Americans when determining the eligibility for welfare services for all people, including the elderly.) Critics point out that while the elderly might eat less than younger people, they have greater needs in other areas, which are not considered when their food needs are simply multiplied by three. Probably the most notable difference between the needs

of the elderly and non-elderly is in the area of health care. The Bureau of Labor Statistics, in *Consumer Expenditures in 1995*, found that while the total population interviewed spent about 5.4 percent of their income on health care, those over 65 years of age spent about 12 percent. These critics feel that the poverty level should be the same for everyone, no matter what the age.

A 1995 report prepared by the National Research Council's Panel on Poverty and Family Assistance raised several important issues regarding poverty thresholds or measurement of need. The panel recommended that new thresholds be developed, using consumer expenditure data to represent a budget for basic needs: food, clothing, shelter (including utilities), and a small allowance for miscellaneous needs. This budget would be adjusted to reflect the needs of different family types and geographic differences in costs. Research and discussion continue on these issues.

How Should Income Be Defined?

The Panel on Poverty and Family Assistance also recommended that family resources be redefined to reflect the net amount available to buy goods and services in that budget for basic needs. Critics have pointed out that the definition of income used to set the poverty figure is not accurate because it does not include the value of all welfare services as income. If the value of these services were counted as income, they believe the proportion of Americans considered to be living in poverty would be lower.

Over the past decade the Bureau of the Census has tried to develop several experimental methods of estimating income for evaluating poverty levels, but it has had considerable difficulty determining the value of many of these subsidies. For example, they first tried to consider Medicare and Medicaid at full market value (this meant taking the total amount of money that the government spent on medical care for a particular group and then dividing it by the number of people in that group). The value often was greater than the actual earnings of the low-income family, which meant that, although their total family earnings may not have been enough to cover food and housing, adding the market value of Medicare or Medicaid to their earnings put them above the poverty threshold.

This did not make much sense, so the Census Bureau has been trying a "fungible value" (giving equivalent value to units) for Medicare and Medicaid. When the Bureau measures a household income, if the earners cannot cover the cost of housing and food, Medicare and Medicaid are given no value. However, if the family can cover the cost of food and shelter, the Census Bureau figures the difference between the household income and the amount needed to meet basic housing and food costs. It then values the health services at this difference (up to the amount of market value of the medical benefits). This is very complicated, but the Bureau of the Census believes it gives a fair value to these services. Similar problems have developed in trying to determine the value of housing subsidies, school lunches, and other benefits.

Still other observers point out that most income definitions do not include assets and liabilities. Perhaps the poor household has some assets, including a home or car, that could be converted into income. One experimental definition of income includes capital gains on earnings, although it seems to make little difference—about 90 percent of all capital gains are earned by those in the upper fifth of the earnings scale. Including assets generally means little since the overwhelming majority of poor families have few financial assets. The Bureau of the Census reports that over half the poor have no assets at all and about four-fifths have assets of less than $1,000, a relatively insignificant amount from which to earn income.

Another major issue is the question of income before and after income taxes. While the Tax Reform Act of 1986 (PL 99-514) has removed most poor households from the federal income tax rolls, many poor households still pay state and local taxes. Naturally, some critics claim, the taxes paid to local and state governments are funds that are no longer available for feeding and housing the family and, therefore, should not be counted as income.

Table 3.7 lists the various experimental definitions for income that the Bureau of the Census has considered. Table 3.8 shows the effects of selected definitions on the poverty rate.

HUNGER IN AMERICA

Often, when a person thinks of the consequences of poverty, he or she visualizes poor people being poorly housed, or in the worst case, homeless, and of people not having enough to eat. While it may be hard to conceive of Americans not having enough to eat, many Americans go to bed hungry or experience times when there is not enough food for the family.

During the 1980s a growing number of reports found that Americans, especially children, were suffering from hunger. Many observers did not believe these reports or thought they had been exaggerated. President Ronald Reagan appointed a President's Task Force on Food Assistance. In 1984 the Task Force found that it could not "report definitive evidence on the extent of hunger" because there was no agreed-upon way to measure hunger.

To determine the amount of hunger in the United States, the Food Research and Action Center (FRAC) in Washington, D.C., an advocacy group for the poor, coordinated a study of seven sites. The method for this survey was based on a comprehensive study, the Community Childhood Hunger Identification Project (CCHIP), per-

TABLE 3.7

Definitions of Money Income Excluding Capital Gains Before Taxes

1. **Money Income excluding capital gains before taxes.** This is the official definition used in Census Bureau reports.
2. **Definition 1 less government cash transfers.** Government cash transfers include nonmeans-tested transfers such as Social Security payments, unemployment compensation, and government educational assistance (e.g., Pell Grants) as well as means-tested transfers such as Aid to Families with Dependent Children (AFDC) and Supplemental Security Income (SSI).
3. **Definition 2 plus capital gains.** Realized capital gains and losses are simulated as part of the Census Bureau's Federal individual income tax estimation procedure.
4. **Definition 3 plus health insurance supplements to wage or salary income.** Employer-provided health insurance coverage is treated as part of total worker compensation.
5. **Definition 4 less Social Security Payroll taxes.**
6. **Definition 5 less Federal income taxes.** The effect of the Earned Income Tax Credit is shown separately in Definition 7.
7. **Definition 6 plus the Earned Income Tax Credit.**
8. **Definition 7 less State income taxes.**
9. **Definition 8 plus nonmeans-tested government cash transfers.** Nonmeans-tested government cash transfers include Social Security payments, unemployment compensation, worker's compensation, nonmeans-tested Veteran's payments, U.S. Railroad Retirement, Black Lung payments, Pell Grants, and other government educational assistance (Pell Grants are income-tested but are included here because they are very different from the assistance programs that are included in the means-tested category).
10. **Definition 9 plus the value of Medicare.** Medicare is counted at its fungible value.
11. **Definition 10 plus the value of regular-price school lunches.**
12. **Definition 11 plus means-tested government cash transfers.** Means-tested government cash transfers include AFDC, SSI, other public assistance programs, and means-tested Veteran's payments.
13. **Definition 12 plus the value of Medicaid. Medicaid is counted at its fungible value.**
14. **Definition 13 plus the value of other means-tested government noncash transfers.** These include food stamps, rent subsidies, and free and reduced-price school lunches.
15. **Definition 14 plus net imputed return on equity in own home.** This definition includes a calculated annual benefit of converting one's home equity into an annuity, net of property taxes.

SOURCE: *Measuring the Effect of Benefits and Taxes on Income and Poverty.* U.S. Bureau of the Census: Washington, D.C., 1993

formed by the Connecticut Association for Human Services. This first FRAC survey interviewed 2,335 households with incomes at or below 185 percent of poverty and with at least one child under 12 years of age.

The results of the first survey, released in 1991, concluded that 32 percent of the U.S. households with incomes at or below 185 percent of the poverty level were hungry. At least one child out of every eight under 12 years of age suffered from hunger. Another 40 percent of low-income children were at risk for hunger.

Between 1992 and 1994 the FRAC sponsored the second set of CCHIP surveys at 11 sites (5,282 households with at least one child below the age of 12). The results were reported in *Community Childhood Hunger Identification Project: A Survey of Childhood Hunger in the United States* (Washington, D.C., 1995).

TABLE 3.8

The Cumulative Effect of Taxes and Transfers on Poverty Estimates: 1995 and 1996

[Numbers in thousands]

Selected income definitions		1996		1995		Difference 1996 less 1995	
		Number below poverty	Poverty rate	Number below poverty	Poverty rate	Number below poverty	Poverty rate
Definition 1	(current measure)	36,529	13.7	36,425	13.8	104	-0.1
Definition 2	(definition 1 less government cash transfers)	57,476	21.6	57,643	21.9	-167	-0.3
Definition 4	(definition 2 plus capital gains and employee health benefits)	55,447	20.8	55,558	21.1	-111	-0.3
Definition 6	(definition 4 less social security payroll and federal income taxes*)	58,598	22.0	58,388	22.1	210	-0.1
Definition 7	(definition 6 plus the earned income credit (EIC))	54,644	20.5	55,061	20.9	-417	-0.4
Definition 8	(definition 7 less state income taxes)	55,119	20.7	55,505	21.0	-386	-0.3
Definition 9	(definition 8 plus nonmeans-tested government cash transfers)	37,075	13.9	37,176	14.1	-101	-0.2
Definition 11	(definition 9 plus the value of medicare and regular-price school lunch)	36,017	13.5	36,177	13.7	-160	-0.2
Definition 14	(definition 12 plus the value of medicaid and other means-tested government noncash transfers)	27,133	10.2	27,190	10.3	-57	-0.1

*This definition refers to social security and federal income tax liabilities before taking into account refundable credits i.e. EIC.

Note: No differences between 1995 and 1996 were statistically significant at the 90 percent confidence level.

SOURCE: *Poverty in the United States: 1996*. U.S. Bureau of the Census: Washington, D.C., 1997

For the purposes of its report, the FRAC defined hunger as food insufficiency—skipping meals, eating less, running out of food—that occurs because of limited household resources.

Eight key questions in both CCHIP surveys were designed to determine whether a household was short of food and whether members of the household were hungry. The eight questions were:

1. Does your household ever run out of money to buy food to make a meal?

2. Do you or adult members of your household ever eat less than you feel you should because there is not enough money for food?

3. Do you or adult members of your household ever cut the size of meals or skip meals because there is not enough money for food?

4. Do your children ever eat less than you feel they should because there is not enough money for food?

5. Do you ever cut the size of your children's meal, or do they ever skip meals because there is not enough money for food?

6. Do your children ever say they are hungry because there is not enough food in the house?

7. Do you ever rely on a limited number of foods to feed your children because you are running out of money to buy food for a meal?

8. Do any of your children ever go to bed hungry because there is not enough money to buy food?

The CCHIP study defines hunger as a score of five "yes" answers to any of these eight questions on hunger. A score of one to four "yes" answers to the questions means that the household is at risk for suffering from hunger.

Not surprisingly, households suffering from hunger tended to be poorer than those that were not. About 62 percent of hungry households had incomes below the poverty level. Their average income was 86 percent ($12,341) of the poverty line for a family of four in 1993 ($14,350). Furthermore, the less the family earned, the more likely it was to suffer from hunger. (See Figure 3.5.)

Housing costs took up a higher percentage of income in hungry families than in those that were not hungry (34 percent compared to 28 percent). Although hungry households spent more than one-third of their remaining income on food (counting the value of food stamps and other food-assistance programs), this averaged only $74.78 per person per month.

Based on the findings of the CCHIP study, the FRAC concluded that about 4 million children under the age of 12 years experienced hunger in some part of one or more months during the previous year. Another 9.6 million children were at risk of becoming hungry.

The Urban Institute's "Snapshots of America's Families" conducted 44,000 interviews and found that nearly

FIGURE 3.5

Hunger Rates in Relation to Income

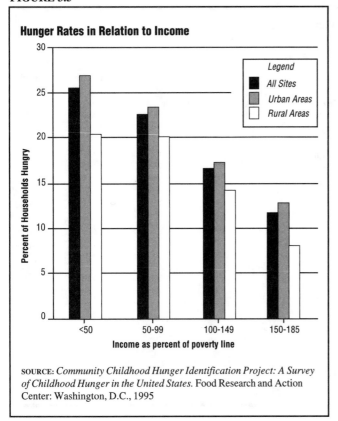

SOURCE: *Community Childhood Hunger Identification Project: A Survey of Childhood Hunger in the United States.* Food Research and Action Center: Washington, D.C., 1995

TABLE 3.9

Characteristics of Hungry Households, Households at Risk of Hunger, and Households That are Not Hungry

Characteristics	Percent of Households		
	Hungry Households	Households at Risk of Hunger	Households Not Hungry
Income equal to or below the poverty line[1]	62.3%	50.0%	41.8%
Employment Status[1]			
At least one household member employed	60.2%	69.2%	71.3%
At least one full-time worker	48.4%	57.5%	62.4%
Employed, but not full-time	11.8%	11.7%	8.9%
No one employed	39.8%	30.8%	28.6%
Receives AFDC benefits[1]	37.8%	30.8%	27.4%
At least one high school graduate[1]	72.2%	78.6%	78.6%
Household Type[2]			
Two-parent households	46.5%	54.8%	55.0%
Female-headed households	39.2%	31.7%	28.0%
Other type households	14.3%	13.4%	17.0%
Geographic Residence[1]			
Urban households	81.7%	77.3%	75.4%
Rural households	18.3%	22.7%	24.6%
Race[2]			
White (non-Hispanic) households	43.9%	59.2%	55.0%
African-American (Black, non-Hispanic) households	29.4%	20.2%	25.0%
Hispanic households	13.7%	10.4%	10.6%
Other households	13.1%	10.2%	9.3%
Average household size	4.4	4.1	4.2
Average number of children	2.6	2.3	2.3'

[1]Test for trend performed is significant at p < .001 among hungry households, households at risk of hunger, and households not hungry.

[2]Test of association performed is significant at p < .00I among hungry households, households at risk of hunger, and households not hungry.

SOURCE: *Community Childhood Hunger Identification Project: A Survey of Childhood Hunger in the United States.* Food Research and Action Center: Washington, D.C.,

half of low-income families (those with family incomes two times the federal poverty line) reported in 1997 that the food they purchased ran out before they got money to buy more or they worried they would run out of food. Four out of five of these families with food problems reported suffering actual food shortages, and one out of five worried about food shortages. More children than adults lived in families that worried about or had trouble affording food, so that 54 percent of low-income children experienced the problem.

In a 1997 study of families no longer receiving Temporary Assistance for Needy Families (TANF) in ten large states (California, Florida, Illinois, Massachusetts, Michigan, New Jersey, New York, Ohio, Pennsylvania, and Texas), 36 percent of families surveyed reported that their children were eating less or skipping meals due to cost.

Table 3.9 compares the characteristics of hungry, at-risk, and non-hungry households. The majority (60.2 percent) of hungry households have at least one employed household member, and half (48.4 percent) have at least one full-time worker. Almost two in five (39.2 percent) households were headed by women. More than half (56.1 percent) were non-white. The large majority (81.7 percent) lived in urban areas.

The CCHIP survey studied one child in each household (the child with the most recent birthday) and found that, in comparison with non-hungry children, hungry children were:

- More than three times as likely to suffer from unwanted weight loss.
- More than four times as likely to suffer from fatigue.
- Almost three times as likely to suffer from irritability.
- More than three times as likely to have frequent headaches.
- Almost one and one-half times as likely to have frequent ear infections.
- Four times as likely to suffer from concentration problems.
- Almost twice as likely to have frequent colds.

Based on the findings from the CCHIP, the FRAC concluded that although federal food programs are target-

TABLE 3.10

Food Assistance Program Participation Rates for Hungry, at Risk, and Non-Hungry Households
(Percent of Eligible Households Participating)[1]

Food Assistance Program	Hungry Households	Households At Risk of Hunger	Non-Hungry Households
Food Stamp Program	68.5%	66.2%	65.0%
WIC Program	45.9%	50.1%	47.9%
National School Lunch Program[2][3]	94.1%	89.2%	84.9%
School Breakfast Program[2][3]	59.0%	43.9%	38.5%
Summer Food Service Program[3]	15.3%	10.1%	8.7%

[1]Households are considered eligible for the Food Stamp Program if they would quality based on income. Households must be income and categorically eligible for the WIC Program. Households are considered eligible for the School Lunch and School Breakfast Programs if they have school-aged children. Since the Summer Food Service Programs available to all children in communities where it operates, all households are considered eligible to participate in it.

[2]Participation rates for the School Lunch and Breakfast Programs are for low-income households with children eligible for and receiving free or reduced-price lunches.

[3]Test for trend performed is siginticant at p<.00 l.

SOURCE: *Community Childhood Hunger Identification Project: A Survey of Childhood Hunger in the United States.* Food Research and Action Center: Washington, D.C., 1995

ed to households most in need, a common barrier to program participation is a lack of information, particularly about eligibility guidelines. (See Table 3.10 for a comparison of program participation by hungry, at-risk, and non-hungry households.) The FRAC believes that if federal, state, and local governments made a greater effort to ensure that possible recipients were aware of their eligibility for food programs, such as Women, Infants, and Children (WIC) and the School Breakfast Program, there would be a large drop in hunger in this country.

In 1997 the United States Department of Agriculture (USDA) released the government's first national data on the prevalence of hunger and food insecurity in the United States. A questionnaire, developed jointly by the United States Census Bureau and the USDA, was administered to nearly 45,000 nationally representative households in April 1995. Based on answers to 18 key questions, households were characterized in one of four categories: "food secure," "food insecure without hunger," "food insecure with moderate hunger," or "food insecure with severe hunger." The results showed that the prevalence of food insecurity, which included all three levels of severity, was 11.9 percent, nearly 12 million households or a total of over 34 million persons.

GROWING DEMAND FOR EMERGENCY FOOD ASSISTANCE

Second Harvest National Research Study

Second Harvest, the nation's largest charitable hunger-relief organization, published the results of its study on the charitable response to hunger in *Hunger 1997: The Faces and Facts.* Seventy-nine of its regional food banks conducted local research from January through March of 1997. They found the following characteristics of recipients of emergency food assistance:

- More than 21 million people (including 8 million children and more than 3.5 million elderly) sought emergency food assistance during that time period. Approximately 62 percent were female, 38 percent male. (See Figure 3.6.)

- Single-parent households represented more than one half (54 percent) of the families with children who sought food assistance.

- More than a third (38.6 percent) of all emergency client households had at least one member working.

- Eighty-six percent earned less that $15,500 annually. (The poverty level for a family of 3 was $13,330.)

- Forty-seven percent of the recipients were white; 32 percent, black; 15 percent, Hispanic; and 3 percent, Native American. (See Figure 3.7.)

- Forty percent had not completed high school, while 36 percent had a high school diploma or its equivalent. Only 5 percent had attended college or received a college degree.

- Forty-one percent received food stamps, 64 percent of households with children participated in School Breakfast and Lunch Programs, and 31 percent participated in the Special Supplement Nutrition Program for Women, Infants, and Children (WIC). (See Figure 3.8.)

FIGURE 3.6

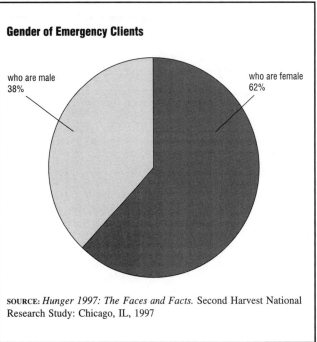

Gender of Emergency Clients

who are male 38%

who are female 62%

SOURCE: *Hunger 1997: The Faces and Facts.* Second Harvest National Research Study: Chicago, IL, 1997

FIGURE 3.7

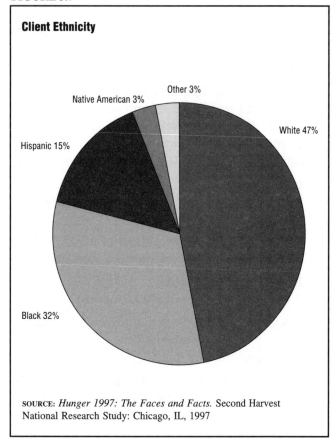

Client Ethnicity

SOURCE: *Hunger 1997: The Faces and Facts.* Second Harvest National Research Study: Chicago, IL, 1997

FIGURE 3.8

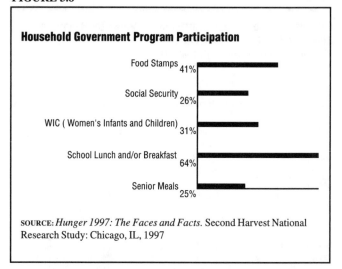

Household Government Program Participation

SOURCE: *Hunger 1997: The Faces and Facts.* Second Harvest National Research Study: Chicago, IL, 1997

FIGURE 3.9

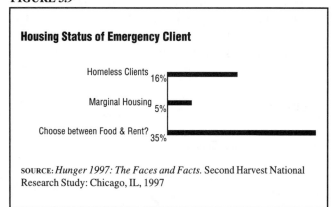

Housing Status of Emergency Client

SOURCE: *Hunger 1997: The Faces and Facts.* Second Harvest National Research Study: Chicago, IL, 1997

• Thirty-five percent had to choose between buying food and paying their rent or mortgage. Sixteen percent were homeless. (See Figure 3.9.)

• Thirty-six percent reported that at least one household member was in poor health; 41 percent had unpaid medical or hospital bills.

• More than one in eight persons requesting emergency food had been cut from cash assistance in the prior two years.

U.S. Conference of Mayors Status Report

In 1998 the United States Conference of Mayors reported a continuing, growing demand for emergency food assistance. The *Status Report on Hunger and Homelessness in America's Cities: 1998* (The United States Conference of Mayors, Washington, D.C., 1998) reported that 78 percent of cities surveyed found that demand for emergency food assistance had increased by an average of 14 percent from the previous year. Eighty-four percent of cities surveyed reported increased demand of emergency food among families with children. Thirty-seven percent of persons requesting emergency food assistance were employed. The causes of hunger, according to officials in the surveyed cities, included low-paying jobs, unemployment, food stamp cuts, high housing costs, poverty or lack of income, and low benefits in public assistance programs.

CHAPTER 4
A CHANGING NATION—
WEALTH AND INCOME DISTRIBUTION

The number of Americans living in poverty grew in the 1980s and 1990s. As a result, the cost of welfare has been rising. A key factor contributing to the increase in poverty and welfare outlays has been the changing economic structure of the nation.

The Bureau of the Census has released a number of studies showing a change in the distribution of wealth and earnings in the United States. This change has resulted in an increase in the gap between the rich and the poor. Unlike many short-term economic changes that are often the product of normal economic cycles of growth and recession, these changes seem to indicate fundamental changes in American society.

GROWING INCOME INEQUALITY

In the 1980s and 1990s the Bureau of the Census tracked a growing inequality in income in the United States. For comparison purposes, the Bureau of the Census divides the population into five income groups (quintiles). In 1998 the income differences were close to record highs, with only the top fifth having increased its percentage of the nation's income in the past 20 years. The average income of the top fifth of families, after adjusting for inflation, was 11 percent higher than in 1990. In contrast, the average income of the poorest fifth of families was only 3 percent higher than in 1990. Census data shows that in 1998 the quintile of families with the highest incomes received 50 percent of the national income, about the same as that received by the other 80 percent of the population combined. (See Table 4.1.)

Why Is the "Income Gap" Growing?

There are many reasons for the growing inequality, although observers disagree on which are more important. One reason is that the proportion of the elderly population, who are likely to earn less, is growing. In 1998, 21 percent of all households had a householder 65 years of age or older. (A "household" may consist of a single individual or a group of related or nonrelated people living together, while a "family" is made up of related individuals.) In addition, more people are living in nonfamily situations (either alone or with nonrelatives). In 1998, 31.1 percent lived in nonfamily households, which tend to earn about half that of family households. (See Table 4.2 for the characteristics of households by income in 1998.)

Also contributing to growing income inequality is the increase in the number of households headed by females with no husband as well as the increase in labor force participation of women. In 1998 the proportion of female-headed households with no husband present made up 17.8 percent of all family households, and female householders (either in family or nonfamily living arrangements or living alone) constituted 25 percent of all households in the nation. Female-headed households typically earn significantly less than other types of households. (On average, women earn 70 percent of what men earn because women's labor is devalued.)

Other factors that contribute to the growing income gap include the decline in the influence of unions and the changing occupational structure, in general, from better-paying manufacturing positions to lower-paying service jobs. The average wage paid to less-educated workers (after adjusting for inflation) has actually dropped in the past 20 years. In 1996 workers with less than a high school education earned an hourly wage that was 26 percent lower than in 1979. High-school graduates experienced a 13 percent wage decline. In addition, the proportion of low-wage workers that receive employer-based health insurance and pension benefits dropped significantly between 1979 and 1996.

MEDIAN HOUSEHOLD INCOMES

In real value (in comparative dollars, accounting for inflation), the median income of the country's households

TABLE 4.1

Selected Measures of Household Income Dispersions, 1990, 1997, and 1998

(Income in 1998 dollars)

Measures of Income Dispersion	1998	1997	1996	1995	1990	1985	1980[2]	1975 [3]	1970	1968	1967
Household Income at Selected Percentiles											
20th percentile upper limit	16,116	15,640	15,342	15,402	15,589	15,149	14,965	14,574	14,552	14,367	13,471
50th (median)	38,885	37,581	36,872	36,446	37,343	35,778	35,076	34,224	34,471	33,478	32,075
80th percentile upper limit	75,000	72,614	70,659	69,654	68,848	66,365	62,784	59,446	57,863	54,858	53,170
95th percentile lower limit	132,199	128,521	124,187	120,860	118,163	110,984	101,999	94,787	91,477	85,824	85,317
Household Income Ratios of Selected Percentiles											
95th/20th	8.20	8.22	8.09	7.85	7.58	7.33	6.82	6.50	6.29	5.97	6.33
95th/50th	3.40	3.42	3.37	3.32	3.16	3.10	2.91	2.77	2.65	2.56	2.66
80th/50th	1.93	1.93	1.92	1.91	1.84	1.85	1.79	1.74	1.68	1.64	1.66
80th/20th	4.65	4.64	4.61	4.52	4.42	4.38	4.20	4.08	3.98	3.82	3.95
20th/50th	0.41	0.42	0.42	0.42	0.42	0.42	0.43	0.43	0.42	0.43	0.42
Mean Household Income of Quintiles											
Lowest quintile	9,223	9,010	8,930	8,931	8,973	8,782	8,879	8,800	8,008	7,921	7,301
Second quintile	23,288	22,442	21,917	21,816	22,486	21,708	21,428	20,894	21,293	20,935	19,906
Third quintile	38,967	37,756	36,866	36,478	37,141	35,955	35,268	34,186	34,289	33,201	31,783
Fourth quintile	60,266	58,479	57,057	56,076	55,997	54,072	51,928	49,645	48,336	46,319	44,468
Highest quintile	127,529	124,676	120,005	117,021	108,671	99,741	91,211	86,457	85,581	81,120	80,584
Shares of Household Income of Quintiles											
Lowest quintile	3.6	3.6	3.7	3.7	3.9	4.0	4.3	4.4	4.1	4.2	4.0
Second quintile	9.0	8.9	9.0	9.1	9.6	9.7	10.3	10.5	10.8	11.1	10.8
Third quintile	15.0	15.0	15.1	15.2	15.9	16.3	16.9	17.1	17.4	17.5	17.3
Fourth quintile	23.2	23.2	23.3	23.3	24.0	24.6	24.9	24.8	24.5	24.4	24.2
Highest quintile	49.2	49.4	49.0	48.7	46.6	45.3	43.7	43.2	43.3	42.8	43.8
Gini coefficient of income inequality	0.456	0.459	0.455	0.450	0.428	0.419	0.403	0.397	0.394	0.388	0.399

[1] Reflects the implementation of 1990 census adjusted population controls, 1990 census sample re-design, a change in data collection method from paper-pencil to computer-assisted interviewing (CAI), and changes in income reporting limits. For detailed information concerning the impact of these changes, see Current Population Reports, Series P60 - 191, "A Brief Look at Postwar U.S. Income Inequality."

[2] Reflects implementation of 1980 census population controls.

[3] Reflects implementation of 1970 census population controls.

SOURCE: U.S. Census Bureau, Current Population Surveys, selected March Supplements

declined 5 percent from 1990 to 1993. But the median income had nearly returned to the 1990 level by 1997. (See Table 4.3.) ("Median" means that half the measured values are above the specified value and half are below.) Table 4.3 shows the distribution of household income from 1967 to 1998 in 1998 equivalent dollars. In 1967, 22.3 percent of households earned less than $15,000 per year, and 22.6 percent earned $50,000 or more. By 1998, 18.1 percent earned less than $15,000 while 38.7 percent earned $50,000 or more.

Types of Households

In 1998 family households made up nearly 69 percent of all households in the United States. Their median income was $47,469. The type of household, however, made a big difference in income level. The median income of families headed by married couples was $54,276. But male householders with no wife present made only $39,414, and female householders with no husband present earned only $24,393. Nonfamily house-

holds showed consistently lower median incomes. Females living alone earned only $16,406, the lowest median income. (See Table 4.2.)

Race and Hispanic Origin

The level of income also varied widely by race and ethnicity. In 1998 the median income for white households was $40,912; for African American households, $25,351; and for Hispanic households, $28,330. Black households were overrepresented in the lower-income categories; while they made up 12 percent of all households, they accounted for 21 percent of households earning less than $15,000 in income. Households of Hispanic origin were also overrepresented in lower-income levels, making up 8.7 percent of all households but comprising 12.2 percent of households earning less than $15,000. Minorities were also less likely to have large incomes. While 11.3 percent of white households earned over $100,000, only 4 percent of blacks and 4.5 percent of Hispanic households earned that much. (See Table 4.2.)

TABLE 4.2

Selected Characteristics—Households by Total Money Income in 1998

[Numbers in thousands. Households as of March of the following year.]

Characteristic	Total	Less than $5,000	$5,000 to $9,999	$10,000 to $14,999	$15,000 to $24,999	$25,000 to $34,999	$35,000 to $49,999	$50,000 to $74,999	$75,000 to $99,999	$100,000 and over	Median income Value (dollars)	Median income Standard error (dollars)	Mean income Value (dollars)	Mean income Standard error (dollars)
All households	103,874	3,373	7,332	8,093	14,587	13,698	16,660	19,272	9,934	10,926	38,885	230	51,855	280
TYPE OF RESIDENCE														
Inside metropolitan areas	83,441	2,687	5,408	6,193	11,103	10,669	13,091	15,643	8,636	10,012	40,983	215	54,725	330
Inside central cities	32,144	1,562	2,909	3,042	4,878	4,320	4,931	5,134	2,581	2,788	33,151	388	46,467	460
1 million or more	20,513	997	1,954	1,987	2,999	2,628	3,065	3,269	1,686	1,928	33,559	500	47,529	595
Under 1 million	11,631	566	955	1,054	1,879	1,692	1,867	1,865	895	859	32,488	535	44,593	716
Outside central cities	51,297	1,125	2,499	3,151	6,225	6,349	8,159	10,509	6,055	7,224	46,402	311	59,901	449
1 million or more	35,028	671	1,523	1,974	3,830	4,083	5,452	7,312	4,421	5,762	49,940	395	63,998	571
Under 1 million	16,269	454	976	1,177	2,395	2,266	2,707	3,198	1,634	1,462	39,428	564	51,079	693
Outside metropolitan areas	20,433	686	1,924	1,900	3,484	3,029	3,569	3,629	1,298	914	32,022	383	40,131	547
REGION														
Northeast	19,877	687	1,468	1,580	2,614	2,358	3,007	3,582	2,048	2,532	40,634	469	55,041	624
Midwest	24,489	646	1,541	1,834	3,304	3,353	3,940	5,032	2,418	2,422	40,609	365	52,430	592
South	36,959	1,391	2,989	2,925	5,683	5,100	5,907	6,473	3,168	3,323	35,797	304	48,284	467
West	22,549	648	1,334	1,755	2,985	2,887	3,806	4,185	2,300	2,648	40,983	403	54,274	632
RACE AND HISPANIC ORIGIN OF HOUSEHOLDER														
White	87,212	2,263	5,352	6,468	11,937	11,480	14,230	16,862	8,730	9,889	40,912	205	54,207	319
Black	12,579	918	1,773	1,338	2,183	1,700	1,795	1,659	708	507	25,351	397	34,139	456
Hispanic origin[1]	9,060	441	912	989	1,620	1,477	1,432	1,271	503	416	28,330	546	38,280	814
TYPE OF HOUSEHOLD														
Family households	71,535	1,650	2,537	3,653	8,639	8,996	12,192	15,676	8,489	9,702	47,469	249	60,406	371
Married-couple families	54,770	627	914	1,841	5,488	6,329	9,454	13,301	7,739	9,077	54,276	322	68,010	452
Male householder, no wife present	3,976	97	138	209	641	675	759	845	319	293	39,414	993	48,306	1,053
Female householder, no husband present	12,789	925	1,486	1,603	2,510	1,992	1,979	1,530	431	333	24,393	398	31,608	496
Nonfamily households	32,339	1,723	4,795	4,440	5,948	4,701	4,468	3,596	1,444	1,224	23,441	285	32,938	319
Male householder	14,368	726	1,358	1,364	2,475	2,237	2,415	2,128	849	816	30,414	340	40,127	565
Living alone	10,966	642	1,283	1,201	2,119	1,783	1,768	1,338	425	408	26,021	334	34,572	626
Female householder	17,971	998	3,437	3,076	3,473	2,464	2,053	1,467	595	408	18,615	281	27,190	342
Living alone	15,640	947	3,366	2,951	3,155	2,144	1,638	959	295	186	16,406	236	23,362	321
AGE OF HOUSEHOLDER														
Under 65 years	82,286	2,741	4,128	4,645	9,694	10,627	14,029	17,386	9,104	9,930	44,697	274	56,688	327
15 to 24 years	5,770	493	582	668	1,325	944	932	551	151	123	23,564	445	30,947	995
25 to 34 years	18,819	673	833	1,193	2,521	2,932	3,502	4,192	1,713	1,260	40,069	423	47,960	540
35 to 44 years	23,968	606	888	1,132	2,426	2,950	4,387	5,529	3,002	3,049	48,451	444	60,103	616
45 to 54 years	20,158	475	813	790	1,831	2,119	3,123	4,621	2,724	3,663	54,148	534	67,293	729
55 to 64 years	13,571	494	1,013	863	1,590	1,681	2,086	2,494	1,515	1,835	43,167	601	57,952	865
65 years and over	21,589	632	3,204	3,448	4,893	3,071	2,631	1,886	829	995	21,729	240	33,432	468
65 to 74 years	11,373	306	1,406	1,353	2,400	1,742	1,645	1,257	587	678	26,112	399	38,580	691
75 years and over	10,216	327	1,798	2,095	2,493	1,329	986	629	243	317	17,885	283	27,700	609
Mean age of householder	48.6	45.8	57.0	55.6	51.7	47.9	46.1	45.0	46.0	47.8	(X)	(X)	(X)	(X)
SIZE OF HOUSEHOLD														
One person	26,606	1,588	4,649	4,151	5,273	3,926	3,406	2,297	720	594	20,154	221	27,982	324
Two people	34,262	872	1,310	2,051	5,115	4,991	5,936	6,871	3,327	3,788	41,512	301	54,930	515
Three people	17,386	411	661	844	1,941	2,014	2,999	3,971	2,247	2,297	49,069	518	60,356	708
Four people	15,030	255	381	544	1,241	1,567	2,536	3,723	2,206	2,578	55,886	607	67,691	770
Five people	6,962	167	204	310	622	729	1,161	1,680	976	1,113	53,706	911	66,523	1,336
Six people	2,367	46	95	126	256	299	383	473	330	360	49,080	1,500	63,626	2,125
Seven people or more	1,261	33	33	66	138	171	239	256	128	196	46,646	1,676	62,922	3,063
Mean size of household	2.61	2.06	1.74	1.98	2.23	2.45	2.72	2.97	3.18	3.25	(X)	(X)	(X)	(X)
NUMBER OF EARNERS														
No earners	21,263	2,056	5,005	3,984	4,702	2,400	1,594	893	299	330	14,442	147	20,946	242
One earner	36,216	1,150	2,007	3,350	7,134	6,787	6,670	5,121	1,947	2,050	31,162	183	42,498	461
Two earners or more	46,396	167	321	759	2,752	4,511	8,396	13,257	7,687	8,545	60,787	258	73,323	453
Two earners	36,501	146	308	712	2,527	3,935	7,117	10,427	5,481	5,848	57,388	319	69,238	486
Three earners	7,409	21	12	47	213	506	1,066	2,223	1,558	1,763	70,012	816	84,455	1,326
Four earners or more	2,485	0	1	0	12	71	213	608	648	933	86,676	1,640	100,147	1,953
Mean number of earners	1.41	0.45	0.37	0.62	0.90	1.23	1.55	1.88	2.11	2.18	(X)	(X)	(X)	(X)

TABLE 4.2

Selected Characteristics—Households by Total Money Income in 1998 [CONTINUED]

[Numbers in thousands. Households as of March of the following year.]

Characteristic	Total	Less than $5,000	$5,000 to $9,999	$10,000 to $14,999	$15,000 to $24,999	$25,000 to $34,999	$35,000 to $49,999	$50,000 to $74,999	$75,000 to $99,999	$100,000 and over	Median income Value (dollars)	Median income Standard error (dollars)	Mean income Value (dollars)	Mean income Standard error (dollars)
WORK EXPERIENCE OF HOUSEHOLDER														
Total	103,874	3,373	7,332	8,093	14,587	13,698	16,660	19,272	9,934	10,926	38,885	230	51,855	280
Worked	74,296	1,177	2,038	3,571	8,487	9,867	13,421	16,937	8,929	9,869	48,179	263	60,766	353
Worked at full~time jobs	64,566	690	1,179	2,485	6,882	8,626	11,941	15,419	8,298	9,046	50,562	223	63,102	383
50 weeks or more	54,963	283	448	1,676	5,302	7,240	10,323	13,853	7,542	8,296	53,033	301	66,088	420
27 to 49 weeks	6,194	60	301	447	998	968	1,136	1,103	599	582	39,041	808	52,071	1,211
26 weeks or less	3,409	346	430	363	581	418	482	463	158	167	24,525	1,140	34,993	1,078
Worked at part~time jobs	9,730	487	859	1,086	1,605	1,241	1,480	1,518	631	823	31,470	618	45,266	857
50 weeks or more	4,867	118	363	561	872	667	721	763	337	465	32,276	852	47,585	1,244
27 to 49 weeks	2,325	89	217	234	384	268	407	371	147	209	33,945	1,312	47,049	1,791
26 week or less	2,538	280	280	290	349	306	352	384	147	149	27,249	1,194	39,184	1,540
Did not work	29,578	2,196	5,294	4,522	6,100	3,831	3,239	2,335	1,005	1,056	19,093	193	29,471	362
EDUCATIONAL ATTAINMENT[2]														
Total	9 104	2,880	6,750	7,425	13,262	12,754	15,727	18,721	9,783	10,802	40,296	194	53,084	290
Less than 9th grade	7,047	414	1,573	1,327	1,537	918	668	402	104	104	16,154	347	23,501	610
9th to 12th grade (no diploma)	9,407	586	1,473	1,346	2,056	1,304	1,289	890	286	177	20,724	336	28,234	479
High school graduate (includes equivalency)	30,613	1,010	2,258	2,613	4,840	4,831	5,534	5,729	2,347	1,450	34,373	334	42,352	370
Some college, no degree	17,833	437	771	1,126	2,357	2,579	3,330	3,852	1,842	1,539	41,658	374	51,220	597
Associate degree	7,468	146	246	387	772	918	1,376	1,875	924	824	48,604	818	57,317	1,066
Bachelor's degree or more	25,738	287	430	626	1,700	2,204	3,531	5,973	4,280	6,707	66,474	499	83,096	755
Bachelor's degree	16,781	191	323	422	1,251	1,616	2,465	4,070	2,758	3,684	62,188	549	75,213	796
Master's degree	5,961	60	71	134	340	429	805	1,337	1,061	1,723	71,086	955	87,497	1,692
Professional degree	1,623	23	19	51	64	81	132	282	200	771	95,309	3,560	127,499	4,787
Doctorate degree	1,373	13	17	18	45	77	129	284	261	528	84,100	3,491	107,847	3,700

[1]Hispanics may be of any race.

[2]Restricted to people 25 years and over.

SOURCE: *Money Income in the United States: 1998.* Current Population Reports, P60-206. U.S. Bureau of the Census: Washington, D.C., 1999.

Age and Income

The age of the householder was also a factor in the level of income. In 1998 householders age 65 and older, who are usually past their peak earning years, had a median income of only $21,729, while householders under age 65 had a median income of $44,697. Those from 45 to 54, the highest-earning age group, had a median income of $54,148. (See Table 4.2.)

Work Experience and Income

Although working is an important factor in avoiding poverty, working in itself may not be enough to save a household from poverty. Of the 74.3 million households with a working householder in 1998, 9.1 percent earned less than $15,000, below the poverty threshold for a family of four ($16,450). While the majority (86.9 percent) of working householders worked full-time, a significant proportion (13.1 percent) held part-time jobs. As expected, the wages of part-time working householders were lower; 25 percent earned less that $15,000 in 1998. (See Table 4.2.)

Education

Not surprisingly, the more education a householder had, the more likely he or she was to earn a higher income. For example, for men with doctoral degrees, the median income in 1998 was $69,188, and for women with doctoral degrees, the median income was $52,167. For those with less than a ninth grade education, men earned a median income of $18,553, and women earned a median income of $14,132. High-school graduates (including those with general equivalency diplomas) fared better, with men earning $30,868 and women earning $21,963.

Ratio of Income to Poverty Levels

For analysis purposes, the Bureau of the Census uses income-to-poverty ratios, which measure the relative size of income in relation to the respective poverty threshold for each family size. Poor persons have a poverty ratio below 1.00. Persons above the poverty level are divided into two groups: the "near-poor" and the "non-poor." The "near-poor" have a poverty ratio between 1.00 and 1.24 (100 percent to 124 percent of the poverty level), and the "non-poor" have an income-to-poverty ratio of 1.25 (125 percent of the poverty level) and above.

In 1998, 12.7 percent of the total population had income-to-poverty ratios under 1.00; in other words, 34.4 million persons in the United States had incomes below

TABLE 4.3

Households by Total Money Income, Race, and Hispanic Origin of Householder, 1967 to 1998

[Income in 1998 CPI~U~X1 adjusted dollars. Households as of March of the following year.]

Race and Hispanic origin of householder and year	Number (1,000)	Total	Under $5,000	$5,000 to $9,999	$10,000 to $14,999	$15,000 to $24,999	$25,000 to $34,999	$35,000 to $49,999	$50,000 to $74,999	$75,000 to $99,999	$100,000 and over	Median income Value (dollars)	Median income Standard error (dollars)	Mean income Value (dollars)	Mean income Standard error (dollars)
ALL RACES															
1998	103,874	100.0	3.2	7.1	7.8	14.0	13.2	16.0	18.6	9.6	10.5	38,885	230	51,855	280
1997	102,528	100.0	3.4	7.4	8.0	14.8	13.2	16.3	18.0	9.1	9.8	37,581	167	50,464	274
1996	101,018	100.0	3.3	8.0	8.2	15.1	13.4	16.2	18.1	8.7	9.0	36,872	186	48,955	274
1995	99,627	100.0	3.3	7.8	8.4	15.1	13.8	16.7	17.8	8.5	8.5	36,446	211	48,064	263
1994	98,990	100.0	3.6	8.4	8.3	15.3	13.6	16.5	17.3	8.3	8.5	35,486	162	47,440	255
1993	97,107	100.0	3.8	8.5	8.4	15.3	13.9	16.2	17.5	8.2	8.1	35,241	165	46,732	253
1992	96,426	100.0	3.8	8.5	8.3	15.3	13.9	16.6	18.0	8.2	7.5	35,593	168	45,124	189
1991	95,669	100.0	3.5	8.5	7.9	14.9	14.1	17.0	18.1	8.5	7.6	36,054	174	45,384	187
1990	94,312	100.0	3.4	8.0	7.7	14.5	13.8	17.6	18.3	8.7	8.0	37,343	191	46,646	197
1989	93,347	100.0	3.1	7.9	7.5	14.6	13.4	17.0	18.8	9.0	8.6	37,997	209	48,006	209
1988	92,830	100.0	3.3	8.4	7.3	14.8	13.2	17.0	19.0	8.9	8.1	37,512	183	46,870	209
1987	91,124	100.0	3.3	8.3	7.7	14.5	13.3	16.9	19.1	9.0	7.8	37,394	178	46,504	191
1986	89,479	100.0	3.6	8.4	7.6	14.6	13.4	17.4	18.8	8.7	7.5	37,027	192	45,746	186
1985	88,458	100.0	3.6	8.6	7.8	15.3	13.9	17.7	18.1	8.5	6.5	35,778	194	44,031	174
1984	86,789	100.0	3.5	8.7	8.0	15.6	14.2	17.6	18.3	8.0	6.2	35,165	160	43,086	158
1983	85,290	100.0	3.8	8.9	8.0	16.1	14.4	17.9	17.8	7.5	5.6	34,397	155	41,910	155
1982	83,918	100.0	3.6	9.0	8.3	15.9	14.6	18.1	17.8	7.3	5.4	34,392	155	41,447	153
1981	83,527	100.0	3.4	9.0	8.2	16.1	14.1	18.2	18.5	7.4	5.0	34,507	181	41,224	150
1980	82,368	100.0	3.1	9.0	8.2	15.6	14.0	19.0	18.6	7.5	5.1	35,076	180	41,717	153
1979	80,776	100.0	3.0	8.7	7.6	15.3	13.8	18.5	19.7	7.6	5.6	36,259	172	43,072	163
1978	77,330	100.0	2.8	8.7	8.1	15.2	13.7	18.8	19.8	7.7	5.3	36,377	147	42,815	164
1977	76,030	100.0	2.9	8.9	8.5	15.5	14.2	18.9	19.3	7.1	4.7	35,004	132	41,524	126
1976	74,142	100.0	3.0	9.0	8.3	15.8	14.3	19.6	19.0	6.8	4.3	34,812	129	40,948	126
1975	72,867	100.0	3.1	9.2	8.6	15.8	15.0	19.4	18.6	6.3	4.0	34,224	139	39,964	125
1974	71,163	100.0	3.0	8.8	7.8	15.2	15.4	19.5	19.1	6.9	4.4	35,166	135	41,124	129
1973	69,859	100.0	3.5	8.0	8.1	14.7	14.6	19.5	19.7	7.1	4.8	36,302	138	41,983	128
1972	68,251	100.0	3.9	8.4	7.9	14.5	14.7	20.2	19.1	6.6	4.6	35,599	136	41,433	128
1971	66,676	100.0	4.5	8.8	7.5	15.4	15.5	20.9	17.8	5.8	3.7	34,143	132	39,267	125
1970	64,778	100.0	4.6	8.6	7.5	14.9	15.4	21.5	18.1	5.7	3.7	34,471	126	39,471	126
1969	63,401	100.0	4.6	8.5	7.2	14.8	15.8	21.7	18.3	5.6	3.5	34,706	128	39,484	124
1968	62,214	100.0	4.9	8.4	7.6	15.1	17.2	21.6	17.4	4.8	2.9	33,478	121	37,875	121
1967	60,813	100.0	5.7	8.9	7.7	15.9	17.0	22.1	15.3	4.4	2.9	32,075	117	35,873	117
WHITE															
1998	87,212	100.0	2.6	6.1	7.4	13.7	13.2	16.3	19.3	10.0	11.3	40,912	205	54,207	319
1997	86,106	100.0	2.8	6.5	7.7	14.4	13.1	16.5	18.7	9.7	10.5	39,579	240	52,708	305
1996	85,059	100.0	2.5	7.1	7.8	14.8	13.5	16.6	18.9	9.1	9.7	38,606	199	50,899	301
1995	84,511	100.0	2.6	6.9	8.0	14.9	13.8	17.0	18.6	9.0	9.2	38,254	200	49,979	290
1994	83,737	100.0	2.9	7.4	8.0	15.1	13.7	17.0	18.0	8.9	9.1	37,426	210	49,531	288
1993	82,387	100.0	3.0	7.3	8.0	15.1	14.0	16.8	18.4	8.7	8.7	37,180	217	48,827	282
1992	81,795	100.0	2.9	7.4	7.8	15.1	13.9	17.0	18.9	8.8	8.1	37,420	181	47,162	210
1991	81,675	100.0	2.6	7.3	7.6	14.6	14.2	17.4	18.9	9.1	8.1	37,781	183	47,300	206
1990	80,968	100.0	2.6	7.0	7.3	14.3	14.0	17.9	19.2	9.2	8.6	38,949	178	48,528	217
1989	80,163	100.0	2.4	6.8	7.1	14.3	13.5	17.4	19.8	9.5	9.2	39,969	195	50,006	231
1988	79,734	100.0	2.7	7.1	6.8	14.5	13.2	17.7	19.9	9.4	8.7	39,656	234	48,870	230
1987	78,519	100.0	2.7	7.1	7.2	14.2	13.3	17.5	20.0	9.6	8.4	39,398	199	48,491	209
1986	77,284	100.0	2.9	7.4	7.2	14.2	13.5	17.9	19.7	9.2	8.0	38,928	189	47,651	204
1985	76,576	100.0	3.0	7.5	7.4	14.9	14.0	18.2	18.9	9.0	7.1	37,732	201	45,838	192
1984	75,328	100.0	2.9	7.6	7.5	15.2	14.3	18.1	19.3	8.5	6.7	37,098	187	44,863	174
1983	74,170	100.0	3.1	7.7	7.5	15.8	14.6	18.5	18.6	8.0	6.1	36,061	162	43,661	169
1982	73,182	100.0	3.0	8.0	7.8	15.5	14.8	18.6	18.6	7.9	5.9	36,005	164,	43,156	169
1981	72,845	100.0	2.8	7.9	7.7	15.7	14.2	18.8	19.4	8.0	5.4	36,459	168	42,952	163
1980	71,872	100.0	2.6	8.0	7.7	15.2	14.1	19.5	19.6	7.9	5.5	37,005	190	43,400	166
1979	70,766	100.0	2.5	7.8	7.1	14.8	13.9	19.0	20.7	8.1	6.0	38,016	181,	4,770	178
1978	68,028	100.0	2.5	7.7	7.6	14.8	13.6	19.3	20.8	8.1	5.7	37,816	167	44,401	179
1977	66,934	100.0	2.6	7.9	8.0	14.9	14.2	19.5	20.4	7.5	5.1	36,809	155	43,146	139
1976	65,353	100.0	2.6	8.0	7.7	15.4	14.3	20.1	20.0	7.2	4.7	36,466	151	42,523	137
1975	64,392	100.0	2.7	8.2	8.1	15.5	14.9	19.9	19.6	6.7	4.4	35,790	131	41,440	136
1974	62,984	100.0	2.6	7.9	7.3	14.6	15.4	20.1	20.0	7.3	4.7	36,777	138	42,647	138
1973	61,965	100.0	3.1	7.3	7.5	14.1	14.5	20.0	20.8	7.6	5.1	38,046	145	43,606	138
1972	60,618	100.0	3.4	7.7	7.3	13.9	14.7	20.9	20.0	7.1	5.0	37,347	143	43,044	140
1971	59,463	100.0	4.0	8.0	7.0	14.8	15.4	21.7	18.8	6.2	4.0	35,713	136	40,689	132
1970	57,575	100.0	4.1	7.9	7.0	14.3	15.4	22.2	19.0	6.1	4.0	35,903	138	40,853	134
1969	56,248	100.0	4.1	7.9	6.7	14.0	15.8	22.4	19.4	5.9	3.9	36,220	132	40,949	137
1968	55,394	100.0	4.4	7.8	7.0	14.4	17.4	22.4	18.4	5.1	3.2	34,857	130	39,237	130
1967	54,188	100.0	5.2	8.3	7.1	15.2	17.1	23.1	16.3	4.6	3.2	33,449	121	37,185	126

SOURCE: *Money Income in the United States: 1998.* Current Population Reports, P60-206. U.S. Bureau of the Census: Washington, D.C., 1999.

TABLE 4.4

Ratio of Family Income to Poverty Threshold for People by Selected Characteristics, 1998

[Numbers in thousands]

Characteristic	Total	Under 0.50		Under 1.00		Under 1.25	
		Number	Percent of total	Number	Percent of total	Number	Percent of total
PERSONS							
Total	271,059	13,914	5.1	34,476	12.7	46,036	17.0
Age							
Under 18 years	71,338	5,774	8.1	13,467	18.9	17,135	24.0
18 to 24 years	25,967	2,006	7.7	4,312	16.6	5,654	21.8
25 to 34 years	38,474	1,990	5.2	4,582	11.9	6,103	15.9
35 to 44 years	44,744	1,575	3.5	4,082	9.1	5,470	12.2
45 to 54 years	35,232	999	2.8	2,444	6.9	3,283	9.3
55 to 59 years	12,601	498	4.0	1,165	9.2	1,521	12.1
60 to 64 years	10,308	322	3.1	1,039	10.1	1,422	13.8
65 years and over	32,394	750	2.3	3,386	10.5	5,447	16.8
Race[1] and Hispanic Origin[2]							
White	222,837	9,012	4.0	23,454	10.5	31,916	14.3
White, not Hispanic	192,754	6,182	3.2	15,799	8.2	21,930	11.4
Black	34,877	3,901	11.2	9,091	26.1	11,662	33.4
Other races	13,345	1,000	7.5	1,931	14.5	2,458	18.4
Asian and Pacific Islander	10,873	748	6.9	1,360	12.5	1,748	16.1
Hispanic origin,[2] all races	31,515	3,079	9.8	8,070	25.6	10,484	33.3
FAMILY STATUS							
In families	227,229	9,892	4.4	25,370	11.2	34,022	15.0
Householder	71,551	2,873	4.0	7,186	10.0	9,714	13.6
Related children under 18	70,253	5,355	7.6	12,845	18.3	16,447	23.4
Related children under 6	23,160	2,172	9.4	4,775	20.6	6,043	26.1
Unrelated individual	42,539	3,640	8.6	8,478	19.9	11,293	26.5
Male	20,394	1,668	8.2	3,465	17.0	4,504	22.1
Female.	22,145	1,972	8.9	5,013	22.6	6,789	30.7

[1]Data for American Indians, Eskimos, and Aleuts are not shown separately. Data for this population group should not be tabulated from the CPS because of its small sample size.

[2]People of Hispanic origin may be of any race.

SOURCE: Joseph Dalaker. *Poverty in the United States: 1998.* Current Population Reports, Series P60-207. U.S. Bureau of the Census: Washington, D.C., 1999

TABLE 4.5

Median Measured Net Worth and Distribution of Measured Net Worth by Monthly Household Income Quintiles, 1993 and 1991

[Number of households in thousands]

Monthly household income quintlies[1]	1993			1991 (in 1993 dollars)		
	Number of households	Median Measured net worth (dollars)	Distribution of measured networth	Number of households	Median measured net worth (dollars)	Distribution of measured net worth
Total	96,468	37,587	100.0	94,692	38,500	100.0
Lowest quintile	19,327	4,249	7.2	18,977	5,406	7.0
Second quintile	19,306	20,230	12.2	18,912	20,315	12.2
Third quintile	19,279	30,788	15.9	18,969	30,263	15.8
Fourth quintile	19,304	50,000	20.6	18,928	51,779	20.4
Highest quintile	19,251	118,996	44.1	18,905	121,423	44.6

[1]Quintile upper limits for 1993 were: lowest quintile - $1,071; second quintile - $1,963; third quintile - $2,995: fourth quintile - $4,635. Upper limits for 1991 were: lowest quintile - $1,135; second quintile - $2,027; third quintile - $3,089; fourth quintile - $4,721.

SOURCE: T.J. Eller and Wallace Fraser. *Asset Ownership of Households.* U.S. Bureau of the Census: Washington, D.C., 1995

TABLE 4.6

Median Measured Net Worth by Race and Hispanic Origin of Householder and Monthly Household Income Quintile, 1993 and 1991

[Excludes group quarters]

Monthly household income quintile	Total		White		Black		Hispanic origin[1]	
	1993	1991 (in 1993 dollars)	1993	1991 (in 1993 dollars)	1993	1991 (in 1993 dollars)	1993	1991 (in 1993 dollars)
All households (thousands)	96,468	94,692	82,190	81,409	11,248	10,768	7,403	6,407
Median measured net worth (dollars)	37,587	38,500	45,740	47,075	4,418	4,844	4,656	5,557
Measured Net Worth by Quintile[2]								
Lowest quintile:								
Households (thousands)	19,327	18,977	14,662	14,480	4,066	4,041	2,272	1,835
Median measured net worth (dollars)	4,249	5,406	7,605	10,743	250	0	499	529
Second quintile:								
Households (thousands)	19,306	18,912	16,162	16,006	2,663	2,436	1,760	1,557
Median measured net worth (dollars)	20,230	20,315	27,057	26,665	3,406	3,446	2,900	3,214
Third quintile:								
Households (thousands)	19,279	18,969	16,591	16,388	2,126	2,124	1,437	1,312
Median measured net worth (dollars)	30,788	30,263	36,341	35,510	8,480	8,302	6,313	7,501
Fourth quintile:								
Households (thousands)	19,304	18,928	17,218	17,043	1,454	1,353	1,115	1,009
Median measured net worth (dollars)	50,000	51,779	54,040	55,950	20,745	21,852	20,100	20,564
Highest quintile:								
Households (thousands)	19,252	18,905	17,558	17,492	937	814	819	694
Median measured net worth (dollars)	118,996	121,423	123,350	128,298	45,023	56,922	55,923	72,168

[1]Persons of Hispanic origin may be of any race.

[2]Quintile upper limits for 1993 were: lowest quintile - $1,071 ; second quintile - $1 ,963; third quintile - $2,995; fourth quintile - $4,635. Upper limits for 1991 were: lowest quintile- $1,135; second quintile - $2,027; third quintile - $3,089; fourth quintile - $4,721.

SOURCE: T.J. Eller and Wallace Fraser. *Asset Ownership of Households.* U.S. Bureau of the Census: Washington, D.C., 1995

---

the poverty threshold. Those under 18 years of age were most likely to be poor (18.9 percent), followed by those ages 18 to 24 (16.6 percent). African Americans (26.1 percent) and Hispanics (25.6 percent) were nearly three times as likely to have ratios below 1.00 as were whites (10.5 percent). (See Table 4.4.)

Almost 20.6 percent of families with children under six years of age had income-to-poverty ratios below 1.00, driven by the large number of female-headed households, which typically have lower incomes. (See Table 4.4.) In addition, 31.5 percent of all single females had ratios below the poverty threshold.

Of the total population, 4.26 percent (11.5 million people) had an income classified as "near poor," between 100 and 125 percent of the poverty threshold. (In Table 4.4, the right-hand column labeled "Under 1.25" includes all those earning less than 1.25. Consequently, this figure includes both poor and near-poor. To calculate the figures on only the near-poor, figures in the middle column, "Under 1.00," must be subtracted from figures in the column, "Under 1.25.") Eighteen percent of the 11.6 million "near-poor" were 65 years old or older. (See Table 4.4.)

NET WORTH OF HOUSEHOLDS

Income is one measure of a household's economic well being; another measure is net worth, that is, the value of assets (what a person owns) minus any debts (what a person owes). In *Asset Ownership of Households: 1993* (Washington, D.C., 1995), the Bureau of the Census reported in the publication on the net worth of United States households. It reported that the 1993 median net worth of households was $37,587, down 2.4 percent from $38,500 in 1991 (in 1993 dollars). (See Table 4.5.) Unless otherwise indicated, all figures include a household's equity in their house. The Bureau of the Census cautions that these figures might be somewhat low because the financial holdings of certain types of wealth tend to be underreported, and a large amount of wealth is concentrated in the hands of a very few people who are underrepresented in the survey.

As was the case with income, the highest quintile (the upper one-fifth) controlled the most wealth (44.1 percent) in 1993. While the median net worth of the lowest quintile was only $4,249, the median net worth of the highest quintile was $118,996. (See Table 4.5.)

Net Worth by Race and Hispanic Origin

The Census Bureau found huge disparities in net worth among the various sectors of society. The overall median net worth of a white household ($45,740) was more than 10 times that of an African American household ($4,418) and almost 10 times that of an Hispanic household ($4,656). Overall net worth, however, decreased for

FIGURE 4.1

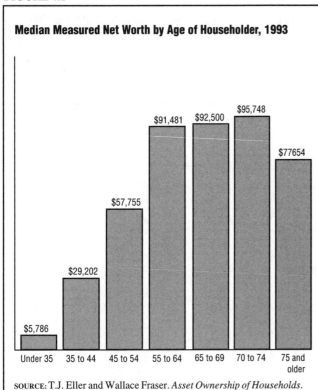

Median Measured Net Worth by Age of Householder, 1993

SOURCE: T.J. Eller and Wallace Fraser. *Asset Ownership of Households.* U.S. Bureau of the Census: Washington, D.C., 1995

TABLE 4.7

Median Measured Net Worth by Type of Household and Age of Householder, 1993 and 1991
[Excludes group quarters]

Type of household by age of householder	1993 Median measured net worth (dollars)			1991 Median measured net worth (in 1993 dollars)		
	Number households (thousands)	Total	Excluding equity in own home	Number of households (thousands)	Total	Excluding equity in own home
Married-couple households	52,891	61,905	17,051	52,616	63,599	19,557
Less than 35 years	12,141	12,941	5,677	12,247	12,702	5,548
35 to 54 years	23,983	61,874	17,436	23,080	64,047	19,801
55 to 64 years	7,568	127,752	43,543	7,849	123,138	47,158
65 years and over	9,199	129,790	44,410	9,040	142,517	59,200
Male householders	15,397	13,500	5,157	15,297	12,698	5,963
Less than 35 years	5,285	4,300	2,890	5,746	5,027	3,668
35 to 54 years	6,157	18,426	6,156	5,409	18,391	7,420
55 to 64 years	1,437	44,670	10,905	1,514	32,330	5,988
65 years and over	2,518	60,741	12,927	2,627	69,157	17,489
Female householdes	28,180	13,294	3,363	27,179	15,518	3,762
Less than 35 years	6,935	1,342	790	7,038	1,383	953
35 to 54 years	8,908	8,405	2,652	7,959	11,294	3,308
55 to 64 years	3,286	44,762	6,475	3,211	41,635	6,229
65 years and over	9,050	57,679	9,560	8,972	62,746	13,015

SOURCE: T.J. Eller and Wallace Fraser. *Asset Ownership of Households.* U.S. Bureau of the Census: Washington, D.C., 1995

all racial and ethnic groups between 1991 and 1993, in constant 1993 dollars. (See Table 4.6.) For white households, the decrease was 2.8 percent; for African Americans and Hispanics, those who were poorer to start with, the decreases were 8.8 percent and 16.2 percent, respectively.

In 1993 the highest quintile among whites had a median worth of $123,350, while among blacks, the median net worth of the highest one-fifth was only $45,023. Among Hispanics, the median net worth of the highest quintile was $55,923. These relative positions held for all five quintiles: in the lowest quintile, the median net worth of whites was $7,605, blacks had only $250, and Hispanics were a little better off with $499. (See Table 4.6.)

Age and Household Type

As householders age, they have greater opportunity to accumulate wealth. In 1993 net worth increased with age through age 74 and then dropped. (See Figure 4.1.) Households headed by married couples ($61,905) were worth considerably more in 1993 than were households headed by single men ($13,500) or women ($13,294). As expected, younger persons, many of whom are starting their working careers, tend to have lower net worth than older, more established persons. (See Table 4.7.)

Assets

In its 1993 survey the Bureau of the Census asked respondents what type of financial assets they owned.

The researchers found that almost 3 out of 4 Americans (71.1 percent) had some type of interest-bearing account at a financial institution, while almost 1 in 11 (8.6 percent) owned other interest-bearing assets. Almost two-thirds (64.3 percent) owned their own homes, which represented the largest single asset held by most age groups. Overall, a home accounted for about 75 percent of total net worth. An overwhelming majority (86 percent) owned their own vehicles. About 1 in 5 (20.9 percent) held either stocks or mutual fund shares (which are usually invested in stocks), 1 in 11 (8.4 percent) held rental property, almost 1 in 4 (23.1 percent) had an IRA or Keogh account for retirement, and 1 in 6 (18.5 percent) had U.S. savings bonds. (See Table 4.8.)

Households with considerable net worth generally have the opportunity to offer their members greater opportunities. They are better able to send their children to college, to travel, to help their children out as they get started, to buy the things they want, and to feel more secure. Considerable net worth can buy political influence and power, or at least present the opportunity to meet those who have that power. Net worth is a major factor determining a household's position and power in American society.

On the other hand, those with the fewest assets and net worth have the least to fall back on if they become ill or lose a job. They are the least able to financially help

TABLE 4.8

Ownership Rates, Median Value of Asset Holdings, and the Distribution of Measured Net Worth by Asset Type: 1993, 1991, 1988, and 1984
[Excludes group quarters]

Asset type	1993			1991 (in 1993 dollars)			1988 (in 1993 dollars)			1984 (in 1993 dollars)		
	Percent of households that own asset type	Median values of holdings for asset owners (dollars)	Distribution of measured net worth	Percent of households that own asset type	Median values of holdings for asset owners (dollars)	Distribution of measured net worth	Percent of households that own asset type	Median values of holdings for asset owners (dollars)	Distribution of measured net worth	Percent of households that own asset type	Median values of holdings for asset owners (dollars)	Distribution of measured net worth
All assets	(X)	37,587	100.00	(X)	38,500	100.00	(X)	43,617	100.00	(X)	445,411	100.00
Interest-earning assets at financial institutions	71.1	2,999	11.4	73.2	3,709	14.3	72.9	4,263	14.1	71.8	4,262	14.5
Savings accounts	60.1	(NA)	(NA)	62.4	(NA)	(NA)	61.6	(NA)	(NA)	62.9	(NA)	(NA)
Money market deposit accounts	12.6	(NA)	(NA)	14.9	(NA)	(NA)	15.2	(NA)	(NA)	15.7	(NA)	(NA)
Certificates of deposits	16.0	(NA)	(NA)	22.0	(NA)	(NA)	17.7	(NA)	(NA)	19.1	(NA)	(NA)
Interest-earning checking	36.9	(NA)	(NA)	37.8	(NA)	(NA)	34.3	(NA)	(NA)	24.8	(NA)	(NA)
Other Interest-earning assets	8.6	12,998	4.0	9.0	16,058	5.0	9.4	13,311	4.2	8.5	13,165	3.2
Money market funds.	3.9	(NA)	(NA)	4.2	(NA)	(NA)	3.6	(NA)	(NA)	3.8	(NA)	(NA)
Government securities .	2.1	(NA)	(NA)	2.2	(NA)	(NA)	2.2	(NA)	(NA)	1.4	(NA)	(NA)
Corporate or municipal bonds	3.1	(NA)	(NA)	3.4	(NA)	(NA)	2.8	(NA)	(NA)	2.6	(NA)	(NA)
Other interest-earning assets	2.2	(NA)	(NA)	2.2	(NA)	(NA)	3.3	(NA)	(NA)	2.8	(NA)	(NA)
Checking accounts	45.9	499	0.5	46.0	529	0.5	48.3	594	0.6	53.9	624	0.6
Stocks and mutual fund shares	20.9	6,960	8.3	20.7	5,490	7.1	21.8	5,502	6.5	20.0	5,410	6.8
Own home	64.3	46,669	44.4	64.7	43,070	42.6	63.6	52,545	43.0	64.3	56,430	41.3
Rental property	8.4	29,300	6.7	9.0	31,270	6.5	9.0	45,676	7.9	9.8	48,033	9.0
Other real estate	9.3	19,415	4.6	10.7	20,140	5.4	10.5	22,038	4.3	10.0	20,559	4.4
Vehicles	85.7	5,140	6.4	86.4	5,555	6.4	86.3	5,388	5.8	85.8	5,705	5.9
Business or profession.	10.8	7,000	6.4	11.7	10,203	7.3	12.5	12,744	8.8	12.9	8,754	1.03
U.S. savings bonds	18.5	775	0.8	18.1	610	0.6	17.5	666	0.6	15.0	417	0.5
IRA or Keogh accounts	23.1	12,985	6.7	22.9	11,886	5.2	24.2	11,000	4.2	19.5	6,679	2.2
Other financial investmerits[1]	5.2	21,001	3.0	2.8	19,769	3.1	6.6	19,769	3.0	7.0	17,777	5.0

X Not applicable. NA Not available because separate questions were not asked about the amount held in these Individual assets.

[1]Includes mortgages held from sale of real estate, amount due from sale of business, unit trusts, and other financial investments.

SOURCE: T.J. Eller and Wallace Fraser. *Asset Ownership of Households.* U.S. Bureau of the Census: Washington, D.C., 1995

their children get started in life. In addition, they are the least likely to have political power. These are the Americans most likely to fall into poverty if misfortune strikes.

ENTERING AND LEAVING POVERTY

For most poor Americans, poverty is not a static condition. Some people improve their economic status within two years or less, while others at near-poverty levels become poor through economic catastrophes, such as illness or job loss. The Bureau of the Census collects annual poverty data in its *Current Population Surveys* (CPS). But these surveys do not reflect the dynamic nature of poverty for individual persons and families. In its *Survey of Income and Program Participation* (SIPP), the Bureau of the Census gathers longitudinal information (measurements over time for specific individuals or households) that examines poverty over a 30-month period. This makes it possible to measure particular individuals and families and their movement into and out of poverty over a 30-month period.

In "Who Stays Poor? Who Doesn't?" (*Current Population Reports*, June 1996), T. J. Eller of the Bureau of the Census studied data from the 1992 SIPP, which covered the period from October 1991 through April 1994. He focused on monthly measures of poverty, distinguishing between short- and long-term poverty. Some highlights of the survey were:

- About 52.9 million persons were poor at least 2 months in 1992, and about 52.7 million were poor at least 2 months in 1993, not a significant difference.

- Approximately 11.9 million persons (about 13 percent of those who were poor and 4.8 percent of the total population) were poor all 24 months of 1992 and 1993.

- About 21.6 percent of persons who were poor in 1992 were not poor in 1993.

- Nonelderly adults were more likely to exit poverty than children and the elderly.

- Half of all poverty spells lasted 4.9 months or longer.

FIGURE 4.2

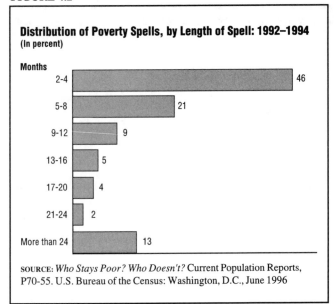

Distribution of Poverty Spells, by Length of Spell: 1992–1994
(In percent)

SOURCE: *Who Stays Poor? Who Doesn't?* Current Population Reports, P70-55. U.S. Bureau of the Census: Washington, D.C., June 1996

FIGURE 4.4

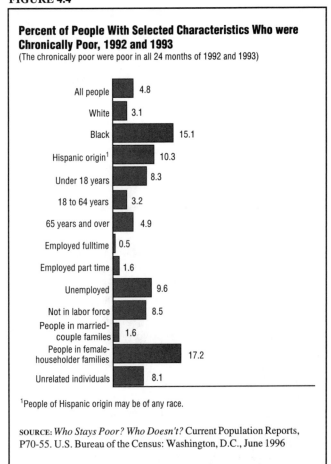

Percent of People With Selected Characteristics Who were Chronically Poor, 1992 and 1993
(The chronically poor were poor in all 24 months of 1992 and 1993)

[1]People of Hispanic origin may be of any race.

SOURCE: *Who Stays Poor? Who Doesn't?* Current Population Reports, P70-55. U.S. Bureau of the Census: Washington, D.C., June 1996

FIGURE 4.3

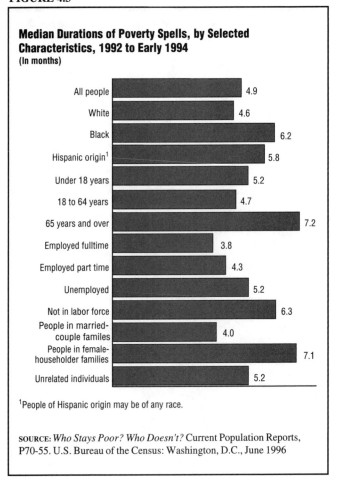

Median Durations of Poverty Spells, by Selected Characteristics, 1992 to Early 1994
(In months)

[1]People of Hispanic origin may be of any race.

SOURCE: *Who Stays Poor? Who Doesn't?* Current Population Reports, P70-55. U.S. Bureau of the Census: Washington, D.C., June 1996

FIGURE 4.5

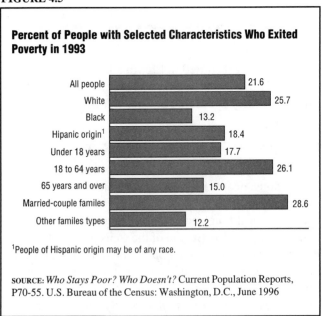

Percent of People with Selected Characteristics Who Exited Poverty in 1993

[1]People of Hispanic origin may be of any race.

SOURCE: *Who Stays Poor? Who Doesn't?* Current Population Reports, P70-55. U.S. Bureau of the Census: Washington, D.C., June 1996

Spells of poverty reported from 1992 through 1993 lasted for varying lengths of time. Forty-six percent lasted from 2 to 4 months, while 13 percent lasted throughout both years of the study. (See Figure 4.2.) African Americans (with a median duration of 6.2 months) and Hispanics (with one of 5.8 months) had significantly longer poverty spells than whites (4.6 months). For the elderly, the median poverty spell lasted 7.2 months. The shortest poverty spells were for those employed full-time (3.8 months) and families headed by married couples (4 months). (See Figure 4.3.)

FIGURE 4.6

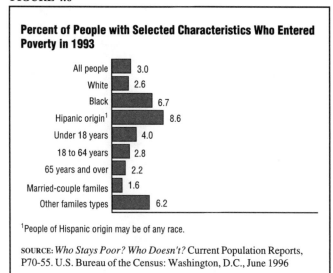

Percent of People with Selected Characteristics Who Entered Poverty in 1993

All people	3.0
White	2.6
Black	6.7
Hispanic origin[1]	8.6
Under 18 years	4.0
18 to 64 years	2.8
65 years and over	2.2
Married-couple familes	1.6
Other familes types	6.2

[1]People of Hispanic origin may be of any race.

SOURCE: *Who Stays Poor? Who Doesn't?* Current Population Reports, P70-55. U.S. Bureau of the Census: Washington, D.C., June 1996

Nearly 5 percent of the population were poor all 24 months of 1992 and 1993. Figure 4.4 shows the characteristics of these chronically poor. African Americans (15.1 percent) were significantly more likely to be chronically poor (for a long duration or frequently recurring) than people of Hispanic origin (10.3 percent), who, in turn, were more chronically poor than whites (3.1 percent). Seventeen percent of people in female-householder families were poor continuously for 24 months. Not surprisingly, those not working were more likely to be chronically poor than those who were employed. (See Figure 4.4.)

Characteristics of Those Changing Their Poverty Status

Based on the SIPP interviews, 22.7 million people who were poor in 1992 were also poor in 1993. Between 1992 and 1993, the number of people who exited poverty (6.3 million) was similar to the number of people who entered poverty (6.5 million).

RACE AND AGE. Of the poor in 1992, whites (25.7 percent) were more likely to leave poverty in 1993 than either African Americans (13.2 percent) or Hispanics (18.4 percent). (See Figure 4.5.) Figure 4.6 shows the newly poor as a percent of the population that was not poor in 1992. Whites were less likely to enter poverty in 1993 than blacks or Hispanics.

The elderly (often on fixed incomes) and children were less likely to exit from poverty than were persons of other ages. Only 15 percent of the elderly and 17.7 percent of children under 18 years of age who were poor in 1992 were able to escape poverty in 1993. Adults 18 to 64 years of age were the most likely to escape—26.1 percent moved out of poverty. (See Figure 4.5.) Only 2.2 percent of the elderly entered poverty in 1993, compared to 4 percent of children under 18 years of age. (See Figure 4.6.)

FAMILY STATUS. Families headed by married couples were much more likely than other family types to leave poverty in 1993. Of the poor families headed by married couples in 1992, 28.6 percent were able to escape poverty during 1993. Only 12.2 percent of the poor families of other types recovered from poverty in 1993. (See Figure 4.5.) Families headed by married couples were also significantly less likely to enter poverty in 1993. (See Figure 4.6.) With at least two adults in the household, a family headed by a married couple is more likely to have at least one person working than a family headed by a single person.

CHAPTER 5

FACTORS AFFECTING POVERTY AND WELFARE USE

Poverty is the largest single factor that drives people to apply for the governmental assistance commonly called "welfare". Many researchers agree that the major factors that create poverty are family size, family background, educational achievement, unemployment (or underemployment, such as part-time workers who want to work full-time), low earnings, and the prevailing economic conditions in the labor market.

Children are the poorest group in America, having replaced the elderly in 1974. The major reason for the decline in elderly poverty rates was social insurance benefits, nearly all of which come from Social Security. In 1998, 18.3 percent of all children lived in families with incomes below the poverty level. Changes in household and family composition, particularly the increase in the number of single-parent families, have contributed to higher poverty rates, especially the higher rates of child poverty. In 1996 over half (58.8 percent) of children under the age of six who lived in female-headed families were poor, compared to 11.5 percent of children in families headed by married couples.

ASSISTANCE FROM THE GOVERNMENT

Women and children are most affected by poverty. The two largest cash assistance programs for families with children have been Temporary Aid to Needy Families (TANF), which replaced Aid to Families with Dependent Children or AFDC, under the 1996 welfare reform law and the Earned Income Tax Credit (EITC). States currently provide cash assistance from their TANF block grants to families that meet the work requirements (mandatory after two years on assistance) and who have not exceeded the five-year limit for assistance. The EITC is available to needy working households, most of which goes to families with children. (See Chapter 3 for more information about EITC.)

Other cash and noncash programs targeted at helping women, children, and the elderly include Supplemental Security Income (SSI), the Low Income Home Energy Assistance Program (LIHEAP), Medicaid, the Food Stamp Program, the National School Lunch Program, the Child Care Food Program, the School Breakfast Program, the Summer Food Service Program, and Supplemental Food for Women, Infants, and Children (WIC). (For more information on these programs, see Chapter 8.)

Many poor families do not qualify for welfare benefits because of their income or resources. Most of these families are more likely to receive income from social insurance programs such as social security (benefits for children whose parents are dead, retired, or disabled) and unemployment compensation. Even though social security benefits are not means-tested, they help reduce the child poverty rate.

Poor Families More Likely to Need Government Assistance

In "Income and Spending of Poor Households with Children" (*Family Economics and Nutrition Review*, vol. 9, no. 1, 1996), Mark Lino analyzed the 1990–92 *Consumer Expenditure Survey*, conducted by the U.S. Bureau of the Census for the U.S. Bureau of Labor Statistics. He found that, as one would expect, poor households counted far more heavily on government assistance to survive than nonpoor households. (In his analysis, Lino defined poverty as having either income or total expenditures below the poverty level.)

About half (54 percent) of poor households earned wages or salaries, compared to 94 percent of nonpoor households. Fifty-four percent of poor households also received public assistance, while only 4 percent of nonpoor families did. Poor households depended much more on food stamps (69 percent) and slightly more on alimony/child support (14 percent) to supplement their incomes.

TABLE 5.1

Percentage of Poor and Non-Poor Households with Children with Income Source,* 1990–92

Income source	Poor	Nonpoor
Wages or salary	54	94
Public assistance	54	4
Food stamps	69	6
Alimony, child support, or regular contributions[1]	14	11
Interest or dividends	2	30
Social Security	8	4
Other[2]	24	30

[1]Regular contributions are periodic payments from a nongovernment, nonhousehold source.

[2]Includes income from pensions, Supplemental Security Income, unemployment compensation, or owned businesses.

*All differences in income sources between poor and nonpoor households were statistically significant at $p \leq .01$ based on unweighted data.

SOURCE: Family Economics and Nutrition Review, vol 9, no 1, 1996

TABLE 5.2

Income of Poor and Nonpoor Households with Children, 1990–92

Income source	Poor	Nonpoor
Before-tax income*	$8,633	$41,670
Per capita*	1,962	10,685
After-tax income*	8,688	37,873
Per capita*	1,975	9,711
	Percentage of before-tax income	
Wages and salary*	35.1	86.9
Public assistance*	26.7	0.4
Food stamps*	21.2	0.3
Alimony, child support, and regular contributions*[1]	2.7	1.1
Interest and dividends*	0.1	1.1
Social Security	4.8	0.8
Other*[2]	9.4	9.4

[1]Regular contributions are periodic payments from a nongovernment, nonhousehold source.

[2]Includes income from pensions, Supplemental Security Income, unemployment compensation, and owned businesses.

*Differences in dollar amounts between poor and nonpoor households were statistically significant at $p \leq .01$ based on unweighted data.

SOURCE: Family Economics and Nutrition Review, vol 9, no 1, 1996

TABLE 5.3

Households by Type and Selected Characteristics, 1998

Numbers are in thousands, except averages and percentages.

Characteristics	All households	Family households Total	Married couple	Other families Female householder	Other families Male householder	Nonfamily households Total	Female householder	Male householder
All households	102,528	70,880	54,317	12,652	3,911	31,648	17,516	14,133
Race and Hispanic origin								
White	86,106	59,511	48,066	8,308	3,137	26,596	14,871	11,725
White not Hispanic	77,936	52,871	43,423	6,826	2,622	25,065	14,164	10,901
Black	12,474	8,408	3,921	3,926	562	4,066	2,190	1,876
Hispanic[1]	8,590	6,961	4,804	1,612	545	1,630	754	875
Size of household								
1 person	26,327	(X)	(X)	(X)	(X)	26,327	15,317	11,010
2 people	32,965	28,722	21,833	5,290	1,598	4,243	1,850	2,393
3 people	17,331	16,640	11,595	3,858	1,187	691	232	459
4 people	15,358	15,090	12,427	2,008	654	268	76	192
5 people	7,048	6,972	5,743	924	306	76	17	59
6 people	2,232	2,195	1,807	293	95	37	21	15
7 or more people	1,267	1,260	911	278	70	7	3	4
Average size	2.62	3.24	3.26	3.18	3.22	1.24	1.17	1.33
Percent with own children under 18	33.9	49.0	46.5	60.8	46.0	(X)	(X)	(X)
Age of householder								
Under 25	5,435	3,019	1,373	1,095	551	2,417	1,080	1,336
25 to 34	19,033	13,639	9,886	2,887	866	5,394	2,070	3,325
35 to 44	23,943	18,872	14,180	3,637	1,055	5,072	1,863	3,208
45 to 54	19,547	14,694	11,734	2,260	701	4,853	2,421	2,431
55 to 64	13,072	9,387	7,936	1,099	352	3,685	2,336	1,348
65 to 74	11,272	6,989	5,841	938	210	4,283	3,080	1,203
75 and over	10,225	4,282	3,368	738	176	5,944	4,664	1,280
Median age	46.3	45.0	46.4	41.4	40.4	50.8	60.8	42.5

[1]People of Hispanic origin may be of any race.

(X) Not applicable.

SOURCE: *Household and Family Characteristics: March 1998 (Update)*. P20-525. Summary Tables

Nonpoor households were more likely to receive income from interest or dividends (30 percent) or from pensions, owned businesses, unemployment compensation, or Supplemental Security Income (30 percent). (See Table 5.1.)

The average before-tax income of poor households ($8,633) was only one-fifth (20.7 percent) that of nonpoor households ($41,670). A little over one-third (35.1 percent) of the income of poor households came from wages and salaries, compared to 86.9 percent for nonpoor families. Not surprisingly, a far larger percentage of income for poor households came from public assistance and food stamps. While these two categories accounted for 47.9 percent of the income of poor households, they made up less than 1 percent of income for nonpoor households. (See Table 5.2.)

FAMILY STRUCTURE OF WELFARE RECIPIENTS
Single-Parent Families

An increasing number of children are being raised by one parent, usually the mother. The proportion of single-parent families grew rapidly between 1970 and 1990, while the proportion dropped for families headed by married couples. Since then the structure of American households and families has remained relatively stable. In 1998, 76.6 percent of all families were families headed by married couples, down from 82.5 percent in 1980 and 87 percent in 1970. Meanwhile, the proportion of single-parent families headed by males rose from 2.4 percent in 1970 to 2.9 percent in 1980 and 5.5 percent in 1998. (See Table 5.3.)

The proportion of single-parent families headed by females grew from 11 percent in 1970 to 15 percent in 1980 and to 17.8 percent in 1998. (See Table 5.3.) Single-parent families, especially single-parent families headed by women, usually earn much less than families headed by married couples. (See also Chapters 3 and 4.)

The increase in the number of single-parent families was most dramatic among African Americans and Hispanics and less so among whites. From 1970 to 1998, the proportion of white families headed by married couples declined from 89 percent to 81 percent. During the same period, the proportion of white single-parent families headed by males rose from 2.2 to 5 percent, and the percent of white single-parent families headed by females grew from 9 to 13 percent. (See Table 5.3.)

Among Hispanics, the proportion of families headed by married couples dropped from 81 percent in 1970 to 69 percent in 1998, while the proportion of single-parent families headed by males rose from 4 to 8 percent, and the percentage of single-parent families headed by females increased from 15 to 23 percent. (See Table 5.3.)

The largest increase in the proportion of single-parent families occurred among African Americans. While the proportion of families headed by married couples fell from 68 percent in 1970 to less than half (46.6 percent) in 1998, the proportion of single-parent families headed by men grew from 4 to nearly 6.7 percent, and the percentage of single-parent families headed by women nearly doubled from 28 percent to make up almost half (47 percent) of all black families. (See Table 5.3.)

Families with Children

Single parents make up an even larger proportion of families with children under 18 years of age. In 1998, 27 percent of families with minor children were single-parent families; 19 percent of those single-parent families were family groups with a father and child (or children). Two-parent families made up 70 percent of all family groups with children, down from 87.1 percent in 1970 and 78.5 percent in 1980. Meanwhile, the proportion of families with children headed by men rose from 1.3 percent in 1970 and 2.1 percent in 1980 to 5.6 percent in 1998. Similarly, the proportion of families with children headed by women rose from 11.5 percent in 1970 to 25 percent in 1998. (See Table 5.4.)

BY RACE. Figure 5.1 shows the living arrangements of children by race in 1996. African American children are far more likely to live with a single parent than either white or Hispanic children. In 1996 a majority of black children (57 percent) lived in a single-parent family. About one-third (32 percent) of Hispanic children lived with one parent; sixty-two percent lived in two-parent families. Twenty-two percent of white children lived with one parent, while nearly 75 percent lived with two parents.

A higher percentage of black children (9.3 percent) than whites and Hispanics lived with neither parent. In part, this is because black children are more likely to live with grandparents without the presence of either parent. (See Figure 5.1.)

FIGURE 5.1

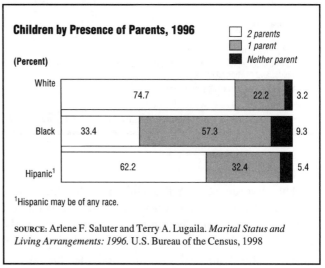

1Hispanic may be of any race.

SOURCE: Arlene F. Saluter and Terry A. Lugaila. *Marital Status and Living Arrangements: 1996.* U.S. Bureau of the Census, 1998

TABLE 5.4

Families by Type, Race, and Hispanic Origin[1], by Selected Characteristics 1998

Numbers are in thousands, except averages and medians

| | | Married couple families | | | | Other families | | | | Male householder |
| | | | | | | Female householder | | | | |
Characteristics	All families	All races	White	Black	Hispanic	All races	White	Black	Hispanic	All races
All families	70,880	54,317	48,066	3,921	4,804	12,652	8,308	3,926	1,612	3,911
Size of family[2]										
2 people	30,282	22,042	20,228	1,196	974	6,016	4,337	1,505	546	2,225
3 people	16,231	11,639	10,190	869	1,012	3,628	2,341	1,179	493	964
4 people	14,633	12,402	10,715	1,030	1,307	1,777	1,004	699	283	454
5 people	6,555	5,633	4,829	535	891	756	417	303	180	167
6 people	2,047	1,746	1,440	186	360	239	117	117	65	63
7 or more people	1,130	855	663	105	259	237	92	122	45	39
Average size	3.18	3.24	3.18	3.58	4.10	3.04	2.89	3.32	3.52	2.86
Own children under 18										
Without own children under 18	36,120	29,048	26,156	1,865	1,683	4,960	3,396	1,357	491	2,113
With own children under 18	34,760	25,269	21,910	2,055	3,121	7,693	4,912	2,569	1,121	1,798
One own child under 18	14,363	9,507	8,231	723	1,001	3,739	2,539	1,104	445	1,117
Two own children under 18	13,122	10,241	8,913	830	1,174	2,425	1,498	865	384	456
Three or more own children under 18	7,275	5,521	4,766	502	946	1,529	875	600	292	225
Total own children under 18	64,323	47,931	41,265	3,996	6,834	13,656	8,438	4,751	2,349	2,736
Average per family with own children under 18	1.85	1.90	1.88	1.94	2.19	1.78	1.72	1.85	2.10	1.52
Age of own children[3]										
Of any age	44,979	31,288	27,057	2,586	3,680	11,175	7,353	3,486	1,434	2,516
Under 25 years	40,006	28,871	25,057	2,323	3,434	9,026	5,799	2,955	1,294	2,110
Under 18 years	34,760	25,269	21,910	2,055	3,121	7,693	4,912	2,569	1,121	1,798
Under 12 years	26,030	19,279	16,739	1,549	2,611	5,513	3,433	1,935	866	1,238
Under 6 years	15,532	11,773	10,278	880	1,747	3,000	1,811	1,108	511	759
Under 3 years	8,927	7,053	6,205	507	1,023	1,428	883	498	272	446
Under 1 year	3,160	2,527	2,240	163	361	435	245	174	67	198
Six to 17 years	26,298	8,927	16,360	1,609	2,314	6,137	3,882	2,086	870	1,234
Members 65 and older										
Without members 65 and older	57,338	43,542	38,31	3,275	4,229	10,566	6,719	3,490	1,421	3,230
With members 65 and older	13,542	10,775	9,750	646	575	2,086	1,589	436	191	681
Family without own children under 18	12,873	10,252	9,371	598	504	1,975	1,525	401	164	648
Family with own children under 18	669	524	379	47	71	112	65	35	26	33
Householder's age										
Under 25 years	3,019	1,373	1,221	111	300	1,095	612	429	180	551
25 to 34 years	13,639	9,886	8,557	858	1,345	2,887	1,725	1,085	435	866
35 to 44 years	18,872	14,180	12,382	1,066	1,427	3,637	2,371	1,146	461	1,055
45 to 54 years	14,694	11,734	10,324	884	812	2,260	1,551	607	284	701
55 to 64 years	9,387	7,936	7,125	485	507	1,099	748	314	135	352
65 to 74 years	6,989	5,841	5,338	369	282	938	710	214	78	210
75 years and over	4,282	3,368	3,118	149	130	738	591	132	39	176
Median age	45.0	46.4	46.7	44.3	40.2	41.4	42.8	38.4	39.0	40.4
Householder's marital status										
Married, spouse present	54,317	54,317	48,066	3,921	4,804	(X)	(X)	(X)	(X)	(X)
Married, spouse absent	2,506	(X)	(X)	(X)	(X)	1,977	1,269	617	399	529
Separated	1,905	(X)	(X)	(X)	(X)	1,586	1,032	502	317	319
Other	601	(X)	(X)	(X)	(X)	392	236	116	82	209
Widowed	2,698	(X)	(X)	(X)	(X)	2,325	1,767	493	200	373
Divorced	5,910	(X)	(X)	(X)	(X)	4,518	3,486	914	457	1,391
Never married	5,449	(X)	(X)	(X)	(X)	3,831	1,787	1,901	557	1,618

[1] People of Hispanic origin may be of any race.

[2] Note that "size of family" and "size of household" are different. Household members include all persons living in the household, whereas family members include only the householder and his/her relatives.

[3] Age categories are not mutually exclusive.

(X) Not Applicable

SOURCE: *Household and Family Characteristics: March 1998 (Update).* P20-525. Summary Tables

DIVORCE

The divorce rate in the United States has risen markedly in every decade since the 1950s and is one of the major factors contributing to women receiving welfare. In 1985 almost one-quarter of those living in the United States who had ever married had also been divorced at one time or another. Divorce is a major factor in why women receive welfare, as divorced women are seldom as well off financially as they were when they were married. (In part, this is due to the fact that because women's work is devalued, on average, they receive 70 percent of what men earn for their labor.) The fact that

TABLE 5.5

Child Support Payments Agreed to or Awarded Custodial Parents

(Numbers in thousands. Parents living with own children under 21 years of age whose other parent is absent from the home. Amounts in dollars)

Characteristic	Number	Number	Number	Child support agreed to or awarded					Child support not awarded	
				Supposed to receive child support payments in 1995						
				Received payments in 1995			Received no payments in 1995			
				Number	Average child support	Average total money income	Number	Average total money income	Number	Average total money income
All Custodial Parents										
Total	**13,739**	**7,967**	**6,966**	**4,769**	**$3,732**	**$22,543**	**2,198**	**$17,398**	**5,772**	**$18,927**
Standard error	287	222	208	173	$187	$546	118	$577	190	$591
Custodial mothers	11,634	7,123	6,233	4,353	$3,767	$21,829	1,880	$16,093	4,511	$14,068
Standard error	265	210	197	165	$200	$539	109	$575	168	$375
Custodial fathers	2,105	844	733	416	$3,370	$30,030	318	$25,122	1,261	$36,312
Standard error	116	73	69	52	$471	$2,628	45	$1,917	90	$2,141
Poverty Status in 1995:										
Family income below poverty level	4,172	2,103	1,761	1,067	$2,531	$6,855	694	$6,043	2,069	$5,660
Standard error	162	116	106	83	$510	$202	67	$272	115	$147
Visitation and Joint Custody Arrangements With Non-custodial Parents in 1995:										
Visitation privileges only	7,469	4,683	4,074	2,924	$3,297	$21,110	1,150	$17,460	2,555	$20,084
Joint custody only[1]	121	95	73	39	(B)	(B)	35	(B)	26	(B)
Visitation and joint custody	3,044	2,089	1,901	1,487	$4,592	$26,836	414	$21,082	908	$29,404
Neither	3,105	1,100	917	318	$3,770	$15,630	599	$14,767	1,953	$13,012
Custodial Mothers										
Race and Hispanic origin:										
White	7,970	5,403	4,782	3,488	$4,100	$23,067	1,294	$17,642	2,567	$15,517
White, not Hispanic origin	6,545	4,709	4,191	3,149	$4,274	$23,958	1,041	$19,083	1,836	$17,965
Black	3,323	1,509	1,273	749	$2,116	$16,614	524	$12,376	1,814	$11,916
Hispanic origin[2]	1,530	725	613	354	$2,420	$14,801	259	$11,744	806	$9,567
Current Marital Status:										
Married	2,216	1,516	1,368	981	$3,546	$19,968	387	$16,289	699	$15,418
Divorced	4,003	3,028	2,692	2,044	$3,990	$26,521	648	$21,257	975	$19,243
Separated	1,791	942	798	552	$4,182	$18,432	246	$13,157	850	$14,881
Widowed[3]	316	178	163	94	$9,624	$21,641	69	(B)	138	$17,490
Never Married	3,309	1,459	1,212	683	$2,271	$13,224	530	$10,862	1,850	$10,201
Educational Attainment:										
Less than high school diploma	2,419	1,145	945	523	$2,106	$9,299	422	$8,368	1,274	$7,172
High school graduate	4,396	2,702	2,350	1,586	$3,179	$16,827	764	$15,385	1,694	$13,531
Some college, no degree	2,545	1,682	1,467	1,085	$3,932	$22,505	383	$16,492	863	$16,107
Associate degree	953	634	586	459	$4,899	$28,484	126	$22,935	318	$17,587
Bachelors degree or more	1,322	960	885	700	$5,338	$37,109	186	$31,086	362	$32,907

(B) Represents base less than 75,000.

[1] Joint custody may be physical, legal or both. Legal custody does not necessarily include visitation.

[2] Persons of Hispanic origin may be of any race.

[3] Widowed parents have children from a previous marriage that ended in divorce or from a previous nonmarried relationship.

SOURCE: Lydia Scoon Rogers. *Child Support for Custodial Mothers and Fathers: 1995.* Current Population Reports. U.S. Bureau of the Census: Washington, D.C., March 1999

---

divorced women are more likely than men to receive custody of their children adds an additional financial burden. In 1996 women were about 85 percent of divorced parents with custody of their children. (See Table 5.5.)

By 1996 the number of people who had been divorced more than quadrupled from 1970, from 4.3 million to 18.3 million. This translated to 9.5 percent of the total U.S. adult population, compared to 3.2 percent in 1970. Further, there were more single women then men because men are more likely to marry after divorce. (See Table 5.6.)

NEVER-MARRIED ADULTS

The number of adults aged 18 or older who had never married more than doubled from 1970 to 1996, from 21.4 million to 44.9 million. Twenty-three percent of all adults had never married, making up the largest share of the unmarried population in 1996. (See Table 5.6.)

A majority of single mothers with children under six years of age have never been married—85 percent of blacks, 73 percent of Hispanics, and 56 percent of whites. In 1997, 44 percent of never-married black mothers, 30

TABLE 5.6

Marital Status of People 18 Years and Over, 1970 and 1996
(Numbers in thousands)

Marital status	1996	1970
Total, 18 years and over	193,166	132,507
Percent who are:		
Married	60.3	71.7
Unmarried	39.7	28.3
Never married	23.3	16.2
Widowed	7.0	8.9
Divorced	9.5	3.2

SOURCE: Arlene F. Saluter and Terry A. Lugaila. *Marital Status and Living Arrangements: 1996.* U.S. Bureau of the Census, 1998

percent of never-married Hispanic mothers, and 14 percent of never-married white mothers had children between the ages of 6 and 17. In addition to a growing trend away from marriage, these percentages could also be explained by marriages following the birth of the first child.

CHILD SUPPORT

In 1996, 22.8 million children under the age of 21 (28 percent of all children under 21) lived with a custodial parent. Most of these children lived with their mother. Of the 13.7 custodial parents in 1996, about 11.6 million, or 85 percent, were women, according to the U.S. Census Bureau. (See Table 5.5.)

Child support is becoming an increasingly important source of income for women with the increasing number of families headed by women, coupled with the time limits now in place for receiving cash assistance (see Chapter 2). In 1996, 8 million out of the 13.7 million custodial parents (58 percent) were given child support. Approximately 61 percent of mothers and 40 percent of fathers received child support of some amount. The other 5.8 million custodial parents did not receive financial support from an ex-partner. Of the 92 percent of those custodial parents receiving child support, 7.3 million had legal agreements established by a court or other government institution. The other 700,000 had some sort of extralegal agreement. (See Figure 5.2.)

According to the U.S. Census Bureau, 87 percent of the 8 million custodial parents who were awarded child support actually received payments in 1995. Seventy percent of the women and 57 percent of the men due payments received at least part of the amount during that year.

Those Living in Poverty

While most custodial mothers receive child support, often it is not enough to keep them and their children out of poverty. According to the U.S. Census Bureau, in 1996 about 30 percent (4.2 million) of custodial parents had family incomes considered below the poverty level, compared to 16 percent of all parents. Thirty-three percent, or 3.9 million,

FIGURE 5.2

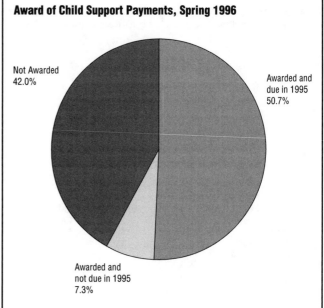

Award of Child Support Payments, Spring 1996

Not Awarded 42.0%

Awarded and due in 1995 50.7%

Awarded and not due in 1995 7.3%

Base: 13.7 million people with children from absent parents (custodial parents)

SOURCE: Lydia Scoon Rogers. *Child Support for Custodial Mothers and Fathers: 1995.* Current Population Reports. U.S. Bureau of the Census: Washington, D.C., March 1999

custodial mothers lived below the poverty threshold. Only 14 percent, or 300,000, custodial fathers were below the poverty threshold during the same period. (See Figure 5.3.)

The U.S. Census Bureau also reported that approximately 32 percent of custodial parents who were due child support, but did not receive it in 1995, were poor. In addition, a similar percentage (36 percent) of custodial parents who were not awarded child support at all were considered poor in 1995. This compares to a poverty rate of 22 percent for custodial parents who received some form of child support in 1995. On the other hand, only about 22 percent of custodial parents who did receive some or all of the child support that was owed them were poor. (See Figure 5.4.)

Child Support Received

In 1995 custodial mothers received an average amount of $3,767 in child support for the year. The average amount for custodial fathers was $3,370. (See Table 5.5.)

According to the U.S. Census Bureau, custodial mothers who actually received child support had total individual incomes of about three-fourths the amount of custodial fathers who received child support ($21,829 versus $30,030). On average, these support payments constituted 17 percent of the women's income and only 11 percent of the men's. (See Table 5.5.)

One of the reasons women tend to have lower incomes than men is because there are fewer women par-

FIGURE 5.3

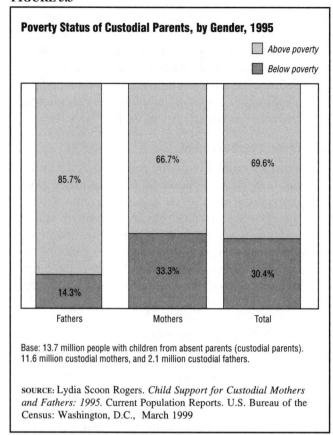

Poverty Status of Custodial Parents, by Gender, 1995

Base: 13.7 million people with children from absent parents (custodial parents). 11.6 million custodial mothers, and 2.1 million custodial fathers.

SOURCE: Lydia Scoon Rogers. *Child Support for Custodial Mothers and Fathers: 1995.* Current Population Reports. U.S. Bureau of the Census: Washington, D.C., March 1999

FIGURE 5.4

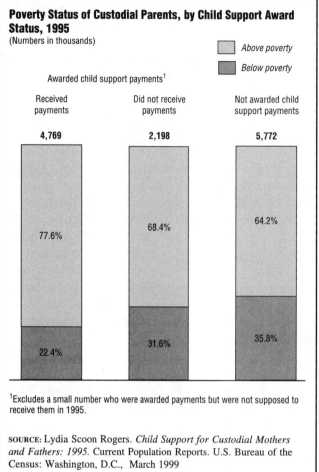

Poverty Status of Custodial Parents, by Child Support Award Status, 1995
(Numbers in thousands)

[1]Excludes a small number who were awarded payments but were not supposed to receive them in 1995.

SOURCE: Lydia Scoon Rogers. *Child Support for Custodial Mothers and Fathers: 1995.* Current Population Reports. U.S. Bureau of the Census: Washington, D.C., March 1999

ticipating in the workforce permanently and full-time. Though about 82 percent of custodial mothers who received child support worked in 1995 (statistically the same as custodial fathers, 82 percent), only 51 percent of them worked full-time, year round (compared to 72 percent of custodial fathers). And when both custodial mothers and fathers did work full-time, year-round, the average income of custodial mothers with child support was still lower ($29,672) in 1995, compared to custodial fathers ($36,834).

Socioeconomic factors

Other socioeconomic factors that prevent custodial mothers from lifting themselves out of poverty were highlighted by the U.S. Census Bureau in 1996. They included:

• Of the poor women due child support payments in 1995, 62 percent actually received payments. For nonpoor women, the receipt rate for due payments was 73 percent.

• Seventy-three percent of white women received child support payments that were due to them, compared to 59 percent of African American women and 58 percent of Hispanic women.

• Women ages 30 and over were more likely to receive child support payments owed to them (71 percent) than women under age 30 (65 percent).

• The percentage of never-married women who received payments in 1995 was much lower (56 percent), compared with 73 percent for ever-married women.

• Women with at least a bachelor's degree were more likely to receive the child support due them (79 percent) than women with less education (68 percent).

Government Assistance in Obtaining Child Support

In 1975 Congress established the Child Support Enforcement program to ensure that children had financial support from both parents. Though improvements in paternity establishment and child support collections have followed, much more needs to be done. Only about one-half of the custodial parents due child support receive full payments. About 25 percent receive partial payment, and 25 percent get none at all. Provisions in the Personal Responsibility and Work Reconciliation Act of 1996 (PL 104-193, or PRWORA) strengthened and improved child support collection and enforcement activities.

Under the PRWORA, states must have child support assignment (requirement that families receiving assistance must assign child support rights to the state) and good faith cooperation requirements for TANF participants. The cooperation provision requires the custodial parent to provide the name and other identifying information about the absent parent. However, states have the flexibility to develop their own "good cause" exceptions to the cooperation requirements, such as a serious threat of domestic violence and/or sexual abuse. In addition, they may decide the penalty for non-cooperation, although the PRWORA mandates a minimum penalty of 25 percent of the monthly cash assistance.

The welfare-reform law (PRWORA) also required states to have child support automation systems in place by October 1, 2000. Each state must have in effect a computerized child support enforcement system to account for funds, to record data, to facilitate the collection and disbursement of support payments, and to keep records that improve the state's ability to locate missing parents and/or their assets. Enforcement procedures include denying or revoking driver's licenses, withholding wages, and seizing income tax refunds or unemployment compensation benefits. Data must be kept confidential for several reasons, including the possibility of family violence.

Child Support Assurance

A family that receives assistance in the state's TANF program must assign any child support rights to the state in order to reimburse some of the cost of that assistance. If child support is then collected on the case, the state is required to give a predetermined portion to the federal government. As an alternative to this provision, a state may choose to use its maintenance of effort funds (the 80 percent of its historic welfare expenditure level states are required to spend on welfare) to run a Child Support Assurance program (CSA). Any eligible family with a support order could then choose to participate in the CSA program rather than the TANF.

In a CSA program, children with child support orders are guaranteed to receive a minimum amount of support each month. The child support agency will collect the ordered support and, if necessary, supplement it up to the assured level. If the support is not paid by the non-custodial parent, the CSA agency pays the family the guaranteed support and steps up its enforcement efforts for non-payment. In return, the custodial parent would have to use the state's child support system, which keeps records of support collections and disbursements. Collecting back payments would allow the state to recover or partially recover the cost of the guaranteed payment. In addition, states would determine at what point assistance should be phased out as a family's income increases.

With a Child Support Assurance program, the state saves money. When the state is using federal money from the TANF program, it must turn over a portion (maximum 50 percent) of the child support it gets from the TANF recipient to the federal government. In a state-funded CSA program, the child support payment is kept by the recipient, and the state pays the difference between the TANF assistance amount and the assured child support. The state saves money in this case because no money goes to the federal government. In addition, the CSA program recipient continues getting the assured support payment each month following employment, encouraging single parents to enter and stay in the paid labor force.

Government Enforcement

About 5.9 million custodial parents made 13 million contacts to a child support enforcement office (IV-D office), department of social services, or other government agency for assistance. The most common reasons for the contacts were to collect due child support (3.4 million contacts), to establish a legal agreement (3.1 million contacts), to receive Aid to Families with Dependent Children or Medicaid (2.4 million contacts), or to locate the other parent (1.6 million contacts).

UNEMPLOYMENT COMPENSATION

In order to qualify for unemployment compensation benefits, an unemployed person usually must have worked recently for a covered employer for some period of time and for a certain amount of pay. In 1995 about 111 million individuals were covered by unemployment compensation—97 percent of all wage and salary workers and 84 percent of the civilian labor force. Most of those not covered were the self-employed, agricultural or domestic workers, certain alien farm workers, and railroad workers (who have their own unemployment program).

Although the unemployment compensation system covers 97 percent of all wage and salary workers, on average, only 36 percent of unemployed workers received unemployment benefits in 1994. This compares with a peak of 75.5 percent of the unemployed receiving benefits in 1975 and a low of 31.5 percent in 1987 and 1988. (See Table 5.7.)

Unemployment compensation varies widely by state. Table 5.8 shows the average unemployment rates from May to December 1994 and the percentages of unemployed receiving benefits in each state.

In 1995 almost 2.3 percent of the workforce covered by unemployment compensation were receiving benefits when the total civilian unemployment rate was about 5.6 percent. The average weekly unemployment compensation benefit was $179. Average compensation was between $170 and $189 per week (in 1996 dollars) from 1983 to 1995. (See Table 5.9.)

While the maximum a state may offer is 39 weeks of coverage (except for special programs), all states provide up to 26 weeks of benefits, except Massachusetts and Washington, which offer 30 weeks. Benefits vary dramatically from state to state. The average 1995 weekly bene-

TABLE 5.7

Unemployed Workers Receiving Unemployment Insurance, 1955–1994

Year	Percentage of Unemployed Receiving Benefits	Unemployment Rate
1955	49.1%	4.4%
1956	48.1	4.1
1957	54.9	4.3
1958	60.3	6.8
1959	49.7	5.5
1960	53.8	5.5
1961	63.5	6.7
1962	49.8	5.5
1963	48.5	5.7
1964	46.3	5.2
1965	43.1	4.5
1966	39.3	3.8
1967	42.7	3.8
1968	42.1	3.6
1969	41.6	3.5
1970	50.6	4.9
1971	52.0	5.9
1972	44.9	5.6
1973	41.1	4.9
1974	49.6	5.6
1975	75.5	8.5
1976	67.4	7.7
1977	56.3	7.1
1978	43.3	6.1
1979	42.1	5.8
1980	50.4	7.1
1981	41.4	7.6
1982	45.3	9.7
1983	43.9	9.6
1984	34.1	7.5
1985	32.9	7.2
1986	32.7	7.0
1987	31.5	6.2
1988	31.5	5.5
1989	33.0	5.3
1990	36.8	5.5
1991	41.6	6.7
1992	51.1	7.4
1993	46.8	6.8
1994, Total Year	36.1	6.1
January to April	42.2	6.5
May to December	32.5	5.9

Note: Data for years before 1985 are from historical tables that include Puerto Rico and the Virgin Islands in the tabulation of unemployment insurance beneficiaries but not in the tabulation of the unemployed. The pre-1985 data thus overstate coverage in these years by an estimated one-half to one percentage point. None of the data for 1985 through 1994 include beneficiaries in Puerto Rico and the Virgin Islands.

SOURCE: Marion Nichols and Isaac Shapiro. *Unemployment Insurance Protection in 1994*. Center on Budget and Policy Priorities: Washington, D.C., 1995

TABLE 5.8

Unemployment and Unemployment Insurance Protection by State, May–December 1994

State	Percentage of Unemployed Receiving Benefits	State Rank from Highest to Lowest	Average Unemployment Rate from May to December 1994
Alabama	25.5%	36	5.7%
Alaska	60.7	2	7.8
Arizona	24.2	40	6.2
Arkansas	36.4	18	5.3
California	38.2	16	8.3
Colorado	27.3	29	4.3
Connecticut	49.8	6	5.3
Delaware	33.7	20	4.6
District of Columbia	39.6	12	7.8
Florida	24.2	40	6.4
Georgia	21.4	46	5.2
Hawaii	44.4	7	5.8
Idaho	40.6	11	5.2
Illinois	34.0	19	5.4
Indiana	18.4	48	4.8
Iowa	29.2	28	3.3
Kansas	26.6	31	5.0
Kentucky	30.3	25	5.0
Louisiana	18.8	47	7.9
Maine	39.1	13	6.7
Maryland	29.9	27	5.2
Massachusetts	41.0	10	5.8
Michigan	30.1	26	5.4
Minnesota	33.4	22	3.6
Mississippi	22.8	43	6.4
Missouri	37.4	17	4.5
Montana	42.8	9	4.8
Nebraska	26.0	34	2.7
Nevada	32.3	24	5.8
New Hampshire	23.8	42	4.4
New Jersey	39.1	13	6.6
New Mexico	25.1	37	5.4
New York	38.5	15	6.5
North Carolina	26.3	32	4.3
North Dakota	25.9	35	3.5
Ohio	27.1	30	5.3
Oklahoma	18.4	48	5.9
Oregon	51.3	4	5.3
Pennsylvania	43.4	8	6.2
Rhode Island	63.9	1	6.8
South Carolina	24.8	38	6.0
South Dakota	17.6	51	3.0
Tennessee	33.1	23	4.4
Texas	21.9	45	6.3
Utah	22.5	44	3.6
Vermont	50.4	5	4.4
Virginia	17.7	50	5.0
Washington	60.3	3	6.1
West Virginia	24.3	39	8.5
Wisconsin	33.6	21	4.4
Wyoming	26.3	32	5.2
U.S. Total	**32.5**		**5.9**

SOURCE: Marion Nichols and Isaac Shapiro. *Unemployment Insurance Protection in 1994*. Center on Budget and Policy Priorities: Washington, D.C., 1995

fits in Hawaii ($262), New Jersey ($245), Massachusetts ($239), Minnesota ($217), Rhode Island ($217), Michigan ($215), and Connecticut ($202) were about twice as much as those offered by Alabama ($135), Mississippi ($130), and Louisiana ($119). (See Table 5.10.)

Unemployment Compensation Important in Avoiding Poverty

In the latest study available, *Family Incomes of Unemployment Insurance Recipients and the Implications for Extending Benefits* (Washington, D.C., 1990), the Congres-

sional Budget Office (CBO) concluded that unemployment compensation prevented many families from falling into poverty. The CBO study found that about 9 percent of unemployed workers had been earning a poverty wage before they became unemployed and started receiving unemployment compensation. The poverty rate increased to 19 percent during their spell of unemployment. Howev-

TABLE 5.9

Unemployment Compensation Program Statistics, Selected Years 1983–97

Statistic	Fiscal years											
	1983	1985	1987	1989	1990	1991	1992	1993	1994	1995	1996 (estimated)	1997 (projected)[1]
Total civilian unemployment rate (%)	10.1	7.2	6.4	5.3	5.4	6.5	7.3	7.0	6.3	5.6	5.7	5.7
Insured unemployment rate (%)[2]	4.3	2.9	2.5	2.1	2.3	3.1	3.1	2.7	2.6	2.3	2.4	2.4
Coverage (millions)	86.3	93.5	98.0	104.3	106.1	105.1	104.9	106.6	109.7	112.6	113.6	115.0
Average weekly benefit amount:												
Current dollars	120	123	134	145	154	163	167	172	175	179	184	192
In 1996 dollars[3]	179	170	186	184	186	189	188	188	186	185	184	186
State unemployment compensation:												
Beneficiaries (millions)	9.9	8.4	7.5	7.0	8.1	10.2	9.6	7.8	8.2	7.9	8.7	9.1
Regular benefit exhaustions (millions)	4.6	2.5	2.5	1.9	2.2	3.2	3.9	3.3	3.1	2.7	2.7	2.8
Regular benefits paid (billions of dollars)	20.8	14.3	15.0	13.5	16.8	24.4	25.6	21.9	21.7	20.9	23.1	24.2
Extended benefits (State share: billions of dollars)	1.21	0.03	0.04	(6)	0.03	0.01	0.02	0.00	0.15	0.04	0.05	0.07
State tax collections (billions)	14.4	20.0	19.1	17.3	16.0	15.3	17.6	21.0	22.5	23.2	24.0	25.0
State trust fund impact (income-outlays: billions)[4]	−7.62	+5.65	+4.11	+3.80	−0.88	−9.13	−8.03	−0.93	+0.66	+2.24	+0.89	+0.79
Federal unemployment compensation accounts:												
Federal tax collections (billions of dollars)[5]	3.58	4.44	5.08	4.45	5.36	5.33	5.41	[7]4.23	5.46	5.70	5.74	5.81
Outlays: Federal extended benefits share plus Federal supplemental benefits (billions of dollars)	6.80	1.27	0.04	(6)	0.03	0.01	11.15	13.17	4.37	0.05	0.05	0.07
State administrative costs (billions):												
Unemployment Insurance Service	1.70	1.58	1.56	1.71	1.74	1.95	2.49	2.52	2.43	2.38	2.31	2.50
Employment Service	0.72	0.92	0.90	1.00	1.01	1.05	1.02	0.90	0.90	1.05	1.06	1.02
Total administrative costs	2.42	2.50	2.46	2.71	2.75	3.00	3.51	3.42	3.33	3.43	3.37	3.51

[1] Based on President Clinton's 1997 budget.
[2] The average number of workers claiming State unemployment compensation benefits as a percent of all workers covered.
[3] Adjusted using CPI-U.
[4] Excludes interest earned.
[5] Net of reduced credits.
[6] Less than $5 million
[7] Reflects a book adjustment of minus $967 million.

SOURCE: Office of Research, U.S. Department of Labor

---

er, the CBO concluded that 46 percent of these families would have been living in poverty had they not been receiving unemployment compensation.

The Center on Budget and Policy Priorities, a non-profit organization that "studies government spending and the programs and public policy issues that have an impact on low-income Americans," agrees that unemployment insurance is an important part of the nation's "safety net" for families. In the Center's *Unemployment Insurance Protection in 1994* (Washington, D.C., 1995), Marion Nichols and Isaac Shapiro concluded that the April 1994 expiration of the federal temporary emergency unemployment compensation program weakened the nation's safety net. About one-third (32.5 percent) of unemployed workers received benefits from May to December 1994.

Minorities Hardest Hit by Unemployment

The unemployment rate for African American and Hispanic workers is about double that of whites. In 1997 the unemployment rate for white workers 20 years old and over was 4.2 percent, compared to 10 percent for blacks and 7.7 percent for Hispanics in the same age group. The unemployment rate among African American teenagers (16 to 19 years old) was 32.4 percent, while that of white teenagers was 13.6 percent. (See Table 5.11.)

THE FEDERAL MINIMUM WAGE—A RELATIVE DECLINE

The federal minimum wage dates back to the passage of the Fair Labor Standards Act (PL 75-718) in 1938, which established basic national standards for minimum wages, overtime pay, and the employment of child workers. (The minimum wage is a "cash wage" only and does not include any fringe benefits. Consequently, the total compensation for minimum wage workers is even lower than the total compensation for higher-paid workers, who generally receive some kind of benefits in addition to wages. Most minimum wage workers do not receive any benefits.) The provisions of the Act have been extended to cover many other areas of employment since 1938.

The first minimum wage instituted in 1938 was $0.25 an hour. Over the years, it gradually increased, reaching $3.35 hour in 1981. For almost a decade there was no increase in the minimum wage, the longest period for

FIGURE 5.5

Real Minimum Wage in 1997 Dollars, 1955–97

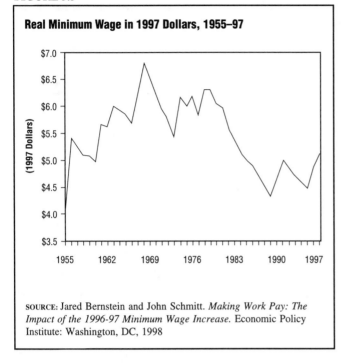

SOURCE: Jared Bernstein and John Schmitt. *Making Work Pay: The Impact of the 1996-97 Minimum Wage Increase.* Economic Policy Institute: Washington, DC, 1998

TABLE 5.10

Amount and Duration of Weekly Benefits for Total Unemployment Under the Regular State Programs, 1995 and 1996

State	1995 average weekly benefit	1996 weekly benefit amount[1] Minimum	Maximum	1995 average duration (weeks)	1996 potential duration (weeks) Minimum	Maximum
Alabama	$135	$22	$180	11	15	26
Alaska	167	44-68	212-284	15	16	26
Arizona	146	40	185	14	12	26
Arkansas	158	47	264	12	9	26
California	148	40	230	17	14	26
Colorado	196	25	272	13	13	26
Connecticut	202	15-25	350-400	17	26	26
Delaware	186	20	300	15	24	26
District of Columbia	223	50	359	20	20	26
Florida	170	10	250	14	10	26
Georgia	155	37	205	10	9	26
Hawaii	262	5	347	17	26	26
Idaho	161	44	248	13	10	26
Illinois	206	51	251-332	18	26	26
Indiana	176	87	217	11	8	26
Iowa	184	33-40	224-274	12	11	26
Kansas	191	65	260	14	10	26
Kentucky	158	22	238	14	15	26
Louisiana	119	10	181	14	26	26
Maine	155	35-52	202-303	14	21	26
Maryland	186	25-33	250	17	26	26
Massachusetts	239	14-21	347-521	17	10	30
Michigan	215	42	293	13	15	26
Minnesota	217	38	303	16	10	26
Mississippi	130	30	180	12	13	26
Missouri	146	45	175	13	11	26
Montana	139	57	228	15	8	26
Nebraska	149	20	184	12	20	26
Nevada	185	16	237	14	12	26
New Hampshire	146	32	216	12	26	26
New Jersey	245	60	362	18	15	26
New Mexico	151	42	212	17	19	26
New York	193	40	300	20	26	26
North Carolina	174	25	297	9	13	26
North Dakota	162	43	243	13	12	26
Ohio	192	66	253-339	15	20	26
Oklahoma	168	16	247	14	20	26
Oregon	169	70	301	16	4	26
Pennsylvania	202	35-40	352-360	17	16	26
Puerto Rico	90	7	133	19	26	26
Rhode Island	217	41-51	324-404	17	15	26
South Carolina	155	20	213	11	15	26
South Dakota	140	28	180	11	15	26
Tennessee	147	30	200	12	12	26
Texas	177	42	252	16	9	26
Utah	185	17	263	12	10	26
Vermont	157	25	212	15	26	26
Virginia	162	65	208	11	12	26
Virgin Islands	170	32	214	20	13	26
Washington	190	75	350	19	116	30
West Virginia	166	24	290	15	2 6	26
Wisconsin	174	52	274	13	12	26
Wyoming	174	16	233	15	82	26
U.S. average	**186**	**NA**	**NA**	**15**	**NA**	**NA**

[1]A range of amounts is shown for those States that provide dependents' allowances.
NA-Not applicable.

SOURCE: U.S. Department of Labor

which there was no rise in the minimum wage. The minimum wage was increased to $3.80 in 1990 and $4.25 in 1991. (See Table 5.12.) In July 1996, Congress passed legislation, which raised the minimum wage to $5.15 in 1997 by means of two 45 cent increases. President Bill Clinton signed the bill into law in early August 1996. In 2000 the minimum wage was still $5.15, although states like California, Alaska, and Connecticut had minimum wage rates higher than the federal rate, and states like Texas, Ohio, and Wyoming had minimum wage rates lower than the federal rate.

The decade of no increase in the minimum wage meant that the minimum wage actually lost about half its value between 1978 and 1990, when it was finally raised. The increases in 1996 and 1997 still left the real value of the minimum wage well below the 1978 value. (See Figure 5.5.) A person working 40 hours a week for 50 weeks a year at minimum wage would gross $206 per week or $10,300 per year, well below the poverty level for a family of three ($13,330 in 1997). For adults, this means that "day laborers" (those without a permanent job) who look for a job every day and those employed in many service jobs for minimum wages are unlikely to earn enough to escape from poverty.

The number of people working at or below the minimum wage dropped sharply from 7.8 million in 1981 to 3.2 million in 1989. The decrease was caused mainly by the sharp decline in the purchasing power of the minimum wage. As the value of the minimum wage dropped, the number of those hired at that minimum level also fell. After the recession of 1990–91 and the slow recovery in 1992, 4.2 million workers in 1993 earned the minimum wage or less. In 1996 nearly 10 million workers were directly affected by the minimum wage increase. Often employers use the minimum wage as a standard for low-paying jobs, perhaps paying $1 or $2 above minimum wage for a particular job.

TABLE 5.11

Selected Unemployment Indicators, Monthly Data Seasonally Adjusted
[Unemployment rates]

Selected categories	Annual average 1996	1997	1997 Jan.	Feb.	Mar.	Apr.	May	June	July	Aug.	Sept.	Oct.	Nov.	Dec.	1998 Jan.
Characteristic															
Total, all workers	**5.4**	**4.9**	**5.3**	**5.3**	**5.2**	**5.0**	**4.8**	**5.0**	**4.9**	**4.9**	**4.9**	**4.8**	**4.6**	**4.7**	**4.7**
Both sexes, 16 to 19 years	16.7	16.0	16.9	17.3	16.5	15.6	15.7	16.5	16.3	16.2	16.4	15.5	15.2	14.3	14.1
Men, 20 years and over	4.6	4.2	4.5	4.4	4.4	4.2	3.9	4.2	4.1	4.1	4.1	4.1	3.9	4.1	3.8
Women, 20 years and over	4.8	4.4	4.7	4.7	4.7	4.4	4.5	4.4	4.3	4.3	4.3	4.1	4.0	4.0	4.4
White, total	4.7	4.2	4.5	4.5	4.4	4.2	4.1	4.3	4.2	4.2	4.2	4.1	3.9	3.9	4.0
Both sexes, 16 to 19 years	14.2	13.6	14.1	14.6	14.1	13.5	12.9	14.4	14.4	14.2	14.1	13.4	12.3	11.2	11.6
Men, 16 to 19 years	15.5	14.3	15.1	14.8	15.1	14.6	13.0	15.8	15.0	15.1	14.4	14.3	12.8	11.3	14.2
Women, 16 to 19 years	12.9	12.8	13.1	14.4	13.0	12.2	12.7	12.8	13.7	13.1	13.7	12.3	11.6	11.1	8.8
Men, 20 years and over	4.1	3.6	3.9	3.8	3.8	3.6	3.3	3.6	3.5	3.6	3.6	3.6	3.4	3.6	3.3
Women, 20 years and over	4.1	3.7	3.9	3.9	3.9	3.7	3.7	3.7	3.5	3.7	3.7	3.5	3.4	3.4	3.7
Black, total	10.5	10.0	10.7	11.0	10.5	9.9	10.3	10.3	9.6	9.5	9.6	9.6	9.7	9.9	9.3
Both sexes, 16 to 19 years	33.6	32.4	34.1	33.6	32.1	31.9	33.9	32.2	30.0	30.4	32.7	29.5	33.3	34.4	30.1
Men, 16 to 19 years	36.9	36.5	40.9	36.8	40.5	37.7	34.5	39.1	34.6	33.9	37.6	30.1	35.0	36.2	31.8
Women, 16 to 19 years	30.3	28.7	27.7	30.4	34.6	26.3	33.3	25.5	25.9	27.2	28.6	28.8	31.9	33.1	28.5
Men, 20 years and over	9.4	8.5	9.0	8.8	8.9	8.4	8.4	9.0	8.3	7.9	7.9	8.3	7.8	8.6	7.9
Women, 20 years and over	8.7	8.8	9.3	10.0	9.2	8.6	9.2	9.0	8.4	8.4	8.4	8.3	8.4	8.1	8.0
Hispanic origin, total	8.9	7.7	8.2	8.1	8.3	8.0	7.6	7.7	7.9	7.3	7.6	7.8	6.9	7.5	6.9
Married men, spouse present	3.0	2.7	2.8	2.8	2.8	2.7	2.7	2.7	2.6	2.6	2.6	2.6	2.4	2.6	2.6
Married women, spouse present	3.6	3.1	3.3	3.4	3.3	3.2	3.2	3.2	3.1	3.0	3.1	2.8	2.8	2.8	3.1
Women who maintain families	8.2	8.1	8.7	8.8	8.7	7.9	7.9	8.0	7.6	8.0	7.8	7.8	8.1	7.7	7.6
Full-time workers	5.3	4.8	5.2	5.1	5.1	4.8	4.8	4.9	4.8	4.7	4.7	4.7	4.4	4.6	4.5
Part-time workers	5.8	5.5	5.7	5.9	5.7	5.6	5.3	5.3	5.4	5.5	5.5	5.3	5.4	5.0	5.4
Industry															
Nonagricultural wage and salary workers	5.5	5.0	5.4	5.3	5.2	5.0	5.0	5.0	4.9	5.0	5.0	4.8	4.7	4.8	4.7
Mining	5.1	3.8	5.3	4.0	3.9	2.3	3.3	2.8	4.1	4.9	3.4	4.5	3.3	3.3	4.0
Construction	10.1	9.0	9.8	9.1	9.4	a.8	8.6	8.8	8.7	9.0	8.7	8.7	7.9	a.9	7.9
Manufacturing	4.8	4.2	4.6	4.5	4.3	4.4	4.3	4.2	4.3	4.1	4.1	3.8	3.6	3.8	3.9
Durable goods	4.5	3.5	4.3	4.0	3.7	3.6	3.6	3.6	3.5	3.5	3.3	3.1	3.1	3.1	3.4
Nondurable goods	5.2	5.1	5.0	5.3	5.3	5.5	5.3	5.0	5.4	5.0	5.3	4.8	4.4	4.9	4.5
Transportation and public utilities	4.1	3.5	4.0	4.1	3.9	2.9	3.6	3.0	3.4	3.7	3.8	3.3	3.1	3.3	3.8
Wholesale and retail trade	6.4	6.2	6.4	6.4	6.3	6.2	6.1	6.4	6.1	6.2	6.2	6.1	6.2	5.8	5.9
Finance, insurance, and real estate	2.7	3.0	3.4	3.1	3.2	3.3	3.1	2.5	3.1	3.0	3.0	2.9	2.4	2.8	2.6
Services	5.4	4.6	4.9	4.9	4.9	4.6	4.7	4.7	4.4	4.5	4.6	4.3	4.4	4.5	4.3
Government workers	2.9	2.6	2.9	2.9	2.8	2.4	2.5	2.8	2.7	2.6	2.6	2.4	2.3	2.1	2.4
Agricultural wage and salary workers	10.2	9.1	8.7	9.0	9.3	9.5	7.6	10.4	8.4	8.9	9.0	9.6	8.6	9.7	10.6
Educational attainment[1]															
Less than a high school diploma	8.7	8.1	8.9	8.8	8.4	8.2	8.2	8.2	7.8	7.7	8.0	7.7	7.5	7.6	7.2
High school graduates, no college	4.7	4.3	4.4	4.5	4.4	4.2	4.2	4.4	4.2	4.3	4.2	4.2	3.8	4.1	3.9
Some college, less than a bachelor's degree	3.7	3.3	3.5	3.5	3.6	3.3	3.0	3.2	3.2	3.2	3.2	2.9	3.1	3.2	3.2
College graduates	2.2	2.0	2.1	2.1	2.1	2.0	2.1	2.1	2.1	2.1	2.0	1.9	1.8	1.8	1.9

[1]Data refer to persons 25 years and over.

SOURCE: Monthly Labor Review, vol 121, no 3, March 1998

Who Works for Minimum Wage?

In *Making Work Pay: The Impact of the 1996–1997 Minimum Wage Increase* (Economic Policy Institute, Washington, D.C., 1998), Jared Bernstein and John Schmitt report that most workers affected by minimum wage increases are adults (71.4 percent), and most live in low-income households. They believe that these factors suggest that minimum wage increases are accomplishing the goal of raising the earnings of low-wage workers in lower-income households. Table 5.13 shows the characteristics of low-wage workers in the year prior to the increase. A majority (58.2 percent) were female workers, and nearly two-thirds (62.8 percent) were white. While 46 percent worked full-time (35 hours per week or more), another 33.3 percent worked between 20 and 34 hours a week.

Comparing the workers directly affected by the new minimum wage (see column 1 of Table 5.13) to all workers (last column) shows the characteristics of the population with the lowest earnings. Female and minority workers are overrepresented in the affected range, as are teenagers, who typically earn low wages. Affected workers are more likely to be in retail trade jobs, especially service providers such as clerks or waiters, and they are nearly all (96 percent) nonunion workers.

The percentages at the bottom of Table 5.13 show the average and median share of weekly earnings that minimum wage earners contribute to their households. When one-person families are excluded, the average minimum wage worker brings home 44 percent of the family's

TABLE 5.12

Federal Minimum Wage Rates, 1938–1991

	Effective date	Minimum wage	Value of 1978 minimum wage[1]
Public Law 75-718 enacted June 25, 1938.	October 1938	$0.25	
	October 1939	.30	
	October 1945	.40	
Public Law 81-393 enacted October 26, 1949.	January 1950	.75	
Public Law 84-381 enacted August 12, 1955.	March 1956	1.00	
Public Law 87-30 enacted May 5, 1961.	September 1961	1.15	
	September 1963	1.25	
Public Law 89-601 enacted September 23, 1966.	February 1967	1.40	
	February 1968	1.60	
Public Law 93-259 enacted April 8, 1974.	May 1974	2.00	
	January 1975	2.10	
	January 1976	2.30	
Public Law 95-151, enacted November 1, 1977.	January 1978	2.65	2.65
	January 1979	2.90	2.95
	January 1980	3.10	3.35
	January 1981	3.35	3.69
Public Lawn 101-157 enacted November 17, 1989.	April 1990	3.80	5.31
	April 1991	4.25	5.54

[1]1978 statutory minimum wage adjusted for inflation (Consumer Price index for All Urban Consumers) using calendar year CPI's.

SOURCE: U.S. Department of Labor

weekly earnings. (By definition, one person in a family would contribute 100 percent of that family's earnings.)

While workers must receive at least the minimum wage for most jobs, there are some exceptions, in which a person may be paid less than the minimum wage. Full-time students working on a part-time basis in the service and retail industries or at the student's academic institution, certain handicapped persons, and workers who are "customarily and regularly" tipped may receive less than the minimum wage.

A DECLINE IN MALE EARNINGS

In the 1980s and 1990s the median personal income of American men declined substantially. For all males, median earnings (half earned more and half earned less) reached $27,821 in 1973 (in constant 1998 dollars) and then began dropping, hitting a low of $23,785 in 1982, a year of deep recession. Male earnings then began a slow recovery, reaching $26,150 in 1989. Since then, male earnings have been falling, dipping to $23,765 in 1992, lower than the median earnings during the recession of the early 1980s, and more than 14 percent below male earnings in 1973. In 1998 median male earnings reached $26,492. This trend applied to white, African American, and Hispanic men. (See Table 5.14.)

Female earnings rose 33 percent from 1973 to 1998. It should be noted, however, that the median income of female workers in 1998 was still only about half (54 percent) that of male workers. (See Table 5.14.)

TABLE 5.13

Characteristics of Minimum Wage and Other Workers, October 1995–September 1996

Characteristic	Workers Directly Affected by New Minimum ($4.25–$5.14)	Other Low-Wage Workers ($5.15–$6.14)	Higher-Wage Workers ($6.15+)	All Workers
Average Wage	$4.73	$5.72	$14.64	$12.73
Employment	9,886,158	9,610,926	89,079,931	110,999,085
Share of Total	8.9%	8.7%	80.3%	100.0%
Demographics				
Male	41.8%	41.9%	54.9%	52.3%
16-19	13.7	8.1	1.0	2.9
20+	28.2	33.8	53.9	49.4
Female	58.2	58.1	45.1	47.7
16-19	14.9	7.9	0.7	2.8
20+	43.2	50.2	44.4	44.9
White	62.8	67.7	77.9	75.4
Male	24.6	26.2	42.8	39.4
Female	38.2	41.5	35.1	36.0
Black	16.1	13.8	10.4	11.3
Male	6.4	5.5	5.1	5.3
Female	9.8	8.3	5.3	6.0
Hispanic	17.5	14.8	7.9	9.5
Male	9.3	8.6	4.9	5.7
Female	8.2	6.2	3.0	3.8
Teens (16-19)	28.6%	16.0%	1.7%	5.6%
Work Hours				
Full Time (35+)	46.0%	62.7%	87.7%	81.1%
Part Time				
20-34 hours	33.3%	25.4%	9.0%	13.0%
1-19 hours	20.7	11.9	3.3	5.9
Industry				
Manufacturing	8.8%	12.7%	19.7%	17.8%
Retail Trade	42.6	35.8	12.2	17.3
Union*				
Union	4.4%	6.3%	19.1%	16.4%
Nonunion	95.6	93.7	80.9	83.6

Addendum: The Share of Weekly Earnings Contributed by Minimum Wage Workers, 1997

	Average	Median
All Families With an Affected Worker	54%	41%
Excluding One-Person Families	44	27

*Includes both union members and nonmembers covered by union contracts.

SOURCE: Jared Bernstein and John Schmitt. *Making Work Pay: The Impact of the 1996-97 Minimum Wage Increase.* Economic Policy Institute: Washington, D.C., 1998

SOMETIMES HAVING A JOB DOES NOT GET A PERSON OUT OF POVERTY

In *A Profile of the Working Poor, 1996* (Bureau of Labor Statistics, Washington, D.C., 1997), Samantha Quan studied the working poor. The term "working poor" refers to those who participated in the labor force for at least 27 weeks (either working or looking for work) and who lived in families with incomes below the official poverty level. She found that for 7.4 million workers in 1996, 5.8 percent of those in the labor force, their jobs were not enough to keep them out of poverty.

Quan reported that working women (6.5 percent) had a somewhat higher poverty rate than working men (5.2

TABLE 5.14

Persons by Total Money Income, Race, Hispanic Origin, and Sex: 1967 to 1998

[Income in 1996 CPI-U-X1 adjusted dollars. Persons 15 years old and over beginning with March 1980, and persons 14 years old and over as of March of the following year for previous years.]

Race, Hispanic origin, sex, and year	Number (thous.)	Number with income (thous.)	With income — Percent distribution									Median income Value (dollars)	Median income Standard error (dollars)	Mean income Value (dollars)	Mean income Standard error (dollars)
			Total	$1 to $2,499 or less	$2,500 to $4,999	$5,000 to $9,999	$10,000 to $14,999	$15,000 to $24,999	$25,000 to $49,999	$50,000 to $74,999	$75,000 and over				
All Races															
Male															
1998	102,048	94,948	100.0	5.3	3.5	9.6	10.1	18.6	31.5	12.4	9.0	26,492	128	36,315	257
1997	101,123	94,168	100.0	5.4	3.6	10.1	11.2	19.0	31.0	11.6	8.1	25,605	120	35,332	254
1996	100,159	93,439	100.0	5.7	3.8	10.7	11.5	19.2	30.6	11.1	7.4	24,761	163	34,075	257
1995	98,593	92,066	100.0	5.8	4.2	10.3	11.5	19.6	30.3	11.1	7.3	24,131	156	33,642	248
1994[1]	97,704	91,254	100.0	6.2	4.0	10.9	11.7	19.4	30.1	10.6	7.3	23,889	121	33,400	235
1993[2]	96,768	90,194	100.0	6.6	4.3	10.7	11.0	19.6	29.6	10.8	6.7	23,804	120	32,644	231
1992[3]	95,652	90,175	100.0	6.5	4.6	11.1	11.2	19.7	30.1	10.5	6.5	23,765	124	31,148	161
1991	93,760	88,653	100.0	6.0	4.4	10.8	11.0	19.0	31.0	11.0	6.4	24,497	126	31,558	160
1990	92,840	88,220	100.0	5.9	4.2	10.8	10.4	19.3	31.3	11.4	6.8	25,308	127	32,477	171
1989	91,955	87,454	100.0	5.6	4.3	10.2	9.9	18.8	31.4	12.5	7.2	26,150	162	33,844	185
1988	91,034	86,584	100.0	5.9	4.4	10.3	9.5	18.9	31.9	12.2	6.8	26,052	180	33,143	182
1987[4]	90,256	85,713	100.0	6.3	4.5	10.0	10.5	18.1	30.9	13.1	6.7	25,520	176	32,712	165
1986	89,368	84,471	100.0	6.6	4.5	10.0	10.5	17.7	31.6	12.4	6.7	25,452	137	32,454	161
1985	88,474	83,631	100.0	6.8	4.8	10.5	9.7	19.4	30.9	11.6	6.4	24,709	138	31,285	151
1984	87,034	82,183	100.0	7.1	4.9	11.1	9.7	18.4	31.5	11.3	6.0	24,474	141	30,495	135
1983[5]	86,014	80,795	100.0	7.7	5.1	11.0	9.9	19.0	31.3	10.5	5.5	23,993	(NA)	29,756	(NA)
1982	84,955	79,722	100.0	7.5	4.7	10.9	10.1	19.1	31.5	10.7	5.5	23,785	155	29,635	133
1981	83,958	79,688	100.0	7.0	4.8	11.0	10.1	18.2	32.8	11.2	5.0	24,374	165	29,877	132
1980	82,949	78,661	100.0	6.8	4.4	10.9	9.5	18.8	33.4	11.0	5.2	24,816	154	30,382	135
1979[6]	81,947	78,129	100.0	6.3	4.7	10.4	9.4	17.9	33.6	12.1	5.6	25,946	132	31,523	143
1978	80,969	75,609	100.0	6.9	4.4	10.6	9.3	17.2	33.7	12.3	5.5	26,406	152	31,665	147
1977	79,863	74,015	100.0	7.0	4.5	10.5	9.6	17.0	34.2	11.9	5.4	26,108	121	31,112	134
1976	78,782	72,775	100.0	7.1	4.6	10.5	9.5	17.9	34.3	11.3	4.9	25,866	145	30,638	132
1975	77,560	71,234	100.0	6.9	4.4	10.8	9.7	17.6	35.2	10.8	4.6	25,677	133	30,248	133
1974[7]	76,363	70,863	100.0	7.0	4.6	10.2	8.7	16.9	35.9	11.4	5.3	26,545	(NA)	30,970	(NA)
1973	75,040	69,387	100.0	7.1	4.7	9.6	8.6	16.4	35.3	12.4	5.9	27,821	(NA)	32,079	(NA)
1972	73,572	67,474	100.0	6.9	4.9	9.6	8.8	16.2	36.9	11.3	5.3	27,350	(NA)	31,701	(NA)
1971	72,469	66,486	100.0	7.6	5.0	10.2	8.5	17.5	37.1	9.6	4.5	26,106	(NA)	29,847	(NA)
1970	70,592	65,008	100.0	7.6	5.4	10.0	8.5	16.9	37.6	9.7	4.4	26,325	(NA)	29,747	(NA)
1969	69,027	63,882	100.0	7.5	5.6	10.0	8.4	16.7	37.9	9.5	4.3	26,597	(NA)	29,795	(NA)
1968	67,611	62,501	100.0	7.4	5.9	9.9	8.2	17.7	38.7	8.5	3.7	25,855	(NA)	28,648	(NA)
1967	66,519	61,444	100.0	7.8	6.3	10.4	8.6	18.7	37.6	7.1	3.5	24,935	(NA)	27,185	(NA)
Female															
1998	109,628	98,694	100.0	11.3	7.1	18.7	14.3	19.3	21.9	5.2	2.2	14,430	102	20,462	139
1997	108,168	97,447	100.0	11.0	7.8	19.4	14.5	20.1	20.7	4.5	2.1	13,916	105	19,814	122
1996	107,076	96,558	100.0	11.4	8.3	20.2	14.4	19.9	20.0	4.1	1.8	13,313	110	19,083	130
1995	106,031	96,007	100.0	12.3	8.4	20.3	14.4	19.5	19.6	4.0	1.6	12,974	80	18,466	118
1994[1]	105,028	95,147	100.0	13.0	8.7	20.6	14.4	18.8	19.3	3.7	1.5	12,611	78	18,124	119
1993[2]	104,032	94,417	100.0	13.3	9.3	20.3	14.5	18.9	18.8	3.7	1.2	12,460	80	17,779	118
1992[3]	102,954	93,517	100.0	13.5	9.4	20.1	14.1	18.8	19.4	3.3	1.2	12,447	81	17,336	91
1991	101,483	92,569	100.0	13.4	9.2	20.5	14.3	19.0	19.2	3.3	1.2	12,537	84	17,292	89
1990	100,680	92,245	100.0	13.8	9.8	19.5	14.1	19.1	19.1	3.5	1.2	12,559	89	17,351	91

TABLE 5.14

Persons by Total Money Income, Race, Hispanic Origin, and Sex: 1967 to 1998 [CONTINUED]

[Income in 1996 CPI-U-X1 adjusted dollars. Persons 15 years old and over beginning with March 1980, and persons 14 years old and over as of March of the following year for previous years.]

Race, Hispanic origin, sex, and year	Number (thous.)	Number with income (thous.)	With income									Median income		Mean income	
			Percent distribution									Value (dollars)	Standard error (dollars)	Value (dollars)	Standard error (dollars)
			Total	$1 to $2,499 or less	$2,500 to $4,999	$5,000 to $9,999	$10,000 to $14,999	$15,000 to $24,999	$25,000 to $49,999	$50,000 to $74,999	$75,000 and over				
All Races															
Female (cont.)															
1989	99,838	91,399	100.0	13.8	9.6	19.5	13.6	19.5	19.3	3.6	1.1	12,651	91	17,386	91
1988	99,019	90,593	100.0	14.6	9.7	20.1	13.0	19.4	19.1	3.1	1.0	12,241	105	16,963	95
1987[4]	98,225	89,661	100.0	15.0	9.9	19.6	14.2	18.9	18.5	3.0	1.0	11,902	96	16,555	86
1986	97,320	87,822	100.0	16.1	10.0	20.2	13.7	18.3	18.2	2.6	0.9	11,318	82	15,974	82
1985	96,354	86,531	100.0	16.6	10.6	20.3	13.1	19.2	17.2	2.3	0.8	10,933	82	15,411	79
1984	95,282	85,555	100.0	17.2	10.1	20.7	13.5	18.9	16.8	2.0	0.7	10,775	71	15,036	74
1983[5]	94,269	83,781	100.0	17.8	10.8	20.8	13.3	19.2	15.7	1.9	0.6	10,482	(NA)	14,564	(NA)
1982	93,145	82,505	100.0	18.4	10.3	21.4	13.9	18.9	15.0	1.6	0.5	10,037	65	13,973	70
1981	92,228	82,139	100.0	18.5	10.8	21.9	13.8	18.9	14.3	1.5	0.3	9,874	69	13,460	65
1980	91,133	80,826	100.0	19.1	11.1	21.6	13.6	19.1	13.9	1.3	0.4	9,744	65	13,412	67
1979[6]	89,914	79,921	100.0	19.9	11.3	20.9	13.2	19.2	13.8	1.3	0.4	9,586	77	13,273	68
1978	88,617	71,864	100.0	17.2	12.2	22.1	13.9	19.1	13.9	1.3	0.4	9,823	87	13,521	70
1977	87,399	65,407	100.0	14.4	12.5	22.9	14.9	19.4	14.3	1.1	0.4	10,164	72	13,646	64
1976	86,153	63,170	100.0	15.2	12.9	23.0	14.5	19.7	13.2	1.1	0.3	9,813	77	13,378	66
1975	84,982	60,807	100.0	15.2	13.0	22.8	15.3	19.4	13.1	1.0	0.2	9,818	61	13,089	61
1974[7]	83,599	59,642	100.0	15.9	13.2	23.0	13.9	19.2	13.5	1.1	0.3	9,679	(NA)	13,068	(NA)
1973	82,244	57,029	100.0	16.5	14.0	21.3	14.7	18.9	13.3	1.1	0.3	9,656	(NA)	13,119	(NA)
1972	80,896	54,487	100.0	16.8	14.2	21.0	14.4	18.6	13.7	1.1	0.3	9,541	(NA)	13,132	(NA)
1971	79,565	52,603	100.0	17.4	15.3	20.5	13.2	20.2	12.1	0.9	0.3	9,107	(NA)	12,605	(NA)
1970	77,649	51,647	100.0	19.0	15.1	20.3	13.0	19.4	12.0	0.8	0.3	8,829	(NA)	12,385	(NA)
1969	76,277	50,224	100.0	19.1	15.9	19.4	13.6	20.0	10.9	0.8	0.3	8,820	(NA)	12,184	(NA)
1968	74,889	48,544	100.0	19.3	16.0	19.9	13.6	19.4	10.8	0.7	0.2	8,729	(NA)	11,812	(NA)
1967	73,584	46,843	100.0	21.3	16.8	19.1	13.9	18.5	9.2	0.7	0.4	8,087	(NA)	11,150	(NA)

SOURCE: *Money Income in the United States: 1998.* Current Population Reports, P60-206. U.S. Bureau of the Census: Washington, D.C., 1999.

TABLE 5.15

Persons in the Labor Force for 27 Weeks or More: Poverty Status by Age, Sex, Race, and Hispanic Origin, 1996
(Numbers in thousands)

Age and sex	Total	White	Black	Hispanic origin	Below poverty level				Poverty rate[1]			
					Total	White	Black	Hispanic origin	Total	White	Black	Hispanic origin
Total, 16 years and older	128,320	108,431	14,225	12,433	7,421	5,432	1,647	1,788	5.8	5.0	11.6	14.4
16 to 19 years	4,881	4,169	583	538	581	428	134	125	11.9	10.3	23.0	23.2
20 to 24 years	11,892	9,853	1,497	1,642	1,448	1,060	334	294	12.2	10.8	22.3	17.9
25 to 34 years	32,166	26,557	3,955	4,081	2,180	1,588	512	597	6.8	6.0	13.0	14.6
35 to 44 years	35,954	30,153	4,179	3,295	1,865	1,335	407	494	5.2	4.4	9.7	15.0
45 to 54 years	26,825	23,083	2,658	1,803	910	681	187	189	3.4	2.9	7.0	10.5
55 to 64 years	12,729	11,145	1,093	894	377	296	62	77	3.0	2.7	5.7	8.6
65 years and older	3,873	3,471	260	180	61	44	10	12	1.6	1.3	3.8	6.5
Men, 16 years and older	69,626	59,921	6,649	7,596	3,633	2,855	574	1,121	5.2	4.8	8.6	14.8
16 to 19 years	2,483	2,157	266	331	243	184	53	72	9.8	8.5	20.0	21.6
20 to 24 years	6,304	5,388	641	1,072	642	512	102	188	10.2	9.5	15.9	17.6
25 to 34 years	17,823	14,977	1,903	2,571	1,090	879	166	386	6.1	5.9	8.7	15.0
35 to 44 years	19,515	16,675	1,969	1,958	958	726	150	316	4.9	4.4	7.6	16.2
45 to 54 years	14,277	12,488	1,249	1,045	453	357	68	104	3.2	2.9	5.4	9.9
55 to 64 years	6,988	6,211	497	507	210	172	29	49	3.0	2.8	5.8	9.6
65 years and older	2,236	2,025	124	112	38	24	7	6	1.7	1.2	5.3	5.3
Women, 16 years and older	58,694	48,510	7,576	4,836	3,788	2,577	1,073	667	6.5	5.3	14.2	13.8
16 to 19 years	2,398	2,012	317	206	338	244	81	53	14.1	12.1	25.5	25.8
20 to 24 years	5,588	4,466	856	570	806	548	232	106	14.4	12.3	27.1	18.6
25 to 34 years	14,344	11,580	2,052	1,510	1,090	709	347	211	7.6	6.1	16.9	14.0
35 to 44 years	16,439	13,478	2,210	1,337	907	609	257	177	5.5	4.5	11.6	13.2
45 to 54 years	12,548	10,595	1,410	758	456	323	120	86	3.6	3.1	8.5	11.3
55 to 64 years	5,740	4,934	596	386	167	124	33	28	2.9	2.5	5.6	7.2
65 years and older	1,637	1,445	136	68	23	20	3	6	1.4	1.4	2.3	(2)

[1] Number below the poverty level as a percent of the total in the labor force for 27 weeks or more who worked during the year.

[2] Data not shown where base is less than 75,000.

NOTE: Detail for race and Hispanic-origin groups will not sum to totals because data for the "other races" group are not presented and Hispanics are included in both the white and black population groups.

SOURCE: *A Profile of the Working Poor, 1996*. Bureau of Labor Statistics: Washington, D.C., 1997

percent). Nearly three-fourths of the working poor were white workers, but African American and Hispanic workers continued to experience poverty rates at more than twice the rates of whites. Blacks (11.6 percent) and Hispanics (14.4 percent) with at least six months in the labor force had a far higher poverty rate than whites (5 percent). Younger workers were more likely to be in poverty than older workers. Much of the reason for this is that many younger workers are still in school and work at part-time or entry-level jobs that often do not pay well. (See Table 5.15.)

In general, the lower the educational level, the higher the risk of poverty. Among workers in the labor force for at least half of the year 1996, those with less than a high school diploma had a much higher poverty rate (16.2 percent) than high school graduates (6.3 percent). Far lower poverty rates were reported for workers with an associate degree (3.2 percent) or a four-year college degree (1.5 percent). African American workers, regardless of education levels, had higher poverty rates than white workers. The highest poverty rate (30.6 percent) was for black women workers with less than a high school diploma.

In 1996 families headed by married couples without children were least likely to be poor (1.8 percent), while the presence of children under age 18 increased the married-couple poverty rate to 6 percent. Single women with families were most likely to be living in poverty (26.6 percent), although the poor population included a significant proportion of single men with children (13.7 percent). (See Table 5.16.)

In a family headed by a married couple, there is a greater likelihood that two people are working than with a single-parent family. Two-income families are rarely poor. Only 1.6 percent of families headed by married couples with two wage earners were poor in 1996. Of the 4.1 million working poor families, nearly half were families maintained by women. Working women who were the sole supporters of their families had the highest poverty rate, 26.8 percent. (See Table 5.16.)

Several factors affect the poverty status among working families: the size of the family, the number of workers in the family, the characteristics of the worker, and various labor market problems. The addition of a child puts a financial strain on the family and increases the chances that a parent might have to stay home to care for the child. A child in a single-parent family may work. But children usually work for lower pay and at part-time jobs. In addition, the more education a person has, the better

TABLE 5.16

Primary Families: Poverty Status, Presence of Related Children, and Work Experience of Family Members in the Labor Force for 27 Weeks or More, 1996

(Numbers in thousands)

Characteristic	Total families	At or above poverty level	Below poverty level	Poverty rate[1]
Total primary families	58,087	54,003	4,084	7.0
With related children under 18	33,753	30,226	3,527	10.4
Without children	24,333	23,777	557	2.3
With one member in the labor force	23,307	19,900	3,407	14.6
With two or more members in the labor force	34,780	34,103	677	1.9
With two members	29,026	28,426	599	2.1
With three or more members	5,754	5,676	7 8	1.4
Married-couple families:				
With related children under 18	25,295	23,782	1,512	6.0
Without children	19,778	19,420	358	1.8
With one member in the labor force	14,366	12,982	1,384	9.6
Husband	10,894	9,760	1,134	10.4
Wife	2,763	2,569	194	7.0
Relative	709	653	56	7.9
With two or more members in the labor force	30,706	30,221	486	1.6
With two members	25,770	25,337	433	1.7
With three or more members	4,936	4,884	53	1.1
Families maintained by women:				
With related children under 18	6,637	4,872	1,765	26.6
Without children	3,014	2,869	145	4.8
With one member in the labor force	6,879	5,128	1,751	25.5
Householder	5,689	4,165	1,524	26.8
Relative	1,190	963	227	19.1
With two or more members in the labor force	2,772	2,612	160	5.8
Families maintained by men:				
With related children under 18	1,822	1,572	250	13.7
Without children	1,541	1,488	53	3.5
With one member in the labor force	2,062	1,790	272	13.2
Householder	1,746	1,500	246	14.1
Relative	316	291	26	8.1
With two or more members in the labor force	1,302	1,270	32	2.5

[1] Number below the poverty level as a percent of the total in the labor force for 27 weeks or more.

NOTE: Data relate to primary families with at least one member in the labor force for 27 weeks or more.

SOURCE: *A Profile of the Working Poor, 1996.* Bureau of Labor Statistics: Washington, D.C., 1997

TABLE 5.17

Persons in the Labor Force for 27 Weeks of More: Poverty Status and Labor Market Problems of Full-Time Wage and Salary Workers, 1996

(Numbers in thousands)

Poverty status and labor market problems	Total	At or above poverty level	Below poverty level	Poverty rate[1]
Total, full-time wage and salary workers	100,278	96,377	3,902	3.9
No unemployment, involuntary part-time employment, or low earnings[2]	78,989	78,501	488	0.6
Unemployment only	5,845	5,404	441	7.5
Involuntary part-time employment only	2,374	2,336	38	1.6
Low earnings only	8,324	6,698	1,626	19.5
Unemployment and involuntary part-time employment	1,171	1,078	93	7.9
Unemployment and low earnings	1,986	1,253	733	36.9
Involuntary part-time employment and low earnings	983	742	241	24.5
Unemployment, involuntary part-time employment, and low earnings	606	364	242	39.9

[1] Number below the poverty level as a percent of the total in the labor force for 27 weeks or more.

[2] The low earnings threshold in 1996 was $230.93 per week.

NOTE: Data refer to persons 16 years and over.

SOURCE: *A Profile of the Working Poor, 1996.* Bureau of Labor Statistics: Washington, D.C., 1997

his or her job is likely to pay. Single mothers are more likely to have less education than married women.

Finally, the labor market plays a major role in whether a working family lives in poverty. Quan named three major labor market problems contributing to poverty among workers in 1996—unemployment, low earnings, and involuntary part-time employment. Only 0.6 percent of workers who did not suffer from any of these problems were poor in 1996, while 19.5 percent of low-paid workers were in poverty. Unemployment (7.5 percent) and involuntary part-time work (1.6 percent) were also important reasons. However, it was the combination of two or more factors that had the most devastating effect on families. (See Table 5.17.)

CHAPTER 6
WHO RECEIVES BENEFITS?

AN OVERVIEW OF WELFARE PROGRAM PARTICIPATION

With few exceptions, the demand for welfare assistance has increased sharply in the 1990s. Nonetheless, close to a quarter of the poor received no benefits in 1998. There are several reasons why over one-fourth of those living below the poverty line did not receive the assistance available to them. Some were ineligible because they had assets, such as a car or a savings account, which brought them above permitted limits. Others did not know they were eligible for benefits, while some knew they were eligible but chose not to accept benefits or felt the effort was not worth the small amount of benefits they would receive.

How Many People Receive Benefits

In *Poverty in the United States: 1998* (Washington, D.C., 1999), the Bureau of the Census reported that about 65 million people, or 24 percent of the population, lived in households that received some form of means-tested assistance—assistance that is based on earning below a certain amount. (See Table 6.1.) This number is considerably higher than the 53.2 million people, or 21 percent, who received assistance in 1990.

In 1998, among the 34.4 million people living below the poverty level, almost 24 million, or 69.7 percent, were receiving some form of means-tested aid. (See Table 6.1.)

The Bureau of the Census reported that in 1998 about 20.4 million persons, or 7.5 percent of the population (down from 22.8 million, or 9 percent, in 1990), lived in households that received food stamps. Among the population living below the poverty level, 13.4 million people received food stamps. (See Table 6.2.)

In 1997 Medicaid covered about 34.8 million people (up from 25.3 million in 1990), about 12.8 percent of the population. (See Table 6.3.)

What Type of Households Receive Assistance?

Certain types of households were more likely than others to receive means-tested assistance. Poor families with children under 18 years of age were most likely to receive government assistance. In 1998, 61 percent of poor children (nearly 67 percent of those under 6 years of age) who lived in single female-headed families received assistance. In unrelated subfamilies (two or more people living in the same household who are related to each other but are not related to the householder), 66.4 percent of poor children under the age of 6 received assistance. (See Table 6.1.)

Gender of Welfare Recipients

In 1998 there were somewhat more female than male welfare recipients. (See Table 6.1.) About 35.5 million females received program assistance for at least a short time during 1998. Among poor females, 13.9 million received benefits during some part of the year. About 29.6 million males received some assistance during the period, and 10 million poor males received welfare assistance during the survey.

One reason for the difference was that women are more likely to live in a family without a spouse present. Another reason is that women, on average, earn only 70 percent of what men earn. Age may also play a role in the higher number of women in poverty; there are far more elderly women then men.

USE OVER A PERIOD A TIME

In its *Survey of Income and Program Participation* (SIPP), the Census Bureau periodically surveys sample households over a period of time to measure their economic activity. Among the many areas covered in the 1993–94 survey, the Bureau studied the use of major means-tested programs: Aid to Families with Dependent Children (AFDC), General Assistance, Supplemental Security Income (SSI), Medicaid, Food Stamps, and rent

TABLE 6.1

Ratio of Income to Poverty Threshold for People in Households that Received Means-Tested Assistance, by Age, Sex, and Household Relationship, 1998

[Numbers in thousands. People, families, and unrelated individuals as of March of the following year.]

Characteristic	Total	Under .50		Under 1.00		Under 1.25		Under 1.50		Under 1.75		Under 2.00	
		Number	Percent of total	Number	Percent of total	Number	Percent of total	Number	Percent of total	Number	Percent of total	Number	Percent of total
People In Households That Received Means-Tested Assistance													
Both Sexes													
Total	65,080	8,917	13.7	23,866	36.7	30,574	47.0	36,873	56.7	42,005	64.5	46,445	71.4
Under 18 years	26,353	4,885	18.5	11,489	43.6	14,269	54.1	16,981	64.4	19,000	72.1	20,865	79.2
18 to 24 years	6,623	979	14.8	2,345	35.4	3,009	45.4	3,559	53.7	4,139	62.5	4,540	68.6
25 to 34 years	8,774	1,218	13.9	3,199	36.5	4,099	46.7	4,995	56.9	5,716	65.1	6,358	72.5
35 to 44 years	9,270	960	10.4	2,813	30.3	3,681	39.7	4,580	49.4	5,410	58.4	6,128	66.1
45 to 54 years	5,229	417	8.0	1,429	27.3	1,894	36.2	2,276	43.5	2,620	50.1	2,924	55.9
55 to 59 years	1,798	145	8.0	549	30.5	684	38.0	839	46.6	958	53.2	1,064	59.2
60 to 64 years	1,667	111	6.7	545	32.7	699	41.9	826	49.5	958	57.4	1,034	62.0
65 years and over	5,366	203	3.8	1,496	27.9	2,240	41.7	2,819	52.5	3,205	59.7	3,530	65.8
65 to 74 years	2,907	124	4.3	769	26.4	1,179	40.6	1,489	51.2	1,660	57.1	1,842	63.4
75 years and over	2,460	79	3.2	728	29.6	1,061	43.1	1,330	54.1	1,545	62.8	1,689	68.7
Male													
Total	29,588	3,666	12.4	10,015	33.8	13,021	44.0	15,902	53.7	18,384	62.1	20,534	69.4
Under 18 years	13,374	2,475	18.5	5,751	43.0	7,182	53.7	8,572	64.1	9,670	72.3	10,600	79.3
18 to 24 years	2,899	297	10.3	866	29.9	1,154	39.8	1,407	48.5	1,692	58.4	1,904	65.7
25 to 34 years	3,542	291	8.2	1,022	28.9	1,348	38.0	1,686	47.6	2,009	56.7	2,305	65.1
35 to 44 years	4,086	289	7.1	1,005	24.6	1,377	33.7	1,785	43.7	2,160	52.9	2,519	61.6
45 to 54 years	2,346	152	6.5	570	24.3	800	34.1	970	41.3	1,133	48.3	1,270	54.1
55 to 59 years	769	45	5.8	215	28.0	264	34.3	322	41.8	352	45.7	394	51.2
60 to 64 years	681	44	6.4	188	27.6	248	36.4	298	43.8	365	53.6	408	59.9
65 years and over	1,891	73	3.9	398	21.0	648	34.3	863	45.6	1,004	53.1	1,135	60.0
65 to 74 years	1,162	59	5.1	258	22.2	406	34.9	550	47.4	619	53.3	696	59.9
75 years and over	730	14	2.0	140	19.2	243	33.2	312	42.8	385	52.8	439	60.2
Female													
Total	35,492	5,251	14.8	13,851	39.0	17,553	49.5	20,971	59.1	23,620	66.6	25,911	73.0
Under 18 years	12,979	2,409	18.6	5,738	44.2	7,086	54.6	8,409	64.8	9,330	71.9	10,266	79.1
18 to 24 years	3,724	682	18.3	1,479	39.7	1,856	49.8	2,152	57.8	2,448	65.7	2,636	70.8
25 to 34 years	5,232	927	17.7	2,177	41.6	2,751	52.6	3,309	63.2	3,706	70.8	4,053	77.5
35 to 44 years	5,184	672	13.0	1,809	34.9	2,304	44.4	2,795	53.9	3,250	62.7	3,610	69.6
45 to 54 years	2,882	265	9.2	859	29.8	1,094	38.0	1,306	45.3	1,487	51.6	1,655	57.4
55 to 59 years	1,029	100	9.7	334	32.4	420	40.8	517	50.2	606	58.9	671	65.2
60 to 64 years	987	67	6.8	357	36.2	451	45.7	527	53.4	593	60.1	627	63.5
65 years and over	3,475	130	3.7	1,099	31.6	1,591	45.8	1,956	56.3	2,201	63.3	2,395	68.9
65 to 74 years	1,745	65	3.7	511	29.3	773	44.3	939	53.8	1,041	59.6	1,145	65.6
75 years and over	1,730	65	3.7	588	34.0	818	47.3	1,017	58.8	1,160	67.1	1,250	72.2
Household Relationship													
Total	65,080	8,917	13.7	23,866	36.7	30,574	47.0	36,873	56.7	42,005	64.5	46,445	71.4
65 years and over	5,366	203	3.8	1,496	27.9	2,240	41.7	2,819	52.5	3,205	59.7	3,530	65.8
In families	57,274	7,553	13.2	19,818	34.6	25,603	44.7	31,331	54.7	36,015	62.9	40,100	70.0
Householder	15,285	2,023	13.2	5,262	34.4	6,825	44.6	8,302	54.3	9,577	62.7	10,634	69.6
Under 65 years	13,668	1,975	14.4	4,965	36.3	6,373	46.6	7,662	56.1	8,815	64.5	9,752	71.3
65 years and over	1,618	48	3.0	297	18.4	452	27.9	640	39.6	763	47.2	882	54.5
Related children under 18 years	25,788	4,649	18.0	11,087	43.0	13,824	53.6	16,513	64.0	18,508	71.8	20,338	78.9
Under 6 years	8,402	1,858	22.1	3,987	47.5	4,887	58.2	5,733	68.2	6,259	74.5	6,823	81.2
6 to 17 years	17,386	2,791	16.1	7,100	40.8	8,937	51.4	10,780	62.0	12,249	70.5	13,515	77.7
Own children 18 years and over	5,611	314	5.6	1,161	20.7	1,709	30.5	2,158	38.5	2,625	46.8	2,995	53.4

TABLE 6.1

Ratio of Income to Poverty Threshold for People in Households that Received Means-Tested Assistance, by Age, Sex, and Household Relationship, 1998 [CONTINUED]

[Numbers in thousands. People, families, and unrelated individuals as of March of the following year.]

Characteristic	Total	Under .50		Under 1.00		Under 1.25		Under 1.50		Under 1.75		Under 2.00	
		Number	Percent of total	Number	Percent of total	Number	Percent of total	Number	Percent of total	Number	Percent of total	Number	Percent of total
Household Relationship (cont.)													
In married-couple families	32,000	1,828	5.7	7,436	23.2	10,513	32.9	14,095	44.0	16,909	52.8	19,622	61.3
Husbands	7,679	394	5.1	1,658	21.6	2,365	30.8	3,177	41.4	3,871	50.4	4,504	58.7
Under 65 years	6,666	377	5.6	1,522	22.8	2,126	31.9	2,815	42.2	3,431	51.5	3,988	59.8
65 years and over	1,012	17	1.7	136	13.4	239	23.6	361	35.7	440	43.5	516	51.0
Wives	7,679	394	5.1	1,658	21.6	2,365	30.8	3,177	41.4	3,871	50.4	4,504	58.7
Under 65 years	6,949	385	5.5	1,569	22.6	2,207	31.8	2,940	42.3	3,567	51.3	4,143	59.6
65 years and over	730	9	1.2	89	12.2	158	21.6	237	32.5	304	41.6	361	49.5
Related children under 18 years	13,041	958	7.3	3,662	28.1	5,082	39.0	6,724	51.6	7,907	60.6	9,079	69.6
Under 6 years	4,211	338	8.0	1,310	31.1	1,787	42.4	2,340	55.6	2,653	63.0	3,048	72.4
6 to 17 years	8,830	621	7.0	2,352	26.6	3,295	37.3	4,384	49.7	5,254	59.5	6,031	68.3
Own children 18 years and over	2,594	64	2.5	321	12.4	495	19.1	688	26.5	855	33.0	1,054	40.6
In families with female householder, no spouse present	21,823	5,332	24.4	11,286	51.7	13,715	62.8	15,521	71.1	17,086	78.3	18,103	83.0
Householder	6,527	1,511	23.1	3,269	50.1	4,029	61.7	4,587	70.3	5,084	77.9	5,399	82.7
Under 65 years	5,989	1,483	24.8	3,131	52.3	3,833	64.0	4,325	72.2	4,780	79.8	5,064	84.6
65 years and over	538	28	5.2	138	25.7	196	36.5	261	48.6	304	56.6	335	62.3
Related children under 18 years	11,288	3,484	30.9	6,864	60.8	8,058	71.4	8,932	79.1	9,632	85.3	10,105	89.5
Under 6 years	3,665	1,432	39.1	2,452	66.9	2,822	77.0	3,076	83.9	3,254	88.8	3,354	91.5
6 to 17 years	7,623	2,052	26.9	4,411	57.9	5,236	68.7	5,856	76.8	6,378	83.7	6,751	88.6
Own children 18 years and over	2,656	234	8.8	762	28.7	1,103	41.5	1,336	50.3	1,594	60.0	1,755	66.1
In unrelated subfamilies	715	258	36.1	472	66.0	532	74.4	572	80.0	603	84.3	662	92.5
Under 18 years	422	149	35.4	277	65.7	312	73.9	335	79.5	354	84.0	389	92.2
Under 6 years	152	62	40.6	101	66.0	110	71.8	124	81.4	134	87.6	140	91.9
6 to 17 years	269	87	32.4	176	65.4	202	75.0	211	78.4	221	81.9	249	92.5
18 years and over	293	109	37.2	195	66.6	220	75.1	237	80.7	249	84.8	273	92.9
Unrelated individuals	7,091	1,106	15.6	3,576	50.4	4,440	62.6	4,970	70.1	5,386	76.0	5,684	80.1
Male	3,067	475	15.5	1,370	44.7	1,715	55.9	1,895	61.8	2,076	67.7	2,227	72.6
Under 65 years	2,497	429	17.2	1,147	45.9	1,370	54.9	1,507	60.4	1,655	66.3	1,774	71.0
Living alone	919	117	12.7	526	57.2	623	67.8	679	73.9	733	79.7	751	81.7
65 years and over	570	46	8.0	223	39.1	344	60.4	388	68.1	421	73.9	453	79.5
Living alone	452	17	3.8	161	35.7	269	59.5	298	65.9	326	72.1	358	79.2
Female	4,025	631	15.7	2,206	54.8	2,725	67.7	3,075	76.4	3,310	82.2	3,457	85.9
Under 65 years	2,320	550	23.7	1,399	60.3	1,589	68.5	1,758	75.8	1,887	81.3	1,959	84.4
Living alone	1,243	189	15.2	763	61.4	877	70.6	985	79.2	1,052	84.6	1,091	87.7
65 years and over	1,705	81	4.7	807	47.3	1,137	66.7	1,317	77.3	1,423	83.5	1,498	87.9
Living alone	1,638	73	4.5	775	47.3	1,091	66.6	1,266	77.3	1,372	83.7	1,446	88.3

SOURCE: Joseph Dalaker. *Poverty in the United States: 1998.* Current Population Reports, Series P60-207. U.S. Bureau of the Census: Washington, D.C., 1999

TABLE 6.2

Ratio of Income to Poverty Threshold for People in Households that Received Food Stamps, by Age, Sex, and Household Relationship, 1998

[Numbers in thousands. People, families, and unrelated individuals as of March of the following year.]

Characteristic	Total	Under .50		Under 1.00		Under 1.25		Under 1.50		Under 1.75		Under 2.00	
		Number	Percent of total	Number	Percent of total	Number	Percent of total	Number	Percent of total	Number	Percent of total	Number	Percent of total
People In Households That Received Food Stamps													
Both Sexes													
Total	20,368	5,689	27.9	13,451	66.0	15,687	77.0	17,160	84.2	18,241	89.6	18,827	92.4
Under 18 years	9,685	3,357	34.7	7,025	72.5	8,016	82.8	8,646	89.3	9,029	93.2	9,252	95.5
18 to 24 years	2,132	605	28.4	1,282	60.2	1,515	71.1	1,672	78.4	1,832	85.9	1,915	89.9
25 to 34 years	2,805	771	27.5	1,789	63.8	2,098	74.8	2,321	82.7	2,471	88.1	2,553	91.0
35 to 44 years	2,383	537	22.5	1,409	59.1	1,676	70.3	1,877	78.7	2,057	86.3	2,153	90.3
45 to 54 years	1,273	230	18.1	747	58.7	877	68.9	992	78.0	1,095	86.0	1,123	88.3
55 to 59 years	431	69	15.9	262	60.7	307	71.3	338	78.5	356	82.6	368	85.5
60 to 64 years	449	51	11.3	279	62.2	311	69.4	348	77.5	380	84.6	394	87.7
65 years and over	1,211	69	5.7	658	54.4	887	73.3	966	79.8	1,021	84.4	1,068	88.2
65 to 74 years	683	43	6.2	358	52.4	502	73.5	543	79.6	576	84.3	602	88.1
75 years and over	528	27	5.1	300	56.9	385	73.0	422	80.1	446	84.4	466	88.4
Male													
Total	8,627	2,298	26.6	5,487	63.6	6,454	74.8	7,076	82.0	7,639	88.5	7,904	91.6
Under 18 years	4,851	1,693	34.9	3,486	71.9	4,008	82.6	4,330	89.3	4,548	93.7	4,643	95.7
18 to 24 years	805	171	21.3	432	53.7	517	64.3	582	72.3	675	83.9	710	88.2
25 to 34 years	891	154	17.3	477	53.5	575	64.5	641	72.0	717	80.4	756	84.8
35 to 44 years	860	129	15.0	417	48.5	519	60.4	595	69.3	691	80.3	747	86.9
45 to 54 years	519	87	16.8	293	56.5	356	68.6	405	77.9	450	86.8	464	89.4
55 to 59 years	166	23	13.9	108	65.2	120	72.4	130	78.2	133	79.8	137	82.4
60 to 64 years	158	23	14.7	98	62.1	105	66.7	120	76.1	129	82.0	135	85.3
65 years and over	377	18	4.7	176	46.7	253	67.0	272	72.1	296	78.4	313	82.8
65 to 74 years	246	15	6.2	121	49.0	165	67.1	177	71.8	192	77.9	202	82.0
75 years and over	131	2	1.8	56	42.3	88	66.8	95	72.7	104	79.3	111	84.3
Female													
Total	11,741	3,391	28.9	7,964	67.8	9,233	78.6	10,084	85.9	10,602	90.3	10,923	93.0
Under 18 years	4,834	1,664	34.4	3,538	73.2	4,007	82.9	4,316	89.3	4,481	92.7	4,609	95.3
18 to 24 years	1,327	434	32.7	851	64.1	997	75.2	1,090	82.1	1,157	87.2	1,206	90.9
25 to 34 years	1,914	617	32.3	1,313	68.6	1,524	79.6	1,680	87.8	1,755	91.7	1,797	93.9
35 to 44 years	1,523	407	26.7	993	65.1	1,157	75.9	1,281	84.1	1,366	89.7	1,406	92.3
45 to 54 years	754	143	18.9	454	60.2	521	69.1	588	78.0	644	85.5	659	87.5
55 to 59 years	265	46	17.2	153	57.9	187	70.7	208	78.6	223	84.3	231	87.4
60 to 64 years	291	28	9.5	181	62.2	206	70.8	228	78.2	250	86.0	259	89.1
65 years and over	834	52	6.2	482	57.8	634	76.1	694	83.3	726	87.1	756	90.7
65 to 74 years	437	27	6.2	238	54.3	337	77.0	367	83.9	384	87.9	400	91.5
75 years and over	396	25	6.2	244	61.7	298	75.1	327	82.5	341	86.1	356	89.8
Household Relationship													
Total	20,368	5,689	27.9	13,451	66.0	15,687	77.0	17,160	84.2	18,241	89.6	18,827	92.4
65 years and over	1,211	69	5.7	658	54.4	887	73.3	966	79.8	1,021	84.4	1,068	88.2
In families	17,788	5,115	28.8	11,637	65.4	13,644	76.7	14,985	84.2	15,963	89.7	16,488	92.7
Householder	4,732	1,346	28.4	3,096	65.4	3,656	77.3	4,002	84.6	4,268	90.2	4,402	93.0
Under 65 years	4,362	1,325	30.4	2,932	67.2	3,429	78.6	3,736	85.7	3,980	91.2	4,089	93.7
65 years and over	370	21	5.6	165	44.6	228	61.6	266	71.9	288	77.9	312	84.5
Related children under 18 years	9,491	3,274	34.5	6,858	72.3	7,849	82.7	8,474	89.3	8,844	93.2	9,058	95.4
Under 6 years	3,607	1,343	37.2	2,620	72.6	2,981	82.6	3,226	89.4	3,343	92.7	3,451	95.7
6 to 17 years	5,884	1,931	32.8	4,238	72.0	4,868	82.7	5,248	89.2	5,501	93.5	5,607	95.3
Own children 18 years and over	1,353	197	14.5	617	45.6	798	59.0	917	67.8	1,058	78.2	1,129	83.4

TABLE 6.2

Ratio of Income to Poverty Threshold for People in Households that Received Food Stamps, by Age, Sex, and Household Relationship, 1998 [CONTINUED]

[Numbers in thousands. People, families, and unrelated individuals as of March of the following year.]

Characteristic	Total	Under .50		Under 1.00		Under 1.25		Under 1.50		Under 1.75		Under 2.00	
		Number	Percent of total	Number	Percent of total	Number	Percent of total	Number	Percent of total	Number	Percent of total	Number	Percent of total
People In Households That Received Food Stamps													
Household Relationship (cont.)													
In married-couple families	6,174	899	14.6	3,473	56.3	4,214	68.2	4,886	79.1	5,328	86.3	5,569	90.2
Husbands	1,389	188	13.5	765	55.1	942	67.8	1,085	78.1	1,195	86.1	1,257	90.5
Under 65 years	1,232	185	15.0	698	56.7	842	68.4	975	79.1	1,077	87.4	1,128	91.6
65 years and over	157	3	1.7	67	42.8	100	63.6	110	70.3	119	75.5	129	82.0
Wives	1,389	188	13.5	765	55.1	942	67.8	1,085	78.1	1,195	86.1	1,257	90.5
Under 65 years	1,275	185	14.5	720	56.4	872	68.4	1,007	79.0	1,111	87.1	1,163	91.2
65 years and over	114	3	2.3	46	40.1	70	61.7	78	68.3	84	74.2	93	81.9
Related children under 18 years	2,798	474	16.9	1,712	61.2	2,049	73.2	2,359	84.3	2,537	90.7	2,627	93.9
Under 6 years	1,098	180	16.4	667	60.7	795	72.4	917	83.5	973	88.6	1,024	93.2
6 to 17 years	1,700	294	17.3	1,045	61.5	1,254	73.8	1,442	84.8	1,564	92.0	1,603	94.3
Own children 18 years and over	409	43	10.5	167	40.8	201	49.2	243	59.4	277	67.7	301	73.5
In families with female householder, no spouse present	10,664	3,998	37.5	7,613	71.4	8,799	82.5	9,401	88.2	9,848	92.3	10,059	94.3
Householder	3,063	1,098	35.8	2,174	71.0	2,527	82.5	2,712	88.5	2,842	92.8	2,899	94.6
Under 65 years	2,888	1,083	37.5	2,094	72.5	2,420	83.8	2,579	89.3	2,697	93.4	2,742	94.9
65 years and over	175	15	8.4	80	45.6	107	61.0	132	75.6	144	82.4	156	89.3
Related children under 18 years	6,235	2,685	43.1	4,842	77.7	5,464	87.6	5,746	92.2	5,917	94.9	5,996	96.2
Under 6 years	2,313	1,118	48.3	1,832	79.2	2,049	88.6	2,161	93.4	2,213	95.7	2,244	97.0
6 to 17 years	3,922	1,567	39.9	3,010	76.7	3,415	87.1	3,585	91.4	3,704	94.4	3,753	95.7
Own children 18 years and over	870	145	16.7	421	48.3	564	64.7	637	73.2	732	84.1	774	88.9
In unrelated subfamilies	232	83	35.6	192	82.4	192	82.4	201	86.6	218	93.8	232	100.0
Under 18 years	144	47	32.6	118	81.8	118	81.8	124	85.9	134	93.2	144	100.0
Under 6 years	59	23		47		47		49		57		59	
6 to 17 years	85	24	28.3	71	83.0	71	83.0	74	87.4	77	90.5	85	100.0
18 years and over	88	36	40.5	74	83.4	74	83.4	77	87.6	84	94.7	88	100.0
Unrelated individuals	2,347	491	20.9	1,623	69.1	1,851	78.9	1,973	84.1	2,059	87.7	2,107	89.8
Male	1,032	228	22.0	650	63.0	737	71.4	791	76.7	837	81.0	866	83.9
Under 65 years	908	216	23.8	561	61.7	625	68.8	678	74.6	723	79.6	753	82.9
Living alone	316	43	13.7	248	78.7	279	88.5	293	93.0	298	94.3	298	94.3
65 years and over	124	12	9.5	89	72.0	112	90.4	113	91.5	113	91.5	113	91.5
Living alone	98	5	5.4	72	73.5	90	92.1	91	93.5	91	93.5	91	93.5
Female	1,315	264	20.0	973	74.0	1,114	84.8	1,182	89.9	1,223	93.0	1,240	94.4
Under 65 years	883	241	27.2	650	73.6	715	81.0	772	87.4	806	91.3	819	92.8
Living alone	544	92	16.9	407	74.9	448	82.5	487	89.7	512	94.1	517	95.2
65 years and over	431	23	5.3	323	74.9	399	92.5	410	95.1	416	96.5	421	97.6
Living alone	413	23	5.6	312	75.7	387	93.8	395	95.8	401	97.2	406	98.4

SOURCE: Joseph Dalaker. *Poverty in the United States: 1998*. Current Population Reports, Series P60-207. U.S. Bureau of the Census: Washington, D.C., 1999

TABLE 6.3

Unduplicated Number of Recipients, Total Vendor Payments, and Average Amounts, by Type of Eligibility Category, Fiscal Years 1972–97[1,2]

Fiscal year	Total	Aged 65 or older	Blind	Permanent and total disability	Dependent children under age 21	Adults in families with dependent children	Other
				Number (in thousands)			
1972	17,606	3,318	108	1,625	7,841	3,137	1,576
1975	22,007	3,615	109	2,355	9,598	4,529	1,800
1980	21,605	3,440	92	2,819	9,333	4,877	1,499
1985	21,814	3,061	80	2,937	9,757	5,518	1,214
1986	22,515	3,140	82	3,100	10,029	5,647	1,362
1987	23,109	3,224	85	3,296	10,168	5,599	1,418
1988	22,907	3,159	86	3,401	10,037	5,503	1,343
1989	23,511	3,132	95	3,496	10,318	5,717	1,175
1990	25,255	3,202	83	3,635	11,220	6,010	1,105
1991	28,280	3,359	85	3,983	13,415	6,778	658
1992	30,926	3,742	84	4,378	15,104	6,954	664
1993	33,432	3,863	84	4,932	16,285	7,505	763
1994	35,053	4,035	87	5,372	17,194	7,586	779
1995	36,282	4,119	92	5,767	17,164	7,604	1,537
1996	36,118	4,285	95	6,126	16,739	7,127	1,746
1997	34,872	3,955	...	6,129	15,266	6,803	2,719
				Amount (in millions)			
1972	$6,300	$1,925	$45	$1,354	$1,139	$962	$875
1975	12,242	4,358	93	3,052	2,186	2,062	492
1980	23,311	8,739	124	7,497	3,123	3,231	596
1985	37,508	14,096	249	13,203	4,414	4,746	798
1986	41,005	15,097	277	14,635	5,135	4,880	980
1987	45,050	16,037	309	16,507	5,508	5,592	1,078
1988	48,710	17,135	344	18,250	5,848	5,883	1,198
1989	54,500	18,558	409	20,476	6,892	6,897	1,268
1990	64,859	21,508	434	23,969	9,100	8,590	1,257
1991	77,048	25,453	475	27,798	11,690	10,439	1,193
1992	90,814	29,078	530	33,326	14,491	12,185	1,204
1993	101,709	31,554	589	38,065	16,504	13,605	1,391
1994	108,270	33,618	644	41,654	17,302	13,585	1,467
1995	120,141	36,527	848	48,570	17,976	13,511	2,708
1996	121,685	36,947	869	51,196	17,544	12,275	2,746
1997	124,430	37,721	...	54,130	15,658	12,307	4,612
				Average amount			
1972	$358	$580	$417	$833	$145	$307	$555
1975	556	1,205	850	1,296	228	455	273
1980	1,079	2,540	1,358	2,659	335	663	398
1985	1,719	4,605	3,104	4,496	452	860	658
1986	1,821	4,808	3,401	4,721	512	864	719
1987	1,949	4,975	3,644	5,008	542	999	761
1988	2,126	5,425	4,005	5,366	583	1,069	891
1989	2,318	5,926	4,317	5,858	668	1,206	1,079
1990	2,568	6,717	5,212	6,595	811	1,429	1,138
1991	2,725	7,577	5,572	6,979	871	1,540	1,813
1992	2,936	7,770	6,298	7,612	959	1,752	1,813
1993	3,042	8,168	7,036	7,717	1,013	1,813	1,824
1994	3,089	8,331	7,412	7,755	1,006	1,791	1,884
1995	3,311	8,868	9,256	8,422	1,047	1,777	1,762
1996	3,369	8,622	9,143	8,357	1,048	1,722	1,635
1997	3,568	9,538	...	8,832	1,026	1,809	3,597

[1]Fiscal year 1977 began in October 1976 and was the first year of the new federal fiscal cycle. Before 1977, the fiscal year began in July.

[2]Beginning in fiscal year 1980, recipients' categories do not add to unduplicated total because of the small number of recipients that are in more than one category during the year.

SOURCE: *Annual Statistical Supplement, 1999.* Social Security Administration: Washington, D.C., 1999

subsidies. In "Who Gets Assistance?" (*Current Population Reports*, July 1998), the Bureau of the Census reported some of the highlights of the SIPP.

According to the survey, 15.2 percent of those living in the United States, about 40 million people, received some type of assistance during an average month in both 1993 and 1994. This average monthly participation rate increased considerably from the 11.4 percent, or 27.4 million people, in 1987. (See Figure 6.1.) The increase in the monthly participation rate was consistent with the increase in the poverty rate, from 12.8 percent between

1987 and 1989, a strong economic period, to 14.5 percent in 1994.

Most benefit recipients, however, participated in means-tested programs on a short-term basis only. About 10 percent, primarily children and the elderly, received benefits for all 24 months of the 1993–94 period of the survey.

Racial and Ethnic Characteristics of Welfare Recipients

In an average month in 1994, 9.4 percent of the 39 million recipients in means-tested programs were white and not of Hispanic origin; 36 percent were African American; and 31.7 percent were Hispanic (persons of Hispanic origin can be of any race). (See Table 6.4.) Though the median length of time participants received benefits from means-tested programs was 7.4 months, the median for blacks (7.9 months) was slightly longer than for non-Hispanic whites (7.2 months) or for Hispanics (7.4 months). (See Table 6.5.) Moreover, the median monthly benefit for blacks ($542) was higher than the median benefits for all groups ($476). (See Table 6.4.) This seemed to result from having relatively lower incomes and larger families.

Age of Welfare Recipients

Over one-fourth (26.5 percent) of children under 18 years old received assistance at some time during 1994. Approximately 1 out of 8 of the elderly (11.7 percent) received assistance. (See Table 6.4.) However, those who were 65 years old and over tended to receive much lower median monthly benefits ($200 in 1994) than younger recipients ($443 for ages 18 to 64). (See Table 6.4.)

Family Relationships of Welfare Recipients

The 1993–94 SIPP found that only 8.9 percent of recipients who received benefits for some part of 1994 were living in families headed by married couples. In contrast, 44.3 percent of all individuals in female-headed families with no spouse present received benefits. About 12.4 percent of unrelated individuals received benefits of some kind and for some duration in 1994. (See Table 6.4.)

In addition, female-headed families were likely to receive higher median monthly benefits in 1994 ($599) than families headed by married couples ($380) or individuals ($188). (See Table 6.4.) This is probably because their earned income is generally much lower than those of the other two groups.

Likewise, female-headed families experienced longer spells of receiving benefits—a median duration of 9.8 months, compared to 6 months for families headed by married couples. But unrelated individuals had the longest spells of receiving benefits at 10.5 months. (See Table 6.5.)

Education Levels of Welfare Recipients

The SIPP found a strong correlation between a low level of education and receipt of welfare benefits. (See

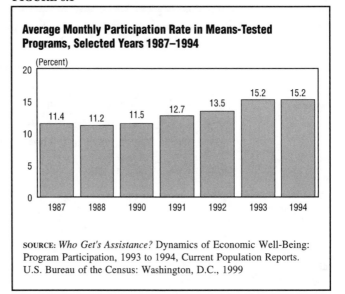

FIGURE 6.1

Average Monthly Participation Rate in Means-Tested Programs, Selected Years 1987–1994

source: *Who Get's Assistance?* Dynamics of Economic Well-Being: Program Participation, 1993 to 1994, Current Population Reports. U.S. Bureau of the Census: Washington, D.C., 1999

Table 6.4.) Adults who did not graduate from high school were most likely to receive assistance:

- Those who did not finish high school—25.6 percent;

- Those who were high school graduates—10.5 percent;

- Those with one or more years of college—4.5 percent.

The median duration of welfare assistance to recipients without a high school diploma (11 months) is much longer than the median for high school graduates (7.2 months) and people with some college experience (7.1 months). (See Table 6.5.)

Employment Status of Welfare Recipients

More than one-quarter (26.9 percent) of the unemployed and more than one-fifth (21.3) of those individuals not in the labor force received welfare assistance in an average month of 1994. On the other hand, only 3.8 percent of full-time employees and 9.2 percent of part-time workers received these benefits. The median monthly benefit from means-tested programs was $446 for unemployed recipients. (See Table 6.4.)

Regional Relationship to Welfare

In addition, the survey found that people living outside metropolitan areas were more likely to receive welfare assistance than those living in metropolitan areas. Furthermore, the participation rates are significantly higher for central city residents, compared to non-central city residents in metropolitan areas (See Table 6.4.):

- 22.4 percent of central city residents received aid.

- 16.6 percent of non-metropolitan residents received aid.

- 9.5 percent of non-central city residents received aid.

TABLE 6.4

Average Monthly Participation Rates and Median Family Benefits by Selected Characteristics, 1993 and 1994

Characteristic	Any means-tested program[1]		AFDC/GA		SSI		Food stamps		Medicaid		Housing assistance		1993		1994	
													Median	Standard error	Median	Standard error
	1993	1994	1993	1994	1993	1994	1993	1994	1993	1994	1993	1994				
Total number of recipients[3]	39,162	39,514	14,675	14,438	4,841	5,106	25,713	25,383	27,984	29,332	13,044	12,206	(X)	(X)	(X)	(X)
As percent of the population	15.2	15.2	5.7	5.5	1.9	2.0	10.0	9.7	10.9	11.3	5.1	4.7	485	4.0	476	3.0
Race and Hispanic Origin[4]																
White	11.7	11.8	3.8	3.7	1.4	1.5	7.4	7.2	8.1	8.5	3.5	3.3	444	4.5	435	3.5
Not of Hispanic origin	9.4	9.4	2.8	2.6	1.3	1.3	5.7	5.4	6.4	6.8	2.8	2.6	400	6.0	399	5.0
Black	36.6	36.0	16.4	16.4	4.5	4.7	26.0	25.6	26.8	27.5	14.9	13.2	560	4.0	542	9.0
Hispanic origin	32.3	31.7	13.7	12.9	3.0	2.9	22.9	21.9	23.4	23.0	10.9	10.0	557	18.0	556	12.5
Not of Hispanic origin	13.3	13.2	4.8	4.7	1.8	1.8	8.5	8.3	9.4	9.9	4.4	4.1	466	4.5	460	3.0
Age																
Under 18 years	26.2	26.5	13.2	12.9	0.0	0.0	19.6	19.3	21.2	22.1	8.0	7.4	604	4.5	587	6.0
18 to 64 years	11.0	10.8	3.4	3.3	2.0	2.1	6.9	6.6	6.8	7.1	3.8	3.4	444	2.0	443	3.0
65 years and over	12.0	11.7	0.2	0.2	5.5	5.4	4.2	4.1	8.1	8.0	5.2	5.2	204	3.5	200	5.0
Sex																
Male	13.0	13.0	4.5	4.3	1.4	1.4	8.4	8.2	8.8	9.2	4.4	3.9	490	7.5	479	5
Female	17.2	17.3	6.8	6.7	2.4	2.5	11.5	11.2	12.8	13.2	5.7	5.4	483	5	473	5.5
Educational Attainment (people 18 years old and over)																
Less than 4 years of high school	25.8	25.6	6.5	5.9	7.5	7.7	15.3	14.8	17.5	17.8	9.0	8.4	432	7	433	5.5
High school graduate, no college	10.5	10.5	2.9	3.0	1.9	2.0	6.2	6.1	6.4	6.7	3.6	3.5	396	10	386	10.5
1 or more years of college	4.6	4.5	1.2	1.2	0.8	0.9	2.4	2.3	2.7	2.8	1.9	1.7	420	13	433	11
Disability Status (people 15 to 64 years old)																
With a work disability	25.0	25.5	6.4	6.3	9.3	10.0	15.1	14.6	18.9	20.0	6.6	6.5	459	5	454	7
With no work disability	8.7	8.5	3.2	3.1	0.3	0.4	5.7	5.6	4.8	5.0	3.4	3.0	466	9.5	448	7
Residence																
Metropolitan	14.7	14.7	5.9	5.9	1.7	1.9	9.5	9.4	10.6	11.1	5.3	4.9	517	5.5	521	6
Central city	23.0	22.4	10.4	9.9	2.7	2.7	15.8	15.2	17.0	17.0	9.1	8.3	574	7.5	564	5.5
Noncentral city	9.3	9.5	3.1	3.2	1.1	1.3	5.5	5.5	6.5	7.0	2.9	2.6	444	5	447	8
Nonmetropolitan	17.0	16.6	4.8	4.4	2.4	2.3	11.5	10.7	11.6	11.9	4.2	3.9	401	9.5	354	7
Region																
Northeast	14.8	14.6	6.4	6.0	1.9	1.9	8.9	8.6	10.9	10.9	5.9	5.6	599	11	610	13
Midwest	12.5	12.6	5.4	5.3	1.2	1.3	8.7	8.5	9.1	9.5	4.6	4.4	538	9.5	486	5
South	16.5	16.4	4.5	4.3	2.4	2.5	11.5	11.4	10.5	11.1	5.0	4.2	377	2	368	5.5
West	16.7	16.8	7.3	7.4	2.0	2.0	10.0	9.6	13.4	13.9	4.9	4.9	630	7	624	7.5
Family Status																
In families	15.6	15.6	6.5	6.4	1.4	1.5	10.8	10.6	11.4	11.8	4.8	4.4	531	6	512	6.5
In married-couple families	9.1	8.9	2.2	2.2	0.9	0.9	5.5	5.2	5.8	6.1	2.5	2.0	377	2	380	4.5
In families with a female householder, no spouse present	44.3	44.3	26.3	24.9	3.4	3.4	34.9	33.8	36.1	36.3	15.4	15.0	614	4	599	3
Unrelated individuals	12.8	12.4	0.7	0.6	4.5	4.7	5.2	4.9	7.7	7.9	6.3	6.1	169	13.5	188	12.5
Employment and Labor Force Status (people 18 years old and over)																
Employed full time	4.0	3.8	0.4	0.5	0.2	0.3	1.8	1.7	1.2	1.4	1.8	1.6	235	6.5	239	10
Employed part time	8.6	9.2	1.8	2.0	0.9	1.1	4.9	5.4	4.6	5.4	3.1	3.0	297	6.5	299	6
Unemployed	26.6	26.9	10.4	11.3	1.9	1.5	19.9	20.2	16.0	17.0	9.1	9.0	455	6.5	446	10.5
Not in labor force	21.3	21.3	6.3	6.0	6.9	7.1	12.6	12.3	15.9	16.1	7.1	6.7	460	3.5	458	3.5

TABLE 6.4

Average Monthly Participation Rates and Median Family Benefits by Selected Characteristics, 1993 and 1994 [CONTINUED]

Characteristic	Program participation rates (percent)												Monthly family benefits[2] (dollars)			
	Any means-tested program[1]		AFDC/GA		SSI		Food stamps		Medicaid		Housing assistance		1993		1994	
	1993	1994	1993	1994	1993	1994	1993	1994	1993	1994	1993	1994	Median	Standard error	Median	Standard error
Marital Status (people 18 years old and over)																
Married	6.6	6.2	1.4	1.3	1.0	1.1	3.9	3.7	3.5	3.5	2.1	1.7	604	7.5	587	9
Separated, divorced, or widowed	19.6	19.6	5.0	4.8	5.9	6.1	11.2	11.1	13.6	13.9	7.4	7.3	358	10.5	359	8.5
Never married	15.6	15.6	5.1	4.9	3.6	3.8	8.9	8.6	10.5	11.0	6.0	5.6	363	11.5	371	9.5
Family Income-to-Poverty Ratio																
Under 1.00	60.5	60.3	29.7	28.3	6.2	6.7	49.6	48.3	47.0	47.7	20.8	20.0	558	6.5	541	6.5
1.00 and over	6.7	7.0	1.2	1.4	1.1	1.1	2.6	2.8	4.1	4.6	2.1	1.9	349	11.5	364	8

X Not applicable.

[1]Means-tested programs include AFDC, general assistance, SSI, food stamps, medicaid, and housing assistance.

[2]Median monthly family benefits include AFDC, general assistance, SSI, and food stamps only.

[3]In thousands.

[4]Hispanics may be of any race.

SOURCE: *Who Get's Assistance?* Dynamics of Economic Well-Being: Program Participation, 1993 to 1994, Current Population Reports. U.S. Bureau of the Census: Washington, D.C., 1999

By region, welfare participation rates ranged from 1 in 8 inhabitants in the Midwest to 1 in 6 in the South (See Table 6.4.):

- 16.4 percent of Southern residents received aid.

- 16.8 percent of Western residents received aid.

- 14.6 percent of Northeastern residents received aid.

- 12.6 percent of Midwestern residents received aid.

Poor versus Non-poor Welfare Recipients

As would be expected, over half (60.3 percent) of the poor received assistance in 1994, compared to just 6.7 percent of the non-poor. (See Table 6.4.) In addition, the poor received more months of support (10.1) than the median of 9.6 months of assistance for the non-poor. (See Table 6.5.)

Participation Rates for Welfare Programs

Medicaid was the most used welfare program. In 1994 the monthly participation rate for Medicaid was 11.3 percent, higher then any of the other means-tested programs. The 1994 monthly average for food stamp recipients was 9.7 percent and for AFDC (Aid to Families with Dependent Children) or General Assistance, 5.5 percent. About 4.7 percent of the nation received housing assistance during an average month, while 2 percent received SSI (Supplemental Security Income). (See Fig-

ure 6.2.) This was the same pattern for persons who participated in these programs all 24 months of the 1993–94 period—the most receiving Medicaid and the least getting SSI. (See Table 6.4.)

OVERLAPPING SERVICES

Not surprisingly, poor individuals who receive one form of social welfare are likely to qualify for and receive others. For example, during 1995, 31 percent of those people receiving AFDC lived in public or subsidized housing, about 63 percent received free or reduced school meals, about 87 percent received food stamps, and almost all (97 percent) were on Medicaid. Similarly, among SSI recipients, 50 percent received food stamps, 25 percent received free or reduced school meals, 24 percent lived in public or subsidized rental housing, and 100 percent were on Medicaid. About 14 percent of those receiving Social Security and Medicare were also on Medicaid. (See Table 6.6.)

At the same time, among the households receiving food stamps, half (48.9 percent) received AFDC, 27.6 percent received SSI, 25.6 percent received Social Security, and 22.5 percent were on Medicare. (The figures do not add up to 100 percent because some people received more than one benefit.) About 42 percent of those receiving WIC (Special Supplemental Nutrition Program for Women, Infants, and Children) also got AFDC. The largest proportion of those living in public or subsidized

TABLE 6.5

Median Duration of Participation and Standard Errors by Program, 1993 and 1994

Characteristic	Any means-tested program[1] Median	Standard error	AFDC/GA Median	Standard error	SSI Median	Standard error	Food stamps Median	Standard error	Medicaid Median	Standard error	Housing assistance Median	Standard error
All persons	7.4	0.22218	8.3	0.79405	(X)	(X)	8.2	1.00416	8.0	0.18135	16.1	1.31521
Race and Hispanic Origin[2]												
White	7.3	0.24837	7.6	0.52661	(X)	(X)	7.6	0.40906	7.9	0.21114	11.8	1.0888
Not of Hispanic origin	7.2	0.30979	7.2	0.66564	(X)	(X)	7.6	0.5598	8.4	2.01193	11.0	1.06865
Black	7.9	0.30321	11.2	0.55659	(X)	(X)	11.2	0.4974	9.0	1.02362	18.0	1.13099
Hispanic origin	7.4	0.39864	8.6	1.29495	(X)	(X)	7.6	0.51089	7.5	0.33358	(X)	(X)
Not of Hispanic origin	7.4	0.26354	8.1	0.97106	(X)	(X)	8.6	0.1124	8.6	1.2717	14.0	1.84038
Age[3]												
Under 18 years	7.0	0.29579	9.8	1.55256	(X)	(X)	10.1	1.92349	7.4	0.22398	19.9	2.18595
18 to 64 years	7.5	0.30135	7.6	0.47854	(X)	(X)	7.5	0.35678	11.1	0.42482	11.5	0.88704
65 years and over	19.5	3.35537	(B)	(B)	(X)	(X)	14.4	3.94844	(X)	(X)	(X)	(X)
Sex												
Male	7.1	0.27064	7.3	0.55756	(X)	(X)	7.5	0.39061	7.7	0.24285	12.6	21.0952
Female	7.8	0.3638	9.8	1.73589	(X)	(X)	9.9	1.24348	8.9	1.40133	18.2	1.47466
Educational Attainment (people 18 years old and over)												
Less than 4 years of high school	11.0	0.70525	7.4	0.62194	(X)	(X)	8.7	2.20665	12.7	2.66229	21.5	4.58025
High school graduate, no college	7.2	0.4382	8.5	2.1211	(X)	(X)	7.4	0.54764	11.5	1.15493	11.0	2.10206
1 or more years of college	7.1	0.60594	6.8	6.2284	12.8	8.17021	7.1	0.77092	8.6	2.9504	9.0	6.27684
Disability Status (people 15 to 64 years old)												
With a work disability	11.1	1.31667	7.5	0.69958	(X)	(X)	9.7	2.36988	17.8	7.42448	21.9	4.68369
With no work disability	7.0	0.33104	7.5	0.5768	(X)	(X)	7.3	0.39049	7.8	0.34871	8.0	0.79504
Residence												
Metropolitan	7.6	0.25709	8.9	1.00242	(X)	(X)	10.0	1.70288	8.2	1.44454	18.6	1.38412
Central city	7.7	0.33959	9.2	1.47948	(X)	(X)	11.2	0.6975	9.4	6.25239	19.9	1.79573
Noncentral city	7.4	0.38586	8.4	1.57093	(X)	(X)	8.4	1.15938	8.0	0.29192	11.4	1.13945
Nonmetropolitan	6.7	1.31011	7.0	4.55103	(X)	(X)	6.8	1.07261	7.8	0.40092	7.8	0.99204
Region												
Northeast	7.3	0.44999	8.0	0.54801	25.6	2.28723	10.6	3.71621	7.7	0.34646	(X)	(X)
Midwest	6.0	0.98197	8.1	1.64662	(X)	(X)	7.7	0.86382	9.8	1.58659	13.1	3.66224
South	7.5	0.42478	7.8	0.8718	(X)	(X)	8.6	1.13991	7.8	0.33785	7.0	1.10906
West	7.7	0.3904	11.5	1.75971	(X)	(X)	7.7	0.58606	8.8	3.4856	(X)	(X)
Family Status												
In families	7.3	0.22602	8.6	0.81977	(X)	(X)	8.0	1.03657	7.8	0.18941	16.3	1.23242
In married-couple families	6.0	0.2385	9.0	0.82206	(X)	(X)	7.2	1.37234	7.5	0.23022	7.5	1.26258
In families with a female householder, no spouse present	9.8	1.871	11.0	0.59151	(X)	(X)	11.7	0.71355	10.5	1.70927	(X)	(X)
Unrelated individuals	10.5	1.95171	4.0	0.95566	(X)	(X)	9.9	3.12797	20.5	5.90563	14.3	2.38853
Employment and Labor Force Status (people 18 years old and over)												
Employed full time	4.3	0.99373	3.9	0.18634	3.9	0.24163	4.8	0.92289	7.2	0.42438	5.2	2.03562
Employed part time	9.1	2.39752	7.1	4.37907	(X)	(X)	6.2	2.27387	11.9	0.62936	11.5	1.34208
Unemployed	7.4	0.6129	8.1	1.11922	(X)	(X)	7.5	0.66937	8.7	1.30151	13.9	2.53526
Not in labor force	11.8	0.74419	10.4	20.8445	(X)	(X)	11.1	0.72093	15.2	1.06796	(X)	(X)
Family Income-to-Poverty Ratio												
Under 1.00	10.1	1.08174	9.1	1.26663	(X)	(X)	10.5	1.02283	11.4	0.3862	(X)	(X)
1.00 and over	9.6	0.90115	7.4	0.51679	(X)	(X)	6.8	0.74421	7.2	0.2262	7.1	0.93348

B Base less than 200,000. X Not applicable.

[1] Means-tested programs include AFDC, general assistance, SSI, food stamps, medicaid, and housing assistance.

[2] Hispanics may be of any race.

[3] Age, educational attainment, and other variables are measured at the time the spells begin, excluding people already on programs at the start of the survey.

SOURCE: *Who Get's Assistance?* Dynamics of Economic Well-Being: Program Participation, 1993 to 1994, Current Population Reports. U.S. Bureau of the Census: Washington, D.C., 1999

FIGURE 6.2

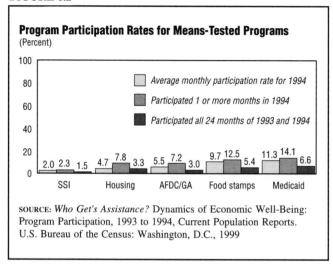

Program Participation Rates for Means-Tested Programs
(Percent)

SOURCE: *Who Get's Assistance?* Dynamics of Economic Well-Being: Program Participation, 1993 to 1994, Current Population Reports. U.S. Bureau of the Census: Washington, D.C., 1999

TABLE 6.7

Percent of Recipients in Other Major Federal Assistance Programs Receiving Assistance Under Programs Within the Jurisdiction of the Committee on Ways and Means, 1995

Ways and Means assistance program	Other assistance program					
	Food stamps	WIC	Free or reduced school meals	Public or subsidized rental housing	Medicaid	VA compensation or pensions
AFDC	48.9	41.7	30.3	28.7	35.6	1.6
SSI	27.6	9.3	11.9	22.0	36.1	6.7
Social Security	25.6	9.9	11.4	37.6	30.6	59.3
Unemployment compensation	2.5	3.6	3.8	1.8	2.9	1.6
Medicare	22.5	5.8	6.8	36.2	28.4	57.7
Number of households receiving benefits (in thousands)	8,298	2,757	9,681	5,031	12,685	2,465

Note.—Table shows households in the first quarter of 1995. Table reads that 48.9 percent of food stamp recipient households receive AFDC. SSI recipients living in California receive a higher SSI payment in lieu of food stamps, and thus are not included in the food stamp percentages.

SOURCE: U.S. Bureau of the Census.

---

rental housing were older Americans receiving Social Security or Medicare. Over one-third of the Medicaid recipients received other benefits as well. (See Table 6.7.)

Between 1984 and 1995 there were fluctuations in the percentage of AFDC and SSI households who received other benefits. But basically the coverage for all benefits, except VA (veterans) compensation or pensions, increased. However, the proportion of AFDC recipients living in public or subsidized rental housing increased dramatically from 19.4 percent in 1987 to 34.7 percent in 1990 but then dropped to 31.1 percent in 1995. (See Table 6.8.)

TABLE 6.6

Percent of Recipients in Programs Within the Jurisdiction of the Committee on Ways and Means Receiving Assistance from Other Major Federal Assistance Programs, 1995

Other assistance program	Ways and Means assistance program				
	AFDC	SSI	Social Security	Unemployment compensation	Medicare
Food stamps	87.2	50.0	7.7	9.1	7.4
WIC	24.7	5.6	1.0	4.4	0.6
Medicaid	97.2	100.0	14 0	16.2	14.3
Free or reduced-price school meals	63.1	25.2	4.0	16.5	2.6
Public or subsidized rental housing	31.1	24.1	6.8	4.1	7.2
VA compensation or pensions	0.8	3.6	5.3	1.7	5.6
Number of households receiving benefits (in thousands)	4,652	4,580	27,654	2,246	25,271

Note: Table shows number of households in the first quarter of 1995. Table reads that 87.2 percent of AFDC households, also receive food stamps. SSI recipients living in California receive a higher SSI payment in lieu of food stamps, and thus are not included in the food stamp percentages.

SOURCE: U.S. Bureau of the Census.

TABLE 6.8

Percent of Households Receiving AFDC or SSI and also Receiving Assistance from Other Programs for Selected Time Periods

Assistance program	Year						
	1984	1987	1990	1992	1993	1994	1995
AFDC:							
Food stamps	81.4	81.7	82.7	86.2	88.9	88.3	87.2
WIC	15.3	18.6	18.7	21.5	18.5	21.4	24.7
Free or reduced-price school meals	49.2	55.6	52.7	55.5	56.9	57.5	63.1
Public or subsidized rental housing	23.0	19.4	34.7	29.5	33.1	30.3	31.1
Medicaid	93.2	95.5	97.6	96.2	97.6	96.4	97.2
VA compensation or pensions	2.8	1.9	1.3	1.9	1.1	1.1	0.8
Number of households receiving benefits (in thousands)	3,585	3,527	3,434	4,057	4,831	4,906	4,652
SSI:							
Food stamps	46.5	39.7	41.3	46.2	48.0	50.1	50.0
WIC	2.5	2.5	3.0	4.3	3.7	5.4	5.6
Free or reduced-price school meals	12.7	11.9	15.3	18.2	21.3	23.8	25.2
Public or subsidized rental housing	21.6	20.0	21.4	23.8	23.9	24.9	24.1
Medicaid	100.0	99.6	99.7	99.8	99.5	100.0	100.0
VA compensation or pensions	4.7	7.7	5.7	4.0	4.5	3.9	3.6
Number of households receiving benefits (in thousands)	3,008	3,341	3,037	3,957	3,861	4,223	4,580

Note: SSI recipients living in California receive a higher SSI payment in lieu of food stamps, and thus are not included in the food stamp percentages.

SOURCE: U.S. Bureau of the Census

CHAPTER 7

COMPARING THE NEW (TANF) WITH THE OLD (AFDC)

The Personal Responsibility and Work Opportunity Reconciliation Act (PL 104-193), the welfare-reform law enacted in 1996, ended the Aid to Families with Dependent Children (AFDC) program and replaced it with the Temporary Assistance for Needy Families (TANF) program. AFDC was an entitlement program that guaranteed benefits to all recipients whose income and resources were below state-determined eligibility levels. However, state-determined tests of financial need for cash assistance were subject to federal guidelines and limits. Under TANF, a federal block grant program, states have the authority to determine eligibility requirements and benefit levels. Unlike AFDC, TANF is not an entitlement program. Because of this, there is no requirement that states aid, or apply uniform rules to, all families determined financially needy. (See Chapter 2 for the specific provisions regarding TANF.)

For several years prior to the passage of the controversial welfare-reform law, critics challenged many aspects of the existing program. On the one hand, many thought that the new welfare-to-work system merely pushed welfare recipients deeper into poverty after former recipients tended to gain employment in low-wage service-sector jobs. On the other hand, many felt that the old entitlement system did not reward hard work and that it discouraged the formation and stability of two-parent families. Others charged that the program actually harmed recipients by creating "welfare dependency." Welfare dependency refers to individuals who spend a good part of their potential working lives on welfare and to the passing of welfare dependency from one generation to another. Tied to the issue of welfare dependency was a growing belief that the living patterns of many of the poor supposedly contributed to their condition.

Gallup Public Opinion Polls

In 1994 a Gallup poll surveyed Americans concerning welfare and welfare reform. The survey found that 64 percent of those sampled believed that a congressional candidate's stand on welfare reform was most or very important, compared to 35 percent who felt it was only moderately or not very important.

When asked whether the welfare system should be replaced with a new system or just have its existing problems fixed, 63 percent voted to just fix the problems, and 36 percent felt the system should be replaced. On the other hand, another question asked whether respondents would favor or oppose replacing the current system with a new one that would "help poor people get off welfare, if that new system would cost the government more money in the next few years." In response to this question the survey found that 68 percent favored a new system, while 27 percent were opposed, and 5 percent had no opinion. (See Table 7.1.)

TABLE 7.1

Should Welfare System be Replaced?

Which of the following statements comes closer to your view—the welfare system is fundamentally flawed and should be replaced with a completely new system; the welfare system may have problems which need to be fixed, but it should not be completely replaced.

Replace entirely	36%
Fix problems	63
No opinion	1
	100%

Would you favor or oppose replacing the current welfare system with a completely new system to help poor people get off welfare, if that new system would cost the government more money in the next few years than the current system?

Favor	68%
Oppose	27
No opinion	5
	100%

SOURCE: The Gallup Poll Monthly, May 1994

About two-thirds (68 percent) of the respondents felt that most welfare recipients were taking advantage of the system, rather than truly needing help. As a result, 44 percent wanted to reduce welfare payments, and another 10 percent wanted to cut off payments altogether.

When asked what government could do to "help recipients get off welfare" and become self-sufficient, respondents most often favored job training (94 percent) and child care (90 percent). Other actions favored by the respondents included financing welfare reform with funds taken from existing welfare benefits, cutting off all benefits to welfare recipients after two years, paying transportation costs to a job or job training class, and providing government-paid jobs when there is a lack of private sector jobs. (See Table 7.2.)

In November 1996, following the passage of the welfare-reform law, Americans were asked their opinion of the new law and its probable success or failure in improving the welfare system. The majority (54 percent) of the respondents felt it would be a success, while 31 percent thought it would be a failure, and 15 percent had no opinion. (See Table 7.3.)

A BRIEF BACKGROUND OF AFDC

Because the nation's welfare system was based on the Aid to Families with Dependent Children program for about 60 years, it is important to understand that program before comparing TANF to it. Following this brief background, the rest of the chapter will compare the old system with the new.

Part of the Social Security Act

The Great Depression of the 1930s brought enormous suffering to most Americans. The administration of President Franklin Delano Roosevelt (1933–45) introduced a large amount of social legislation designed to ease some of that misery. The Social Security Act (August 14, 1935) was the most significant piece of legislation passed during that time. Title IV of the act was a cash grant program that would enable states to aid needy children who lacked one or both parents. Renamed Aid to Families with Dependent Children (AFDC) in the 1950s, the program became active in all 50 states, the District of Columbia, Guam, Puerto Rico, and the Virgin Islands in the 1960s.

Helping Widows

The primary goal of Title IV of the Social Security program was to provide economic support for children whose parent (usually the father) had died, had left, or had become disabled. The AFDC program was modeled after the many state Mother's Pension funds, which had provided assistance to single mothers, mainly widows.

The AFDC program was not a controversial issue at the time. At that time, widows were generally considered

TABLE 7.2

Things Government Could Do to Get People Off Welfare

Next, I am going to read a list of some things government could do as part of a plan to help welfare recipients get off welfare and become self-sufficient. Please tell me whether you would favor or oppose each one. First . . . help provide child care so a parent on welfare can work or look for work; provide job training to teach welfare recipients new skills; pay the costs of commuting to a job or job training classes; provide a government-paid job to welfare recipients when there are not enough private sector jobs available; cut off all benefits to people who had not found a job or become self-sufficient after two years; finance welfare reform by reducing or eliminating some existing welfare benefits. (RANDOM ORDER)

	Favor	Oppose	No opinion
Job training	94%	5%	1%
Provide child care	90	9	1
Finance from within	78	18	4
Cut off after 2 years	67	30	3
Pay commuting costs	66	32	2
Provide job if needed	60	37	3
	100%	100%	100%

SOURCE: The Gallup Poll Monthly, May 1994

unemployable and morally deserving of aid. After all, it was not their fault that their husbands had died. Furthermore, during a time when there were few jobs, legislators, having a bias toward providing jobs to male breadwinners first, considered it wiser to pay a widow a small pension than to have her take a "man's" job. Finally, they believed that a mother belonged in the home, raising her children, and the AFDC support helped to maintain that situation. Since that time, widows and their children have been increasingly covered under the survivor's insurance provided by the Social Security Act. By 1961 widows made up barely 7 percent of the AFDC caseload.

Although congressmen were thinking mostly of widows, benefits were granted to poor mothers who were alone for reasons other than the deaths of their spouses. They did not expect that a significant percentage of those eligible for AFDC would be single mothers other than widows. Furthermore, no one at the time could have foreseen the huge increase in the number of female-headed households that would later lead to the large growth in the AFDC program. Finally, many legislators thought paying AFDC to mothers was a better alternative than having to pay to care for the children in orphanages, where many poor mothers had been forced to put their children when they could not afford to take care of them.

Growing AFDC Caseloads Lead to Reevaluation

In 1962, 3.5 million Americans were receiving AFDC. Just five years later, in 1967, the number had grown to five million. Eligibility rules had been expanded. Poor rural blacks who had often been denied benefits were moving to the cities, which added to urban poverty. Community action groups and advocates for the needy were helping the poor get benefits for which they were

TABLE 7.3

Will New Law Improve Welfare System?

As you may know, this past summer Congress passed a new law which made major changes in the nation's welfare system. In terms of improving the welfare system over the next few years, do you think this new law will mostly be a success or a failure?

Success	54%
Failure	31
No opinion	15
	100%

SOURCE: The Gallup Poll Monthly, May 1994

eligible. Divorces were increasing, and more babies were being born outside marriage. All these factors contributed to the increase in AFDC recipients, as well as a growing concern about the number of caseloads, the cost, and the characteristics of the recipients.

CHANGING ATTITUDES TOWARD WOMEN. The AFDC rolls and programs grew as divorced, separated, and never-married women sought help. While these women were still generally considered unemployable and best suited to staying at home with their children, many Americans considered that the behavior that led to their receiving AFDC should disqualify them. They believed that a mother's single status was immoral and threatening to the ideal of the traditional family of a father, mother, and children. This led legislators and many others to look upon welfare as a moral issue. Since the 1970s, the stigma once attached to divorce and separation has virtually disappeared, and those concerned about the moral issues have focused primarily on the never-married mother.

Several other factors contributed to the changing attitudes toward women on welfare. In the 1960s the number of black women on the AFDC rolls began to increase. Discriminatory practices had often prevented their receiving the assistance to which they were legally entitled. However, as these barriers slowly fell, the number of black women receiving support began to grow. The eventual over-representation of black women receiving AFDC payments tended to reinforce existing racial stereotypes and to lessen support for the AFDC program.

Finally, as the number of women entering the work force grew, it seemed increasingly difficult to justify poor women's receiving AFDC payments that allowed them to stay at home with their children. The "traditional" value that the mother belonged at home with her children was beginning to erode as a greater number of women began entering the workforce. Many people reasoned that welfare recipients should not be at home when many millions of nonpoor women were out in the labor force, either supporting themselves or increasing the family income. This attitude contributed greatly to the idea sometimes known as "workfare," in which the welfare recipient is expected

to do some kind of work for his or her assistance, an old idea that has reappeared throughout American history. (See Chapter 9.)

AFDC-UP

As of October 1, 1990, states that operated AFDC had to offer AFDC to children in two-parent families who were needy because one or both of their parents were unemployed. This program was called AFDC-UP (unemployed parent). Eligibility for AFDC-UP was limited to families in which the principal wage earner was unemployed but had a history of working. States that did not have an unemployed parent program as of September 26, 1988, could limit benefits under the AFDC-UP program to as few as 6 months in any 13-month period. AFDC-UP was intended to eliminate one of the major criticisms of the AFDC program. Previously, in many cases, recipients were eligible for AFDC only when there was no father in the house. This contributed to many poor fathers as a survival strategy leaving home in order to permit their families to get welfare support. Many observers believed this weakened the structure of numerous poor families.

After years of criticism and suggested modifications, the controversial 1996 Personal Responsibility and Work Opportunity Reconciliation Act (PL 104-193) replaced the AFDC program with the TANF block grant program. The rest of this chapter discusses the differences between the two programs.

FEDERAL SPENDING ON AFDC AND TANF

Under the prior law, the federal government reimbursed states for a portion of AFDC, the related expenditures for Emergency Assistance (EA), and Job Opportunity and Basic Skills (JOBS). Federal funds paid from 50 to 80 percent of the state AFDC benefit costs, depending on per capita income. In addition, the federal government paid 50 percent of the administrative costs for the programs. Figure 7.1 shows the federal and state shares of the $28 billion spent on these programs in 1996. Federal funds accounted for 54 percent ($15 billion), while state funds made up the remaining 46 percent ($13 billion).

States were required to end the AFDC program and begin TANF by July 1, 1997, but many began the new system earlier. The $16.5 billion federal block grant for TANF is based on each state's peak level of federal expenditures for AFDC and related programs; for most, this was the 1994 level. Federal conditions apply to the federally-funded TANF, such as work participation requirements, 5-year time limits, child support assignment and distribution, and aid to only those unwed minor parents living in an adult-supervised setting. (For the specific requirements, see Chapter 2.)

FIGURE 7.1

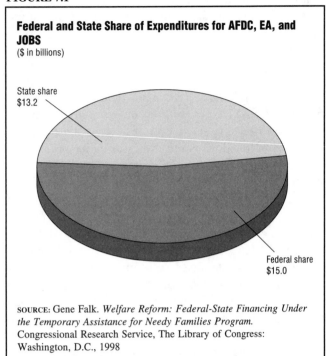

Federal and State Share of Expenditures for AFDC, EA, and JOBS
($ in billions)

State share
$13.2

Federal share
$15.0

SOURCE: Gene Falk. *Welfare Reform: Federal-State Financing Under the Temporary Assistance for Needy Families Program.* Congressional Research Service, The Library of Congress: Washington, D.C., 1998

Though TANF is called a block grant program, it combines seven different grants, each having capped (limited maximums) federal funding:

• State family assistance grant—the $16.5 billion grant based on historic state welfare expenditures.

• Bonus to reward decreases in illegitimacy—$20 million grant to each of the five states with the largest reduction in out-of-wedlock birth rates combined with a decline in abortion rates.

• Supplemental grants for population increases in certain states—formula grants to states with above-average population growth and below average federal spending per poor person in AFDC and related programs.

• Bonus to reward high performance states—bonus funds for states meeting the goals of the TANF program (in 1999, based on job entry rates and workfare success).

• Welfare-to-work formula grants—matching grants to states to fund welfare-to-work initiatives targeting long-term welfare recipients, with an 85 percent pass-through of funds to localities (Job Training Partnership Act Service Delivery areas).

• Welfare-to-work competitive grants—grants competitively awarded to private industry councils and cities or counties with welfare-to-work projects.

• Contingency—fund matching grants to states that experience high unemployment rates or increased food stamp caseloads.

Almost all of the TANF program funds the state family assistance grant. This grant is capped at $16.5 billion for fiscal years 1997 through 2002 and is $1.5 billion more than the federal share of the AFDC and related programs in 1996. (See Table 7.4.)

Figure 7.2 compares the federal share of expenditures under the prior system with its share of total TANF funding. The lighter bars show federal expenditures under AFDC, EA, and JOBS, while the darker bars show the total TANF available grants through fiscal year 2002. The figure at the bottom represents the expenditures in constant dollars, showing an actual decrease of funds when adjusted for inflation. Using constant 1996 dollars, the estimated federal share of TANF funding in 2002 will be $14.7 billion, a lower amount than the AFDC expenditures for each year from 1991 to 1996.

The funds for the state family assistance grant are distributed to each state according to its historic welfare spending under the prior law. Table 7.5 shows the amount granted to each state and its percentage of the total grant.

TABLE 7.4

Summary of Total TANF Expenditures Funding for 50 States and the District of Columbia
($ in millions)

Grant	Fiscal Year						Total: FY1997 to FY2002
	1997	1998	1999	2000	2001	2002	
State family assistance grant (403(a)(1))	$16,489	$16,489	$16,489	$16,489	$16,489	$16,489	$98,932
Bonus to reward decrease in illegitimacy (403(a)(2))	–	–	100	100	100	100	400
Supplemental grant for population increases in certain states (403(a)(3))	–	79	161	244	315	–	800
Bonus to reward high performance states (403(a)(4))	–	–	200	300	200	200	900
Welfare-to-Work formula grants (403(a)(5)(A))	–	1,069	996	–	–	–	2,135
Welfare-to-Work competitive grants (403(a)(5)(B))	–	368	343	–	–	–	712
Contingency fund (403(b))							1.960
Total TANF	**16,489**	**18,005**	**18,289**	**17,133**	**17,104**	**16,789**	**105,768**

SOURCE: Gene Falk. *Welfare Reform: Federal-State Financing Under the Temporary Assistance for Needy Families Program.* Congressional Research Service, The Library of Congress: Washington, D.C., 1998

FIGURE 7.2

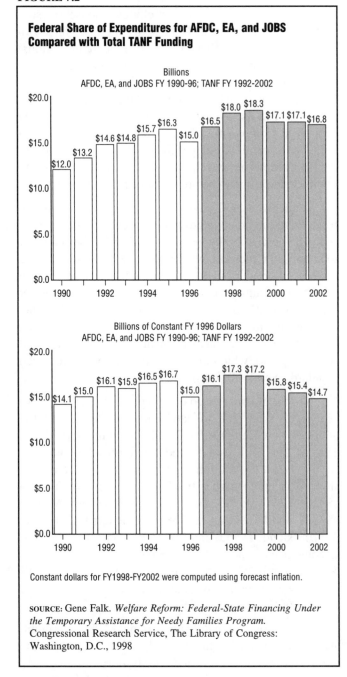

Federal Share of Expenditures for AFDC, EA, and JOBS Compared with Total TANF Funding

Billions
AFDC, EA, and JOBS FY 1990-96; TANF FY 1992-2002

Billions of Constant FY 1996 Dollars
AFDC, EA, and JOBS FY 1990-96; TANF FY 1992-2002

Constant dollars for FY1998-FY2002 were computed using forecast inflation.

SOURCE: Gene Falk. *Welfare Reform: Federal-State Financing Under the Temporary Assistance for Needy Families Program.* Congressional Research Service, The Library of Congress: Washington, D.C., 1998

TABLE 7.5

State Family Assistance Grants, by State
($ in thousands)

State	State family assistance grant	% of total for 50 states and D.C.
Alabama	93,315	0.6%
Alaska	63,609	0.4%
Arizona	222,420	1.3%
Arkansas	56,733	0.3%
California	3,733,818	22.6%
Colorado	136,057	0.8%
Connecticut	266,788	1.6%
Delaware	32,291	0.2%
District of Columbia	92,610	0.6%
Florida	562,340	3.4%
Georgia	330,742	2.0%
Hawaii	98,905	0.6%
Idaho	31,938	0.2%
Illinois	585,057	3.5%
Indiana	206,799	1.3%
Iowa	131,525	0.8%
Kansas	101,931	0.6%
Kentucky	181,288	1.1%
Louisiana	163,972	1.0%
Maine	78,121	0.5%
Maryland	229,098	1.4%
Massachusetts	459,371	2.8%
Michigan	775,353	4.7%
Minnesota	267,985	1.6%
Mississippi	86,768	0.5%
Missouri	217,052	1.3%
Montana	45,534	0.3%
Nebraska	58,029	0.4%
Nevada	43,977	0.3%
New Hampshire	38,521	0.2%
New Jersey	404,035	2.5%
New Mexico	126,103	0.8%
New York	2,442,931	14.8%
North Carolina	302,240	1.8%
North Dakota	26,400	0.2%
Ohio	727,968	4.4%
Oklahoma	148,014	0.9%
Oregon	167,925	1.0%
Pennsylvania	719,499	4.4%
Rhode Island	95,022	0.6%
South Carolina	99,968	0.6%
South Dakota	21,894	0.1%
Tennessee	191,524	1.2%
Texas	486,257	2.9%
Utah	76,829	0.5%
Vermont	47,353	0.3%
Virginia	158,285	1.0%
Washington	404,332	2.5%
West Virginia	110,176	0.7%
Wisconsin	318,188	1.9%
Wyoming	21,781	0.1%
TOTAL	**16,488,667**	**100.0%**

SOURCE: Gene Falk. *Welfare Reform: Federal-State Financing Under the Temporary Assistance for Needy Families Program.* Congressional Research Service, The Library of Congress: Washington, D.C., 1998

California (22.6 percent) and New York (14.8 percent) together receive over one-third of the total grant while 26 states each receive less than 1 percent of the funding. Indian tribes are permitted to administer their own tribal assistance programs with funds deducted from their state's family assistance grant.

STATE SPENDING ON AFDC AND TANF

State expenditures accounted for 46 percent of total expenditures for AFDC, EA, and JOBS in 1996. The welfare-reform law requires states to maintain at least 75 percent of their "historic state expenditures" (the state share of 1994 AFDC, EA, and JOBS expendi-

tures). This cost-sharing requirement (in order to receive the full family assistance grant) is called the maintenance of effort (MOE) level. If a state fails to meet the federal work requirements, its MOE level becomes 80 percent. Failure to meet the MOE level results in a dollar-for-dollar reduction of the state's family assistance grant. Table 7.6 provides historic state expenditures for each state as well as the 75 percent and 80 percent MOE thresholds.

TABLE 7.6

TANF Maintenance of Effort Thresholds
($ in thousands)

State	100% of historic state expenditures	75% of historic state expenditures	80% of historic state expenditures
Alabama	52,285	39,214	41,828
Alaska	65,257	48,942	52,205
Arizona	126,704	95,028	101,363
Arkansas	27,785	20,839	22,228
California	3,635,855	2,726,892	2,908,684
Colorado	110,495	82,871	88,396
Connecticut	244,561	183,421	195,649
Delaware	29,028	21,771	23,222
District of Columbia	93,932	70,449	75,146
Florida	494,559	370,919	395,647
Georgia	231,158	173,369	184,926
Hawaii	97,309	72,981	77,847
Idaho	18,238	13,679	14,591
Illinois	573,451	430,088	458,761
Indiana	151,367	113,526	121,094
Iowa	82,618	61,963	66,094
Kansas	82,333	61,750	65,866
Kentucky	89,891	67,418	71,913
Louisiana	73,887	55,415	59,109
Maine	50,032	37,524	40,026
Maryland	235,954	176,965	188,763
Massachusetts	478,597	358,948	382,877
Michigan	624,691	468,518	499,753
Minnesota	239,660	179,745	191,728
Mississippi	28,966	21,724	23,173
Missouri	160,161	120,121	128,129
Montana	20,955	15,716	16,764
Nebraska	38,173	28,629	30,538
Nevada	33,985	25,489	27,188
New Hampshire	42,820	32,115	34,256
New Jersey	400,213	300,160	320,171
New Mexico	49,795	37,346	39,836
New York	2,291,438	1,718,578	1,833,150
North Carolina	205,568	154,176	164,454
North Dakota	12,092	9,069	9,674
Ohio	521,108	390,831	416,887
Oklahoma	81,667	61,250	65,334
Oregon	123,006	92,255	98,405
Pennsylvania	542,834	407,126	434,267
Rhode Island	80,489	60,367	64,392
South Carolina	47,902	35,927	38,322
South Dakota	11,699	8,774	9,359
Tennessee	110,413	82,810	88,331
Texas	319,301	235,726	251,441
Utah	33,721	25,291	26,977
Vermont	34,067	25,550	27,253
Virginia	170,898	128,173	136,718
Washington	362,748	272,061	290,198
West Virginia	43,058	32,294	34,446
Wisconsin	22,638	169,229	180,511
Wyoming	14,220	10,665	11,376
U.S. Totals	**13,911,583**	**10,433,687**	**11,129,266**

SOURCE: Gene Falk. *Welfare Reform: Federal-State Financing Under the Temporary Assistance for Needy Families Program.* Congressional Research Service, The Library of Congress: Washington, D.C., 1998

ELIGIBILITY AND BENEFIT PAYMENTS

Aid to Families with Dependent Children

Under the Aid to Families with Dependent Children program, states determined the eligibility of needy families with children. But it had to be done within federal guidelines. If the state determined that a family was financially needy, the family was guaranteed AFDC benefits.

The individual states defined "need" as what a person must have to exist: food, shelter, clothing, household supplies, utilities, and personal care items. States set their own benefits levels, established (within federal limitations) income and resource limits, and administered the program or supervised its administration. Eligible recipients received benefits no matter what the status of the economy, even in recessions and fiscal downturn. Eligibility for AFDC ended at a child's eighteenth birthday or, at state option, at a child's nineteenth birthday if the child was a full-time student in a secondary or technical school and was expected to complete the program before she or he reached age 19.

To receive AFDC payments, a family had to pass two tests. First, the family's gross income could not be greater than 185 percent of the need standard set by the state. For example, in Colorado, where the state had established a 1996 need standard of $421 per month for a three-person family, the family could earn no more than $779 per month to be eligible for AFDC. Second, the family's net income (income after taxes and certain other deductions) had to be below the state's payment standard (the amount the state pays), which in most states was below the need standard. (See Table 7.7.)

Need standards, based on 100 percent of "need," varied widely from state to state. For example, in 1996 the states of New Hampshire ($2,034), Washington ($1,252), Hawaii ($1,140), and Vermont ($1,148) believed the monthly cost of maintaining a basic life for a family of three was much higher than did the states of Indiana ($320), Delaware ($338), Nebraska ($364), New Mexico ($389), and Mississippi ($368) and the territories of the Virgin Islands ($300) and Puerto Rico ($360). The U.S. average need standard for a 3-person family in 1996 was $675 a month, while the median (half were higher; half were lower) need standard among the 50 states and the District of Columbia was $645. (See Table 7.7.)

In addition, Table 7.7 shows typical 1996 maximum AFDC payments for three-member families. As in the need standards, states varied widely in typical monthly payments. In all cases, the typical annual AFDC payments were well below the 1996 federal poverty guidelines for a family of three ($12,516, or $1,043 per month). The typical 1996 AFDC payments for a family of three in Alaska ($923), Hawaii ($712), New York, Suffolk County ($703), Connecticut ($636), Vermont ($650), and California ($607) were much higher than Mississippi ($120), Alabama ($164), Tennessee ($185), Texas ($188), and Louisiana ($190). The U.S. average payment for a family of three was $399, and the median payment was $389.

Most AFDC families were eligible for and received food stamps, an important supplement to the cash assistance paid under AFDC. Table 7.7 shows the combined benefits amounts and their percentage of 1996 poverty guidelines (based on the guideline for a family of three in

TABLE 7.7

Gross Income Limit, Need Standard, and Maximum Monthly Potential Benefits, AFDC and Food Stamps, One-Parent Family of Three Persons, January 1996

State	Gross income limit (185 percent of need standard)	100 percent of "need"	Maximum AFDC grant[2]	Food stamp benefit[3]	Combined benefits	Combined benefits as a percent of 1996 poverty guidelines[4]	AFDC benefits as a percent of 1996 poverty guidelines[4]
Alabama	$1,245	$ 673	$164	$313	$ 477	44	15
Alaska	1,902	1,028	923	321	1,244	92	68
Arizona	1,783	964	347	313	660	61	32
Arkansas	1,304	705	204	313	517	48	19
California	1,351	730	607	245	852	79	56
Colorado	779	421	421	301	722	67	39
Connecticut	1,613	872	636	236	872	81	59
Delaware	625	338	338	313	651	60	31
District of Columbia	1,317	712	420	301	721	67	39
Florida	1,943	1,050	303	313	616	57	28
Georgia	784	424	280	313	593	55	26
Guam	611	330	330	461	791	73	31
Hawaii	2,109	1,140	712	471	1,183	95	57
Idaho	1,833	991	317	313	630	58	29
Illinois	1,782	963	[5]377	313	690	64	35
Indiana	592	320	288	313	601	56	27
Iowa	1,571	849	426	299	725	67	39
Kansas	794	429	[5]429	313	742	69	30
Kentucky	973	526	262	313	575	53	24
Louisiana	1,217	658	190	313	503	47	18
Maine	1,023	553	418	301	719	66	39
Maryland	956	517	[5]373	313	686	63	34
Massachusetts	1,045	565	565	257	822	76	52
Michigan:							
(Washtenaw Co.)	1,086	587	489	280	769	71	45
(Wayne Co.)	1,019	551	459	289	748	69	42
Minnesota	984	532	532	267	799	74	49
Mississippi	681	368	120	313	433	40	11
Missouri	1,565	846	292	313	605	56	27
Montana	1,001	541	425	299	724	67	39
Nebraska	673	364	364	313	677	63	34
Nevada	1,293	699	348	313	661	61	32
New Hampshire	3,763	2,034	550	262	812	75	51
New Jersey	1,822	985	[5]424	307	731	68	39
New Mexico	720	389	389	310	699	65	36
New York:							
(New York City)	1,067	577	[5]577	270	847	78	53
(Suffolk Co.)	1,301	703	[5]703	232	935	86	65
North Carolina	1,006	544	272	313	585	54	25
North Dakota	797	431	431	298	729	67	40
Ohio	1,709	924	[5]341	313	654	60	32
Oklahoma	1,193	645	307	313	620	57	28
Oregon	851	460	[5]460	313	773	71	43
Pennsylvania	1,136	614	421	301	722	67	39
Puerto Rico	666	360	180	NA	180	NA	17
Rhode Island	1,025	554	[5]554	299	853	79	51
South Carolina	969	524	200	313	513	47	18
South Dakota	938	507	430	298	728	67	40
Tennessee	1,079	583	185	313	498	46	17
Texas	1,389	751	188	313	501	46	17
Utah	1,051	568	426	299	725	67	39
Vermont	2,124	1,148	650	232	882	82	60
Virgin Islands	555	300	246	402	642	59	22
Virginia	727	393	354	313	667	62	33
Washington	2,316	1,252	[5]546	289	835	77	50
West Virginia	1,833	991	253	313	566	52	23
Wisconsin	1,197	647	517	272	789	73	48
Wyoming	1,247	674	360	313	673	62	33
Median AFDC State	720	645	389	310	699	65	36

[1] In most States these benefit amounts apply also to two-parent families of three (where the second parent is incapacitated or unemployed). Some, however, increase benefits for such families.

[2] In States with area differentials, figure shown is for area with highest benefit.

TABLE 7.7

Gross Income Limit, Need Standard, and Maximum Monthly Potential Benefits, AFDC and Food Stamps, One-Parent Family of Three Persons, January 1996 [CONTINUED]

[3] Food stamp benefits are based on maximum AFDC benefits shown and assume deductions of $381 monthly ($134 standard household deduction plus $247 maximum allowable deduction for excess shelter cost) in the 48 contiguous States and the District of Columbia. In the remaining four jurisdictions these maximum allowable food stamp deductions are assumed: Alaska, $658, Hawaii, $542, Guam, $569; and Virgin Islands, $300. If only the standard deduction were assumed, food stamp benefits would drop by about $74 monthly in most of the 48 contiguous States and the District of Columbia. Maximum food stamp benefits from October 1995 through September 1996 are $313 for a family of three except in these four jurisdictions, where they are as follows: (urban) Alaska, $401; Hawaii, $522; Guam, $461; and Virgin Islands, $402.

[4] This column is based on the 1996 poverty guideline for a family of three persons in the 48 contiguous States, $12,980, converted to a monthly rate of $1,082. For Alaska, the guideline is $16,220; for Hawaii, $14,930.

[5] In these States part of the AFDC cash payment has been designated as energy aid and is disregarded by the State in calculating food stamp benefits. Illinois disregards $18. Kansas disregards $57. Maryland disregards $43. New Jersey disregards $25. New York disregards $53. Ohio disregards $14. Oregon disregards $118. Rhode Island disregards $127.85. Washington disregards $86.

NA—Not available

Note: Puerto Rico does not have a food stamp program; instead a cash nutritional assistance payment is given to recipients.

SOURCE: Table prepared by Congressional Research Service from information provided by a telephone survey of the States.

the 48 contiguous states). Mississippi had the lowest combined benefits ($433), which amounted to 40 percent of the poverty rate ($1,082 a month). Hawaii had the highest at $1,183, or 95 percent of Hawaii's poverty rate of $1,244 per month.

In 1996, in almost four-fifths (78 percent) of the states and territories, typical payment amounts were well below the state-established need standards. Only one-fifth (22 percent), which included Delaware, Guam, Kansas, Massachusetts, Minnesota, Nebraska, New Mexico, New York, North Dakota, Oregon, and Rhode Island, had typical payment amounts equal to their need standard for a three-person family. In 1980 payments were more likely to equal need standards; 32 states and territories (60.4 percent) had payments equal to need standards. Measured in constant (1996) dollars, the average need standard declined by 30 percent from 1970 to 1996, while the maximum benefit declined by 51 percent. (See Table 7.8.)

Similarly, typical monthly AFDC payments dropped sharply in real value (buying power). The typical monthly payment per four-person family changed from $178 in

1970 to $377 in 1995. However, in constant 1995 dollars, the typical benefit fell from $704 in 1970 to $377 in 1995, a 46 percent drop. Because the average family size became smaller over this period, average benefits per person dropped less sharply (26 percent). (See Table 7.8.)

Temporary Assistance to Needy Families (TANF)

Under the Temporary Assistance to Needy Families program, states decide how much to aid a needy family. There are no federal guidelines for determining eligibility and no requirement that states aid all needy families. Though TANF does not require states to have a need standard or a gross income limit, as did AFDC, many states have based their TANF programs in part on their earlier practices. The asterisks indicate that a state no longer has that particular program feature. Through January 1998, 13 states had eliminated the need standard. (See Table 7.9.)

The maximum benefit is the amount paid to a family with no countable income. (Federal law specifies what income counts toward figuring benefits and what income, such as child support, is to be disregarded by the state.)

TABLE 7.8

Historic Trends in Average Payment Per Recipient and Per Family and Maximum and Median Benefits for a Family of Four, Selected Years 1970-95

AFDC payments	Year									
	1970	1975	1980	1985	1987	1989	1991	1992	1993	1995
Average monthly benefit per family	$178	$210	$274	$331	$359	$381	$388	$389	$373	$377
In 1995 dollars[2]	704	601	518	470	484	471	434	423	394	377
Average monthly benefit per person	46	63	94	113	123	131	135	136	131	135
In 1995 dollars[2]	182	180	178	160	166	162	151	148	138	135
Median State benefit in July for a family unit of four with no income[1]	221	264	350	399	420	432	435	435	435	435
In 1995 dollars[2]	874	756	662	566	566	534	487	473	459	435

[1] Among 50 States and the District of Columbia.

[2] The constant dollar numbers were calculated using the CPI-U.

Note: AFDC benefit amounts have not been reduced by child support enforcement collections.

SOURCE: Family Support Administration, U.S. Department of Health and Human Services and the Congressional Research Service.

TABLE 7.9

TANF Gross Income Limits, Countable Income Limits (Need Standards), and Maximum Monthly Benefits for a Family of Three, January 1998

State	Gross income limits	Need standard	Payment standard	Maximum benefits
Alabama	*	*	164	164
Alaska	1,994	1,078	1,078	923
Arizona	1,783	964	347	347
Arkansas	*	*	204	204
California	*	754	565	565
Colorado	778	421	356	356
Connecticut	*	872	636	636
Delaware	1,541	833	338	338
District of Columbia	1,317	712	379	379
Florida	2,105	1,138	303	303
Georgia	784	424	424	280
Hawaii *(Exempt)*	2,109	1,140	712	712
Hawaii *Nonexempt)*	2,109	1,140	570	570
Idaho	*	*	276	276
Illinois	*	*	377	377
Indiana	*	*	288	288
Iowa	1,570	849	426	426
Kansas	793	429	429	429
Kentucky	973	526	262	262
Louisiana	*	658	190	190
Maine	1,023	553	553	418
Maryland	*	*	388	388
Massachusetts *(Exempt)*	1,071	579	579	579
Massachusetts *(Nonexempt)*	1,045	565	565	565
Michigan *Wayne Co.*	*	*	459	459
Michigan *Washtenaw Co.*	*	*	489	489
Minnesota	a	a	a	532
Mississippi	680	368	368	120
Missouri	1,565	846	292	292
Montana	1,060	573	450	450
Nebraska	*	535	364	364
Nevada	1,422	769	348	348
New Hampshire	*	1,892	550	550
New Jersey	636	*	424	424
New Mexico	719	389	389	389
New York *Suffolk Co.*	1,082	703	703	703
New York *New York City*	1,067	577	577	577
North Carolina	1,006	544	544	272
North Dakota	906	490	490	490
Ohio	*	*	362	362
Oklahoma	1,193	645	292	292
Oregon	851	460	460	460
Pennsylvania	*	614	421	421
Puerto Rico	666	360	180	180
Rhode Island	*	554	554	554
South Carolina	1,026	555	555	201
South Dakota	*	*	730	430
Tennessee	1,252	677	677	185
Texas	1,389	751	188	188
Utah	1,050	568	426	426
Vermont	2,314	1251	656	656
Virginia	*	393	354	354
Washington	*	*	546	546
West Virginia	*	991	253	253
Wisconsin *Community Service*	*	*	*	673

The maximum benefit is only to be paid to those families who comply with TANF's work requirements or other program requirements established by the state, such as parental and personal responsibility rules. Some states apply different rules to different categories of recipients. For instance, Massachusetts and Hawaii divide their recipients into "nonexempt" (subject to work requirements and receiving lower benefits) and "exempt" (not subject to work requirements and paid a higher maximum benefit).

TABLE 7.9

TANF Gross Income Limits, Countable Income Limits (Need Standards), and Maximum Monthly Benefits for a Family of Three, January 1998 [CONTINUED]

State	Gross income limits	Need standard	Payment standard	Maximum benefits
Wisconsin *W2 Transition*	*	*	*	628
Wyoming	*	*	340	340
Guam	1,245	673	673	673
Virgin Islands	555	300	240	240

Congressional Research Service, based on a telephone survey of the states.

* Denotes that state no longer has this program feature.

a Minnesota's income eligibility and payment standards are for combined cash (TANF) and food (food stamp) assistance under the Minnesota Family Investment Program (MFIP) program. For a family of three, the MFIP income eligibility and payment standard is $763 for a family without earnings. The cash portion of the benefit is $532 and the food portion of the benefit is $231. Minnesota has a higher income eligibility and payment standard for a family of three with earnings: $839. However, the maximum benefit for families with earnings is $763 ($532 cash and $231 food). so that the higher payment standard results in a larger amount of earnings is disregarded in computing benefits.

SOURCE: Gene Falk et al. *Welfare Reform: Financial Eligibility Rules and Benefit Amounts Under the Temporary Assistance for Needy Families Program.* Congressional Research Service, The Library of Congress: Washington, D.C., 1998

Michigan and New York show benefits in two different areas that vary because of housing costs. (See Table 7.9.)

Though most states vary benefits according to family size, some eliminate or restrict benefit increases due to the birth of a new child to a recipient already receiving benefits. Instead benefits depend on family size at the time of enrollment. Idaho pays $276 a month regardless of family size. Wisconsin pays benefits based on work activity of the recipient and not on family size.

In a comparison of AFDC and TANF maximum benefits for a family of three, 35 states did not change their maximum benefits. Kentucky, Montana, North Dakota, Wisconsin, and Guam significantly increased benefits while 7 states decreased benefits by more than 5 percent. (See Table 7.10.)

Most families receiving TANF benefits are also eligible for food stamps. A single benefit determination is made for both cash and food assistance. Though the eligibility and benefit amounts for TANF are determined by the states, food stamp eligibility and benefit amounts are determined by federal law and are consistent in all states.

Food stamp benefits, administered by the Department of Agriculture, are not counted in determining the TANF cash benefit. However, TANF benefits are considered part of a family's countable income in determining food stamp benefits, which are reduced 30 cents for each dollar of countable income. Therefore, food stamp benefits are higher in states with lower TANF benefits and vice versa. Mississippi had the lowest combined benefits at $441 per month, or 39.8 percent of the 1997 poverty guideline. These figures are nearly the same as Mississippi's 1996

TABLE 7.10

AFDC/TANF Maximum Benefits for a Family of Three, January 1994, 1997, and 1998

State	Jan 94	Jan 97	Jan 98	Change ($)		Change (%)	
				Jan 94 to Jan 98	Jan 97 to Jan 98	Jan 94 to Jan 98	Jan 97 to Jan 98
Alabama	164	164	164	0	0	0.0	0.0
Alaska	923	923	923	0	0	0.0	0.0
Arizona	347	347	347	0	0	0.0	0.0
Arkansas	204	204	204	0	0	0.0	0.0
California	607	565	565	-42	0	-6.9	0.0
Colorado	356	356	356	0	0	0.0	0.0
Connecticut	680	636	636	-44	0	-6.5	0.0
Delaware	338	338	338	0	0	0.0	0.0
District of Columbia	420	398	379	-41	-19	-9.8	-4.8
Florida	303	303	303	0	0	0.0	0.0
Georgia	280	280	280	0	0	0.0	0.0
Hawaii *(Exempt)*	712	712	712	0	0	0.0	0.0
Hawaii *(Nonexempt)*	712	712	570	-142	142	-19 9	19.9
Idaho	317	317	276	-41	-41	-12.9	-12.9
Illinois	367	377	377	10	0	2.7	0.0
Indiana	288	288	288	0	0	0.0	0.0
Iowa	426	426	426	0	0	0.0	0.0
Kansas	429	429	429	0	0	0.0	0.0
Kentucky	228	262	262	34	0	14.9	0.0
Louisiana	190	190	190	0	0	0.0	0.0
Maine	418	418	418	0	0	0.0	0.0
Maryland	366	377	388	22	11	6.0	2.9
Massachusetts *(Exempt)*	579	579	579	0	0	0.0	0.0
Massachusetts *(Nonexempt)*	579	565	565	-14	0	-2.4	0.0
Michigan *Wayne Co.*	459	459	459	0	0	0.0	0.0
Michigan *Washtenaw Co.*	489	489	489	0	0	0.0	0.0
Minnesota	532	532	532	0	0	0.0	0.0
Mississippi	120	120	120	0	0	0.0	0.0
Missouri	292	292	292	0	0	0.0	0.0
Montana	401	438	450	49	12	12.2	2.7
Nebraska	364	364	364	0	0	0.0	0.0
Nevada	348	348	348	0	0	0.0	0.0
New Hampshire	550	550	550	0	0	0.0	0.0
New Jersey	424	424	424	0	0	0.0	0.0
New Mexico	357	389	389	32	0	9.0	0.0
New York *Suffolk Co.*	703	703	703	0	0	0.0	0.0
New York *New York City*	577	577	577	0	0	0.0	0.0
North Carolina	272	272	272	0	0	0.0	0.0
North Dakota	409	431	490	81	59	19.8	13.7
Ohio	341	341	362	21	21	6.2	6.2
Oklahoma	324	307	292	-32	-15	-9.9	-4.9
Oregon	460	460	460	0	0	0.0	0.0
Pennsylvania	421	421	421	0	0	0.0	0.0
Puerto Rico	180	180	180	0	0	0.0	0.0
Rhode island	554	554	554	0	0	0.0	0.0
South Carolina	200	200	201	1	1	0.5	0.5
South Dakota	417	430	430	13	0	3.1	0.0
Tennessee	185	185	185	0	0	0.0	0.0
Texas	184	188	188	4	0	2.2	0.0
Utah	414	426	426	12	0	2.9	0.0
Vermont	638	639	656	18	17	2.8	2.7
Virginia	354	354	354	0	0	0.0	0.0
Washington	546	546	546	0	0	0.0	0.0
West Virginia	249	253	253	4	0	1.6	0.0
Wisconsin *Community Service*	517	517	673	156	156	30.2	30.2
Wisconsin *H'2 Transition*	517	517	628	111	111	21.5	21.5
Wyoming	360	360	340	-20	-20	-5.6	-5.6
Guam	330	673	673	343	0	103.9	0.0
Virgin Islands	240	240	240	0	0	0.0	0.0

SOURCE: Gene Falk et al. *Welfare Reform: Financial Eligibility Rules and Benefit Amounts Under the Temporary Assistance for Needy Families Program.* Congressional Research Service, The Library of Congress: Washington, D.C., 1998

TABLE 7.11

Maximum TANF and Food Stamp Benefits, for a Family of Three with no Other Income, January 1998

State	TANF	Food stamps	Combined benefits	As a percent of the 1997 poverty thresholds		
				TANF	Food stamps	Combined benefits
Alabama	164	321	485	14.8	29.0	43.8
Alaska*	923	327	1,250	66.4	23.5	90.0
Arizona	347	321	668	31.3	29.0	60.3
Arkansas	204	321	525	18.4	29.0	47.4
California	565	266	831	51.0	24.0	75.0
Colorado	356	321	677	32.1	29.0	61.1
Connecticut	636	245	881	57.4	22.1	79.5
Delaware	338	321	659	30.5	29.0	59.5
District of Columbia	379	321	700	34.2	29.0	63.2
Florida	303	321	624	27.3	29.0	56.3
Georgia	280	321	601	25.3	29.0	54.2
Hawaii *(Exempt)**	712	467	1,179	55.7	36.6	92.3
Hawaii *(Nonexempt)**	570	507	1,077	44.6	39.7	84.3
Idaho	276	321	597	24.9	29.0	53.9
Illinois	377	321	698	34.0	29.0	63.0
Indiana	288	321	609	26.0	29.0	54.9
Iowa	426	308	734	38.4	27.8	66.2
Kansas	429	307	736	38.7	27.7	66.4
Kentucky	262	321	583	23.6	29.0	52.6
Louisiana	190	321	511	17.1	29.0	46.1
Maine	418	310	728	37.7	28.0	65.7
Maryland	388	319	707	35.0	28.8	63.8
Massachusetts *(Exempt)*	579	262	841	52.2	23.6	75.9
Massachusetts *(Nonexempt)*	565	266	831	51.0	24.0	75.0
Michigan (Wayne Co.)	459	298	757	41.4	26.9	68.3
Michigan (Washtenaw Co.)	489	289	778	44.1	26.1	70.2
Minnesota	532	231	763	48.0	20.8	68.8
Mississippi	120	321	441	10.8	29.0	39.8
Missouri	292	321	613	26.3	29.0	55.3
Montana	450	301	751	40.6	27.2	67.8
Nebraska	364	321	685	32.8	29.0	61.8
Nevada	348	321	669	31.4	29.0	60.4
New Hampshire	550	271	821	49.6	24.5	74.1
New Jersey	424	309	733	38.3	27.9	66.1
New Mexico	389	319	708	35.1	28.8	63.9
New York (Suffolk Co.)	703	225	928	63.4	20.3	83.7
New York (New York City)	577	263	840	52.1	23.7	75.8
North Carolina	272	321	593	24.5	29.0	53.5
North Dakota	490	289	779	44.2	26.1	70.3
Ohio	362	321	683	32.7	29.0	61.6
Oklahoma	292	321	613	26.3	29.0	55.3
Oregon	460	298	758	41.5	26.9	68.4
Pennsylvania	421	309	730	38.0	27.9	65.9
Rhode Island	554	270	824	50.0	24.4	74.3
South Carolina	201	321	522	18.1	29.0	47.1
South Dakota	430	307	737	38.8	27.7	66.5
Tennessee	185	321	506	16.7	29.0	45.7
Texas	188	321	509	17.0	29.0	45.9
Utah	426	308	734	38.4	27.8	66.2
Vermont	656	239	895	59.2	21.6	80.8
Virginia	354	321	675	31.9	29.0	60.9
Washington	546	272	818	49.3	24.5	73.8
West Virginia	253	321	574	22.8	29.0	51.8
Wisconsin (Community Service)	673	234	907	60.7	21.1	81.8
Wisconsin (W-2 Transitional)	628	247	875	56.7	22.3	78.9
Wyoming	340	321	661	30.7	29.0	59.6

Note: Food stamp benefits assume families have excess shelter costs and receive the maximum allowable maximum shelter deduction in determining food stamp countable income. Minnesota's food stamp benefit is based on schedules provided by the state to CRS. Minnesota has consolidated its cash and food payment standards into a single schedule, but its benefit is divided into a cash portion and a food portion.

*Official poverty income guidelines are 25% higher in Alaska and 15% higher in Hawaii than the guidelines in the 8 contiguous states and the District of Columbia.

SOURCE: Gene Falk et al. *Welfare Reform: Financial Eligibility Rules and Benefit Amounts Under the Temporary Assistance for Needy Families Program.* Congressional Research Service, The Library of Congress: Washington, D.C., 1998

TABLE 7.12

Trends in Total AFDC Enrollments, 1962–1996

Fiscal Year	Average Monthly Number (In thousands)					Children as a Percent of Total Recipients	Average Number of Children per Family
	Total Families[1]	Total Recipients[1]	Unemployed Parent Families	Unemployed Parent Recipients	Total Children		
1962	924	3,593	48	224	2,778	77.3	3.0
1963	950	3,834	54	291	2,896	75.5	3.0
1964	984	4,059	60	343	3,043	75.0	3.1
1965	1,037	4,323	69	400	3,242	75.0	3.1
1966	1,074	4,472	62	361	3,369	75.3	3.1
1967	1,141	4,718	58	340	3,561	75.5	3.1
1968	1,307	5,348	67	377	4,011	75.0	3.1
1969	1,538	6,147	66	361	4,591	74.7	3.0
1970	1,909	7,415	78	420	5,494	74.0	2.9
1971	2,532	9,556	143	726	6,963	72.9	2.8
1972	2,918	10,632	134	639	7,698	72.4	2.6
1973	3,124	11,038	120	557	7,965	72.2	2.6
1974	3,170	10,845	93	429	7,824	72.1	2.5
1975	3,357	11,094	100	446	7,952	71.7	2.4
1976	3,575	11,386	135	593	8,054	70.7	2.3
1977	3,593	11,130	149	659	7,846	70.5	2.2
1978	3,539	10,672	128	568	7,492	70.2	2.1
1979	3,496	10,318	114	506	7,197	69.8	2.1
1980	3,642	10,597	141	612	7,320	69.1	2.0
1981	3,871	11,160	209	881	7,615	68.2	2.0
1982	3,569	10,431	232	976	6,975	66.9	2.0
1983	3,651	10,659	272	1,144	7,051	66.1	1.9
1984	3,725	10,866	287	1,222	7,153	65.8	1.9
1985	3,692	10,813	261	1,131	7,165	66.3	1.9
1986	3,748	10,997	254	1,102	7,300	66.4	1.9
1987	3,784	11,065	236	1,035	7,381	66.7	2.0
1988	3,748	10,920	210	929	7,325	67.1	2.0
1989	3,771	10,934	193	856	7,370	67.4	2.0
1990	3,974	11,460	204	899	7,755	67.7	2.0
1991	4,374	12,592	268	1,148	8,513	67.6	1.9
1992	4,768	13,625	322	1,348	9,226	67.7	1.9
1993	4,981	14,143	359	1,489	9,560	67.6	1.9
1994	5,046	14,226	363	1,510	9,611	67.6	1.9
1995	4,879	13,659	335	1,384	9,280	67.9	1.9
1996	4,552	12,644	301	1,241	8,671	68.6	1.9

[1]Total families and recipients includes unemployed parent families.

SOURCE: *Aid to Families with Dependent Children: The Baseline.* U.S. Department of Health and Human Services: Washington, D.C., 1998

AFDC benefits. Alaska and Hawaii had the highest combined benefits and percentages of their poverty guidelines, which, due to higher costs of living, are higher than the guidelines in the 48 contiguous states and the District of Columbia. (See Table 7.11.)

HOW MANY GET AFDC AND TANF BENEFITS?

The number of AFDC recipients increased sharply in the early 1970s and then generally leveled off somewhat until 1979. During the economic downturn of 1979–81, there was a 10 percent increase in cases. In 1982, following the passage of the Omnibus Budget Reconciliation Act (OBRA), the number of family participants dropped by 8 percent. (See Table 7.12.) The OBRA legislation included provisions that restricted AFDC eligibility.

Participation increased again in 1983 as the country suffered its worst recession since World War II. It

remained fairly steady until increases began again in 1990. By 1994 the number of recipients had swelled to 14.2 million, a 24 percent increase in only four years. In 1996, the last year for AFDC, the number of recipients had dropped to 12.6 million from the record high in 1994. The number of AFDC families also increased between 1990 and 1994, from nearly 4 million to over 5 million (again, a record high). In 1996 AFDC families numbered close to 4.6 million. (See Table 7.12.)

Although both the number of recipients and the number of cases (families) increased until 1994, the number of recipients per case significantly declined since the late 1960s. The number of recipients per case is figured by dividing the number of recipients by the number of families (cases). In 1969 the average AFDC family size was four recipients. By 1973 the number had dropped to 3.6. By 1980 the average number of recipients per family was

FIGURE 7.3

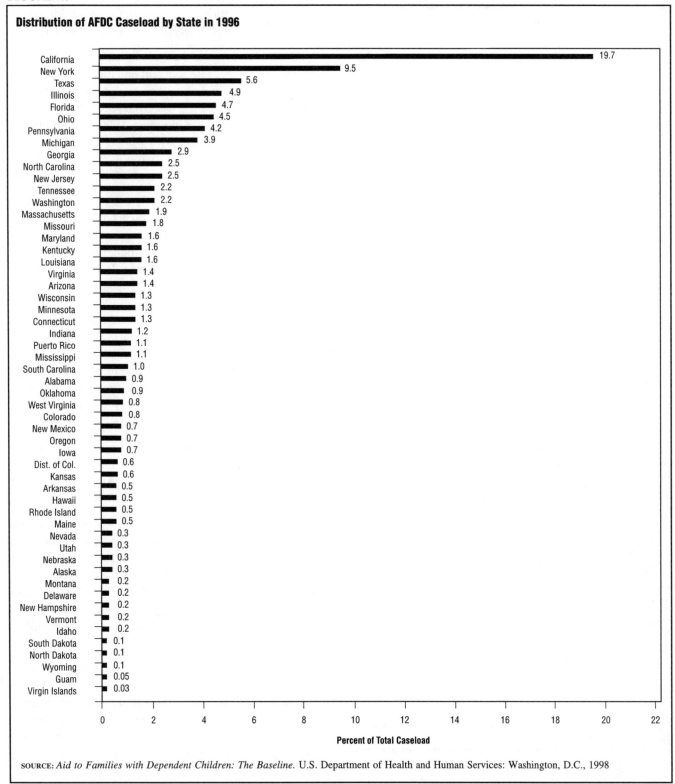

Distribution of AFDC Caseload by State in 1996

SOURCE: *Aid to Families with Dependent Children: The Baseline*. U.S. Department of Health and Human Services: Washington, D.C., 1998

2.9, and in 1996 the average number per family was 2.8, the same as in 1994. (See Table 7.12.)

In the distribution of AFDC caseloads by state in 1996, California had one-fifth (19.7 percent) of the total national caseload, followed by New York with 9.5 percent. (See Figure 7.3.)

With the change in welfare caseloads, as of June 1999, since the welfare-reform law was enacted, the number of caseloads, figured for both families and individual recipients, had dropped by an average of 44 percent. In 18 states, the number fell by 50 percent or more. (See Table 7.13.) However, it is too early to tell the effects of the welfare-reform law on the drop in caseloads. Some

TABLE 7.13

Total TANF Recipients by State

State	Aug-96	June-99	Percent (96-99)
Alabama	100,662	45,472	-55%
Alaska	35,544	25,393	-29%
Arizona	169,442	87,894	-48%
Arkansas	56,343	29,350	-48%
California	2,581,948	1,735,103	-33%
Colorado	95,788	35,469	-63%
Connecticut	159,246	83,458	-48%
Delaware	23,654	15,599	-34%
Dist. of Col.	69,292	46,840	-32%
Florida	533,801	173,341	-68%
Georgia	330,302	130,210	-61%
Guam	8,314	8,864	7%
Hawaii	66,482	44,229	-33%
Idaho	21,780	4,365	-80%
Illinois	642,644	344,320	-46%
Indiana	142,604	108,986	-24%
Iowa	86,146	57,356	-33%
Kansas	63,783	32,532	-49%
Kentucky	172,193	93,444	-46%
Louisiana	228,115	100,577	-56%
Maine	53,873	35,313	-34%
Maryland	194,127	89,003	-54%
Massachusetts	226,030	123,933	-45%
Michigan	502,354	244,621	-51%
Minnesota	169,744	135,202	-20%
Mississippi	123,828	33,853	-73%
Missouri	222,820	125,981	-43%
Montana	29,130	14,079	-52%
Nebraska	38,592	32,228	-16%
Nevada	34,261	18,308	-47%
New Hampshire	22,937	15,416	-33%
New Jersey	275,637	159,721	-42%
New Mexico	99,661	77,896	-22%
New York	1,143,962	795,030	-31%
North Carolina	267,326	124,432	-53%
North Dakota	13,146	8,227	-37%
Ohio	549,312	258,773	-53%
Oklahoma	96,201	50,910	-47%
Oregon	78,419	44,565	-43%
Pennsylvania	531,059	304,451	-43%
Puerto Rico	151,023	103,220	-32%
Rhode Island	56,560	49,897	-12%
South Carolina	114,273	40,293	-65%
South Dakota	15,896	7,625	-52%
Tennessee	254,818	147,137	-42%
Texas	649,018	288,525	-56%
Utah	39,073	28,909	-26%
Vermont	24,331	17,585	-28%
Virgin Islands	4,898	3,531	-28%
Virginia	152,845	83,733	-45%
Washington	268,927	164,323	-39%
West Virginia	89,039	31,032	-65%
Wisconsin	148,888	27,140	-82%
Wyoming	11,398	1,621	-86%
U.S. Total	12,241,489	6,889,315	-44%

SOURCE: The Administration for Children and Families, U.S. Department of Health and Human Services, Washington, D.C., 1999

observers believe it is mostly accountable to the welfare reform while others feel the drop is largely due to the strong national economy.

CHARACTERISTICS OF AFDC RECIPIENTS

Children made up the majority of AFDC recipients. Of the 12.6 million Americans who received AFDC support in each month of 1996, about 8.7 million (68.6 per-cent) were children. In 1980, 69.1 percent of AFDC recipients were children. The proportion of children held relatively steady from 1980 to 1996. (See Table 7.12.)

AFDC was given to families in which a child lacked parental support because a parent had died, was disabled, or was absent from home. The reasons varied for the deprivation of children who received AFDC benefits from October 1995 through September 1996. Most children (60 percent) had mothers who were not married. Over one-fifth (22 percent) had parents who were either divorced or separated. Seven percent had an unemployed parent. (See Table 7.14.)

While one of the major criticisms of the AFDC program was the belief that welfare mothers had many children in order to get additional benefits, the average AFDC family had only 1.9 children. Between 1980 and 1996 the average AFDC family changed very little in the number of children, having only from 1.9 to 2 children. In 1996, 69 percent of AFDC families had only one or two children. (See Table 7.12.) Comparing the number of children in AFDC families with other categories of families, married couples in poverty had the largest average number of children (2.6). However, the number of children in all categories of families has declined over the past generation. (See Figure 7.4.)

Ninety-six percent of the adult recipients were natural or adoptive parents of the youngest child in the AFDC family. Barely 2 percent were grandparents. (See Table 7.15.) Women were 87 percent of all AFDC recipients.

In 1996 African American families were 37 percent of the AFDC cases; white families, 36 percent; Hispanics, 21 percent; Asians, 3 percent; and Native Americans, 1.3 percent. Between 1983 and 1996, fairly equal proportions of cases had either white or black parents. However, the proportion of cases headed by Hispanic parents nearly doubled between 1983 and 1996, from 10.5 percent to 20.7 percent. (See Table 7.16.)

The proportion of black or white AFDC children remained somewhat consistent from 1983 to 1996 as well. During the same period, Hispanic recipient children significantly increased their percentage of the caseload, from 12.6 percent in 1983 to 22.4 percent in 1996. While Asians represented only a small percentage of recipients, this group became an increasing proportion of the caseload throughout this period. (See Table 7.17.)

Since 1983 an increasing proportion of adult AFDC recipients were non-citizens residing legally in the United States. About 13 percent of AFDC adults were non-citizens. Illegal immigrants have never been eligible for assistance. (See Table 7.18.)

AFDC recipients were likely to participate in one or more other programs. TANF recipients are also eligible

TABLE 7.14

Percent Distribution of AFDC Families by Reason for Deprivation of the Youngest Child, October 1995–September 1996

| | | | | ONE OR BOTH PARENTS ABSENT AND | | | | | | | |
| STATE | TOTAL FAMILIES | DIVORCED OR LEGALLY SEPARATED | SEPARATED BUT NOT LEGALLY | NOT MARRIED PATERNITY ESTABLISHED | | OTHER ABSENCE | CHILD UNBORN! | PARENT | | | |
				YES	NO			UNEM-PLOYED	DE-CEASED	INCAPA-CITATED	UN-KNOWN
U.S. TOTAL	4,533,308	10.7%	11.1%	25.2%	35.2%	2.1%	1.1%	7.1%	1.6%	3.7%	2.2%

SOURCE: *Characteristics and Financial Circumstances of AFDC Recipients: FY 1996.* U.S. Department of Health and Human Services: Washington, D.C., n.d.

FIGURE 7.4

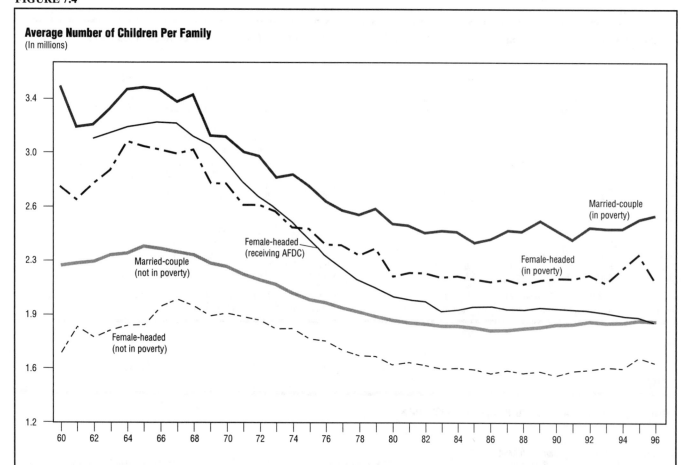

Average Number of Children Per Family
(In millions)

Note: For 1960-74 the average number of children per married-couple family is estimated based on all male-headed families of which during this period they comprised 98-99 percent.

SOURCE: *Aid to Families with Dependent Children: The Baseline.* U.S. Department of Health and Human Services: Washington, D.C., 1998

for these types of assistance. Of the almost 4.6 million families on AFDC in 1996, 89.3 percent received food stamps. (See Table 7.19.) In most states, families qualifying for AFDC also qualified for food stamps.

Though the largest expenditure for most families is for shelter, less than one-third of AFDC families received housing assistance from any source. Most of the 1996 AFDC recipients (62 percent) rented private homes or apartments with no rent subsidies. Only about 9 percent lived in public housing. The Department of Housing and Urban Development (HUD) helped 12 percent pay their rent. (See Chapter 8 for more information on federal housing.) Approximately 7 percent had free housing while only 4 percent owned or were buying their homes. (See Table 7.20.)

TABLE 7.15

Percent Distribution of AFDC Adults in the Assistance Unit by their Relationship to the Youngest Child in the AFDC Unit, October 1995–September 1996

| | | | RELATIONSHIP | | | | | |
STATE	TOTAL ADULTS	NATURAL/ ADOPTIVE PARENTS	STEP- PARENT	GRAND- PARENT	SIB- LING	OTHER RELATIVE	NON- RELATIVE	UN- KNOWN
U.S. TOTAL	3,933,599	96.4%	0.3%	1.7%	0.1%	0.4%	0.3%	0 .7%

SOURCE: *Characteristics and Financial Circumstances of AFDC Recipients: FY 1996.* U.S. Department of Health and Human Services: Washington, D.C., n.d.

TABLE 7.16

Distribution of AFDC Families by Race of Parent, 1983–1996

| | Race of Parent | | | | | |
Fiscal Year	White	African- American	Hispanic	Asian	Native- American	Unknown
1983	36.5	38.3	10.5	1.3	0.9	12.6
1984	36.6	36.7	10.7	1.8	0.9	3.9
1985	40.8	41.6	13.6	2.4	1.2	2.2
1986	39.7	40.7	14.4	2.3	1.3	1.4
1987	38.8	39.8	15.5	2.6	1.3	2.0
1988	38.8	39.8	15.7	2.4	1.4	1.9
1989	38.4	40.1	15.9	2.7	1.3	1.5
1990	38.1	39.7	16.6	2.8	1.3	1.5
1991	38.1	38.8	17.4	2.8	1.3	1.6
1992	38.9	37.2	17.8	2.8	1.4	2.0
1993	38.3	36.6	18.5	2.9	1.3	2.2
1994	37.4	36.4	19.9	2.9	1.3	2.1
1995	35.6	37.2	20.7	3.0	1.3	2.2
1996	35.9	37.2	20.7	3.0	1.3	2.2

SOURCE: *Aid to Families with Dependent Children: The Baseline.* U.S. Department of Health and Human Services: Washington, D.C., 1998

TABLE 7.17

Distribution of AFDC Children by Race, 1983–1996

| | Race of Child | | | | | |
Fiscal Year	White	African- American	Hispanic	Asian	Native- American	Unknown
1983	33.7	40.9	12.6	1.8	1.1	9.9
1984	34.1	40.4	13.0	2.3	1.1	9.2
1985	34.6	41.9	14.5	2.9	1.1	5.0
1986	35.1	42.0	15.6	3.1	1.3	3.0
1987	34.4	41.1	16.9	3.4	1.3	3.0
1988	33.8	41.3	17.4	2.9	1.3	3.2
1989	33.5	41.4	17.1	.3.8	1.3	2.9
1990	33.1	41.4	17.7	3.9	1.3	2.7
1991	33.5	40.1	18.5	3.7	1.3	2.9
1992	33.9	38.5	18.7	3.9	1.6	3.4
1993	33.7	38.0	19.5	3.8	1.4	3.7
1994	33.0	37.9	21.2	3.6	1.4	2.9
1995	31.2	38.5	22.2	4.1	1.5	2.4
1996	31.6	38.4	22.4	3.8	1.4	2.4

SOURCE: *Aid to Families with Dependent Children: The Baseline.* U.S. Department of Health and Human Services: Washington, D.C., 1998

TABLE 7.18

Citizenship Status of Adult AFDC Recipients, 1983–1996

| | Percent of Adult Recipients | | Percent Change | | Number of Adult Recipients | | |
Year	Citizen	Non- Citizen	Citizen	Non- Citizen	Citizen	Non- Citizen	Total
1983	91.0	9.0	–	–	3,310	327	3,637
1984	93.7	6.3	3.0	-30.0	3,373	227	3,600
1985	93.4	6.6	-0.3	4.8	3,373	238	3,612
1986	93.4	6.6	0.0	0.0	3,489	247	3,736
1987	92.9	7.1	-0.5	7.6	3,546	271	3,817
1988	93.4	6.6	0.5	-7.0	3,517	249	3,765
1989	93.0	7.0	-0.4	6.1	3,444	259	3,703
1990	91.9	8.1	-1.2	15.7	3,578	315	3,893
1991	91.2	8.8	-0.8	8.6	3,799	367	4,166
1992	90.7	9.3	-0.5	5.7	4,023	412	4,435
1993	89.2	10.8	-1.7	16.1	4,105	497	4,602
1994	87.3	12.7	-2.1	17.6	4,025	585	4,610
1995	86.8	13.2	-0.6	3.9	3,741	569	4,310
1996	86.7	13.3	-0.1	0.8	3,410	523	3.934

SOURCE: *Aid to Families with Dependent Children: The Baseline.* U.S. Department of Health and Human Services: Washington, D.C., 1998

LENGTH OF TIME ON WELFARE

A number of studies have investigated the length of time welfare recipients receive assistance. While most recipients left the AFDC program after a fairly short period of assistance, many returned later, potentially cycling in and out of welfare a number of times. Therefore, researchers measured not just the length of a given spell but also the total time of all spells in an individual's lifetime.

While 49 percent of AFDC recipients beginning any given spell receive assistance for two or fewer years, only 19 percent have welfare spells longer than seven years. However, for persons beginning their first AFDC spell, 36.5 percent spend less than two years on AFDC in their lifetime, and 29 percent spend eight or more years. (See Table 7.21.)

Despite cycling, over half of those beginning AFDC spells will spend less than a total of five on assistance. At the same time, the study showed that, at any given time, 56 percent of welfare recipients were in the midst of very long periods of welfare (8 years or more) and that these long-term recipients used most of the program's funds. (See Table 7.21.)

In "Targeting Would-Be Long-Term Recipients of AFDC," David T. Ellwood found that marital status was the single most powerful predictor of long-term welfare receipt. Single women receiving welfare averaged 9 years on AFDC and represented 40 percent of those receiving welfare benefits at any one time. Thirty-nine percent were predicted to receive AFDC for 10 years or more.

In "Who Is Affected by Time Limits?" (Urban Institute, Washington D.C., 1995), LaDonna Pavetti presented findings about personal characteristics related to long-term welfare receipt. Persons who had less than 12 years of education were more likely to use AFDC for longer

periods of time. No recent work experience was another factor in long-term use. Those who never married were more likely to spend longer than 60 months on welfare. Other groups likely to use welfare for a long period were those under the age of 24, Hispanics or African Americans, those with a child below age 3, and those who had 3 or more children. (See Table 7.22 and Table 7.23.)

Such statistics will certainly change under the TANF program with its five-year lifetime limit on benefits for

TABLE 7.19

Number and Percent of AFDC Families Receiving Food Stamps, Selected Years, 1967–1996

Fiscal Year	Total AFDC Families (thousands)	AFDC Families Receiving Food Stamps Number (thousands)	Percent
1967	1,141	252	22.1
1969	1,538	455	29.6
1971	2,531	1,339	52.9
1973	3,123	2,136	68.4
1975	3,342	2,510	75.1
1977	3,574	2,645	74.0
1979	3,493	2,623	75.1
1981	3,651	3,030	83.0
1984	3,725	2,984	80.1
1985	3,692	2,998	81.2
1986	3,748	3,024	80.7
1987	3,784	3,137	82.9
1988	3,748	3,171	84.6
1989	3,771	3,213	85.2
1990	3,974	3,402	85.6
1991	4,374	3,814	87.2
1992	4,768	4,163	87.3
1993	4,981	4,408	88.5
1994	5,046	4,476	88.7
1995	4,881	4,383	89.8
1996	4.548	4.062	89.3

SOURCE: *Aid to Families with Dependent Children: The Baseline.* U.S. Department of Health and Human Services: Washington, D.C., 1998

TABLE 7.20

Housing Arrangements of AFDC Families, by Type of Shelter, 1984–1996

Fiscal Year	Proportion of AFDC Families with							
	Public Housing	HUD Rent Subsidies	Other Rent Subsidies	Group Quarters	Free Rent	Own Home	Rental Housing, no Subsidies	Emergency Shelters or Unknown
1984	9.5	7.1	1.4	2.3	5.3	5.8	62.5	6.0
1985	9.4	8.6	1.4	2.0	4.5	4.9	63.9	5.3
1986	9.6	9.1	1.6	1.9	5.3	4.9	63.8	3.9
1987	9.9	9.8	1.6	1.4	5.5	4.8	63.0	3.8
1988	9.6	11.2	1.7	1.6	6.0	5.0	62.3	2.8
1989	9.6	12.1	1.8	1.6	6.5	4.7	62.9	0.7
1990	9.6	12.2	2.1	1.7	6.8	4.5	62.4	0.6
1991	9.5	11.5	1.9	1.6	6.8	4.4	63.8	0.5
1992	9.2	12.1	1.7	1.7	7.2	4.4	63.1	0.6
1993	8.8	12.6	1.7	1.6	7.1	4.3	63.3	0.6
1994	8.3	12.0	2.0	1.6	7.0	4.2	64.2	0.6
1995	8.0	12.1	2.4	1.6	6.9	4.0	64.2	0.6
1996	8.8	12.2	2.6	1.9	7.2	4.3	62.3	7.0

SOURCE: *Aid to Families with Dependent Children: The Baseline.* U.S. Department of Health and Human Services: Washington, D.C., 1998

TABLE 7.21

Distribution of Estimated Time on AFDC Based on Annual Data

	Single spell analysis		Multiple spell analysis	
Total years of AFDC receipt	Proportion of spell beginners	Proportion of current caseload	Proportion of new recipients	Proportion of current caseload
1-2	48.9	14.2	36.5	8.5
3-4	20.0	14.7	18.6	10.4
5-7	12.5	15.3	16.0	15.1
8+	18.6	55.8	29.0	66.0
Total	**100.0**	**100.0**	**100.0**	**100.0**

SOURCE: *Aid to Families with Dependent Children: The Baseline.* U.S. Department of Health and Human Services: Washington, D.C., 1998

adults and the requirement to work after two years in order to continue to receive benefits. In fact, these two provisions concern some observers. One concern is the time limit, especially in regions with high unemployment. Others worry that many women will be unable to compete for and hold onto even low-wage jobs because of a lack of skills and inadequate child care.

TEEN MOTHERS AND WELFARE

The new welfare-reform law contains provisions to encourage two-parent families and reduce out-of-wedlock births. Several provisions deal specifically with the reduction of births among teen mothers. According to Rebecca Maynard, in *Kids Having Kids: A Robin Hood Foundation Special Report on the Costs of Adolescent Childbearing* (The Robin Hood Foundation, New York, 1996), 70 percent of teen mothers received welfare and approximately 40 percent stayed on AFDC for five years or more. Teen mothers tend to have less education and fewer job skills. The Family Planning Councils of America estimate that approximately 80 percent of the children whose unmarried mother did not graduate from high school live in poverty.

TABLE 7.23

Proportion of Recipients With Given Characteristics at Start of First AFDC Spell
[In Percent]

Expected total lifetime receipt of AFDC	High school dropout, no GED	No prior work experience	Under age 25	Never-married	Black	Hispanic
All recipients	47	39	53	58	28	16
Under 24 months	35	30	44	48	23	13
60 or more months	63	50	64	72	34	23

Table reads: 35 percent of individuals whose lifetime total receipt of welfare is 23 months or less are high school dropouts without a GED.

SOURCE: *Aid to Families with Dependent Children: The Baseline.* U.S. Department of Health and Human Services: Washington, D.C., 1998

TABLE 7.22

How Selected Characteristics Affect Expected Total Time on Welfare for a Beginning Cohort of Recipients
[In Percent]

Characteristics at start of first AFDC spell	Proportion of all first-time recipients	Proportion expected to receive AFDC for	
		24+ months	60+ months
All recipients	100.0	57.8	34.8
Education:			
< 9 years	13.0	75.3	63.4
9-11 years	34.0	66.2	40.0
12+ years	53.0	48.2	24.3
Work experience:			
No recent	38.7	67.1	44.9
Recent	61.3	52.0	28.3
Age:			
Under 24	52.7	64.5	41.9
25-30	24.9	51.9	25.6
31-40	19.3	48.4	28.3
Over 40	3.1	51.1	25.2
Race:			
White/other	55.6	50.9	26.7
Black	28.4	66.4	41.4
Hispanic	16.0	66.9	50.7
Marital status:			
Never married	58.2	65.5	43.1
Ever married	41.8	47.2	23.0
Age of youngest child:			
< 12 months	52.1	64.8	39.2
13-36 months	16.6	55.5	37.9
37-60 months	10.9	54.3	29.5
61-120 months	11.2	49.7	29.9
121+ months	9.3	37.1	15.2
Number of children:			
1	57.2	57.0	35.8
2	33.2	58.2	31.9
3	7.5	58.7	35.9
Over 3	2.2	71.0	43.1

Columns 2 and 3 read: 75.3 percent of individuals who begin their first spell of welfare with less than a 9th grade education are expected to receive welfare for 24 months or more over their lifetime.

SOURCE: *Aid to Families with Dependent Children: The Baseline.* U.S. Department of Health and Human Services: Washington, D.C., 1998

The percent of children born to unmarried teens is very high. In 1996, among teen births, over three-quarters (76.4 percent) of children were born outside of marriage, compared to less than half (48.3 percent) in 1980. About 7.7 percent of white births were to unmarried teens, a considerable increase from the 4.4 percent in 1980. On the other hand, the rate of African American births to unmarried teens dropped slightly over the same time period, from 22.2 percent in 1980 to 21 percent in 1996. (See Table 7.24.)

In 1998 five out of every one hundred teenage girls had a baby. About one in four teenage mothers went on to have a second baby within two years after the birth of their first baby.

The approximately 1 million births to teens each year is a concern to society because teen mothers tend to have less education and less ability to support and care for their children. In addition, according to Maynard, in *Kids Having Kids*, babies born to teen mothers are:

TABLE 7.24

Percent of Births to Unmarried Women Within Age Group and Percent of Births to Unmarried Teens Ages 15 to 19

Percent of Births to Unmarried Women Within Age Groups

Year	Under 15	15-17 Yrs.	18-19 Yrs.	All Teens	All Women
1980	88.7	61.5	39.8	48.3	18.4
1981	89.2	63.3	41.4	49.9	18.9
1982	89.2	65.0	43.0	51.4	19.4
1983	90.4	67.5	45.7	54.1	20.3
1984	91.1	69.2	48.1	56.3	21.0
1985	91.8	70.9	50.7	58.7	22.0
1986	92.5	73.3	53.6	61.5	23.4
1987	92.9	75.8	56.0	64.0	24.5
1988	93.6	77.1	58.5	65.9	25.7
1989	92.4	77.7	60.4	67.2	27.1
1990	91.6	77.7	61.3	67.6	28.0
1991	91.3	78.7	63.2	69.3	29.5
1992	91.3	79.2	64.6	70.5	30.1
1993	91.3	79.9	66.1	71.8	31.0
1994	94.5	84.1	70.0	75.9	32.6
1995	93.5	83.7	69.8	75.6	32.2
1996	94.0	84.5	70.9	76.4	32.4

Percent of Births to Unmarried Teens Ages 15 to 19

Year	All Races	White	Black
1980	7.3	4.4	22.2
1981	7.1	4.5	21.5
1982	7.1	4.5	21.2
1983	7.2	4.6	21.2
1984	7.1	4.6	20.7
1985	7.2	4.8	20.3
1986	7.5	5.1	20.1
1987	7.7	5.3	20.0
1988	8.0	5.6	20.3
1989	8.3	5.9	18.6
1990	8.4	6.1	18.3
1991	8.7	6.4	18.1
1992	8.7	6.5	20.2
1993	8.9	6.8	20.2
1994	9.7	7.5	21.1
1995	9.6	7.6	21.1
1996	9.6	7.7	21.0

Notes: Beginning in 1980, births to unmarried women in the United States are based on data from states reporting marital status directly and data from nonreporting states for which marital status was inferred from other information on the birth certificate. Data for 1996 are preliminary.

SOURCE: *Indicators of Welfare Dependence: Annual Report to Congress, October 1997.* U.S. Department of Health and Human Services: Washington, D.C., n.d.

• More likely to be born prematurely and to be of low birth weight.

• At risk for health problems, lower cognitive skills, and behavioral problems.

• Less likely to grow up in homes with their fathers, possibly causing emotional as well as financial problems.

• At greater risk to be abused.

By some estimates, teen parents under age 17 cost the United States close to $7 billion per year. These negative consequences motivated Congress to include provisions in the welfare-reform legislation to encourage the reduction of the incidence of births to unmarried women, with the emphasis on teenagers.

To receive TANF benefits, states must have submitted plans detailing their efforts to reduce out-of-wedlock births, especially among teenagers. In order to be eligible for TANF benefits, unmarried minor parents are required to remain in high school or its equivalent as well as to live in an adult-supervised setting. One provision in the law allows for the creation of second-chance homes for teen parents and their children, a type of home that already existed in some states. These homes require that all residents either enroll in school or participate in a job-training program. They also provide parenting and life skills classes as well as counseling and support services.

A grant separate from the TANF block grant rewards states for the reduction of births outside of marriage combined with a decline in abortion rate. Grant money is also available for states to implement abstinence-only education programs. In addition, the welfare-reform law directs the Department of Health and Human Services to provide a strategy to prevent unmarried teen pregnancies and to ensure that 25 percent of the communities in the United States implement a teen pregnancy prevention program. These measures supplement already-existing federal and state efforts.

The teenage birth rate is declining. Between 1991 and 1998 the rate fell by 18 percent (from 62.1 per 1,000 to 51.1). Still, 1 out of 4 teenage mothers went on to have a second baby within two years of their first baby.

CHAPTER 8

FEDERALLY ADMINISTERED MEANS-TESTED PROGRAMS

"Means-tested" programs provide benefits to those whose income and financial resources meet certain requirements. More than 80 benefit programs provide cash and/or non-cash aid to individuals who meet certain low-income qualifications. Cash assistance programs include the Earned Income Tax Credit (EITC, discussed in Chapter 3) and Supplemental Security Income (SSI).

SUPPLEMENTAL SECURITY INCOME

Supplemental Security Income (SSI) is a means-tested income assistance program authorized by Title XVI of the Social Security Act. The SSI program replaced the combined federal-state programs of Old Age Assistance, Aid to the Blind, and Aid to the Permanently and Totally Disabled in 50 states and the District of Columbia. However, these programs still exist in Guam, Puerto Rico, and the Virgin Islands. Since the first payments in 1974 SSI has provided monthly cash payments to needy aged, blind, and disabled individuals who meet the eligibility requirements. States may supplement the basic federal SSI payment.

Eligibility Requirements for SSI Recipients

There are a number of requirements that must be met in order to get financial benefits from Supplemental Security Income. First, a person must meet the program criteria for age, blindness, or disability. The aged, or elderly, are persons 65 years and older. To be considered legally blind, a person must have vision of 20/200 or less in the better eye with the use of corrective lenses, have tunnel vision of 20 degrees or less (can only see a small area straight ahead), or have met state qualifications for the earlier Aid to the Blind program.

A person is disabled if he or she cannot earn money at a job because of a physical or mental illness or injury that may cause his or her death, or if the condition lasts

for 12 months or longer. Those who met earlier state Aid to the Permanently Disabled requirements may also qualify for assistance.

Children under age 18 (or 22 if a full-time student) and unmarried may qualify for SSI if they have a medically determinable physical or mental impairment that substantially reduces their ability to function independently as well as effectively engage in "age-appropriate" activities. This impairment must be expected to result in death or to last for a continuous period of more than 12 months.

The Personal Responsibility and Work Opportunity Act of 1996 (PL 104-193) abolished Aid to Families with Dependent Children, but it did not eliminate SSI. However, the welfare reform law prohibited all non-citizens from receiving SSI, with the exception of veterans and those who have worked for 10 years and paid Social Security. It also made it harder for disabled children under 18 to get SSI. To be eligible, a disabled child must have "marked and severe functional limitations."

Because SSI is a means-tested benefit, a person's income and property must be counted before he or she can receive benefits. Table 8.1 shows the maximum income that an individual and couple can have, with some income exclusions, and still be eligible for SSI benefits. In 1996 a person could have no more than $2,000 worth of property, and a couple could have no more than $3,000 worth of property (mainly in savings accounts or stocks and bonds). Not included in countable resources are the person's home, as well as household goods and personal effects worth less than $2,000. A car is not counted if a member of the household uses it to go to and from work or to medical treatments or if it has been changed, especially for a handicapped person. A person applying for SSI may have life insurance with a cash value of $1,500 or less and/or a burial policy up to the same value. In 2000 the numbers were the same.

TABLE 8.1

Maximum Income for Eligibility for Federal SSI Benefits, 1996

	Receiving only Social Security		Receiving only wage income	
	Monthly	Annually	Monthly	Annually
Individual	$490	$5,800	$1,025	$12,300
Couple	725	8,700	1,495	17,940

SOURCE: Office of Supplemental Security Income, Social Security Administration

Recipients of SSI Benefits

Over 6.6 million persons received SSI payments in 1999, down 9,425 from 1998 (less than one percent). Of these, about 5.2 million were disabled, 1.4 million were elderly, and 81,000 were blind. (See Figure 8.1.) Among the number of SSI recipients between 1975 and 1998, while the number of elderly recipients has been dropping, the number of disabled receiving SSI has been increasing. In 1998 the leading causes of disability among adults and children were mental disorders and mental retardation. (See Table 8.2.)

About 59 percent of SSI recipients were women, and 41 percent were men. Almost two-thirds (60.3 percent) of those receiving SSI benefits were white, about one fourth (29.3 percent) were black, and 9 percent were "other" races or ethnic groups. (See Table 8.3.)

Cost of the SSI Program

As of January 2000 an individual SSI recipient could receive up to $512 per month. If both people were eligible, a couple could get up to $751. In 1999 the average SSI recipient received $369 per month.

The cost of the program rose from $11 billion in 1985 to $16.6 billion in 1990 and to $30.2 in 1998. (See Table 8.4.) Costs were approximately $31.2 billion in 1999.

NON-CASH MEANS-TESTED BENEFITS

Non-cash benefits are those given in a form other than cash, such as vouchers, coupons, or commodities of some kind. The remainder of this chapter discusses some of the major non-cash means-tested programs, including food stamps, the National School Lunch and School Breakfast Programs, the Women, Infants, and Children (WIC) program, Medicaid, Head Start, home energy assistance, and housing assistance.

Under the Personal Responsibility and Work Opportunity Reconciliation Act (PL 104-193), the welfare-reform law enacted in August 1996, many of these programs will be funded as block grants (lump sums of money) from the federal government to the states. (For more information about this welfare law, see Chapter 2.)

FIGURE 8.1

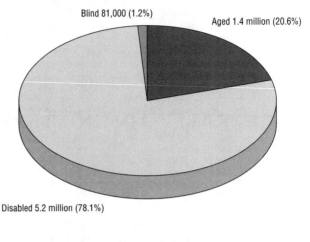

Percent of Recipients of Federally and State-Administered SSI, by Category, December 1998

Blind 81,000 (1.2%)

Aged 1.4 million (20.6%)

Disabled 5.2 million (78.1%)

SOURCE: *Annual Statistical Supplement, 1999.* Social Security Administration: Washington, D.C., 1999

FOOD STAMPS

The Food Stamp Program, administered by the United States Department of Agriculture, is the country's largest food assistance program. Food stamps are designed to help low-income families purchase a nutritionally adequate, low-cost diet. Generally, food stamps may only be used to buy food to be prepared at home. They may not be used for alcohol, tobacco, or hot foods intended to be eaten immediately, such as restaurant or delicatessen food.

Title VIII of the 1996 Personal Responsibility and Work Opportunity Reconciliation Act continues to fund the Food Stamp Program, but the maximum benefits have been reduced. The welfare-reform law lowered the program's expenditures by more than $23 billion from 1997 to 2002. In addition to reduced benefits for many families, it created time limits for benefits to able-bodied adults without dependents and eliminated benefits to most legal immigrants.

In June 1997 the Supplemental Appropriations Act (PL 105-18) gave states the authority to purchase federal food stamps with which to provide state-funded food assistance to those who had been eliminated from the program under the new welfare-reform law. The Agricultural Research, Extension, and Education Reform Act of 1998 (PL 105-185) restored food stamp benefits to 250,000 of the 900,000 immigrants who had earlier lost eligibility.

Participation in the Food Stamp Program

The "typical" American household spends 30 percent of its monthly income on food purchases. The program calculates 30 percent of the family's earnings and then

TABLE 8.2

Number of People Receiving Payments, by Category 1974–98

Month and year	Total	Federally administered	Federal SSI	State supplementation				
				Total	Federally administered		State administered	
					Total	Only	Total	Only
All persons								
January 1974	3,248,949	3,215,632	2,955,959	1,838,602	1,480,309	259,673	358,293	33,317
December:								
1975	4,359,625	4,314,275	3,893,419	1,987,409	1,684,018	420,856	303,391	45,350
1980	4,194,100	4,142,017	3,682,411	1,934,239	1,684,765	459,606	249,474	52,083
1985	4,200,177	4,138,021	3,799,092	1,915,503	1,660,847	338,929	254,656	62,156
1990	4,888,180	4,817,127	4,412,131	2,343,803	2,058,273	404,996	285,530	71,053
1991	5,199,539	5,118,470	4,729,639	2,512,220	2,204,329	388,831	307,891	81,069
1992	5,646,877	5,566,189	5,202,249	2,684,371	2,371,564	363,940	312,807	80,688
1993	6,064,502	5,984,330	5,635,995	2,849,887	2,536,349	348,335	313,538	80,172
1994	6,377,111	6,295,786	5,965,130	2,950,470	2,628,431	330,658	322,039	81,325
1995	6,575,753	6,514,134	6,194,493	2,817,408	2,517,805	319,641	299,603	61,619
1996	6,676,729	6,613,718	6,325,531	2,731,681	2,421,470	288,187	310,211	63,011
1997	6,564,613	6,494,985	6,211,867	3,029,449	2,372,479	283,118	656,970	69,628
1998	6,649,465	6,566,069	6,289,070	3,072,392	2,411,707	276,999	660,685	83,396
Aged								
January 1974	1,889,898	1,865,109	1,690,496	1,022,244	770,318	174,613	251,926	24,789
December:								
1975	2,333,685	2,307,105	2,024,765	1,028,596	843,917	282,340	184,679	26,580
1980	1,838,381	1,807,776	1,533,366	837,318	702,763	274,410	134,555	30,605
1985	1,529,674	1,504,469	1,322,292	698,634	583,913	182,177	114,721	25,205
1990	1,484,160	1,454,041	1,256,623	765,420	649,530	197,418	115,890	30,119
1991	1,497,817	1,464,684	1,278,674	785,366	665,406	186,010	119,960	33,133
1992	1,504,586	1,471,022	1,304,469	792,289	674,463	166,553	117,826	33,564
1993	1,507,463	1,474,852	1,323,577	801,226	685,779	151,275	115,447	32,611
1994	1,499,367	1,465,905	1,326,459	801,257	685,712	139,446	115,545	33,462
1995	1,479,415	1,446,122	1,314,720	777,841	663,390	131,402	114,451	33,293
1996	1,446,321	1,412,632	1,296,462	752,760	638,173	116,170	114,587	33,689
1997	1,395,845	1,362,350	1,251,374	750,168	619,516	110,976	130,652	33,495
1998	1,369,206	1,331,782	1,225,578	756,209	617,984	106,204	138,225	37,424
Blind								
January 1974	73,850	72,390	55,680	45,828	37,326	16,710	8,502	1,460
December:								
1975	75,315	74,489	68,375	36,309	31,376	6,114	4,933	826
1980	79,139	78,401	68,945	39,863	36,214	9,456	3,649	738
1985	82,622	82,220	73,817	41,323	38,291	8,403	3,032	402
1990	84,109	83,686	74,781	43,376	40,334	8,905	3,042	423
1991	85,227	84,549	76,143	44,918	41,323	8,406	3,595	678
1992	86,070	85,400	77,634	45,234	41,682	7,766	3,552	670
1993	86,169	85,456	78,018	45,373	41,771	7,438	3,602	713
1994	85,609	84,911	78,033	44,779	41,253	6,878	3,526	698
1995	84,273	83,545	77,064	42,272	38,695	6,481	3,577	728
1996	82,815	82,137	76,180	40,173	36,759	5,957	3,414	678
1997	81,449	80,778	74,926	40,593	36,050	5,852	4,543	671
1998	81,029	80,243	74,623	40,828	36,193	5,620	4,635	786
Disabled								
January 1974	1,285,201	1,278,122	1,209,783	769,501	672,575	68,350	96,926	7,068
December:								
1975	1,950,625	1,932,681	1,800,279	922,229	808,725	132,402	113,504	17,944
1980	2,276,130	2,255,840	2,080,100	1,050,155	945,788	175,740	104,367	20,290
1985	2,586,741	2,551,332	2,402,983	1,167,326	1,038,643	148,349	128,683	35,409
1990	3,319,911	3,279,400	3,080,727	1,535,007	1,368,409	198,673	166,598	40,511
1991	3,615,438	3,569,237	3,374,822	1,680,590	1,497,600	194,415	182,990	46,201
1992	4,055,105	4,009,767	3,820,146	1,845,464	1,655,419	189,621	190,045	45,338
1993	4,469,711	4,424,022	4,234,400	2,001,855	1,808,799	189,622	193,056	45,689
1994	4,790,658	4,744,970	4,560,638	2,102,711	1,901,466	184,332	201,245	45,688
1995	5,010,326	4,984,467	4,802,709	1,995,262	1,815,720	181,758	179,542	25,859
1996	5,145,850	5,118,949	4,952,889	1,933,493	1,746,538	166,060	186,955	26,901
1997	5,078,995	5,051,857	4,885,567	1,998,187	1,716,913	166,290	281,274	27,138
1998	5,190,815	5,154,044	4,988,869	2,067,530	1,757,530	165,175	310,000	36,771

SOURCE: *Annual Statistical Supplement, 1999.* Social Security Administration: Washington, D.C., 1999

TABLE 8.3

Number and Percentage Distribution of People Receiving Federally Administered Payments, by Race,[1] Sex, and Age, November 1998
[Based on 1-percent sample]

Sex and age	Total	White	Black	Other	Unknown
All recipients	6,589,000	60.3	29.3	9.0	1.4
Under 18	897,500	52.3	41.5	4.7	1.5
18–64	3,639,800	63.1	29.4	6.5	1.0
65 or older	2,051,700	58.8	23.9	15.4	2.0
Male	2,720,900	59.9	29.7	8.9	1.5
Under 18	570,700	52.0	41.7	4.9	1.4
18–64	1,589,100	63.2	29.1	6.6	1.2
65 or older	561,100	58.8	19.1	19.7	2.4
Female	3,868,100	60.5	29.1	9.1	1.4
Under 18	326,800	52.9	41.2	4.3	1.6
18–64	2,050,700	63.0	29.7	6.4	1.0
65 or older	1,490,600	58.7	25.7	13.8	1.9

[1] Codes for parents have been assigned to some recipients under age 42 with missing race codes.

SOURCE: *Annual Statistical Supplement, 1999.* Social Security Administration: Washington, D.C., 1999

issues enough food stamps to make up the difference between that amount and the amount needed to buy an adequate diet. These monthly allotments of coupons are then redeemed for food at retail food stores. Some food stamp programs provide benefits electronically through an electronic benefit transfer (EBT), a debit card similar to a bank card. In an effort to reduce fraud and to save money, the 1996 welfare-reform law requires all states to convert to EBT issuance by fiscal year 2002.

The cash value of these benefits is based on the size of the household and how much the family earns. Households without an elderly or disabled member generally must have a monthly total (gross) cash income at or below 130 percent of the poverty level and may not have liquid assets (cash, savings, or other assets that can be easily sold) of more than $2,000. (If the household has an elderly member, the asset limit is $3,000.) Net monthly income (gross income minus any approved deductions for child care, some shelter costs, and other expenses) must be 100 percent or less of the poverty level, $1,157 per month for a family of three in 1999. (See Table 8.5.)

With some exceptions, food stamps are automatically available to SSI (Supplemental Security Income) and TANF (Temporary Assistance to Needy Families) recipients. Food stamp benefits are higher in states with lower TANF benefits because those benefits are considered a part of a family's countable income. (See Chapter 7.) To receive food stamps, certain household members must register for work, accept suitable job offers, or fulfill work or training requirements (such as looking or training for a job).

While the federal government sets guidelines and provides funding, the Food Stamp Program is actually

TABLE 8.4

Total Annual Amount of Payments, by Category 1974–98
[In thousands]

Calendar year	Total	Federal SSI	State supplementation Federally administered	State administered[1]
All persons				
1974	$ 5,245,719	$ 3,833,161	$1,263,652	$148,906
1975	5,878,224	4,313,538	1,402,534	162,152
1980	7,940,734	5,866,354	1,848,286	226,094
1985	11,060,476	8,777,341	1,972,597	310,538
1990	16,598,680	12,893,805	3,239,154	465,721
1991	18,524,229	14,764,795	3,230,844	528,590
1992	22,232,503	18,246,934	3,435,476	550,093
1993	24,556,867	20,721,613	3,269,540	565,714
1994	25,876,571	22,175,233	3,115,854	585,483
1995	27,627,658	23,919,430	3,117,850	590,378
1996	28,791,924	25,264,878	2,987,596	539,450
1997	29,052,089	25,457,387	2,913,181	681,521
1998	30,216,345	26,404,793	3,003,415	808,137
Aged				
1974	$ 2,503,407	$ 1,782,742	$ 631,292	$ 89,373
1975	2,604,792	1,842,980	673,535	88,277
1980	2,734,270	1,860,194	756,829	117,247
1985	3,034,596	2,202,557	694,114	137,925
1990	3,736,104	2,521,382	1,038,006	176,716
1991	3,890,412	2,691,681	998,652	200,079
1992	4,139,612	2,901,063	1,023,030	215,519
1993	4,250,092	3,097,616	933,852	218,624
1994	4,366,528	3,265,711	876,053	224,764
1995	4,467,146	3,374,772	864,450	227,924
1996	4,507,202	3,449,407	833,091	224,705
1997	4,531,973	3,479,948	823,581	228,444
1998	4,424,877	3,327,856	838,375	258,646
Blind				
1974	$ 130,195	$ 91,308	$ 34,483	$ 4,404
1975	130,936	92,427	34,813	3,696
1980	190,075	131,506	54,321	4,248
1985	264,162	195,183	64,657	4,322
1990	334,120	238,415	90,534	5,171
1991	346,828	254,140	86,437	6,251
1992	370,769	275,606	87,783	7,380
1993	374,998	287,754	79,479	7,765
1994	372,461	292,102	72,596	7,763
1995	375,512	298,238	69,203	8,071
1996	371,869	298,897	65,894	7,077
1997	374,857	302,656	65,189	7,012
1998	366,452	291,050	67,137	8,265
Disabled				
1974	$ 2,601,936	$ 1,959,112	$ 597,876	$ 44,948
1975	3,142,476	2,378,131	694,186	70,159
1980	5,013,948	3,874,655	1,037,137	102,156
1985	7,754,588	6,379,601	1,213,826	161,161
1990	12,520,568	10,134,007	2,110,615	275,946
1991	14,268,192	11,818,974	2,145,755	303,463
1992	17,710,514	15,070,265	2,324,664	315,585
1993	19,925,929	17,336,243	2,256,209	333,477
1994	21,131,001	18,617,421	2,167,205	346,375
1995	22,778,547	20,246,415	2,184,197	347,935
1996	23,905,578	21,516,579	2,088,610	300,389
1997	24,006,254	21,685,421	2,024,410	296,423
1998	25,304,721	22,785,879	2,097,903	420,939

[1] Includes data not distributed by category.

SOURCE: *Annual Statistical Supplement, 1999.* Social Security Administration: Washington, D.C., 1999

carried out by the states. They certify eligibility as well as calculate and issue benefit allotments. Most often, the welfare agency and staff that administer the TANF and Medicaid programs also run the food stamp program. The

TABLE 8.5

Gross and Net Income Eligibility Standards, Food Stamp Program, October 1, 1999–September 30, 2000

People in Household	Gross Income*	Net Income*
1	$ 893	$ 687
2	1,199	922
3	1,504	1,157
4	1,810	1,392
5	2,115	1,627
6	2,421	1,862
7	2,726	2,097

*Amounts are higher in Alaska and Hawaii.

SOURCE: *Food Stamp Program.* FNS-313. Food and Nutrition Service, U.S. Department of Agriculture, October 1999

regular food stamp program operates in all 50 states, the District of Columbia, Guam, and the Virgin Islands. (Puerto Rico is covered under a separate nutrition-assistance program.)

With the exception of some small differences in Alaska, Hawaii, and the territories, the program is run the same way throughout the United States. While the states pay for 50 percent of the administrative costs, the federal government pays for 100 percent of food stamp benefits and the other 50 percent of the operating costs. In 1997 the federal government paid $21.7 billion in food stamp benefits, or an average monthly benefit of about $71 per recipient. By 1999 the federal government paid only 17.7 billion in food stamp benefits. But because the number of recipients was down, the average monthly benefit per recipient actually rose to $72.23.

In federal food stamp funding between 1994 and 1997, the amount spent on food stamps in a given year differs from the Food Stamp Act appropriations (the amount available for spending). The appropriation is based on an estimate of the amount needed to fund the program. In 1997 the total food stamp program expenditure was $22.9 billion, while $27.6 billion was appropriated for that year. (See Table 8.6.)

How Many Receive Food Stamps?

Food stamp participation has increased significantly since 1978, when 6.5 percent of the total population was receiving food stamps. The number increased to about 9.2 percent in 1983 (a period of severe recession), dropped to 7.6 percent in 1988 and 1989, and then rose again in the 1990s. Participation generally peaks in periods of high unemployment, inflation, and recession. In 1995, 26.6 million persons (about 10.1 percent of the population) participated in the food stamp program, a 33 percent increase from the number of recipients in 1990. In 1999 the Food Stamp Program served an average of 18.2 million people each month. (See Table 8.7.)

TABLE 8.6

Recent Federal Food Stamp Funding
(In Millions)

	FY1994	FY 1995	FY1996	FY1997
Regular food stamp program spending[a]	$ 24,434	$ 24,535	$24,351	$21,694
(Benefits)	(22,675)	(22,651)	(22,399)	(19,668)
(Administration & Other costs)[b]	(1,759)	(1,884)	(1,952)	(2,026)
Puerto Rico's nutrition assistance grant[c]	1,091	1,143	1,143	1,174
Total food stamp spending	25,525	25,678	25,494	22,868
Food Stamp Act appropriations[d]	28,137	28,819	27,598	27,618

Note: Figures are from Agriculture Department documents submitted with annual appropriation requests and include federal funding from the food stamp budget account. They do *not* include about $1.6-$1.8 billion a year in state/local funds for administration and work/training programs.

[a] Regular program funding includes grants to American Samoa and the Northern Marianas.

[b] Amounts include federal funding for work/training programs for food stamp recipients, the federal share of state/local administrative costs, and certain federal costs associated with the program (e.g., printing and redeeming food stamp coupons. monitoring program compliance). They do *not* include: (1) approximately $60 million a year attributable to federal administrative activities related to food stamps, but budgeted under a separate Agriculture Department appropriation account for administration of various federal food assistance programs, and (2) federal payments for administrative costs under Puerto Rico's nutrition assistance grant (about $30 million a year, included in the amounts listed in this table for Puerto Rico's grant).

[c] These figures are the specific block grant amounts specified for each year in the Food Stamp Act. Included are federal payments for 50% of administrative costs and funds transferred for a cattle tick eradication project: $12 million a year in 1991 and 1995 and $9 million in 1996.

[d] Annual appropriations include: (1) contingency reserves. (2) a $12 million FY1995 rescission, (3) for FY1997, some $150 million available from the Food Stamp Act appropriation account for the Food Distribution Program on Indian Reservations and the Emergency Food Assistance program. *Additional* funds are available from benefit overpayment recoveries and payments from states choosing to pay for benefits to noncitizens.

SOURCE: Joe Richardson. *Food Stamps: Background and Funding.* Congressional Research Service, the Library of Congress: Washington, D.C., 1998

The food stamp program is the nation's largest source of food assistance, helping 6.5 percent of all Americans. Approximately 70 percent of those who are eligible participate. Half are children, and more than 15 percent are elderly or disabled.

Table 8.8 shows the numbers and percentages of poor households that received food stamps from 1988 to 1994. In 1994, 50.8 percent of all poor households received food stamps. Poor African American households (69.1 percent) were more likely to receive these benefits than were poor Hispanic (51.8 percent) or white (43.9 percent) households.

The number of poor households participating in the food stamp program increased from 14.9 million in 1988 to 19.3 million in 1994. The number of poor Hispanic households receiving food stamps grew by 73.8 percent during this period, while the number of poor white households increased 38.5 percent, and poor black households grew by 16.1 percent. (See Table 8.8.)

TABLE 8.7

Food Stamp Participation Rates in the United States, 1995–99
(Data as of April 27, 2000)

	FY 1995	FY 1996	FY 1997	FY 1998	FY 1999
FOOD STAMP PROGRAM[1]					
People Participating (Thous.)	26,619	25,542	22,858	19,788	18,183
Households Participating (Thous.)	10,879	10,549	9,455	8,249	7,668
Value of Benefits (Mil.$)	22,764	22,441	19,550	16,889	15,762
Average Monthly Benefit Per Person ($)	71.26	73.21	71.27	71.12	72.23
Total Cost (Mil. $)	24,620	24,327	21,487	18,893	17,714

NOTES: All data are provided by Fiscal Year (October through September). FY 1999 data are preliminary; all numbers are subject to revision.

[1]Participation data are 12-month averages. Total cost includes benefits, the Federal share of State administrative expenses, and other Federal costs (e.g., printing and processing stamps).

SOURCE: Food and Nutrition Service, U.S. Department of Agriculture

---

TABLE 8.8

Program Participation Status of Poor Households
(In Thousands)

ALL RACES

	Received Food Stamps	
Year	#	%
1994	19,325	50.8%
1993	20,384	51.9%
1992	19,588	51.5%
1991	17,920	50.2%
1990	16,375	48.8%
1989	15,226	47.0%
1988	14,913	47.0%

WHITE

	Received Food Stamps	
Year	#	%
1994	11,149	43.9%
1993	11,983	45.7%
1992	11,471	45.4%
1991	10,460	44.0%
1990	9,413	42.2%
1989	8,349	39.2%
1988	8,047	38.8%

BLACK

	Received Food Stamps	
Year	#	%
1994	7,046	69.1%
1993	7,434	68.3%
1992	7,230	66.8%
1991	6,654	65.0%
1990	6,391	65.0%
1989	6,077	63.8%
1988	6,070	64.9%

HISPANIC

	Received Food Stamps	
Year	#	%
1994	4,363	51.8%
1993	4,136	50.9%
1992	3,918	51.6%
1991	3,189	50.3%
1990	2,829	47.1%
1989	2,689	44.2%
1988	2,511	46.9%

SOURCE: Richard May and Kathryn H. Porter. *Poverty and Income Trends: 1994.* Center on Budget and Policy Priorities: Washington, D.C., 1996

Increase in Average Monthly Benefits

Average monthly benefits per person have risen from $34.47 in 1980 to $73.00 in 1996, not accounting for inflation. Table 8.9 shows the 1999 maximum monthly food stamp allotments for households of varying sizes within the continental United States.

In the early 1980s, Congress passed many laws designed to hold down the cost of the food stamp program by tightening administrative controls and setting tougher eligibility standards. The Omnibus Budget Rec-

---

TABLE 8.9

Current Maximum Allotment Levels, Food Stamp Program, October 1, 1999–September 30, 2000

People in Household	Maximum Monthly Allotment*
1	$ 127
2	234
3	335
4	426
5	506
6	607
7	671

*Amounts are higher in Alaska and Hawaii.

SOURCE: *Food Stamp Program.* FNS-313. Food and Nutrition Service, U.S. Department of Agriculture, October 1999

onciliation Act of 1981 (PL 97-35), the Agriculture and Food Act of 1981 (PL 97-98), and the Omnibus Budget Reconciliation Act of 1982 (PL 97-253) each contained provisions that held down costs. These measures included delaying inflation adjustments, establishing eligibility at 130 percent of poverty levels, ending eligibility for college students and strikers, and reducing benefits.

In 1985 the Food Security Act (PL 99-198) reversed the earlier trend, making food stamp rules easier and raising some benefits. On the other hand, the law required states to introduce employment and training programs for food stamp recipients. Several other pieces of legislation gave the homeless access to food stamps and increased benefits and accessibility for those receiving student aid, energy assistance, and income from employment programs for the elderly and charitable organizations. The Hunger Prevention Act of 1988 (PL 100-435) increased food stamp benefits and made it easier for people to get food stamps, as did the Mickey Leland Childhood Hunger Relief Act (PL 103-66).

TABLE 8.10

Food Stamp Mothers Versus Nonfood Stamp Mothers

Mothers 15 to 44 years old by food stamp recipiency status and selected fertility and socioeconomic characteristics: summer 1993

Characteristic	Receiving food stamps					Not receiving food stamps				
	Mothers		Births per 1,000 mothers	Mean age of mothers in years-		Mothers		Births per 1,000 mothers	Mean age of mothers in years-	
	Number (thousands)	Confidence interval[1]		at time of survey	at first birth	Number (thousands)	Confidence interval[1]		at time of survey	at first birth
Total	5,303	245	2,577	30.1	19.9	30,473	505	2,101	34.2	22.5
Age										
15 to 19 years	204	49	1,352	18.3	16.7	541	80	1,107	18.0	16.4
20 to 24 years	1,162	117	1,912	22.3	18.3	2,319	165	1,446	22.3	18.9
25 to 29 years	1,150	117	2,413	27.2	19.5	4,734	232	1,869	27.3	21.5
30 to 34 years	1,335	126	2,836	31.8	20.4	7,094	281	2,110	32.1	23.0
35 to 39 years	922	105	3,172	36.9	21.2	8,071	298	2,235	37.0	23.6
40 to 44 years	530	79	3,173	41.8	22.2	7,714	292	2,361	41.9	23.2
Race										
White	3,176	192	2,536	30.2	20.4	25,250	476	2,089	34.3	22.8
Black	1,903	150	2,653	29.9	19.1	3,826	210	2,125	33.4	20.5
Hispanic Origin										
Hispanic [2]	1,060	112	3,020	30.6	20.0	3,129	191	2,378	33.0	21.2
Not Hispanic	4,242	221	2,466	30.0	19.9	27,344	489	2,069	34.3	22.7
Marital Status										
Currently married	1,994	153	2,811	31.0	20.1	24,448	471	2,164	34.5	23.0
Married, husband present	1,087	113	2,838	30.7	19.9	23,212	463	2,159	34.6	23.1
Married, husband absent[3]	906	104	2,778	31.3	20.3	1,236	121	2,250	34.0	21.0
Widowed or divorced	1,244	121	2,653	33.4	20.7	3,617	204	2,033	36.4	21.2
Never married	2,065	156	2,305	27.3	19.3	2,408	168	1,561	26.8	20.0
Educational Attainment										
Not a high school graduate	2,169	159	2,892	29.6	18.8	4,095	217	2,407	32.0	19.4
High school, 4 years	2,141	158	2,377	30.2	20.4	12,182	358	2,075	33.9	21.5
College: 1 or more years	992	108	2,318	31.0	21.3	14,196	382	2,034	35.0	24.3
Enrollment in School										
Enrolled in school	628	86	2,215	29.1	19.8	2,581	174	1,922	31.7	21.3
Not enrolled in school	4,674	231	2,625	30.2	19.9	27,892	492	2,117	34.4	22.6
Labor Force Status										
Worked all or some weeks	1,159	117	2,536	31.2	19.9	21,204	448	2,042	34.8	22.6
No job last month	4,144	218	2,588	29.8	19.9	9,269	318	2,235	32.6	22.3
Monthly Family Income[4]										
Less than $500	1,635	139	2,511	30.0	20.0	605	85	1,965	31.2	20.7
$500 to $999	1,797	145	2,649	30.0	19.9	1,753	144	2,317	32.2	20.5
$1,000 to $1,499	924	105	2,788	31.4	19.9	2,714	178	1,986	32.2	21.2
$1,500 and over	861	101	2,363	29.1	18.9	25,000	475	2,103	34.6	22.9
Poverty Level[4]										
Below poverty level	3,962	214	2,708	30.2	19.8	3,221	193	2,414	31.3	20.4
Above poverty level	1,255	122	2,191	29.8	20.1	26,851	486	2,064	34.5	22.8
Division										
New England	179	46	2,361	28.5	20.1	1,501	133	2,033	35.0	23.8
Middle Atlantic	793	97	2,525	29.9	20.4	4,137	218	2,014	34.5	23.3
East North Central	969	107	2,664	29.9	19.9	5,449	248	2,067	33.8	22.5
West North Central	287	59	2,911	29.3	19.3	2,298	164	2,159	34.3	22.7
South Atlantic	879	102	2,472	30.3	19.4	5,431	248	2,001	34.2	22.3
East South Central	392	68	2,385	31.0	19.2	1,804	146	1,962	34.1	21.4
West South Central	695	91	2,641	30.1	19.7	3,186	192	2,189	34.2	22.0
Mountain	208	50	2,623	28.5	19.3	1,545	135	2,379	34.6	22.5
Pacific	900	103	2,588	30.8	20.9	5,121	241	2,216	33.7	22.5
Metropolitan Residence										
Metropolitan	4,082	217	2,575	29.9	19.9	23,476	465	2,082	34.2	22.8
In central cities	2,766	179	2,673	30.1	19.7	8,040	298	2,087	33.7	22.2
Suburbs	1,316	125	2,368	29.6	20.4	15,436	396	2,080	34.5	23.1
Nonmetropolitan	1,220	120	2,584	30.7	19.9	6,997	279	2,162	33.9	21.6
Place of Birth										
Native born	4,757	233	2,520	29.8	19.7	26,776	486	2,074	34.2	22.5
Foreign born	546	81	3,072	32.7	21.8	3,697	207	2,291	33.9	23.0

[1]Represents the 90-percent confidence interval (1.6 standard error) of the estimated population. [2]Persons of Hispanic origin may be of any race. [3]Includes separated women. [4]Excludes those who did not report income.

SOURCE: *Mothers Who Receive Food Stamps—Fertility and Socioeconomic Characteristics*. Statistical Brief, SB/95-22. U.S. Bureau of the Census: Washington, D.C., August 1995

Average Length of Participation

The average length of a recipient's participation in the food stamp program is less than two years. Half of all new participants remain on the program no more than six months while two-thirds end participation within one year.

Characteristics of Food Stamp Recipients

In 1996 most (92.6 percent) of the food stamp households earned less than the poverty level ($16,036 for a family of four). In fact, about 4 out of 10 (41 percent) earned less than half of the 1996 poverty level. Almost 90 percent of Aid to Families with Dependent Children (AFDC) families participated in the food stamp program. Of all households receiving food stamps in 1996,

- 51 percent were children, over one-third of whom were under six years of age.

- 41 percent were single-parent households with children.

- 12 percent were elderly persons living alone.

- Two-thirds received some type of cash welfare.

- 23 percent had earned income.

Comparing households in 1993 headed by mothers who received food stamps to those who did not, 60 percent of food stamp mothers were white, and slightly more than one-third (35.9 percent) were African American. Approximately 20 percent were Hispanic. Four in 10 (38.9 percent) food stamp mothers had never been married, compared to 7.9 percent of mothers not receiving food stamps. Not surprisingly, mothers participating in the program were much more likely than those not participating to earn less than the poverty level (74.7 percent, compared to 10.6 percent) and to lack high school diplomas (40.9 percent versus 13.4 percent). (See Table 8.10.) Three-quarters of food stamp mothers also received other welfare benefits, primarily AFDC. (See Figure 8.2.)

NATIONAL SCHOOL LUNCH AND SCHOOL BREAKFAST PROGRAMS

The National School Lunch Program (NSLP) and the School Breakfast Program (SBP) provide federal cash and commodity support to participating public and private schools and to nonprofit residential institutions that serve meals to children. Both programs have a three-level reimbursement system. Children from households with incomes at or below 130 percent of the poverty line receive free meals. Children from households with incomes between 130 percent and 185 percent of the poverty level receive meals at a reduced price (no more than 40 cents). Table 8.11 shows the income eligibility guidelines, based on the poverty line, effective from July 1, 1999, to June 30, 2000. The levels are higher for Alaska and Hawaii. Children in TANF families are automatically eligible to receive free breakfasts and lunches.

FIGURE 8.2

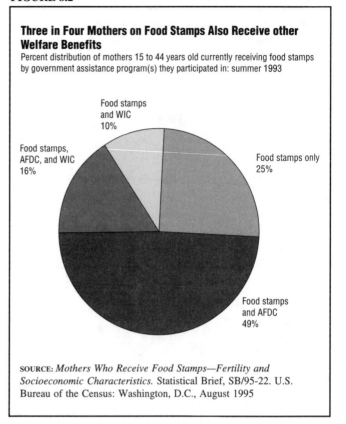

Three in Four Mothers on Food Stamps Also Receive other Welfare Benefits

Percent distribution of mothers 15 to 44 years old currently receiving food stamps by government assistance program(s) they participated in: summer 1993

SOURCE: *Mothers Who Receive Food Stamps—Fertility and Socioeconomic Characteristics.* Statistical Brief, SB/95-22. U.S. Bureau of the Census: Washington, D.C., August 1995

Meals for children from households that do not qualify for free or reduced-price meals are also subsidized. There was a reimbursement of about 32 cents for each full-price school lunch in 1996. Local school food authorities set their own prices for full-price meals. In 1996 the reimbursement for each free school lunch was about $2.00. (See Table 8.12.)

School Lunch Program

The National School Lunch Program (NSLP), created in 1946 under the National School Lunch Act (60 Stat 230), supplies subsidized lunches to children in almost all schools. In fiscal year 1997, about 94,000 elementary and secondary schools, 99 percent of all public schools, participated in the program, and more than half (57.3 percent) of their students received free or reduced-price lunches. On any given day, over 26 million students were receiving subsidized lunches. In April 1998 the monthly cost of the school lunch program was $602 million. (See Table 8.13.)

In the school year 1996–97, the U.S. Department of Agriculture changed certain policies so that school meals would meet the recommendations of the Dietary Guidelines for America, the federal standards for what constitutes a healthy diet. Congress appropriated $4.2 billion for the NSLP for fiscal year 1998, in addition to funds carried over from fiscal year 1997. (See Table 8.14 for 1980–95 statistics.)

TABLE 8.11

Income Eligibility Guidelines
(Effective from July 1, 1999 to June 30, 2000)

Household size	Federal Poverty Guidelines			Reduced Priced Meals-185%			Free Meals-130%		
	Annual	Month	Week	Annual	Month	Week	Annual	Month	Week
	48 CONTIGUOUS UNITED STATES, DISTRICT OF COLUMBIA, GUAM AND TERRITORIES								
1	8,240	687	159	15,244	1,271	294	10,712	893	206
2	11,060	922	213	20,461	1,706	394	14,378	1,199	177
3	13,880	1,157	267	25,678	2,140	494	18,044	1,504	347
4	16,700	1,392	322	30,895	2,575	595	21,710	1,810	418
5	19,520	1,627	376	36,112	3,010	695	25,376	2,115	488
6	22,340	1,862	430	41,329	3,445	795	29,042	2,421	559
7	25,160	2,097	484	46,546	3,879	896	32,708	2,726	629
8	27,980	2,332	539	51,763	4,314	996	36,374	3,032	700
For each add'l family member add	+2,280	+235	+55	+5,217	+435	+101	+3,666	+306	+71
	ALASKA								
1	10,320	860	199	19,092	1,591	368	13,416	1,118	258
2	13,840	1,154	267	25,604	2,134	493	17,992	1,500	346
3	17,360	1,447	334	32,116	2,677	618	22,568	1,881	434
4	20,880	1,740	402	38,628	3,219	743	27,144	2,262	522
5	24,400	2,034	470	45,140	3,762	869	31,720	2,644	610
6	27,920	2,327	537	51,652	4,305	994	36,296	3,025	698
7	31,440	2,620	605	58,164	4,847	1,119	40,872	3,406	786
8	34,960	2,914	673	64,676	5,390	1,244	45,448	3,788	874
For each add'l family member add	+3,520	+294	+68	+6,512	+543	+126	+4,576	+382	+88
	HAWAII								
1	9,490	791	183	17,557	1,464	338	12,337	1,029	238
2	12,730	1,061	245	23,551	1,963	453	16,549	1,380	319
3	15,970	1,331	308	29,545	2,463	569	20,761	1,731	400
4	19,210	1,601	370	35,539	2,962	684	24,973	2,082	481
5	22,450	1,871	432	41,533	3,462	799	29,185	2,433	562
6	25,690	2,141	495	47,527	3,961	914	33,397	2,784	643
7	28,930	2,411	557	53,521	4,461	1,030	37,609	3,135	724
8	32,170	2,681	619	59,515	4,960	1,145	41,821	3,486	805
For each add'l family member add	+3,240	+270	+63	+5,994	+500	+116	+4212	+351	+81

SOURCE: Federal Register, vol 64, no 63. Food and Nutrition Service, U.S. Department of Agriculture, April 1999

TABLE 8.12

Federal Meal Reimbursements from July 1996 to June 1997, Meal Charges, and Participation in FY 1996[a]

Type of Meal	Reimbursements (cents/meal)			Meal Charge	FY1996 7 mo. average Participation
	Cash[b]	Commodity	Total		
Paid (full-price)	17.75	14.5	32.25	No Limit	11,230,000
Reduced Price	143.75	14.5	158.25	40 cents	2,120,000
Free	183.75	14.5	198.25	None	12,570,000

[a] Rates are annually adjusted for inflation each July 1 using the most recent twelve month information available from the Consumer Price Index, series for food away from home. Higher rates are allowed for Alaska and Hawaii. Under the new welfare law, rates for paid lunches will be adjusted down to the nearest one cent beginning with the July 1, 1997 adjustment.

[b] An additional 2 cents is provided in schools where 60 percent or more of meals are served free or at reduced price.

SOURCE: Jean Yavis Jones. *National School Lunch Facts and Issues.* Congressional Research Service, The Library of Congress: Washington, D.C., 1996

TABLE 8.13

National School Lunch Program Participation Rate in the United States, 1995–99
(Data as of April 27, 2000)

	FY 1995	FY 1996	FY 1997	FY 1998	FY 1999
NATIONAL SCHOOL LUNCH PROGRAM[1]					
Children Participating (Thous.)	25,685	25,942	26,341	26,599	26,972
Total Lunches Served (Mil.)	4,253	4,313	4,409	4,425	4,513
Percent Free (%)	49.1	49.3	49.8	49.7	48.9
Percent Reduced-Price (%)	7.3	7.6	7.9	8.2	8.7
Total Snacks Served (Mil.)	0.3	0.3	0.2	0.2	11.3
Cash Payments (Mil. $)	4,466	4,662	4,934	5,102	5,314
Commodity Costs (Mil. $)	694	693	620	728	705
Total Cost (Mil. $)	5,160	5,355	5,554	5,830	6,019

Note: All data are provided by Fiscal Year (October through September). FY 1999 data are preliminary; all numbers are subject to revision.

[1] National School Lunch and School Breakfast participation data are 9-month averages (summer months are excluded). They represent average daily meals served adjusted by an attendance factor. School Lunch costs include cash payments, entitlement commodities, bonus commodities (surplus foods donated by the Dept. of Agriculture), and cash-in-lieu of commodities. School Breakfast costs are cash payments. Cash payments are Federal reimbursements to State agencies based on meals served multipled by reimbursement rates which are adjusted annually to reflect changes in food costs. Free and reduced-price meals served to needy children are reimbursed at much higher rates than full-price meals.

source: Food and Nutrition Service, U.S. Department of Agriculture

TABLE 8.14

School Lunch Federal Spending and Participation from Fiscal Years 1980–1996

Fiscal Year	Children Participating (in millions)			Number of Schools and Res. Instit.	Federal Funding ($ billions)
	Total	Free/Reduced	Paid		
1980	26.6	11.9	14.7	94,100	3.04
1981	25.8	12.5	13.3	94,000	2.96
1982	22.9	11.4	11.5	91,200	2.61
1983	23.0	11.8	11.2	90,600	2.83
1984	23.3	11.8	11.5	89,200	2.95
1985	23.6	11.5	12.1	89,400	3.03
1986	23.8	11.6	12.2	89,900	3.16
1987	24.0	11.6	12.4	90,200	3.25
1988	24.2	11.4	12.8	90,600	3.38
1989	24.2	11.3	12.7	91,400	3.48
1990	24.1	11.5	12.8	91,400	3.68
1991	24.2	12.1	12.1	92,200	4.07
1992	24.5	12.8	11.7	92,300	4.47
1993	24.9	13.5	11.3	92,500	4.66
1994	25.3	14.0	11.3	93,400	4.87
1995	25.6	14.3	11.3	94,200	5.08
1996 est.	26.0	14.6	11.4	93,600	5.50

NOTES: "Schools" includes residential child care institutions; FY 1996 estimate of participants is based on 7 month daily average.

SOURCE: Jean Yavis Jones. *National School Lunch Facts and Issues.* Congressional Research Service, The Library of Congress: Washington, D.C., 1996

School Breakfast Program

The School Breakfast Program (SBP), created under the Child Nutrition Act of 1966 (PL 89-642), serves far fewer students than does the NSLP. The SBP also differs from the NSLP in that most schools offering the program are in low-income areas, and the children who participate in the program are mainly from low- and moderate-income families. In 1999 the program had an average daily participation of nearly 7.4 million students, 85.4 percent of whom received free or reduced-price (up to 30 cents) breakfasts. The cost of this program in April 1999 was $135 million. (See Table 8.15.) (See Table 8.16 for statistics from 1969 to 1999.)

WOMEN, INFANTS, AND CHILDREN (WIC)

The Special Supplemental Food Program for Women, Infants, and Children (WIC) provides food assistance as well as nutrition counseling and health services to low-income pregnant women, to women who have just had a baby and to their babies, and to low-income children up to 5 years old. Participants in the program must have incomes at or below 185 percent of poverty (all but five states use this cutoff level) and must be nutritionally at risk.

Under the Child Nutrition Act of 1966, nutritional risk includes abnormal nutritional conditions, medical conditions related to nutrition, health-impairing dietary deficiencies, or conditions that might predispose a person to these conditions. Pregnant women may receive bene-

TABLE 8.15

School Breakfast Program Participation Rate in the United States, 1995–99
(Data as of April 27, 2000)

	FY 1995	FY 1996	FY 1997	FY 1998	FY 1999
SCHOOL BREAKFAST PROGRAM[1]					
Children Participating (Thous.)	6,318	6,583	6,922	7,142	7,371
Total Breakfasts Served (Mil.)	1,079	1,126	1,191	1,221	1,267
Percent Free or Reduced Price (%)	86.8	86.5	86.5	86.1	85.4
Total Cost (Mil. $)	1,049	1,119	1,214	1,272	1,345

Note: All data are provided by Fiscal Year (October through September). FY 1999 data are preliminary; all numbers are subject to revision.

[1]National School Lunch and School Breakfast participation data are 9-month averages (summer months are excluded). They represent average daily meals served adjusted by an attendance factor. School Lunch costs include cash payments, entitlement commodities, bonus commodities (surplus foods donated by the Dept. of Agriculture), and cash-in-lieu of commodities. School Breakfast costs are cash payments. Cash payments are Federal reimbursements to State agencies based on meals served multiplied by reimbursement rates which are adjusted annually to reflect changes in food costs. Free and reduced-price meals served to needy children are reimbursed at much higher rates than full-price meals.

SOURCE: Food and Nutrition Service, U.S. Department of Agriculture

fits through their pregnancies and for up to six months after childbirth (up to one year for nursing mothers).

Those receiving WIC benefits get supplemental food each month in the form of actual food items or, more commonly, vouchers (coupons) for the purchase of specific items at the store. Permitted foods contain high amounts of protein, iron, calcium, vitamin A, and vitamin C. Items that may be purchased include milk, cheese, eggs, infant formula, cereals, and fruit or vegetable juices. Mothers participating in WIC are encouraged to breastfeed their infants if possible, but state WIC agencies will provide formula for mothers who choose to use it.

The U.S. Department of Agriculture estimated that the national average monthly cost of a WIC food package in 1999 was about $32.50 per participant, plus another $11 for administration. In fiscal year 1999, federal costs for the WIC program totaled $3.95 billion, and the program served approximately 7.3 million women, infants, and children. WIC works in conjunction with the Farmers' Market Nutrition Program, established in 1992 to provide WIC recipients with increased access, in the form of vouchers, to fresh fruits and vegetables.

In 1997 WIC reached about 98 percent of eligible infants, which was 45 percent of all babies born in the United States. Of the 7.4 million participants, 3.8 million were children, 1.9 million were infants, and 1.7 million were women. The WIC program serves the low-income population, whether they are U.S. citizens or not. Almost one-fourth of the participants were women. Half of those women were pregnant, about 10 percent were under 18, and 17 percent were breastfeeding. Nearly one-fifth of women recipients were single-person households, although the average family size was four persons.

TABLE 8.16

TABLE 8.17

School Breakfast Program Participation and Meals Served, 1969–99

Data as of April 27, 2000

Fiscal Years	Total Participation[1]				Meals Served	Free/RP of Total Meals
	Free	Red. Price	Paid	Total		
	Millions					Percent
1969	—	—	—	0.22	39.7	71.0
1970	—	—	—	0.45	71.8	71.5
1971	0.60	—[2]	0.20	0.80	125.5	76.3
1972	0.81	—[2]	0.23	1.04	169.3	78.5
1973	0.99	—[2]	0.20	1.19	194.1	83.4
1974	1.14	—[2]	0.24	1.37	226.7	82.8
1975	1.45	0.04	0.33	1.82	294.7	82.1
1976	1.76	0.06	0.37	2.20	353.6	84.2
1977	2.02	0.11	0.36	2.49	434.3	85.7
1978	2.23	0.16	0.42	2.80	478.8	85.3
1979	2.56	0.21	0.54	3.32	565.6	84.1
1980	2.79	0.25	0.56	3.60	619.9	85.2
1981	3.05	0.25	0.51	3.81	644.2	86.9
1982	2.80	0.16	0.36	3.32	567.4	89.3
1983	2.87	0.15	0.34	3.36	580.7	90.3
1984	2.91	0.15	0.37	3.43	589.2	89.7
1985	2.88	0.16	0.40	3.44	594.9	88.6
1986	2.93	0.16	0.41	3.50	610.6	88.7
1987	3.01	0.17	0.43	3.61	621.5	88.4
1988	3.03	0.18	0.47	3.68	642.5	87.5
1989	3.11	0.20	0.51	3.81	658.4	86.8
1990	3.30	0.22	0.55	4.07	707.5	86.7
1991	3.61	0.25	0.57	4.44	772.1	87.3
1992	4.05	0.26	0.60	4.92	852.6	88.0
1993	4.41	0.28	0.66	5.36	923.6	87.9
1994	4.76	0.32	0.75	5.83	1,001.6	87.4
1995	5.10	0.37	0.85	6.32	1,078.9	86.8
1996	5.27	0.41	0.91	6.58	1,125.7	86.5
1997	5.52	0.45	0.95	6.92	1,191.2	86.5
1998	5.64	0.50	1.01	7.14	1,220.8	86.1
1999	5.71	0.56	1.09	7.37	1,267.1	85.4

Data are subject to revision.

[1] Nine month average: October-May plus September.

[2] Included with free participation.

SOURCE: Food and Nutrition Service, U.S. Department of Agriculture

WIC Program Participation and Costs, 1974–99

Data as of April 27, 2000

Fiscal Year	Total Participation (Thousands)	PROGRAM COSTS			Average Monthly Benefit Per Person (Dollars)
		Food	NSA	Total[1]	
		(Millions in Dollars)			
1974	88	8.2	2.2	10.4	15.68
1975	344	76.7	12.6	89.3	18.58
1976	520	122.3	20.3	142.6	19.60
1977	848	211.7	44.2	255.9	20.80
1978	1,181	311.5	68.1	379.6	21.99
1979	1,483	428.6	96.8	525.4	24.09
1980	1,914	584.1	140.5	727.7	25.43
1981	2,119	708.0	160.6	871.6	27.84
1982	2,189	757.6	190.5	948.8	28.83
1983	2,537	901.8	221.3	1,126.0	29.62
1984	3,045	1,117.3	268.8	1,388.1	30.58
1985	3,138	1,193.2	294.4	1,489.3	31.69
1986	3,312	1,264.4	316.4	1,582.9	31.82
1987	3,429	1,344.7	333.1	1,679.6	32.68
1988	3,593	1,434.8	360.6	1,797.5	33.28
1989	4,118	1,489.5	416.5	1,910.9	30.14
1990	4,517	1,636.9	478.7	2,122.2	30.20
1991	4,893	1,752.0	544.0	2,301.1	29.84
1992	5,403	1,958.6	632.7	2,596.7	30.21
1993	5,921	2,115.1	705.6	2,825.5	29.76
1994	6,477	2,325.2	834.4	3,169.5	29.91
1995	6,894	2,516.6	904.9	3,441.4	30.41
1996	7,188	2,689.9	985.1	3,695.3	31.19
1997	7,407	2,815.3	1,008.2	3,844.1	31.67
1998	7,367	2,807.8	1,061.4	3,889.9	31.75
1999	7,311	2,853.3	1,069.3	3,945.3	32.52

NSA = Nutrition Services and Administrative costs. Nutrition Services includes nutrition education, preventative and coordination services (such as health care), and promotion of breastfeeding and immunization.

Data are subject to revision; FY 1999 numbers are preliminary.

[1] In addition to food and NSA costs, total expenditures includes funds for program evaluation, Farmers Market Nutrition Program (FY 1989 onward), and special projects.

SOURCE: Food and Nutrition Service, U.S. Department of Agriculture

A 1994 study found that over one-third of WIC recipients had a family income less than half the poverty guidelines. The WIC participants were likely to receive other welfare benefits. Twenty-seven percent received cash welfare, 37 percent got food stamps, and 53 percent were covered by Medicaid. (See Table 8.17 for statistics from 1974 to 1999.)

MEDICAID

Medicaid, authorized under Title XIX of the Social Security Act, is a federal-state program that provides medical assistance for low-income people who are aged, blind, disabled, or members of families with dependent children and for certain other pregnant women and children. Within federal guidelines, each state designs and administers its own program. For this reason, there may be considerable differences from state to state as to who is covered, what type of coverage is provided, and how much is paid for medical services. States receive federal

matching payments based on their Medicaid expenditures and the state's per capita income. The federal match ranges from 50 percent to 80 percent of Medicaid expenditures. Table 8.18 shows the number of recipients, the amount of payments, and the average payment per recipient for each state.

Who Gets Medicaid?

Although Medicaid eligibility had been linked to receipt of, or eligibility to receive, benefits under Aid to Families with Dependent Children (AFDC) or Supplemental Security Income (SSI), legislation gradually extended coverage in the 1980s and 1990s. Beginning in 1986, benefits were extended to low-income children and pregnant women not on welfare. States must cover children less than 6 years of age and pregnant women with family incomes below 133 percent of the federal poverty level. Pregnant women are only covered for medical services related to their pregnancies, while children receive full Medicaid coverage. The states may cover infants under one year old and pregnant women with incomes more than 133 percent,

TABLE 8.18

FIGURE 8.3

Number of Recipients, Amount of Payments, and Average Amount per Recipient, by State, Fiscal Year 1997

State	Recipients	Amount (in millions)	Average
Total	34,872,275	$124,430	$3,568
Alabama	546,152	1,571	2,877
Alaska	73,050	321	4,392
Arizona	540,785	246	455
Arkansas	370,386	1,302	3,514
California	4,854,546	11,433	2,355
Colorado	251,423	1,124	4,470
Connecticut	201,779	2,003	9,927
Delaware	83,956	275	3,273
District of Columbia	128,008	696	5,439
Florida	1,597,461	4,885	3,058
Georgia	1,208,445	3,090	2,557
Hawaii	206,081	629	3,051
Idaho	115,087	432	3,757
Illinois	1,399,960	5,783	4,131
Indiana	514,683	2,382	4,628
Iowa	293,596	1,083	3,689
Kansas	232,888	919	3,947
Kentucky	664,454	2,269	3,415
Louisiana	746,461	2,336	3,129
Maine	167,221	780	4,662
Maryland	402,002	2,201	5,474
Massachusetts	723,472	3,855	5,329
Michigan	1,132,783	3,591	3,170
Minnesota	371,483	2,359	6,350
Mississippi	504,017	1,424	2,826
Missouri	540,487	2,097	3,880
Montana	95,562	318	3,325
Nebraska	203,340	696	3,424
Nevada	105,588	373	3,531
New Hampshire	95,215	554	5,818
New Jersey	537,890	3,569	6,635
New Mexico	320,223	822	2,568
New York	3,151,837	21,340	6,771
North Carolina	1,112,931	3,788	3,404
North Dakota	61,117	328	5,373
Ohio	1,395,540	5,848	4,190
Oklahoma	315,801	1,038	3,287
Oregon	531,242	1,475	2,776
Pennsylvania	1,024,993	4,689	4,575
Rhode Island	1,395,540	5,848	4,190
South Carolina	519,875	1,607	3,092
South Dakota	75,444	318	4,221
Tennessee	1,415,612	2,936	2,074
Texas	2,538,655	7,345	2,893
Utah	144,749	424	2,927
Vermont	109,283	309	2,824
Virginia	595,234	1,858	3,121
Washington	630,165	1,393	2,210
West Virginia	359,091	1,257	3,500
Wisconsin	392,223	1,879	4,790
Wyoming	48,865	184	3,771
Outlying areas:			
Puerto Rico	1,087,226	250	230
Virgin Islands	17,154	7	430

SOURCE: *Annual Statistical Supplement, 1999.* Social Security Administration, Washington, D.C., 1999

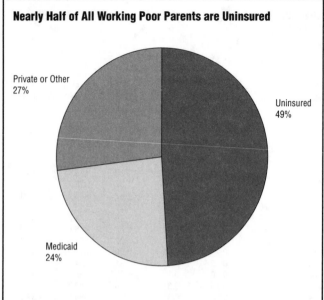

Nearly Half of All Working Poor Parents are Uninsured

Private or Other 27%

Uninsured 49%

Medicaid 24%

Health Insurance Status of Working Poor Parents, 1996
Based on adults in households with children who earn at least $5,150 a year (an amount equivalent to half-time, full-year work at the minimum wage), but whose income still falls below the poverty line.

SOURCE: Jocelyn Guyer and Cindy Mann. *Taking the Next Steps: States Can Now Expand Health Coverage to Low-Income Working Parents Through Medicaid.* Center on Budget and Policy Priorities: Washington, D.C., 1998

law of 1996 requires states to continue benefits to those who would have been eligible under the AFDC requirements each state had in place on July 16, 1996. As with pre-reform law, Medicaid coverage must be continued for one year for those families that have increased their earnings to the point where they are no longer eligible for cash aid and for four months to those who lose eligibility because of child or spousal support.

States may deny Medicaid benefits to adults who lose TANF benefits because they refuse to work. However, the law exempts poor pregnant women and children from this provision, requiring their continued Medicaid eligibility. In addition, the welfare law requires state plans to ensure Medicaid for children receiving foster care or adoption assistance.

The process to determine eligibility can take months. The Balanced Budget Act of 1997 (PL 105-33) gave states the option to grant interim coverage to children who appear to be eligible for Medicaid, based on age and family income. This "presumptive eligibility" option allows children and pregnant women to receive care immediately while waiting for Medicaid approval.

Many states, in an effort to reach the large number of uninsured children (by Census Bureau estimates, over one-third of Medicaid-eligible children), are simplifying the Medicaid application process. According to the Cen-

but not more than 185 percent, of the poverty level. As of January 1, 1991, Medicaid also began to cover aged and disabled persons receiving Medicare whose income was below 100 percent of the poverty level.

Medicaid coverage is not guaranteed for recipients of Temporary Assistance for Needy Families (TANF) as it was for recipients of AFDC. However, the welfare-reform

TABLE 8.19

Unduplicated Number of Recipients, Total Vendor Payments, and Average Amounts, by Type of Eligibility Category, Fiscal Years 1972–97[1,2]

Fiscal year	Total	Aged 65 or older	Blind	Permanent and total disability	Dependent children under age 21	Adults in families with dependent children	Other
				Number (in thousands)			
1972	17,606	3,318	108	1,625	7,841	3,137	1,576
1975	22,007	3,615	109	2,355	9,598	4,529	1,800
1980	21,605	3,440	92	2,819	9,333	4,877	1,499
1985	21,814	3,061	80	2,937	9,757	5,518	1,214
1986	22,515	3,140	82	3,100	10,029	5,647	1,362
1987	23,109	3,224	85	3,296	10,168	5,599	1,418
1988	22,907	3,159	86	3,401	10,037	5,503	1,343
1989	23,511	3,132	95	3,496	10,318	5,717	1,175
1990	25,255	3,202	83	3,635	11,220	6,010	1,105
1991	28,280	3,359	85	3,983	13,415	6,778	658
1992	30,926	3,742	84	4,378	15,104	6,954	664
1993	33,432	3,863	84	4,932	16,285	7,505	763
1994	35,053	4,035	87	5,372	17,194	7,586	779
1995	36,282	4,119	92	5,767	17,164	7,604	1,537
1996	36,118	4,285	95	6,126	16,739	7,127	1,746
1997	34,872	3,955	...	6,129	15,266	6,803	2,719
				Amount (in millions)			
1972	$ 6,300	$ 1,925	$ 45	$ 1,354	$ 1,139	$ 962	$ 875
1975	12,242	4,358	93	3,052	2,186	2,062	492
1980	23,311	8,739	124	7,497	3,123	3,231	596
1985	37,508	14,096	249	13,203	4,414	4,746	798
1986	41,005	15,097	277	14,635	5,135	4,880	980
1987	45,050	16,037	309	16,507	5,508	5,592	1,078
1988	48,710	17,135	344	18,250	5,848	5,883	1,198
1989	54,500	18,558	409	20,476	6,892	6,897	1,268
1990	64,859	21,508	434	23,969	9,100	8,590	1,257
1991	77,048	25,453	475	27,798	11,690	10,439	1,193
1992	90,814	29,078	530	33,326	14,491	12,185	1,204
1993	101,709	31,554	589	38,065	16,504	13,605	1,391
1994	108,270	33,618	644	41,654	17,302	13,585	1,467
1995	120,141	36,527	848	48,570	17,976	13,511	2,708
1996	121,685	36,947	869	51,196	17,544	12,275	2,746
1997	124,430	37,721	...	54,130	15,658	12,307	4,612
				Average amount			
1972	$ 358	$ 580	$ 417	$ 833	$ 145	$ 307	$ 555
1975	556	1,205	850	1,296	228	455	273
1980	1,079	2,540	1,358	2,659	335	663	398
1985	1,719	4,605	3,104	4,496	452	860	658
1986	1,821	4,808	3,401	4,721	512	864	719
1987	1,949	4,975	3,644	5,008	542	999	761
1988	2,126	5,425	4,005	5,366	583	1,069	891
1989	2,318	5,926	4,317	5,858	668	1,206	1,079
1990	2,568	6,717	5,212	6,595	811	1,429	1,138
1991	2,725	7,577	5,572	6,979	871	1,540	1,813
1992	2,936	7,770	6,298	7,612	959	1,752	1,813
1993	3,042	8,168	7,036	7,717	1,013	1,813	1,824
1994	3,089	8,331	7,412	7,755	1,006	1,791	1,884
1995	3,311	8,868	9,256	8,422	1,047	1,777	1,762
1996	3,369	8,622	9,143	8,357	1,048	1,722	1,635
1997	3,568	9,538	...	8,832	1,026	1,809	3,597

[1] Fiscal year 1977 began in October 1976 and was the first year of the new federal fiscal cycle. Before 1977, the fiscal year began in July.

[2] Beginning in fiscal year 1980, recipients' categories do not add to unduplicated total because of the small number of recipients that are in more than one category during the year.

SOURCE: *Annual Statistical Supplement, 1999*. Social Security Administration: Washington, D.C., 1999

ter on Budget and Policy Priorities, as of February 1998, 38 states had dropped the assets test for Medicaid, 30 had developed shorter application forms, and 25 were allowing mail-in applications.

In addition, the 1996 welfare law gives states the option to use Medicaid to provide health care coverage to low-income working parents. About half of the working poor are uninsured. (See Figure 8.3.) Though the income of these households is below the federal poverty line, working poor parents have been ineligible for publicly funded health insurance. In addition, low-wage jobs often do not offer affordable employer-sponsored coverage. The number of uninsured working poor parents is likely

FIGURE 8.4

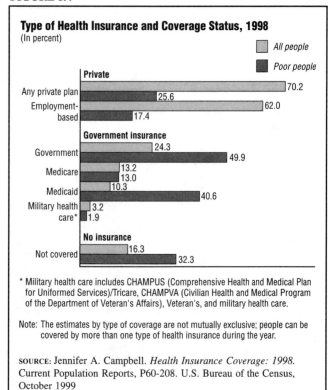

Type of Health Insurance and Coverage Status, 1998
(In percent)

FIGURE 8.5

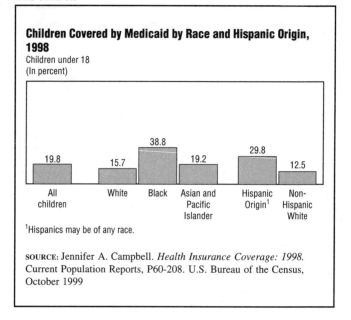

Children Covered by Medicaid by Race and Hispanic Origin, 1998
Children under 18
(In percent)

likely to have Medicaid coverage than were white or Asian and Pacific Islander children. In 1998, 38.8 percent of black children and 29.8 percent of Hispanic children were covered by Medicaid, compared to 15.7 percent of white (not of Hispanic origin) and 19.2 percent of Asian or Pacific Islander children. (See Figure 8.5.)

Medicaid provides health care services, such as long-term care, for many elderly people not covered by Medicare. Medicaid pays for about half of all nursing home expenditures, which accounts for a large percentage of Medicaid expenditures. This proportion of spending on the elderly is expected to increase as more people live longer. The Census Bureau projects a 22 percent increase in the 85-and-over population between 1996 and 2002, from 3.7 million to 4.5 million.

Growth in Medicaid Costs

The rapid growth in spending for Medicaid has contributed to the concern over the rising cost of health care. Not accounting for inflation, spending skyrocketed from $6.3 billion in 1972 to $37.5 billion in 1985 and $124.4 billion in 1997. Of the $124.4 billion spent on Medicaid payments in 1997, most went for the disabled (43.5 percent) and the elderly (30.3 percent). In addition, considerable amounts were spent on dependent children under age 21 (12.5 percent) and adults in families with dependent children (9.9 percent). On average, the Medicaid program spent $9,538 on every elderly recipient, $1,026 on each dependent child under 21, and $8,832 on each disabled person in the program. (See Table 8.19.)

STATE CHILD HEALTH INSURANCE PROGRAM

The Balanced Budget Act of 1997 (PL 105-33) set aside $24 billion over five years to fund the Children's

to grow as welfare recipients move into the work force, as required under the welfare-reform law, unless states expand Medicaid to cover this group.

Medicaid may also cover "medically needy" persons, those with income levels higher than the regular Medicaid levels. Each state may establish a higher income or resource level for the "medically needy" than the standards the states set for those who qualify for other social welfare benefits. They may also limit the categories of the "medically needy" who will receive Medicaid. In 1996, 42 states provided Medicaid to "medically needy" recipients.

MEDICAID RECIPIENTS. In 1997 approximately 34.8 million people were enrolled in Medicaid. Most were dependent children under 21 years of age (43.7 percent) and adults in families with dependent children (19.5 percent). The remainder of Medicaid recipients were permanently and totally disabled (17.5 percent), elderly (11.3 percent), or blind. The number receiving Medicaid coverage stayed around 22 million from 1975 through 1986, when it began to rise, reaching 36 million in 1995 and 1996. (See Table 8.19.)

Poor households were most likely to be covered by Medicaid. About 40 percent of poor persons were covered in 1998. (See Figure 8.4.) One of every five children in the country is covered under Medicaid. It is the single largest source of health insurance coverage for all children from families earning below 200 percent of the poverty line. African American and Hispanic children were far more

Health Insurance Program (CHIP) in an effort to reach the approximately 1 in 7 American children who are uninsured. This was the nation's largest children's health care investment since the creation of Medicaid in 1965. The CHIP requires states to use the funding to cover uninsured children whose families earn too much for Medicaid but too little to afford private coverage. States may use this money to expand their Medicaid programs, design new child health insurance programs, or create a combination of both.

States must enroll all children who meet Medicaid eligibility rules in the Medicaid program rather than in the new CHIP plan. They are not allowed to use the CHIP to replace existing health coverage. In addition, states must decide on what kind of cost-sharing, if any, to require of low-income families without keeping them from access to the program. The only federal requirement is that cost-sharing cannot exceed 5 percent of family income.

HEAD START

Head Start began operating in 1965 under the general authority of the Economic Opportunity Act of 1964 (PL 88-452). Head Start is designed to help low-income children from birth to age 5 improve their social competence, learning skills, health, and nutrition so that they can begin school on a more level footing with more advantaged children.

Education is the service most directly provided by Head Start to enrolled children. Head Start services include language development; medical (including immunizations), dental, and mental health services; and nutritional and social services. Head Start often facilitates access to other social services, such as Medicaid, for siblings and families, as well as for enrolled children. The program tries to involve parents in their children's education, either through volunteer participation or through employment of parents as Head Start staff.

FIGURE 8.6

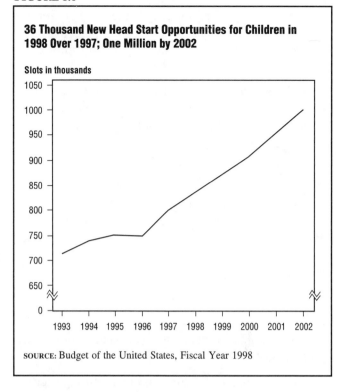

36 Thousand New Head Start Opportunities for Children in 1998 Over 1997; One Million by 2002

Slots in thousands

SOURCE: Budget of the United States, Fiscal Year 1998

Head Start's guidelines require that at least 90 percent of the children enrolled come from families with incomes at or below the poverty income level. At least 10 percent of the enrollment slots must be available for disabled children.

In 1998, 822,316 young children were served in Head Start programs at a total federal cost of nearly $4.2 billion. Money for the program is expected to increase so that an estimated one million children will be served by 2002. (See Figure 8.6.) In 1998 African American children made up 35.8 percent of the enrollment; white children, 31.5 percent; Hispanic children, 26.4 percent;

TABLE 8.20

Characteristics of Children Enrolled in Head Start, Selected Fiscal Years 1980–95
[In Percent]

Fiscal year	Age of children enrolled					Enrollment by race				
	Dis-abled	5 and older	4	3	Under 3	Native Amer-ican	His-panic	Black	White	Asian
1980	12	21	55	24	0	4	19	42	34	1
1982	12	17	55	26	2	4	20	42	33	1
1984	12	16	56	26	2	4	20	42	33	1
1986	12	15	58	25	2	4	21	40	32	3
1988	13	11	63	23	3	4	22	39	32	3
1990	14	8	64	25	3	4	22	38	33	3
1991	13	7	63	27	3	4	22	38	33	3
1992	13	7	63	27	3	4	23	37	33	3
1993	13	6	64	27	3	4	24	36	33	3
1994	13	7	62	28	3	4	24	36	33	3
1995	13	7	62	27	4	4	25	35	33	3

SOURCE: Head Start Bureau, U.S. Department of Health and Human Services

Native Americans, 3.4 percent; and Asians, 2.9 percent. Most of the children participating in the program were 4-year olds (59 percent) or 3-year olds (31 percent), but a significant proportion (13 percent) were disabled children. (See Table 8.20.)

According to Head Start's 1997–98 survey, about 55 percent of Head Start families had incomes of less than $9,000 per year, and 72.7 percent had yearly incomes of less than $12,000.

HELP IN PAYING THE HEATING BILL

What is now the Low-Income Home Energy Assistance Program (LIHEAP) began as Title III of the Crude Oil Windfall Profit Tax Act of 1980 (PL 96-223). The act provided funding for the states to create programs for three types of energy assistance:

- Helping poor households pay their heating and cooling bills.

- Using low-cost insulation to make homes more energy efficient.

- Providing financial aid to households during energy-related emergencies (unusually long cold or hot spells).

In 1981 Title XXVI of the Omnibus Budget Reconciliation Act (OBRA; PL 97-35) gave form and substance to the program. Funding peaked at an estimated $2.1 billion in 1985 and has been declining ever since. In 2000 the Department of Health and Human Services appropriated $1.1 billion in LIHEAP block grants, serving nearly 6 million people.

Home heating assistance benefits, by far the major service of LIHEAP, served 5.2 million households in 1996. Average benefits varied dramatically, ranging from larger grants in colder states with higher costs of heating, such as Connecticut and North Dakota ($411 each), to much lower grants in generally warmer states, such as Kentucky ($64), North Carolina ($80), Arkansas ($87), and Florida ($92). Benefits apply to both heating and cooling in Texas, California, and Florida.

States make payments directly to eligible households or to home energy suppliers to be used for eligible households. The highest level of assistance is given to households with the lowest income and highest energy costs in relation to income, taking into account family size and whether infants, children, or elderly are a part of the household.

FEDERAL HOUSING ASSISTANCE

The primary purpose of federal housing assistance is to improve housing quality and to reduce housing costs for low-income Americans. However, affordability rather than housing quality has become the predominant problem facing low-income renters and homeowners. The number of substandard housing units continues to decline. In 1985, 22 percent of poor renters lived in substandard shelter, such as homes or apartments lacking reliable plumbing. By 1995 the figure had declined to 14 percent.

Affordability problems are nationwide, affecting poor households in every region and in urban, suburban, and rural areas of the country alike. They are spread among all racial and ethnic groups and affect both working and non-working poor renters. In 1995 the typical family of poor renters spent about 60 percent of its income on shelter, twice the percentage the government considers affordable.

Financial Commitments for Housing Assistance

Housing assistance for low-income households comes through a number of programs and can be very confusing. Authorizations for housing assistance, especially for building low-cost public housing, may be committed for a dozen or two dozen years in the future. As a result, a financial authorization made in 1977 may well still affect spending by the U.S. Department of Housing and Urban Development (HUD) in 1996 and into the twenty-first century. Spending patterns have changed dramatically in the 1980s and 1990s. HUD has increasingly turned to using housing vouchers to help low-income families pay the rent in existing housing and has turned away from building low-income housing, which requires larger financial commitments over a longer time.

Vouchers give recipients more flexibility as to where they may live and are particularly helpful to those making the transition from welfare to work. Families can use vouchers to move closer to areas with more job opportunities or better transportation to work.

Housing assistance is not an entitlement to which a person has a legal right if he or she meets certain requirements. The number of people receiving help depends on the amount of money authorized by Congress. Therefore, not all households or families that qualify receive assistance. Approximately one-third of the low-income families that qualify actually receive assistance. In 1995 only about 4.5 million families received federal housing assistance even though about 15 million households qualified for it.

In the 1980s and 1990s the number of new commitments to assist low-income families has dropped dramatically. Between 1977 and 1981 the federal government committed to increase rental assistance by an average of about 260,000 new households per year. From 1982 through 1997 the new assistance commitments fell to an average of 70,000 per year. This limited level of housing assistance means most poor renters desiring housing assistance are placed on waiting lists and sometimes wait several years before receiving aid. In some areas, waiting

FIGURE 8.7

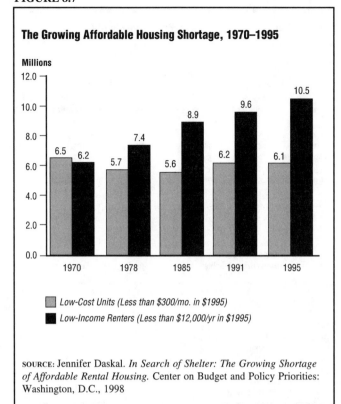

The Growing Affordable Housing Shortage, 1970–1995

Millions

Low-Cost Units (Less than $300/mo. in $1995)

Low-Income Renters (Less than $12,000/yr in $1995)

SOURCE: Jennifer Daskal. *In Search of Shelter: The Growing Shortage of Affordable Rental Housing.* Center on Budget and Policy Priorities: Washington, D.C., 1998

TABLE 8.21

Outlays for Housing Aid Administered by HUD, 1977–96
[In millions of current and 1996 dollars]

	Outlays	
Fiscal year	Current dollars	1996 dollars
1977	2,928	7,312
1978	3,592	8,427
1979	4,189	9,025
1980	5,364	10,399
1981	6,733	11,861
1982	7,846	12,915
1983	9,419	14,846
1984	11,000	16,635
1985	25,064	36,555
1986	12,179	17,332
1987	12,509	17,304
1988	13,684	18,180
1989	14,466	18,352
1990	15,690	18,958
1991	16,897	19,435
1992	18,242	20,370
1993	20,487	22,198
1994	22,183	23,422
1995	24,002	24,651
1996 (estimate)	¹25,954	¹25,954

¹Figures have been adjusted to account for $1.2 billion of advance spending that occurred in 1995 but that should have occurred in 1996.

Note: The bulge in outlays in 1985 is caused by a change in the method of financing public housing, which generated close to $14 billion in one-time expenditures. This amount paid off—all at once—the capital cost of public housing construction and modernization activities undertaken between 1974 and 1985, which otherwise would have been paid off over periods of up to 40 years. Because of this one-time expenditure, however, outlays for public housing since that time have been lower than they would have been otherwise.

SOURCE: Congressional Budget Office, Based on Data Provided by the U.S. Department of Housing and Urban Development

lists are so long that they have been closed, and new families are not allowed to apply.

Availability of Low-Cost Housing

The Center on Budget and Policy Priorities, a non-profit advocacy organization for low-income people, reported in *In Search of Shelter: The Growing Shortage of Affordable Rental Housing* (Jennifer Daskal, Washington, D.C., 1998) that the supply of low-cost housing has dwindled since the 1970s. In 1970 there were approximately 6.5 million low-cost rental units (costing less than $300 per month in 1995 dollars). At the same time, there were about 6.2 million low-income renters (defined as those with incomes less than $12,000 a year in 1995 dollars). Therefore, low-income families had enough housing to choose from, although it might have been less desirable than they would like. However, by 1995 the number of poor renters (10.5 million) had far outstripped the number of low-cost units (6.1 million), resulting in a shortage of 4.4 million affordable units. (See Figure 8.7.) This was the largest shortage on record, about two low-income renters for every low-cost unit.

Observers attribute the decline in low-cost housing to a number of factors, including the conversion of rental units to condominiums, rapidly increasing costs of maintaining apartments, and urban-renewal programs that have destroyed low-cost housing. The decline in federal spending for public housing, both in funding the con-

struction of new facilities and in refurbishing older, sub-standard units, has also contributed to the drop in low-cost housing.

Expenditures on Housing

In 1995 about 82 percent of all poor-renter households and 78 percent of working-poor renters with children spent at least 30 percent of their income on rent and utilities, the level set by the HUD as "affordable housing." Around 4.4 million of these households (three of every five) spent more than 50 percent of their income on housing. The HUD considers these families as "worst-case" and gives them priority for housing assistance.

Most federal housing aid goes to "very-low-income renters" through rental-assistance programs that either provide low-cost public housing or pay rent subsidies so that the low-income families may live in existing private apartments. Under the latter program, the low-income tenant pays 30 percent of his or her household income for rent, and the government pays the rest. The federal government also assists some lower moderate-income households in becoming homeowners by making long-term commitments to reduce their interest rates significantly.

TABLE 8.22

Per Unit Outlays for Housing Aid Administered by HUD, 1977–96
[In current and 1996 dollars]

Fiscal year	Per unit outlays	
	Current dollars	1996 dollars
1977	1,160	2,900
1978	1,310	3,070
1979	1,430	3,070
1980	1,750	3,390
1981	2,100	3,710
1982	2,310	3,800
1983	2,600	4,100
1984	2,900	4,380
1985	6,420	9,360
1986	3,040	4,320
1987	3,040	4,210
1988	3,270	4,340
1989	3,390	4,300
1990	3,610	4,360
1991	3,830	4,410
1992	4,060	4,540
1993	4,450	4,830
1994	4,720	4,980
1995	5,070	5,200
1996 (estimate)	5,480	5,480

Note.—The peak in outlays per unit in 1985 of $6,420 is attributable to the bulge in 1985 expenditures associated with the change in the method for financing public housing. Without this change, outlays per unit would have amounted to around $2,860.

SOURCE: Congressional Budget Office, Based on Data Provided by the U.S. Department of Housing and Urban Development

TABLE 8.23

Program Participation Status of Poor Households
(In Thousands)

ALL RACES

Year	Living in Public or Subsidized Housing	
	#	%
1994	7,179	18.9%
1993	7,496	19.1%
1992r	7,029	18.5%
1991	7,183	20.1%
1990	6,667	19.9%
1989r	6,119	18.9%
1988	5,824	18.3%

WHITE

Year	Living in Public or Subsidized Housing	
	#	%
1994	3,292	13.0%
1993	3,507	13.4%
1992r	3,265	12.9%
1991	1,368	5.8%
1990	3,118	14.0%
1989r	2,816	13.2%
1988	2,790	13.5%

BLACK

Year	Living in Public or Subsidized Housing	
	#	%
1994	3,513	34.5%
1993	3,682	33.8%
1992r	3,415	31 s%
1991	3,536	34.5%
1990	3,292	33.5%
1989r	2,996	31.4%
1988	2,724	29.1%

HISPANIC

Year	Living in Public or Subsidized Housing	
	#	%
1994	1,233	14.7%
1993	1,124	13.8%
1992r	1,144	15.1%
1991	1,056	16.7%
1990	984	16.4%
1989r	967	15.9%
1988	836	15.6%

SOURCE: Richard May and Kathryn H. Porter. *Poverty and Income Trends: 1994.* Center on Budget and Policy Priorities: Washington, D.C., 1996

Federal Funding for Housing

Budget authorizations for these programs also dropped dramatically, from almost $75.5 billion in 1978 to about $11.3 billion in 1989 (in 1996 dollars), but have risen somewhat since then. The budget authority for all housing assistance programs in 1995 was $13.6 billion, and the estimate for 1996 was $14.9 billion.

While the authorizations were declining, the actual yearly outlays, many fueled by earlier commitments, were increasing from $7.3 billion (in 1996 dollars) in 1977 to an estimated $26 billion in 1996, an increase of 256 percent. (See Table 8.21.)

Average annual federal outlays per unit for all programs have generally risen, from about $2,900 in 1977 (in 1996 dollars) to an estimated $5,480 in 1996. (See Table 8.22.) Several factors have contributed to this growth. Rents in subsidized housing have probably risen faster than the income of assisted households, causing the subsidies to rise faster than inflation. In addition, housing aid is being targeted toward a poorer segment of the population, requiring larger subsidies per assisted household.

Increase in the Number of People Served

The number of households who lived in public or subsidized housing increased from 5.8 million in 1988 to 7.2 million in 1994. Much of this increase resulted from financial commitments made long ago, which are currently being processed. This number represented only 18.9 percent of all poor households, which reflected the long time gap between applying and receiving help. Poor black households (34.5 percent) were more likely to live in public or subsidized housing than were poor Hispanic households (14.7 percent) or poor white (13 percent) households. (See Table 8.23.) In 1996, 5.7 million households received housing assistance.

CHAPTER 9
WELFARE-TO-WORK PROGRAMS

WORK, A MAJOR ISSUE OF WELFARE REFORM

The focus of the welfare debate has changed dramatically since the 1980s. During the early 1980s, President Ronald Reagan attacked waste, fraud, and abuse in the welfare system, the conventional attack upon public welfare at the time. Since the late 1980s, however, the issue of welfare reform has focused on work programs as a means of getting people off welfare and keeping them off. Whether Republican or Democrat, a general consensus developed that jobs, either in the private sector, subsidized by the government, or both, were the basic answer to the welfare problem. By the summer of 1996 a number of welfare reform proposals had been offered for consideration in Congress. Virtually all of them contained a basic requirement that welfare recipients get jobs, either on their own or with the help of local welfare agencies. At the same time, the recognition that effective job training can be very expensive led many proposed welfare bills to drop or severely limit job-training funds.

These and similar proposals had been around for at least a generation and had generally been referred to as "workfare" programs. Both liberals and conservatives agree that those able to work for their income should do so. A job allows individuals the independence and sense of accomplishment brought by providing for oneself and a family. Furthermore, finding people jobs reduces the financial burden on state, local, and federal governments.

The passage of the Personal Responsibility and Work Opportunity Reconciliation Act (PL 104-193) in August 1996 laid the foundation for a work-based welfare system. The welfare law replaced Aid to Families with Dependent Children (AFDC) and the JOBS (Job Opportunities and Basic Skills) training program with Temporary Assistance to Needy Families (TANF) and created financial incentives for welfare-to-work programs. States must require TANF recipients to work after two years on assistance or face reductions in funding. In addition, with few exceptions,

they may not use federal funds to assist families for longer than five years. (For more information about the Personal Responsibility and Work Opportunity Reconciliation Act, see Chapter 2.) Funding for the various state work programs is included in federal block grants to states. Within the general guidelines of the act, each state designs its own program to promote job preparation and work.

HISTORY OF WORKFARE

In 1935, in the middle of the Great Depression, President Franklin Delano Roosevelt introduced the nation's first federal welfare program. At that time, 88 percent of welfare families received assistance because the father of the family had died. Since the nation had a surplus of workers and a shortage of work, keeping widows at home allowed mothers to care for their children and also kept these women from competing with men in the job market. Public work programs for men were also created to combat unemployment, such as the Civilian Conservation Corps (CCC) and the Works Progress Administration (WPA).

Community Work and Training Program

The 1962 Public Welfare Amendments (PL 87-543) authorized the first federal workfare program—the Community Work and Training Program (CWTP). At the time, 40,000 fathers were registered in the Aid to Families with Dependent Children for Unemployed Parents (AFDC-UP) program. This new program allowed the states to choose whether or not they wanted to enroll adult AFDC recipients in workfare programs. The CWTP provided standards for health and safety, minimum wages paid as welfare benefits, training, work expenses, and child care. Those enrolled had to work in meaningful public service jobs that did not displace other workers. Between October 1962 and June 1968 CWTP workers received $195 million. When the program ended in June 1968, it had involved 13 states and as many as 27,000 participants.

Economic Opportunity Act

The next major initiative, Title V of the Economic Opportunity Act (EOA) of 1964 (PL 88-452), allowed states to develop "work experience demonstration projects" using EOA funds instead of welfare funds intended for AFDC mothers, unemployed fathers, and other needy adults. If participants in the work-experience program were also AFDC recipients enrolled in the CWTP, Title V funds supplemented welfare benefits. The demonstration projects spent $300 million, with participation peaking at 72,000 persons in 1967. Title V expired in June 1969.

The available information on the EOA and the CWTP is not adequate to evaluate the programs' actual impact on the lives and futures of the participants. The sparse data available showed that 36 to 46 percent of the participants found employment after job training or after leaving a work-experience project. However, the researchers do not know what would have happened without the program's intervention or how long these individuals remained employed.

Work Incentive Program

The Work Incentive (WIN) program was enacted through the 1967 Social Security Amendments (PL 90-248) to make AFDC recipients less dependent on welfare. The 1967 Amendments were in response to a 24 percent increase in the number of female-headed families eligible for AFDC and were intended to provide training for these women.

The WIN program required registration of "appropriate AFDC recipients," with each state defining who was "appropriate." The program included regular counseling, as well as referral and assistance in obtaining basic education and job skills. The recipients in classroom and on-the-job training might receive a small incentive payment. The program was supposed to develop an "employability" plan for each recipient. But by 1971 it became apparent that most participants in the program were not finding jobs.

The Social Security Act was amended in 1971, 1980, 1982, and 1984 to improve the WIN program. The WIN program was phased out by the Job Opportunities and Basic Skills Training Program (JOBS). All states enrolled in WIN had to introduce the JOBS program by October 1990.

Comprehensive Employment and Training Act of 1973

The Comprehensive Employment and Training Act (CETA) of 1973 (PL 93-203) consolidated several federal employment and training programs, some of which did not focus solely on low-income job-seekers. Targeted at economically disadvantaged people, including those on welfare, the CETA training programs lasted about 10 years. In 1979 about 90 percent of the 1.2 million participants in the major CETA programs were economically disadvantaged—71 percent were in poor families, and 18 percent were AFDC recipients.

Food Stamp Workfare

The Food Stamp Act of 1977 (PL 95-400) authorized seven urban and seven rural workfare demonstration projects that operated between 1979 and 1980. The 1981 amendments to the Food Stamp Act (PL 97-98) expanded the program and granted authority to all states and localities to establish workfare programs for food-stamp recipients. The work programs were similar to the previously discussed workfare programs. Noncompliance (not participating in the work program) resulted in the loss of eligibility for food stamps.

After the first year, a U.S. General Accounting Office (GAO) study could not determine the overall costs and benefits. A later GAO study found that during the 1981 expansion phase, those in the workfare demonstration projects reduced their receipt of food stamps at a greater rate than those not on workfare.

Job Training Partnership Act

In 1982 the Job Training Partnership Act (JTPA) of 1982 (PL 97-300) replaced CETA. Title II-A of this act provided block grants to the states for training and related services for economically disadvantaged people, especially those receiving cash assistance and food stamps. State and local governments administered these programs within federal guidelines. The aid was intended to increase the participants' future employment possibilities and earnings and to reduce their dependence on welfare. Services provided by this program included job training, help in finding work, counseling, and other assistance designed to prepare the participant for a job.

The number of terminees (people who have completed the program) dropped sharply between 1990 and 1997, from 307,935 in 1990 to 175,647 in 1994 and 147,717 in 1997. In 1997, 68 percent of those participating in these programs were female and 32 percent were male. Almost half (45 percent) were non-Hispanic whites, about one third (34 percent) were non-Hispanic blacks, 17 percent were Hispanics, and 5 percent were from other races. (See Table 9.1.)

In 1997 the majority (57 percent) of terminees were between 30 and 54 years of age, while 41 percent were between 22 and 29 years of age. Only 2 percent were 55 years and older. In the same year 57 percent of those who completed the program were high school graduates, and 21 percent had an education beyond high school. Of the participants who terminated benefits, 29 percent became employed at an average hourly wage of $5.00 to $7.49, and 13 percent became employed at an average hourly wage of $7.50 or more. (See Table 9.1.)

Just as the number of terminees had dropped, so had the number of new enrollees. In a typical year during the 1970s, over 1 million new people were enrolled in the

TABLE 9.1

Characteristics of Terminees, Trends Over Time
(Universe: PY 97 Title II-A Adult Terminees Who Received Services Beyond Objective Assessment)

	PY 94	PY 95	PY 96	PY 97
Total Terminees	175,647	162,120	151,155	147,717
Gender				
Female	67	67	69	68
Male	33	33	31	32
Age				
22 - 29	42	42	4256	41
30 - 54	56	56	56	57
55 and older	2	2	2	2
Race/Ethnicity				
White (not Hispanic)	52	48	46	45
Black (not Hispanic)	31	32	33	34
Hispanic	14	17	17	17
Amer. Indian or Alaskan Native	1	2	2	2
Asian or Pacific Islander	2	3	3	3
Family Status				
Parent in one-parent family	44	46	47	47
Parent in two-parent family	18	18	17	17
Other family member	8	8	7	7
Not a family member	30	29	29	29
Number of Dependents under Age 18				
None	40	38	38	37
1 or 2	42	43	44	44
3 or more	17	18	19	19
Highest Grade Completed				
Less than high school graduate	23	22	22	21
High school graduate	56	56	56	57
Post high school	21	21	22	21
Reading Skills Grade Level				
Less than 7th grade	16	14	13	13
7th or 8th grade	16	15	16	16
9th grade and above	68	70	71	71
Math Skills Grade Level				
Less than 7th grade	25	24	23	24
7th or 8th grade	28	28	28	28
9th grade and above	48	48	49	48
Veteran				
Total veterans	8	7	7	7
Vietnam era	2	2	2	2
Disabled veteran	0	0	0	0

TABLE 9.1

Characteristics of Terminees, Trends Over Time [CONTINUED]
(Universe: PY 97 Title II-A Adult Terminees Who Received Services Beyond Objective Assessment)

	PY 94	PY 95	PY 96	PY 97
Economically Disadvantaged	98	98	98	98
Cash Welfare Recipient	42	41	39	36
TANF/AFDC	35	35	33	31
GA, RCA, or SSI	8	7	7	6
Food Stamps	57	57	56	53
JOBS/ Welfare to Work Participant	16	16	14	13
Labor Force Status				
Employed	15	15	15	17
Unemployed	52	50	48	49
Not in labor force	33	35	37	34
Weeks Unemployed in Prior 26 Wks				
None - NILF at intake	26	27	29	27
None - employed at intake	11	12	12	13
1 to 14	19	19	19	21
15 to 25	20	19	20	21
26	24	23	20	19
Unemployment Compensation Status				
Claimant	10	8	9	8
Exhaustee	5	4	5	4
None	85	88	87	88
Preprogram Hourly Wage				
Not employed in past 26 weeks	50	52	53	51
$4.99 or less	18	14	11	8
$5.00 to $7.49	23	24	25	29
$7.50 or more	9	10	11	13
Legislatively-Defined Hard to Serve				
Has at least 1 barrier	*87*	*87*	*86*	*86*
Basic skills deficient	58	56	56	57
School dropout	22	22	21	21
Cash welfare recipients	42	41	39	36
Offender (inc. misdemeanors)	12	13	14	15
Disability (substantial barrier)	8	7	7	6
Homeless	2	3	2	3
Other SDA-identified barrier	26	30	31	31
Has 2 or more barriers	*56*	*55*	*54*	*53*
Additional Barriers to Employment				
Limited English proficiency	5	6	6	6
Displaced homemaker	4	4	4	4
Lacks significant work history	35	36	37	36
Long-term welfare recipient	16	16	16	15
Substance abuse	5	6	5	5

Note: Numbers (except Total Terminees) represent percentages. Items in italics are imputed or are based on partial data; '0' denotes a percentage less than 0.5%.

SOURCE: *PY 97 SPIR Data Book*. Prepared for Office of Policy and Research, Employment and Training Administration, U.S. Dept. of Labor: Washington, D.C., June 1999

job training program. By 1984 the number had dropped to 716,200 as budgets were cut in half. Budgets (in 1990 dollars) continued to drop after 1986. As a result, so did the number of new enrollees, which tumbled from 1 million in 1986 to an estimated 329,178 in 1996. (See Table 9.2.)

Critics of the JTPA programs claimed that the most employable individuals from the eligible population were selected to participate in the program. They believed this had been fostered by the heavy use of performance-based contracts, in which the amount paid to a private trainer of JTPA participants was based on the number of participants placed in jobs. Therefore, contractors tended to screen out eligible applicants who might be difficult to place. The strongest evidence of this selection process was in the educational attainment of those in the program. However, it might also have been possible that those people with higher education levels were more likely to apply for the program.

SUMMER EMPLOYMENT. Title II-B of JTPA authorized a summer employment and training program for economically disadvantaged youngsters ages 16 to 21. Under this program, 100 percent of the participants had to be economically disadvantaged. Services included a full range of remedial education, classroom and on-the-job training, and some work experience for which the young people were paid a minimum wage.

As with the training program discussed above, outlays and participation have dropped since 1985. Funding decreased from $776 billion in 1985 to $698 billion (in current dollars) in 1991, while participation dropped from 767,600 in 1985 to 555,200 in 1991, rose to 782,100

TABLE 9.2

Job Training Programs[1] for the Disadvantaged: New Enrollees, Federal Appropriations and Outlays, Fiscal Years 1975–96

Fiscal year	New enrollees	Appropriations (millions)	Outlays (millions)	Budget authority in constant 1990 dollars	Outlays in constant 1990 dollars
1975	1,126,000	$1,580	$1,304	$3,755	$3,099
1976	1,250,000	1,580	1,697	3,515	3,775
1977	1,119,000	2,880	1,756	5,964	3,636
1978	965,000	1,880	2,378	3,658	4,627
1979	1,253,000	2,703	2,547	4,829	4,550
1980	1,208,000	3,205	3,236	5,154	5,203
1981	1,011,000	3,077	3,395	4,493	4,958
1982	N A	1,594	2,277	2,175	3,107
1983	N A	2,181	2,291	2,846	2,990
1984	716,200	1,886	1,333	2,361	1,669
1985	803,900	1,886	1,710	2,279	2,066
1986	1,003,900	1,783	1,911	2,101	2,252
1987	960,700	1,840	1,880	2,108	2,154
1988	873,600	1,810	1,902	1,991	2,092
1989	823,200	1,788	1,868	1,877	1,961
1990	630,000	1,745	1,803	1,745	1,803
1991	[2] 603,900	1,779	1,746	1,694	1,676
1992	[2] 602,300	1,774	1,767	1,637	1,632
1993	[2] 584,547	1,692	1,747	1,530	1,580
Adult	316,687	1,015	1,048	918	948
Youth	267,860	677	699	612	632
1994	[2] 541,463	1,597	1,693	1,415	1,500
Adult	312,297	988	1,016	875	900
Youth	229,166	609	677	540	600
1995	[2] 340,354	1,124	1,534	971	1,325
Adult	310,123	997	934	861	807
Youth	[3] 30,231	127	600	110	518
1996	[2] 329,178	977	1,023	824	862
Adult	254,318	850	866	717	730
Youth	74,860	127	157	107	132

[1] Figures shown in years 1975-83 are for training activities under the Comprehensive Employment and Training Act (CETA); public service employment under CETA IS not included. Figures shown in years 1984-92 are for activities under title II-A of the Job Training Partnership Act (JTPA). For 1993-96 figures are for titles II–A (adult) and II–C (youth) of the JTPA. as amended in 1992.

[2] Estimate.

[3] According to the Department of Labor, reduced budget authority in fiscal year 1995 was insufficient to serve those already enrolled and to enroll a comparable number of new participants. In fiscal year 1996, transfers from II-B (summer youth) enabled more participants to be enrolled.

NA-Not available.

SOURCE: U.S. Department of Labor

in 1992, and dropped again to an estimated 521,000 in 1996. Approximately $625 million was appropriated for the summer of 1996 to serve an estimated 521,000 young people. (See Table 9.3.)

In the summer of 1994, 45 percent of the participants were ages 14 and 15, 37 percent were either 16 or 17 years old, and 18 percent were between 18 and 21. Forty-one percent were African American; 27 percent, white; and 27 percent, Hispanic. Fifteen percent had disabilities.

Job Opportunities and Basic Skills Training Program

The Job Opportunities and Basic Skills Training Program (JOBS) was another program intended to help welfare families obtain education, training, and employment so that they could become self-sufficient. JOBS, administered by the U.S. Department of Health and Human Services (HHS), was also designed to provide these individuals with supportive services, such as child care. Each state was responsible for determining the structure of its JOBS program. This helped direct the training toward unique needs and job opportunities within each state. The Family Support Act of 1988 (PL 100-485) required states to replace any existing WIN programs with JOBS programs.

The target groups for the JOBS program were persons who had received AFDC for at least 36 months over the previous 60 months, parents under 24 years of age who did not have a high school diploma or a GED and who were not in school when they applied for AFDC, parents under 24 years of age with little or no work experience in the previous year, and members of families in which the youngest child was 16 years or older. In a majority of cases, the parent was female. Unlike previous laws, the act required participation in JOBS by parents of children as young as three years old and permitted states to include participation of mothers with children as young as one year old. As described by HHS, the JOBS program:

- Emphasized education, particularly literacy and remedial education. Basic education, in this context, was defined as literacy and remedial education, English as a second language, and a high school diploma or the equivalent.

- Provided training and work experience for jobs that existed. Emphasis was on short-term, goal-oriented training. JOBS was designed to use and coordinate with job training programs that were already in existence. It encouraged community participation in programs such as community-based business and volunteer organizations. Work training programs were targeted at areas that needed specific types of skills to match job opportunities.

- Gave states flexibility in program design. The federal government created the broad standards. But the states designed the programs to best suit their needs.

- Allowed women to choose relatives, independent contractors, or day care centers, within state fiscal constraints, as child-care providers. States used vouchers, direct payments, or other types of financing to compensate child-care workers.

Every state JOBS program was required to include plans to provide education to those without a high school education, offer job skills training, and teach the person how to get and hold a job. With few exceptions, the program had to provide some form of schooling designed to get a high school or equivalent diploma if the person was a parent under 20 years old with no high school education. Similarly, the state had to provide educational programs unless the person had a specific employment goal that did not require a high school diploma if the person was over 20 years of age and without a high school or equivalent diploma.

JOBS required the state to supply child care to mothers who needed it. The state also had to provide transportation and other services if the parent needed them. If the family lost AFDC eligibility because the parent had found a job, the family could get a year of transitional child care and Medicaid. This transition period was intended to help the family adjust to its new situation and be able to somehow replace the child care and health services offered under the JOBS program. Basically, the JOBS program created a new government compact with welfare recipients. It promised to give them more training, supply transportation, furnish day care for their children, and provide Medicaid to protect their health, while the welfare recipient was required to either get an education or a job.

Funding for the JOBS program increased potential federal financing significantly. The federal matching rate was 90 percent, up to a state's WIN allocation for 1987. Funds for JOBS programs beyond that amount were matched at the Medicaid rate or 60 percent, whichever was greater. The total federal financing matched was set

TABLE 9.3

Summer Youth Employment Program: Federal Appropriations, Outlays, and Participants, Fiscal Years 1984–96
[Dollars in millions]

Fiscal or calendar year	Appropriations	Outlays		Participants[1]
		Current dollars	Constant 1990 dollars	
1984	$824	$584	$731	672,000
1985	724	776	938	767,600
1986	636	746	879	785,000
1987	750	723	828	634,400
1988	718	707	778	!22,900
1989	709	697	732	607,900
1990	700	699	639	585,100
1991	683	698	663	555,200
1992	[2] 995	958	[3] 912	782,100
1993	[4] 1,025	915	827	[3] 647,400
1994	[5] 888	834	739	[3] 574,400
1995	[6] 185	883	763	[3] 489,200
1996	[7] 625	N A	N A	[3] 521,000

[1] Because JTPA is an advance-funded program, appropriations for the summer youth program in a particular fiscal year are generally spent the following summer. For example, fiscal year 1991 appropriations were spent during the summer of calendar year 1992. The pattern has varied somewhat in recent years. These variations are noted.

[2] Fiscal year 1992 funding includes a $500 million supplemental appropriation for summer 1992 and $495 million for summer 1993.

[3] Estimate.

[4] Fiscal year 1993 funding includes $354 million for summer 1993 and $671 million for summer 1994.

[5] Fiscal year 1994 funding includes $206 million for summer 1994 and $682 million for summer 1995.

[6] Public Law 104-19 rescinded $682 million in fiscal year 1995 funds which were to be available for the summer of 1996. The remaining $185 million was for the summer of 1995.

[7] Fiscal year 1996 funds are for the summer of 1996.

NA-Not available.

Note.—Appropriations and outlays are for fiscal years; participants are for calendar years.

SOURCE: Employment and Training Administration, U.S. Department of Labor

at a cap of $800 million in 1990 to rise to a cap of $1.3 billion in 1995. There were no limits on child-care funding, which was matched at the Medicaid rate, which ranges from 50 to 80 percent, depending on the state. Generally, federal authorizations permitted about 10 percent of welfare recipients to participate in JOBS programs at any one time. In a typical month in 1994, 579,213 people were participating in JOBS programs.

Job Corps

The Job Corps program was first authorized in 1964 by the Economic Opportunity Act. Since 1982, it was authorized by Title IV-B of JTPA. The program served economically disadvantaged youth ages 14 to 24 who showed both the need for and the ability to benefit from an intensive and wide range of social services provided in a residential setting. In 1996 there were 110 Job Corps centers in the United States offering basic education, vocational skills training, work experience, counseling, health care, and other job-related services.

TABLE 9.4

Job Corps: Federal Appropriations, Outlays, and New Enrollees, Fiscal Years 1982–96
[Dollars in millions]

		Outlays		
	Appropriations	Current dollars	Constant 1990 dollars	New enrollees
1982	$590	$595	$812	53,581
1983	618	563	735	60,465
1984	599	581	727	57,386
1985	617	593	716	63,020
1986	612	594	701	64,964
1987	656	631	723	65,150
1988	716	688	757	68,068
1989	742	689	724	62,550
1990	803	740	740	61,453
1991	867	769	769	62,205
1992	919	834	789	61,762
1993	966	936	846	62,749
1994	1,040	981	869	58,460
1995	1,089	1,011	873	59,422
1996	1,094	¹1,049	¹885	¹63,955

¹ Estimate.

Note.–Appropriations and outlays are for fiscal years; enrollees are for calendar years.

SOURCE: Employment and Training Administration, U.S. Department of Labor

FIGURE 9.1

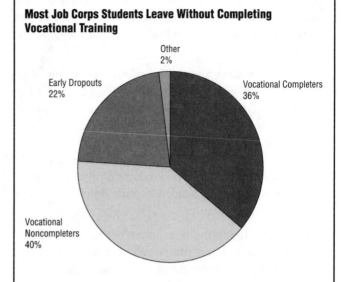

Most Job Corps Students Leave Without Completing Vocational Training

Note: "Other" includes those students who were in the program for at least 60 days but never entered a vocational training program.

SOURCE: *Job Corps: High Costs and Mixed Results Raise Questions About Program's Effectiveness.* U.S. General Accounting Office: Washington, D.C., 1995

In 1994 about 61 percent of the enrollees were male; 51 percent were African American; 28 percent, white; and 15 percent, Hispanic. Seventy-nine percent were high school dropouts, and 69 percent had never worked full time. Forty-three percent of Job Corps enrollees came from families on public assistance. The average enrollee stayed in the program for 7.5 months. An estimated 63 percent of the terminees got a job after leaving, and another 10 percent either continued their education or entered another training program for a total positive termination rate of 73 percent in 1994.

Unlike most work programs, funding for the Job Corps was not cut as dramatically, and participation did not drop. Following a sharp drop between 1982 and 1986, outlays increased gradually each year to an estimated $885 million (in constant 1990 dollars) in 1996. The number of new enrollees stayed within the range of 60,000 from 1983 to 1996. (See Table 9.4.)

In response to congressional questions about the operation and effectiveness of the Job Corps program, the U.S. General Accounting Office (GAO) analyzed data on participants and visited six training sites—in Mammoth Cave, Kentucky; Guthrie, Oklahoma; San Jose, California; Chicopee, Massachusetts; Glide, Oregon; and Laurel, Maryland. In addition, the GAO surveyed employers to check on job retention and their satisfaction with the training the students had received in the program. The data was gathered from December 1994 to May 1995.

In *Job Corps: High Costs and Mixed Results Raise Questions About Program's Effectiveness* (Washington, DC, 1995), the GAO reported that 22 percent of the students who entered the Job Corps program dropped out before they had completed 60 days in 1993. Forty percent stayed at least 60 days but failed to complete their vocational training, and 36 percent completed the training. (See Figure 9.1.)

Those who completed the vocational training were 50 percent more likely to get a job than noncompleters (not including early dropouts) and were more likely (37 percent) to find jobs related to the training they had received, compared to only 7 percent of the noncompleters. (See Figure 9.2.) Furthermore, students who found training-related jobs earned higher average wages ($6.60 per hour) than students who did not find training-related jobs ($5.28 per hour).

Students who took jobs after leaving the six centers tended not to stay in their first job for long. About 30 percent of the students who left had worked less than 1 month for their first employer, while nearly 20 percent worked 6 months or longer. (See Figure 9.3.) Employers reported that 45 percent had quit, 22 percent were fired, and 13 percent were laid off.

WORK REQUIREMENTS FOR TANF RECIPIENTS

The purpose of the TANF provisions differs significantly from the purpose of the JOBS program. The stated

FIGURE 9.2

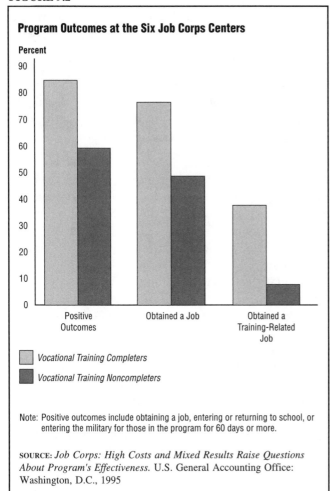

Program Outcomes at the Six Job Corps Centers

Note: Positive outcomes include obtaining a job, entering or returning to school, or entering the military for those in the program for 60 days or more.

SOURCE: *Job Corps: High Costs and Mixed Results Raise Questions About Program's Effectiveness.* U.S. General Accounting Office: Washington, D.C., 1995

FIGURE 9.3

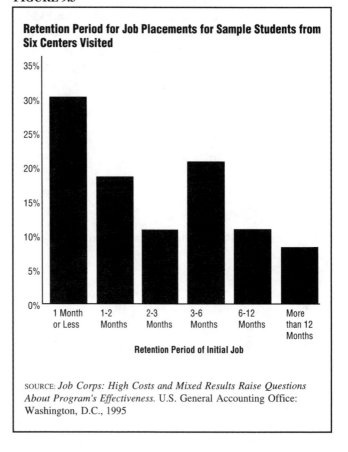

Retention Period for Job Placements for Sample Students from Six Centers Visited

SOURCE: *Job Corps: High Costs and Mixed Results Raise Questions About Program's Effectiveness.* U.S. General Accounting Office: Washington, D.C., 1995

purpose of JOBS was to ensure that needy families with children "obtain the education, training and employment that will help them avoid long-term welfare dependence." The purpose of the TANF is to "end the dependence of needy parents on government benefits by promoting job preparation, work, and marriage." The 1996 welfare law imposed work conditions but did not specifically fund work programs. However, the 1997 Balanced Budget Act established a $3 billion welfare-to-work grant program for 1998–99. (For more information on the Balanced Budget Act, see Chapter 2.) The President's fiscal year 1998 budget proposed funding of $4.1 billion over five years to create or subsidize jobs.

The TANF recipients are expected to participate in work activities while receiving benefits. After 24 months of assistance, states must require recipients to work at least part time in order to continue to receive cash benefits. The only exceptions are parents of very young children (under 3 months) and disabled adults. The TANF law defines the "work activities" that count when determining a state's work participation rate. Table 9.5 lists the work activity requirements for single parents and nonparental caretakers who are at least 20 years old.

TABLE 9.5

Work Activity Requirements for Single Parents at Least 20 Years Old and for Non-Parental Caretakers Who Receive TANF

Work activities	Average Weekly Hours Required		
	FYI997-FY1998	FY1999	FY2000 and later
1. Unsubsidized job	20 hours, all in first 9 activities	25 hours	30 hours
2. Subsidized private job			
3. Subsidized public job			
4. Work experience			
5. On-the-job training		-at least 20 hours in first 9 activities:	-at least 20 hours in first 9 activities:
6. Job search and job readiness (6weeks usual maximum)			
7. Community service			
8. Vocational educational training (12 months maximum)			
9. Caring for child of community service participant			
I0. Job skills training directly related to work		-5 hours countable in last 3 activities	-10 hours countable in last 3 activities
11. Education directly related to work (high school drop-out)			
12. Satisfactory attendance at high school or equivalent (high school drop-out)			

SOURCE: Vee Burke. *New Welfare Law: Role of Education and Training.* Congressional Research Service, The Library of Congress: Washington, D.C., 1997

To be counted as a work participant, a TANF recipient must work at least 20 hours a week in 1997 and 1998. This requirement rises to 25 hours in 1999 and 30 in 2000, unless the recipient has a child under 6. In the first two years, the 20 required hours must be spent in one or more of these nine high-priority activities:

- An unsubsidized job (no government help),

- A subsidized private job,

- A subsidized public job,

- Work experience,

- On-the-job training,

- Job search and job readiness (a usual maximum of six weeks),

- Community service,

- Vocational educational training (a 12-month maximum),

- Providing child care for a community service participant.

Three activities listed—work-related job skills training, work-related education, and satisfactory attendance at high school or its equivalent—become countable only if the parent or caretaker spends 20 hours in the other nine activities. Therefore, after 1998, when recipients must work five or 10 hours more, they may spend the hours beyond 20 in activities 10 to 12 and receive credit for them as a work participant. (In able-bodied two-parent families, one parent must work, or the two parents can share, 35 hours a week, with 30 hours in one or more of the first nine activities.) (See Table 9.5.)

Table 9.6 shows the additional provisions that apply to young parents who are under age 20 and household heads or married that are without a high school diploma. They will be considered "engaged in work" if they either maintain satisfactory attendance in high school (no hours specified) or participate in education directly related to work (20 hours a week).

Education and Training

Reflecting a "work-first" philosophy, the 1996 welfare law limits the number of the TANF recipients who may get work credit through participation in education and training. No more than 30 percent of TANF families who are counted as engaged in work may consist of persons who are participating in vocational educational training. Vocational educational training is the only creditable work activity not explicitly confined to high school dropouts.

In contrast, the prior law funded, and states were required to offer, education and training. Participants in the JOBS program were allowed to count postsecondary education as a JOBS activity. In 1995 higher education activities accounted for nearly 23 percent of the monthly average of JOBS participants. Because very few education and training programs count as work activities, many groups have urged that the definition of vocational educational training be more broadly defined to include training and education for persons beyond high school. For the estimated one-third of welfare recipients with a low literacy level, the National Governors' Association in 1997 urged "greater flexibility to count basic education activities toward the work requirement." On the other hand, the proponents of putting work first believe that education and training are more valuable and meaningful after a recipient is employed. They contend that participation in JOBS education and training programs often became the end in itself, rather than the intended transition to a job.

FINDING AND CREATING JOBS FOR TANF RECIPIENTS

Job availability is one of the most difficult challenges facing states in moving recipients to work from welfare. This includes both the location of job opportunities and the suitability of jobs for the skill levels and past work experience of most welfare recipients. If suitable jobs cannot be found, states must create work activity placements. The problem has been made easier by the current economic prosperity. However, it could become serious again when the economy contracts in a recession, causing a scarcity of jobs.

TABLE 9.6

Qualifying Educational Activities for Parent who is Under Age 20 and Household Head or Married
(without high school diploma)

Work activity	FYI997-FYI998	FY1999	FY2000 and thereafter
11 a. Education directly related to work**	20 hours weekly	20 hours weekly	20 hours weekly
12a. High school attendance (or equivalent)**	"satisfactory attendance"	"satisfactory attendance"	"satisfactory attendance"

**No more thau 30% of TANF recipients who are treated as "engaged in work" may consist of persons who are engaged in activity number 8, vocational educational training. After FY2000, no more than 30%) of persons counted as workers may consist of persons engaged in activities number 8: 11a and 12a.

SOURCE: Vee Burke. *New Welfare Law: Role of Education and Training.* Congressional Research Service, The Library of Congress: Washington, D.C., 1997

Welfare agencies have had to change their focus and train staff to function more as job developers and counselors than as caseworkers. They make an initial assessment of recipients' skills as required by the TANF law. They may then develop personal responsibility plans for recipients, identifying what is needed (training, job placement services, support services) to move them into the workforce.

States have developed a variety of approaches to finding and creating job opportunities. Though most rely on existing unemployment offices, many states have tried other options to help recipients find work:

- Collaboration with the business community to develop strategies that provide recipients with the skills and training employers want.

- Use of several types of subsidies for employers who hire welfare recipients directly (subsidizing wages, providing tax credits to employers, subsidizing workers' compensation and unemployment compensation taxes).

- Targeting state jobs for welfare recipients.

- Financial encouragement for entrepreneurship and self-employment.

- Creation of community service positions, often within city departments, such as parks and libraries. (Recipients usually participate in this "workfare" as a condition of continuing to receive benefits rather than for wages.)

These ideas are not yet fully tested, so their potential to meet the goals of welfare reform is unknown. The different approaches provide an opportunity to learn which programs succeed and which fall short. Careful state evaluation of their programs is crucial.

An In-Depth Evaluation of "Work First" Programs in Five States

A recent Urban Institute study, *Building an Employment Focused Welfare System: Work First and Other Work-Oriented Strategies in Five States* (Washington, D.C., 1998), is one of the first in-depth comparative analyses of how states are succeeding in moving to work-oriented welfare systems. The study of five selected states shows that strategies to promote employment, supported by a strong economy, have been effective in moving significant numbers of welfare recipients into jobs. The report was based on site visits in early 1997 to Indiana, Massachusetts, Oregon, Virginia, and Wisconsin, states that have experienced large caseload declines. These five states had begun reorganizing their welfare systems to emphasize a "work first" approach before Congress passed the 1996 welfare reform law.

Typical practices in all five states included (1) making the job search the first and major activity, (2) restricting participation in education and training, (3) imposing stricter participation and work requirements, (4) enforcing heavy penalties for noncompliance, and (5) setting time limits on assistance. Nonetheless, despite the similarities, each state had its own unique plan for welfare reform. For instance, Virginia gave recipients the greatest opportunity to combine assistance with employment but also imposed harsh penalties for noncompliance. Both Virginia and Massachusetts required work sooner than the other states and depended heavily on community service programs to engage recipients in some form of work. Of the states studied, Oregon had developed the most successful program for creating subsidized job opportunities for welfare recipients.

However, the researchers warn that a "work first" approach by itself cannot help all welfare recipients. It works best for individuals who are already fairly employable. It is less effective in helping those with significant barriers to employment or in helping recipients stay employed. Tracking a sample of recipients over a one-year period, the study found that, by the end of the year, 31 to 44 percent of the participants were still receiving cash assistance or were back on welfare, whether they had a job or not. Pamela Holcomb, the Urban Institute senior research associate who directed the study, said, "It's a strategy that gets a lot of people off the rolls quickly, but that's not the same as keeping them off welfare or moving families out of poverty."

SUPPORT SERVICES NECESSARY FOR MOVING RECIPIENTS TO WORK

Child Care

The offer of affordable child care is one critical enticement that encourages low-income mothers to seek and keep jobs. A recent U.S. General Accounting Office report noted that "any effort to move more low-income mothers from welfare to work will need to take into account the importance of child care subsidies to the likelihood of success." A study in Minneapolis discovered that about one-fourth of the former welfare recipients on the waiting list for child care went back on welfare when the child care services never materialized. According to the 1998 *Kids Count*, an annual report produced by the Annie E. Casey Foundation, child care expenses consume about one-fourth of the earnings of low-income families earning less than $1,200 a month.

Because states may use TANF funds for child care, they have more flexibility than before to design child care programs, not only for welfare recipients but also for working poor families who may need child care support to continue working and stay off welfare. States determine who is

FIGURE 9.4

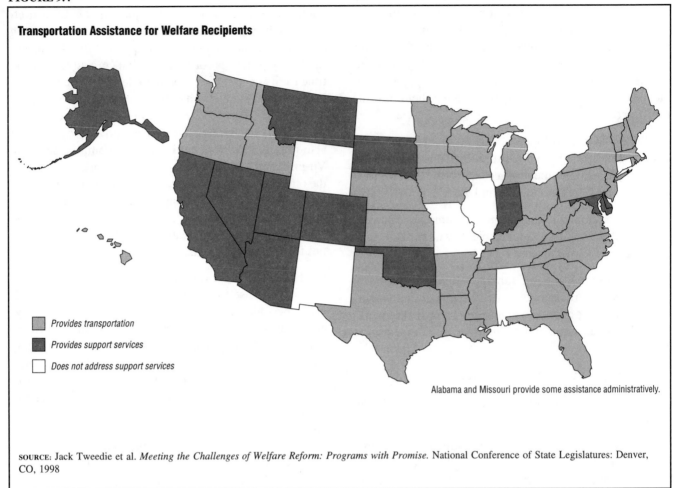

Transportation Assistance for Welfare Recipients

Provides transportation

Provides support services

Does not address support services

Alabama and Missouri provide some assistance administratively.

SOURCE: Jack Tweedie et al. *Meeting the Challenges of Welfare Reform: Programs with Promise.* National Conference of State Legislatures: Denver, CO, 1998

eligible for child care support, how much those parents will pay (often using a sliding fee scale), and the amount a state will reimburse providers of subsidized care.

Transportation, Access to Jobs

Transportation is another critical factor facing welfare recipients moving into a job. Recipients without a car must depend on public transportation. Yet two of three new jobs are in suburban areas, often outside the range of public transportation. Even when jobs are accessible to public transportation, many day-care centers and schools are not. Some jobs require weekend or night shift work, when public transportation schedules are limited. Even for those recipients with cars, less than 6 percent in 1995, the expense of gas and repairs can deplete earnings.

Illustrating the status of state transportation assistance for welfare recipients, states use a variety of approaches to provide transportation for recipients moving into the work force (see Figure 9.4):

- Developing vehicle purchasing agreements so recipients can own their cars.

- Filling transit service gaps, such as new routes or extended hours.

- Providing transit alternatives, such as vanpools or shuttle services.

- Offering entrepreneurial opportunities for recipients to become transportation providers.

CHAPTER 10

WELFARE REFORM—EARLY EVALUATION

A few years after the passage of the Personal Responsibility and Work Opportunity Reconciliation Act (PL 104-193), most observers viewed initial welfare-reform efforts with optimism. In July 1998 the National Governors' Association (NGA) held a press conference to report that the initial success of welfare reform had "far exceeded expectations of proponents and skeptics alike." In August 1998 the Department of Health and Human Services (HHS) issued its First Annual TANF Report to Congress. Giving a preliminary overview of the first two years of welfare, the report suggests that the nation has made "dramatic progress...on the critical goal of moving families from welfare to work."

According to "Tracking Recipients After They Leave Welfare," a report prepared by the staff of the NGA, the NCSL (National Conference of State Legislatures), and the APWA (American Public Welfare Association), states are "in a good situation to make further changes as the caseload reductions in most states means that states have substantial resources to invest in further services to help welfare recipients overcome the barriers to finding work and supporting their families without cash assistance."

Even many welfare recipients appear willing to give welfare reform a try. In *What Welfare Recipients and the Fathers of Their Children Are Saying about Welfare Reform* (Linda Burton et al., Johns Hopkins University, Baltimore, Maryland, 1998), a report about 15 focus group discussions in Baltimore, Boston, and Chicago, the general tone of the focus group interviews was one of cautious optimism. One African-American man in Boston believed that welfare reform is a definite step forward. By giving recipients the necessary assistance to enter the workforce, it not only encourages them to get training and find work, but it also helps build their character and self-esteem.

On the other hand, states are faced with many challenges. The nation's governors have urged Congress and the President to uphold the welfare-reform law and reject any cuts in welfare or Medicaid. States must now track the recipients who leave welfare to see how many are working, what types of jobs they are getting, and whether they are able to support their families. As states learn which programs work and which need adjustment, the programs can be modified. In *Meeting the Challenges of Welfare Reform* (National Conference of State Legislatures, Denver, Colorado, 1998), Jack Tweedie identifies six welfare policy issues he feels are critical in transforming welfare:

- **Creating Jobs**—In many states, there are not enough suitable job opportunities for recipients who have limited education and work experience.

- **Preparing Recipients for Work**—Recipients with low levels of education and limited or no work experience will need programs to train and prepare them for the work force.

- **Child Care**—Any recipients required to work will need child care. States must create and finance enough child care positions for those recipients as well as maintain quality.

- **Transportation**—States will have to provide transportation for many recipients to get their children to child care and to get to work.

- **Safety Net**—States must find ways to protect the children of parents who lose their eligibility for benefits because of time limits or noncompliance of work requirements.

- **Finance and Accountability**—Although the executive branch has primary responsibility for implementing reforms, legislatures must find ways to monitor welfare implementation so they can make changes and adaptations when necessary to ensure that reforms are responsive to their concerns.

Other observers would add the reduction of teen births to the list of critical issues since most teen mothers are on welfare. Welfare-reform legislation required states to submit plans detailing their goals to reduce births outside marriage, especially among teenagers.

CHARACTERISTICS OF THOSE WHO LEAVE WELFARE AND THOSE WHO REMAIN ON THE ROLLS

Welfare caseloads declined 44 percent between August 1996 and June 1999. According to figures compiled by *The New York Times*, white recipients are leaving the welfare rolls much faster than African American and Hispanic recipients. Blacks on welfare now outnumber whites, while the Hispanic proportion is growing the fastest. Combined, African American and Hispanic recipients outnumber whites by about 2 to 1.

The growing minority domination of welfare rolls was unexpected and as yet is largely unexplained. One potential explanation offered was discrimination by employers or by landlords in neighborhoods near jobs. Unpublished data from the Census Bureau, prepared for *The New York Times*, suggest that minority recipients were significantly more disadvantaged than white recipients when the welfare rolls were at their highest in 1994.

The proportion of families with a teen mother has decreased. In 1994, 288,879 mothers who were 19-years old and under received assistance; in 1997 the number had fallen to 201,182. In 1999 the teen birthrate was at its lowest level since 1987. On the other hand, the proportion of child-only cases has increased. The percentage of cases with no adult receiving assistance increased from 17 percent in 1994 to 23 percent in 1997.

Although many recipients leave welfare for work, some have trouble keeping a job. Early data show that about one-fifth of the families who leave welfare come back within several months. Lack of understanding about workplace behavior, problems with child care or transportation, and the instability of the low-skilled labor market are all factors contributing to job loss. States must find ways to keep recipients employed, helping them build a work history so that they can move into higher-skilled, better-paying jobs.

As caseloads decrease, a growing proportion of those who remain on the rolls have significant barriers to employment: low basic skills, learning disabilities, alcohol or substance abuse, and chronic health problems. A number of states are reporting an increasing share of "hard-to-serve" families on welfare. States are beginning to focus more attention on these families. For instance, many states have chosen the Family Violence Option to ensure that victims of domestic violence get both protection and services. Most states exempt mothers of infants from work requirements.

Early information suggests that as welfare caseloads drop, the proportion of long-term welfare cases is increasing. From 1994 to 1997, the proportion of welfare families whose current spell of welfare receipt had been 60 months or more increased from 19 percent to 24 percent, compared to the proportion whose current welfare spell had been one year or less, dropping from 36 percent to 33 percent. This seems to indicate that most state welfare policies have the strongest effect on those who are easiest to employ.

EMPLOYMENT AND EARNINGS

Early data indicate that 1 in 3 families (1.7 million people) who received welfare in 1996 were working in March 1997. In 1992, before welfare reform was begun through federal waivers, only 1 in 5 families who received welfare the previous year moved from welfare to work that quickly.

Reports also show sharp increases in employment for low-income (under 200 percent of poverty levels) single mothers. In 1992, 35 percent of these single mothers with children under 6 were employed, compared to more than 50 percent in 1997. In addition, employment increased among low-income married mothers with children under 6, but not as rapidly. The employment rate for low-income single mothers with young children increased by 15 percent, compared to 5 percent for low-income married women with young children.

Studies from nine states (Indiana, Iowa, Kentucky, Maryland, Michigan, Missouri, New Mexico, South Carolina, and Tennessee) found that from 50 percent to 60 percent of recipients who leave welfare for work find jobs, generally paying between $5.50 and $7.00 an hour. Follow-up studies will track these individuals to see if they stay employed and move on to better jobs.

Earnings have increased for many welfare families. The average earnings per welfare family increased 7 percent from 1996 to 1997. The percentage of welfare families with earned income increased from 9 percent in 1994 to 13 percent in 1997.

Stronger Incentives to Work

States are finding ways to make work more attractive than welfare. In most states both policies and spending choices have focused on work and support for working families. For example, the state of Washington provides welfare recipients with services that help them keep their new jobs, including problem resolution with employers, workplace adjustment skills, job coaching and mentoring. Arizona and Michigan offer vocational and occupation training for former recipients and working recipients to help them acquire more valuable skills to help them keep their jobs or get better ones. Indiana matches recipients' contributions to individual development accounts that can be used for further education or training. And Kansas and Washington have initiatives for clients with learning disabilities that provide a screening tool for welfare staff, help welfare recipients move toward self-sufficiency and identify jobs that are suitable for learning-disabled clients.

Many states provide support, such as child care, transportation, medical care, and even lump sum cash payments to low-income working families to help them avoid welfare. For example, Florida established college accounts for the children of welfare recipients. Ohio and South Carolina are funding home visits to help new parents. Connecticut, Iowa, and Tennessee established a safety net program for families who leave welfare. And Missouri has a "Grandparents as Foster Parents" program funded with TANF. Participating grandparents are eligible for the standard foster care payment and support services including respite and child care.

Hiring Welfare Recipients

In a national survey of 500 employers, the Urban Institute found that nearly 75 percent of employers who have hired a welfare recipient are pleased with that employee's performance. Ninety-four percent of companies who have hired a welfare recipient report they would hire another recipient in the future. More than 80 percent who have not hired someone from welfare say they are likely to in the next year, if they have entry-level job openings. Sixty percent of employers sought "reliability" and "a positive attitude" more than specific skills.

In a meeting of the National Coalition for the Homeless, employers who had hired 135,000 workers moving off welfare reported high retention rates (70 to 79 percent). They credited this to paying livable incomes, providing special training, mentoring and coaching, and offering child care and transportation (funded by state and/or federal government).

The federal government committed to hiring at least 10,000 welfare recipients between 1997 and 2000. By mid-1998, federal agencies had hired over 5,700 people from welfare rolls, more than half of the goal.

WELFARE SAVINGS

Two factors have led to many states having more money then they need in order to fulfill the commitments under TANF provisions. Dramatic reductions in welfare caseloads in recent years have substantially decreased welfare assistance spending. In addition, TANF block grant funding is based on the historically high caseload levels reached in the mid-1990s. As a result, most states now have enough money to fund sev-

TABLE 10.1

The New Math of Block Grants and MOE in an Era of Decreasing Caseloads—The Ohio Example

FY 1994	FY 1998 - Projection
Caseload: 691,000 recipients	Caseload: 481,000 recipients (July 1997)
Total welfare spending - $1,173 m	Welfare money available - $1,173 m
State and local money - $521 m	State and local money - $521 m
Federal money - $652 m	Federal block grant - $652 m
Average cash payment per recipient	
- $116 per month ($1,392/year)	
Spending for benefits - $962 m	Spending for benefits
	(at same rate as FY 1994) - $670 m
Spending for administration and services	Spending for administration and services -
- $221 m ($320 per recipient)	(at same rate as FY 1994) - $154 m
	Total spending - $824 m

If Ohio's cash payment per recipient and admin/service spending per recipient remained the same as in FY 1994, the state would have $349 m left over .
With this money, Ohio could:
- increase benefit payments by 10 percent at a cost of $67 m.
- Increase administration and service spending by SO per cent at a cost of $77 m.
- Leave 10 per cent of the block grant as a reserve fund at a cost of $65 m.
- Transfer $36 m to the child care or social services block grants.
- Reduce its MOE level to 80 percent at a savings of $104 m.

SOURCE: Jack Tweedie et al. *Meeting the Challenges of Welfare Reform: Programs with Promise.* National Conference of State Legislatures: Denver, CO, 1998

eral options, such as child care and transportation programs, to help needy families with children and to strengthen their welfare reforms. For example, Ohio, where caseloads dropped by 33 percent between 1994 and 1998, has several options for the use of its welfare savings. (See Table 10.1.)

Most states have experienced the unexpected excess of funds for welfare. The surplus funds can be used to increase job training and to provide child care and transportation, not just for recipients but also for some of those who have left the welfare rolls. States can also leave block grant money with the federal government to create a reserve fund for when the economy faces a recession.

Flexibility with TANF

Because of the flexibility inherent to TANF, states are realizing that they have the power to decide how to appropriate the money they receive as long as they address at least one of the four TANF purposes.

1. Provide assistance to needy families so children may be cared for in their own homes or in the homes of relatives.

2. End the dependence of needy parents on government benefits by promoting job preparation, work, and marriage.

3. Reduce the incidence of out-of-wedlock pregnancies.

4. Encourage two-parent families.

Federal officials are encouraging states to interpret these requirements broadly, allowing spending for any services that "reasonably" accomplishes their intended purpose. There are a few restrictions that limit the programs states can develop. But the basic principle is that states can use these resources to fund services that strengthen low-income families and help their children.

SUPPORT SERVICES

Because of the additional services offered, overall state spending on welfare efforts has actually increased. According to the National Governors' Association (NGA), states are spending significantly more on child care and other support services to help people find and keep jobs. For example, state spending on child care increased by more than 50 percent. At least 10 states offer child care to all working poor families below a specified income level. Providing child care is a significant aid in getting low-income families into the workforce.

On the other hand, some reports indicate that many families leaving welfare for work have turned to unlicensed, informal types of child care. This type of care is often lower quality than regulated care.

Transportation, too, still seems to be a problem. In the Urban Institute survey, employers noted that their welfare hires had problems getting to work. Thirty-six percent said their entry-level jobs were not accessible by public transportation.

Child Support

In 1997 the state and federal child support enforcement programs collected $13.4 billion for children, an increase of 68 percent from 1992. In addition, the number of families actually receiving their assigned child support increased, from 2.8 million in 1992 to 4.2 million in 1997.

However, a General Accounting Office study looked at the first three states—Virginia, Connecticut, and Florida—to enforce time limits on welfare benefits. The study found that more than 60 percent of families that were owed child support received no payments at all in the year before los-

ing their welfare benefits. Failure to find the absent parent was the most common reason. Some observers feel that child support is more important than any other factor, including wages, in moving people off welfare.

A record 1.3 million paternities were established in 1997, two and a half times the 1992 figure of 510,000. This is due, in large part, to the in-hospital voluntary paternity establishment program begun in 1994. This program encourages fathers to acknowledge paternity at the time of the child's birth. This may indicate that fathers are choosing to take responsibility for their children, a foundation for later emotional and financial support. For the first time, the number of paternities established was equal to the number of out-of-wedlock births.

MANY QUESTIONS STILL UNANSWERED

The impact of the welfare-reform law is still not yet fully understood. In an August 1998 report on welfare-reform developments, according to the Center for Law and Social Policy, an advocacy group in Washington, DC, several questions remain unanswered:

- What part of the welfare caseload decrease can be attributed to increased employment, and what part can be attributed to state policies that have limited eligibility?

- What are the consequences of sanctions (punishment for noncompliance) on affected families?

- What is the impact on child poverty?

As evaluations are made, states will continue to adapt their welfare programs to increase success. Because caseload reductions mean lower expenditures, states have additional resources to offer further services to help welfare recipients overcome the barriers to finding work and supporting their families and avoid a return to welfare. Several state employment-focused strategies, combined with the use of education and training to help recipients become employable and to find better jobs, have been effective in moving substantial numbers of welfare recipients into jobs. These strategies, supported by a strong economy, have resulted in initial welfare-reform successes.

IMPORTANT NAMES
AND ADDRESSES

**Administration for Children
and Families**
U.S. Department of Health and Human
Services
370 L'Enfant Promenade SW
Washington, DC 20447
(202) 401-9200
FAX (202) 401-5770
URL: http://www.acf.dhhs.gov

**American Public Human Services
Association**
810 First St. NE, #500
Washington, DC 20002-4267
(202) 682-0100
FAX (202) 289-6555
URL: http://www.aphsa.org

Bureau of the Census
U.S. Department of Commerce
Washington, DC 20233
(301) 457-4100
FAX (301) 457-4714
URL: http://www.census.gov

Center for Law and Social Policy
1616 P St. NW, #150
Washington, DC20036
(202) 328-5140
FAX (202) 328-5195
URL: http://www.clasp.org

Center for the Study of Social Policy
1250 I St. NW, #503
Washington, DC 20005
(202) 371-1565
FAX (202) 371-1472

Center on Budget and Policy Priorities
820 First St. NE, #510
Washington, DC 20002
(202) 408-1080
FAX (202) 408-1056
URL: http://www.cbpp.org

Child Welfare League of America
440 First St. NW Third Floor
Washington, DC 20001-2085
(202) 638-2952
FAX (202) 638-4004
URL: http://www.cwla.org

Children's Defense Fund
25 E St. NW
Washington, DC 20001
(202) 628-8787
FAX (202) 662-3510
URL: http://www.childrensdefense.org

Families USA
1334 G St. NW
Washington, DC 20005
(202) 628-3030
FAX (202) 347-2417
URL: http://www.familiesusa.org

Food and Nutrition Services
U.S. Department of Agriculture
3101 Park Center Dr.
Alexandria, VA 22302
(703) 305-2286
FAX (703) 305-1117
URL: http://www.fns.usda.gov/fns/

Food Research and Action Center
1875 Connecticut Ave. NW, #540
Washington, DC 20009-5728
(202) 986-2200
FAX (202) 986-2525
URL: http://www.frac.org

Food Stamp Program
U.S. Department of Agriculture
3101 Park Center Dr.
Alexandria, VA 22302
(703) 305-2276
FAX (703) 305-2454

Institute for Research on Poverty
University of Wisconsin
1180 Observatory Dr. 3412

Social Science Building
Madison, WI 53706-1393
(608) 262-6358
FAX (608) 265-3119
URL: http://www.ssc.wisc.edu/irp/

National Association of Social Workers
750 First St. NE, #700
Washington, DC 20002-4241
(202) 408-8600
FAX (202) 336-8310 (800) 638-8799
URL: http://www.naswdc.org

**National Association of State Budget
Officers**
444 North Capitol St. NW, #642
Washington, DC 20001-1511
(202) 624-5382
FAX (202) 624-7745
URL: http://www.nasbo.org

National Conference of State Legislatures
444 North Capitol St. NW, Suite 515
Washington, DC 20001 (202) 624-5400
FAX (202) 737-1069
URL: http://www.ncsl.org

National Urban League
120 Wall Street
New York, NY 10005
(212) 558-5300
FAX (212) 344-5189
URL: http://www.nul.org

**Social Security Administration Research
and Statistics**
6401 Security Blvd.
Baltimore, MD 21235
(410) 965-2841
FAX (410) 965-3308

U.S. House of Representatives
House Ways and Means Committee
1102 Longworth
House Office Bldg.Washington, DC
20515-6348
(202) 225-3625

RESOURCES

The Social Security Administration of the U.S. Department of Health and Human Services (HHS) publishes the quarterly *Social Security Bulletin and the Annual Statistical Supplement to the Social Security Bulletin,* which give a statistical overview of major welfare programs. The annual *Health, United States* published by the HHS is an excellent source of health data. The Administration for Children and Families of the HHS has published an annual *Characteristics and Financial Circumstances of AFDC Recipients,* which describes the families who receive assistance from the now-defunct Aid To Families with Dependent Children (AFDC). Two additional valuable resources were *Indicators of Welfare Dependence, Annual Report to Congress* (October 1997) and *Aid to Families with Dependent Children: The Baseline* (1998).

The Bureau of the Census of the U.S. Department of Commerce periodically publishes studies based upon the *Survey of Income and Program Participation* (SIPP) and *Current Population Surveys* that profile the American population. Some of the publications used in preparing this book include *Poverty in the United States: 1998* (1999), *Money Income in the United States: 1998* (1999), *Income, Poverty, and Valuation of Noncash Benefits: 1994* (1996), *Child Support for Custodial Mothers and Fathers: 1995* (1999), *Household and Family Characteristics: March 1997* (1998), *Marital Status and Living Arrangements: March 1996* (1998), *Dynamics of Economic Well-Being: Program Participation, 1993 to 1994* (1999), and *Asset Ownership of Households: 1993* (1995).

The monthly *Employment and Earnings* of the U.S. Bureau of Labor Statistics (BLS) gives data on wages and work patterns, while the annual *A Profile of the Working Poor* details labor information about low-income workers. Much of the BLS data are published in the *Monthly Labor Review.*

The Food and Nutrition Service of the U.S. Department of Agriculture provided detailed tables about the National School Lunch and School Breakfast Programs, as well as the Food Stamp Program and its participants. The Gale Group offers sincere thanks to the Food Research & Action Center (Washington, DC) for permission to use charts from *Community Childhood Hunger Identification Project: A Survey of Childhood Hunger in the United States* (1995).

The U.S. General Accounting Office (GAO) in Washington, DC, investigates topics as requested by Congress. Some of its publications used in this book are *Job Corps: High Costs and Mixed Results Raise Questions About Program's Effectiveness* (1995), *Waivers and the New Welfare Law: Initial Approaches in State Plans* (1996), and *Poverty Measurement: Issues in Revising and Updating the Official Definition* (1997).

The periodically published *Green Book—Background Material and Data on Programs within the Jurisdiction of the Committee on Ways and Means* (U.S. House of Representatives) provides the most complete information on the nation's welfare system in a single source. The annual *State Expenditure Report* of the National Association of State Budget Officers shows how the states spend their welfare funds.

The Congressional Research Service (CRS) is a government research agency that works exclusively for members and committees of the U.S. Congress. Some of its reports include *Food Stamps: Background and Funding* (Joe Richardson, 1998), *Welfare Reform: Federal-State Financing under the Temporary Assistance for Needy Families Program* (Gene Falk, 1998), *Welfare Reform: Financial Eligibility Rules and Benefit Amounts under TANF* (Gene Falk et al., 1998) and *New Welfare Law: Role of Education and Training* (Vee Burke, 1997).

The Center for Law and Social Policy (CLASP) and the Center on Budget and Policy Priorities (CBPP), two advocacy organizations in Washington, DC, both release reports, papers, updates, and studies on welfare. The Gale Group is grateful to CLASP for timely information on welfare reform, and The Gale Group thanks the CBPP for permission to use tables and figures from several of its publications, including *A Hand Up: How State Earned Income Credits Help Working Families Escape Poverty* (Iris Lav and Edward Lazere, 1996), *Unemployment Insurance Protection in 1994* (Marion Nichols and Isaac Shapiro, 1995), and *In Search of Shelter: The Growing Shortage of Affordable Rental Housing* (Jennifer Daskal, 1998).

The National Conference of State Legislatures presents state welfare-reform programs and analyses in its publication *Meeting the Challenges of Welfare Reform: Programs with Promise* (1998), as well as in its national magazine of state government and policy, *State Legislatures*.

Second Harvest, a charitable hunger-relief organization, graciously permitted the use of information and figures from its national research study *Hunger 1999: The Faces and Facts*. The Gale Group extends a special thank you to the Gallup Organization of Princeton, New Jersey, for the use of Gallup polls regarding welfare in the United States.

INDEX

hunger, 38–41
Medicaid, 115, 117t, 118, 118 (f8.5)
number in family, 99f, 101, 102 (t7.22)
nutrition programs, 18
poverty, 29–31, 31f, 32–33, 70–71
Supplemental Security Income (SSI), 17, 105
time on AFDC, 102 (t7.22)
See also Families; Households
Citizenship, 30t, 35t, 100 (t7.18), 105, 114
See also Immigrants
Community Childhood Hunger Identification Project. *See* CCHIP
Community Work and Training Program (CWTP), 123–124
Comprehensive Employment and Training Act. *See* CETA
Connecticut support services, 135
Contingency funds, 88
Cuban immigrants. *See* Immigrants
Custodial parents, 59t, 60–62, 61f
CWTP. *See* Community Work and Training Program

D

Department of Housing and Urban Development (HUD), 120, 121t, 122 (t8.22)
Disabled
definition, 105
food stamps, 109
Head Start, 119
Medicaid, 117t, 118
Supplemental Security Income (SSI), 106f, 107t, 108 (t8.4)
welfare, 10t–11t, 78t, 80t–81t, 82t, 105, 129
Divorce, 58–59

E

EA. *See* Emergency Assistance
Earned Income Tax Credit (EITC), 36, 37f, 55
EBT (Electronic Benefit Transfer), 108
Economic Opportunity Act (EOA), 124
Education
AFDC recipients, 101, 102, 102 (t7.22)
child support, 59t
food stamp recipients, 111t, 112
income, 45t–46t, 46, 70
Job Corps, 128
Job Training Partnership Act (JTPA), 124, 125t
poverty, 33–34
unemployment, 79
welfare recipients, 79, 80t–81t, 82t
work training, 126–127
EITC. *See* Earned Income Tax Credit
Elderly
food stamps, 109, 112
Medicaid, 115, 117t, 118

poverty, 29, 31f, 37, 52
Supplemental Security Income (SSI), 105, 106f, 107t, 108 (t8.4)
welfare, 78t
Electronic Benefit Transfer. *See* EBT
Eligibility for welfare programs
Medicaid, 115–118
Supplemental Security Income (SSI), 105–106, 106t
Emergency Assistance (EA), 16–17, 87, 89
Emergency food assistance, 41–42, 41f, 42 (f3.7), 42 (f3.9)
Employment
food stamp recipients, 111t
hunger, 40t
poverty, 52, 52 (f4.3), 52 (f4.4), 71 (t5.17)
programs, 123
welfare recipients, 79, 80t–81t, 82t, 134–35
EOA. *See* Economic Opportunity Act
Ethnicty. *See* Race/ethnicity

F

Fair Labor Standards Act, 64
Families
AFDC, 96–97, 96t, 98, 100 (t7.15)
benefit levels, 91t–92t, 92 (t7.8), 93t, 94t, 95t
children, 57, 57f, 58t, 99t, 100 (t7.15)
enrolled in multiple welfare programs, 101 (t7.19)
food stamps, 111t
housing, 101 (t7.20)
income, 34, 44, 48t, 90
Job Training Partnership Act (JTPA), 125t
Medicaid, 117t, 118
nonfamily households, comparison to, 50f
poverty, 30t, 31, 52, 53, 70–71, 71 (t5.16)
poverty guidelines, 24t
race/ethnicity, 57, 57f, 58t
size, 58t
structure, 57–62, 58t, 136
welfare, 57, 79, 80t–81t, 82t
Women, Infants, Children (WIC), 114
Federal funding
food stamps, 108, 109, 109 (t8.6)
housing, 120–122
Medicaid, 115
Supplemental Security Income (SSI), 106f, 106t, 107t, 108 (t8.4)
welfare, 87–89, 88f, 89f, 89t
Females. *See* Gender
Florida support services, 135
Food assistance programs, 41t, 42 (f3.8), 81, 106–115
See also Emergency food assistance; Food stamps

Food stamps, 106–112
benefits, 91t–92t, 95t, 110, 110 (t8.9)
benefits, multiple, 90–92, 93–96, 99, 101 (t7.19), 108, 110, 112, 112f, 115
eligibility, 18, 19
immigrants, 16
participation, 81, 112
poor households, 55
recipients, 41t, 42f, 73, 76t–77t, 80t–81t, 82t, 109, 110 (t8.7), 111
spending, 3t
work requirements, 124
work training programs, 125t
Foster care, 18, 116, 135

G

Gender
divorce, 58–59
emergency food assistance, 41f
food stamps, 76t–77t, 111t
householders, 50f, 80t–81t, 82t, 86
hunger, 40t
income, 67
Job Corps, 128
Job Training Partnership Act (JTPA), 124, 125t
minimum wage, 67 (t5.13)
number of children, 99f
poverty, 30t, 34t, 70t, 74t–75t
Supplemental Security Income (SSI), 106, 108 (t8.3)
unemployment, 66t
welfare recipients, 73, 79, 82t
work experience, 33t
General assistance. *See* AFDC (Aid to Families with Dependent Children)

H

Haitian immigrants. *See* Immigrants
Head Start program, 119–120, 119f, 119t
Health and Human Services, Department of (HHS), 23, 24t, 90–92
Health and medical care
government spending, 2, 3t, 8t, 12t
insurance, 116f, 118 (f8.4)
Heating assistance, 120
HHS. *See* Health and Human Services, Department of
Homeless persons, 110
Households
assets, 50, 51t, 116–117
children, 56 (t5.1), 56 (t5.2)
composition, 56 (t5.1)
food assistance program participation, 41t
food stamps, 76t–77t, 109, 109 (t8.5), 110 (t8.7), 110 (t8.8), 110 (t8.9)
hunger, 40t
income, 34, 35t, 43–49, 44t, 45t–46t, 47t, 48 (t4.4), 56 (t5.1), 56 (t5.2)